Democracy's Moment

People, Passions, and Power
Social Movements, Interest Organizations, and the Political Process
John C. Green, Series Editor

Democracy's Moment

Reforming the American Political System for the 21st Century

Edited by
Ronald Hayduk
and Kevin Mattson

ROWMAN & LITTLEFIELD PUBLISHERS, INC.
Lanham • Boulder • New York • Oxford

ROWMAN & LITTLEFIELD PUBLISHERS, INC.

Published in the United States of America
by Rowman & Littlefield Publishers, Inc.
4720 Boston Way, Lanham, Maryland 20706
www.rowmanlittlefield.com

12 Hid's Copse Road
Cumnor Hill, Oxford OX2 9JJ, England

British Cataloging in Publication Information Available

Library of Congress Cataloging-in-Publication Data

Democracy's moment : reforming the American political system for the 21st century /
edited by Ronald Hayduk and Kevin Mattson.
    p. cm.—(People, passions, power)
  Includes bibliographic references and index.
  ISBN 0-7425-1749-7 (alk. paper)—ISBN 0-7425-1750-0 (pbk. : alk paper)
    1. Democracy—United States. 2. Political participation—United States. 3. United
States—Politics and government—2001– I. Hayduk, Ronald, 1958– II. Mattson, Kevin,
1966– III. Series.

Printed in the United States of America

∞™ The paper used in this publication meets the minimum requirements of
American National Standard for Information Sciences—Permanence of Paper for
Printed Library Materials, ANSI/NISO Z.39.48-1992.

Contents

Foreword

MILES S. RAPOPORT

It is a great honor for me to write the foreword for this book. *Democracy's Moment* is a tremendously important contribution at a time in our nation's history when we can make major progress toward reforming our democratic processes and practices to make them as vibrant, inclusive, and fully participatory as we possibly can. The book contains an incisive assortment of historical analysis, current trends, and particular policy proposals aimed at making democracy truly work.

This book intersects with my own life and work in a number of ways that make it special to me. For fifteen years, I was a community organizer and citizen activist, believing, as several authors in this collection have articulated, that organizing citizens around direct and clear issues was not only a way to win concrete improvements in people's lives, but also a way of enlivening the democratic process and giving it concrete meaning. Beginning in 1984, I spent ten years as a representative in the Connecticut state legislature. While there, I worked hard on election issues, including establishing a state "motor voter" law, fighting for campaign finance reform, opening up the state's nominating process, and making improvements in election administration. I saw a number of legislative changes that made a difference but also learned that no single legislative change can truly revitalize democracy; it takes a well-coordinated, multifaceted approach.

While I was secretary of the state of Connecticut from 1995 to 1999, my office worked to enhance democracy in our state, through an approach that mirrors many of the elements in this book. We worked to register voters, to restore voting rights to ex-offenders, to engage young people in democratic processes, and to modernize election administration. The office even produced its own study, *The State of Democracy in Connecticut*, which enumerated five benchmarks for a well-functioning democracy: knowledge and interest, participation and commitment, social and economic equality, diversity and mutual respect, and the commonweal. These benchmarks track very well with the multiple approaches presented here.

I am now the president of Demos, a national public policy and advocacy organization that works on two intertwined issues: making America's democracy work and dealing with fundamental economic inequalities facing poor and working families. We at Demos are attempting to encourage precisely the kind of multifaceted, experimental, yet optimistic efforts, to lower barriers to participation and create a democracy in which people's voices are truly heard—efforts that are at the core of this book.

Today's moment—and the need for us to seize it and move forward—has been coming for some time. To be sure, the election of 2000 had a great deal to do with putting these issues higher on the nation's political agenda. However, this moment is also the result of a long historical development, in which our nation's understandings of what a democracy must truly mean have evolved through struggle and movement. These steps included early battles, such as the fight against slavery and the women's suffrage movement, and moved on through the procedural reforms of the Progressive Era, the heroic battles of the civil rights movement for full participation by African Americans, the fight for the National Voter Registration Act, and the movement that has developed for campaign finance reform during the past twenty-five years. All these trends have contributed to the broad agenda that has come further forward after the 2000 elections.

Yet we find today that despite the years of struggle and progress, we have a democracy in major need of repair and renewal. Participation levels are at historic lows, and the rates track depressingly with income, race, and age. Political campaigns compete for a narrow slice of likely voters rather than seeking to expand the electorate. Money distorts the playing field mightily, with few signs of abating, despite the work of campaign finance reformers. Civic engagement among young people is alive but disconnected from the political realm. Those of us who care about having a democracy that really works have a tremendous responsibility to fight for change and make this a moment of accomplishment, not just opportunity.

One set of correlations that progressive reformers must face is that between participation and economic inequality. It is not an accident that during the period when we have observed that the democratic system has functioned less and less well, inequality in income and opportunity in America have in fact increased. The correlation between income and participation is a vicious cycle. As long as the political system does not address in a serious way the needs of poor citizens and the more that the nexus between campaign contributions and political decision making becomes part of a popular understanding, the less likely people are to participate. And yet the lack of participation by poor people and working families allows and encourages their needs to be ignored. A recent conversation with a key legislator in Connecticut about the enactment of an Earned Income Tax Credit for the state—an idea whose merit is by this point beyond dispute—made this perfectly clear. I made a passionate argument that this would be the right thing to do, even a "legacy decision" that he and other legislators could make in the latter stages of the state's economic boom. He said, quite bluntly, that it would be good public policy, and indeed a legacy accomplishment. However, he said, "the politics just don't add up. Those people are not going to vote." We cannot separate work on poverty and economic justice issues from work on enhancing democracy. This book helps us make the connection.

Democracy's Moment understands there is no "magic bullet" to enhancing democracy. The broad and varied approaches, all moving together, represent an agenda that can bear fruit over time. Combining reforms will maximize their impact. For example, we at Demos believe strongly that election day voter registration is an important reform. But can it, by itself, make a huge difference in voter turnout? Maybe it can. But it seems obvious that if it were combined with a major civic education program, campaign finance reform that would cut the connection between big private campaign money and political success, and lively civic organizations that are building social capital and educating their members that democracy matters, the results in terms of enhanced participation would be magnified. Similarly, the combination of more accessible entrée for independent candidates to run for office, an instant runoff system that would count people's votes as they intend for them to be counted, and a more open debate process could all work together to widen voters' choices significantly.

The outlook of this book is fundamentally optimistic. The editors and authors firmly believe that all of this activity can make a difference. The essays share and express a faith in people and their ability to make good and important decisions if the means to do so are there. The book encourages experimentation and effort. We cannot always be sure that new approaches will have the effects their architects intend, but *Democracy's Moment* strongly encourages us to try things rather than to throw our hands up in cynicism and resignation. I share this optimism. We can neither guarantee success nor be unaware of the potential for failure and for difficulties along the way. But the continuation of the journey of expanding and perfecting our democracy is a powerful vision, steeped in an impressive history, which calls forth the best efforts in people. This book is both an encouragement for us to step up and try and a most useful guidebook for some promising ways to go about doing it.

As I write this from New York City, the events of September 11, 2001, have cast a pall of uncertainty around the political climate for the country.

Thousands of families have had their lives shattered. Resources are being mobilized for a protracted conflict. Wars have almost always had the effect of polarizing societies very profoundly and of challenging the advances of our democratic progress. The needs of security and armies compete for resources with the needs of people in our own country. With external enemies often come limitations on civil liberties in this country—the pacifists in World War I, Japanese Americans in World War II, Communists and leftists during the Cold War. Issues of resource allocation and of the protection of civil liberties and tolerance may occupy center stage. At the same time, the events of September 11 kindled an enormous outpouring of community and solidarity. Barriers between people, the guardrails we erect in our everyday lives, have come down. We have recognized in a powerful way that we are one society and that our lives and health are intertwined. That spirit is something profoundly democratic and very important to build on for the future. So now is a moment, more than ever, to uphold the values of democracy and indeed to expand participation to bring everyone into the process.

We at Demos are working hard to build the kind of democracy movement envisioned in this book. Our work includes providing research and ideas on democracy issues, building networks of reform advocates in states around the country, attempting to forge a broad agenda from many diverse activists and disparate strands of work, and working to win specific policy changes in states and at the national level. We also want our movement to be fused with the positive sense of the value of democratic engagement and an optimism about its possibility. We want to build, encourage, and nurture a strong democracy movement, not with uniformity of views on every subject, but with a general sense of mission about inclusion and participation.

Democracy's Moment can make a critical contribution to the development of this movement. These essays cover a number of specific reforms and policy proposals. At the same time, the book as a whole keeps the big picture of democratic values in strong view. The combination of these elements makes *Democracy's Moment* a book that everyone concerned about our democracy and wanting to do work on its behalf should certainly read—actually, not just read, but use as a thoughtful guide for democracy work that holds so much importance for the future of our country.

—New York City, October 2001

Acknowledgments

There are many people without whom this book would not have been possible. The editors want to heartily thank the contributors whose time, energy, and wisdom made this anthology what it is—an attempt to move another step in the direction toward the promise of democracy. As editors, we had the privilege of working with scholars and activists who champion political reform and who, along with countless other democracy advocates and organizations, struggle daily to bring about a stronger democracy in the United States. We hope this volume supports their ongoing efforts and the well-spring of activity that has flourished following the 2000 presidential elections and the debacle in Florida. Changes needed to make our political system more democratic will result only from a mass and inclusive movement. Toward that end, we dedicate the proceeds from this book to an organization at the forefront of building linkages among such individuals and organizations—Dēmos: A Network for Ideas and Action (www.demos-usa.org).

Naturally, there are a few people and organizations to whom we owe particular thanks. Foremost is David Kallick, who generously shared with us his democratic acumen and practical experience. Ron Hayduk would especially like to thank the good folks in the New York City Coalition for Voter Participation, the Aspen Institute's Roundtable on Race and Community Revitalization, and Demos, who over the past years helped him think more critically about some of the thorny challenges involved in forging truly democratic projects. Kevin Mattson would like to thank his colleagues at Mount Saint Vincent's Adult Education Institute, where he did much of his editing of this book during the summer of 2001.

Of course, we owe a great debt to the good folks at Rowman & Littlefield who supported our vision and helped us realize this volume—especially Jennifer Knerr and John Green—and their colleagues. Their

xiii

professionalism was matched only by their responsiveness, which made our work manageable and enjoyable.

Finally, we cannot thank enough our dear parents and our partners—Susanna Jones and Vicky Mattson—for their loving support and assistance through the entire process.

CREDITS

An earlier version of Jamin Raskin's essay appeared in the *Texas Law Review*. Similarly, Joel Westheimer's and Joseph Kahne's essay reflects an adaptation of a chapter that appeared in Kahne's *Teaching for Social Justice*, published by Teachers College Press. The cover photos are by Elvert Xavier Barnes and Jacob Sheridan, aka, "Mike Buck."

Part One

Introduction and Historical Background

1

Remembering Florida for the Right Reasons

RONALD HAYDUK AND KEVIN MATTSON

The two-month-long election day in Florida is now permanently sketched into the American political mind-set, no matter how much some people might want to forget it. As the editors of this volume see it, the debate over whether Gore or Bush had more votes in the state of Florida brought to light a more important lesson: We need to find ways to make certain that the American political system is more responsive to the demands of all citizens. In all of the shouting over Florida's "dimpled chads" and legal hairsplitting, there was clear evidence that poorer and historically disenfranchised citizens found it difficult to vote. Throughout most of this imbroglio, the majority of Americans polled expressed their long-held democratic faith by supporting a full and accurate recount while also expressing hopes for an efficient transition of presidential power. What all of this signals is the need to think critically about what can be done to make politics more responsive to America's citizenry in the future. There are many who hold understandable bitterness about George W. Bush's ascendancy to presidential power; we believe it is more constructive to remember what happened in Florida and turn it into a chance to reform our political system in order to make it truly democratic.

If we embark on such a project, we quickly realize that this last election did not just bring the disenfranchisement of poorer minorities and the problems with the ways elections are run to the fore, it alerted us to numerous other problems. First and foremost is the corruption of politics by money. Three billion more dollars was expended in this election than in previous elections. Entire candidacies—Jon Corzine from New Jersey for instance—seemed predicated solely on the wealth of the individuals running for office. Expensive campaign advertisements, cloaked as "issue advertisements," proliferated just days before citizens voted. Those who have examined the numbers believe that the amount spent on winning offices this last election is equal to the amount of money it would cost to update all of the voting machinery across the United States. In the Republican primary, John McCain rightfully raised campaign finance reform to national prominence, where it remains today as of this writing.

On the left, an age-old debate about third parties reached new heights in 2000. As the smoke has cleared, it is now obvious that Ralph Nader's candidacy (though not in and of itself) helped cost Al Gore the election. Nonetheless, many good-hearted progressives continued to support Nader's candidacy even when it was clear just how high the stakes were, expressing their fundamental frustration with the two-party system and the "race to the center" by both major presidential candidates. Many citizens wanted to vote for Nader in order to send a message to Gore but, at the same time, did not want Bush to win. What they were wishing for, even if they did not necessarily articulate it, was an "instant run-off election," a means by which citizens could vote their conscience without feeling like their vote was thrown away. During the 2000 election, progressives in New York State experimented with "fusion," whereby cross-endorsement of candidates allowed voters to send a "message" about their political philosophies to the candidate (i.e., I won't vote for you on the Democratic Party line, which I disagree with, but on the Working Families Party line, which I support). As the fallout has cleared, it is now important to think more seriously about ways to move beyond our "winner-take-all" sort of system. No matter what one thinks of ideas like proportional representation or instant run-off voting, they are getting a well-deserved hearing precisely due to the frustrations expressed by many citizens in this election.

Political debate in the mass media sank to a new low during the 2000 presidential election. Ralph Nader was locked out of the debates altogether, the way Perot had been in the past, thus limiting the spectrum of opinions to which Americans were exposed. During the fairly lackluster Bush–Gore debates, political pundits focused on the styles of the candidates (sighs, smirks, and other assorted body language) rather than the substance of their arguments. In addition to televising these fairly dull debates, the media presented bizarre polling results (changing daily, sometimes hourly) that only engendered more animosity about political reporting. If citizens wanted or demanded helpful political information, they were faced with media corporations more intent on selling sensational stories or being the first to report "groundbreaking"—not necessarily useful—news (as Congress recently learned in a set of hearings about bogus poll reporting). The presidential candidates themselves were no better. The ability of George W. Bush to cloud understanding of his candidacy—as he claimed to support policies he opposed—and the inability of Al Gore to define his own candidacy—as he shifted this way and that—

made clear that political debate is increasingly vapid. This is only confirmed when pollsters find out how little citizens know about political candidates' core standings and views. Few citizens watched the three main debates between Bush and Gore, illustrating just how civic and political knowledge continues to plummet.

If we take these things into account, one response is depression about the doldrums of American politics. We could crack open copies of Walter Lippmann's *Public Opinion* and take cheery relief in his idea that expert-counseled politicians should run the republic while ignoring the ignorant whims of the masses. Another option exists, though, and it is one that the authors collected in this volume are intent on exploring. We want to rediscover and explore an important tradition in American politics—the tradition of political reform in the name of making democracy more participatory. Many have returned to the Progressive Era for inspiration (Levine 2000; Lind 1996; Milkis and Mileur 1999; Isaac 1998; Weisberg 1996); and in chapter 2 of this collection, Kevin Mattson explains why. He shows how progressives from that period grounded their political hopes in the philosophy of pragmatism—with its faith in an open-ended testing of consequences—and believed that democracy required constant reform. Mattson shows how reform can be both dynamic and bold and yet preserve key constitutional and liberal principles at the same time. He also shows how reform requires multifaceted initiatives—including the reform of political institutions as well as nurturing ways ordinary citizens can educate themselves about politics. Most importantly, Mattson argues that today's progressives are not bereft of political traditions that can sustain hope.

The authors of these chapters clearly fit within this tradition of American political reform. All of us place our hopes in reform. Unlike many political scientists today, we are committed to democratic ideals and to the idea that our political system can be improved. In fact, many of us are directly engaged in the reform initiatives discussed here. In order to gain critical perspective, though, we step back to ask what is admittedly an *open-ended* question: What can be done to make American politics more responsive to citizens? This is the same question progressives at the turn of the century asked. But unlike them, we hold no faith in inherent progress. Instead, we recognize that American democracy is not always as conducive to political reform as many might assume—that there is no magical formula of growing improvement that we can rely upon. There are plenty of impediments to reform, and our authors discuss these impediments with openness and honesty. Nonetheless, we always try to think beyond the present and keep our sights focused on a horizon defined by fuller democratic participation and citizen input into public problem solving.

In this introduction, we set out the larger themes around which the work is organized. Central to this book is the idea that reform will not be effective if it limits itself to only one approach (say, for instance, getting money out of politics). The problems of democracy are too large and numerous to think that one reform initiative could constitute a cure. The democracy reform movement today is quite diverse, as is demonstrated in the following chapters. Not all the authors collected here agree with one another; some of us stress certain types of reform that others might shy away from. Some of us emphasize removing barriers at the legal and institutional level while others believe it more important to nurture and create a civic culture that is inclusive and participatory. This collection will document the diversity of approaches that reformers are taking today, precisely with the hope that this will show the healthy state of this diverse movement and emphasize the need for a multilayered approach to America's democratic deficit. What unites our different tactics though is an overall goal of building a stronger and more representative democracy.

FACING AND ERADICATING BARRIERS TO POLITICAL PARTICIPATION

We think it important to begin with a part on the barriers to full political participation. After all, progressives at the turn of the century, when at their best, engaged in the early civil rights movement (W. E. B. Du Bois) and suffrage struggles (Jane Addams)—both of whom aimed to remove barriers to ordinary citizens. In recent history, social movements have produced important electoral reforms. Yet, despite passage of the Voting Rights Act of 1965, the Campaign Finance Act of 1974, and the National Voter Registration Act of 1993 (popularly known as "motor voter"), significant barriers to political participation remain, whether for voters, third parties, or independent candidates. Our opening part examines three barriers in detail: electoral law and administrative policy that pose obstacles to voting, such as restrictive voter registration procedures and practices by partisan elections boards; ballot access laws that limit third parties and insurgent candidates; and the rising costs of elections that prohibit nearly all but the independently wealthy from running for office. More importantly, the chapters in this section explore electoral reforms that would eliminate or ameliorate these barriers.

Though voting might be just one aspect of citizenship, it still stands as crucial. It also stands in a state of crisis. Barely half of the eligible electorate votes in presidential elections and even fewer people vote in state and local elections. Compared to all other democratic advanced industrial nations, the United States continues to rank near the bottom in terms of voter turnout. This lack of participation is most evident in poor, minority and urban communities, and many governmental policies continue to slight these communities (Hill and Leighley 1992). In a political democracy, such disparities raise troubling questions about the legitimacy of public policy and governance.

Ron Hayduk, in the opening chapter for this part, focuses on the historical genesis of election rules and procedures and the ways they continue to play a significant role in producing a bias in political participation. He describes how political conflicts at the turn of the century generated restrictive rules that narrowed possibilities for democratic participation of low-income voters as well as third parties and insurgent candidates. He traces the legacy of turn of the century electoral changes that continue to limit political participation today. He also highlights specific reforms that could eliminate these barriers and hold promise to invigorate the American polity.

Richard Winger focuses on how the rise of ballot access obstacles snuffed out a vibrant third-party tradition in America. Some scholars even suggest that elites within both parties have tried to squelch radical third-party movements of labor, populists, and socialists (Burnham 1970; Keyssar 2000; Piven and Cloward 2000). Though Winger does not necessarily endorse the more conspiratorial of these views, he shows that whatever the intention of ballot access regulation, it has certainly resulted in excluding a wide range of political voices—including progressives. Restrictive ballot access measures worked to marginalize insurgents within the dominant parties and independent campaigns, as Winger shows. He suggests that Americans begin to think of ways to repeal these restrictive measures, while showing the legal barriers to doing so.

Mark Schmitt rounds out this part by examining how the burgeoning prominence of money in elections has provided a crucial impediment to political participation. Much has been said about the corrupting influence of money on the political process. Fortunately, as Schmitt documents, a vibrant campaign finance reform movement has emerged that has the potential to change the political landscape. Campaign finance reform unites environmentalists, labor union activists, advocates of low-income and minority communities, and liberal religious groups. Drawing upon his vast experience in creating campaign finance legislation, Schmitt outlines the history behind the campaign finance struggle that continues at the national level and in a dozen states. He shows just how difficult this struggle really is but also how something can be done about it if reformers become more tough-minded about possibilities.

ENGAGING THE CITIZENRY

These different means of "removing barriers"—making it easier for disenfranchised voters to vote, allowing third parties to mount campaigns,
and reducing the influence of money on politics—are only the first steps
in advancing an overall reform agenda. It is just as important to find ways
to engage citizens in politics once barriers have been removed. In certain
ways, this is a much harder task. It relies upon widening our conception
of democracy beyond the mere act of voting occasionally; it requires that
we find places and institutions where citizens might actually reconnect to
one another and to a wider public good and become, in effect, mindful of
a public interest. In our day and age—with its fetishism of the market and
private well-being—there are fewer and fewer places where citizens in-
teract as equals and as engaged participants in the making of democratic
politics. Progressives cannot simply concern themselves with getting rid
of barriers but must also create viable ways for citizens to reengage in
public life.

Core to the progressive vision at the turn of the century was a deliberative public. Many reformers during the Progressive Era opened up social
centers in public schools where citizens could meet to debate the issues of
the day (Mattson 1998). Progressives believed that citizens capable of deliberation and political learning were also more capable of engaging in reform initiatives, as Peter Levine has shown (Levine 2000). It is important
to rethink the meaning of public deliberation today, a project that many
political theorists have already begun (Fishkin 1991; Bohman 1996; Gutmann and Thompson 1996). R. Claire Snyder opens this section then by
examining the idea popular among political theorists today—that democracy and deliberation are intertwined political concepts. Snyder shows
how central deliberation is to democracy. In many ways, she provides the
political and philosophical foundations for the chapters that follow in this
section. Moving beyond the often abstract sermons about "communicative action" and "deliberative democracy," Snyder also suggests some
ways in which political institutions could better reflect these often lofty-
sounding ideals. The rest of the chapters examine ways in which a more
deliberative democracy might actually become a reality within today's
political culture.

For citizens to deliberate, they of course need information and exposure to key political ideas. Unfortunately, the sort of civic education
democracy requires is in short supply. In large part, this is because the
classical model of civic education—civics courses that stressed memo-
rization of legislative processes—fell into disrepute not too long ago. As
Joel Westheimer and Joseph Kahne point out, America's schools rarely
prepare young people to become active citizens ready for the challenges

of democracy. On the other hand, these authors document some thoughtful experiments carried out by teachers and schools that try to pass on civic skills to students. In the case of C. Wright Mills School, Westheimer and Kahne's central case study, teachers actually opened up political debate during the school day and trained students in how to become political advocates, all the while trying to ensure open educational processes rather than any sort of indoctrination. What the experiment shows is that there are plenty of ways teachers and schools could better prepare young people for the demands of deliberative democracy and active citizenship. At the same time, much stands in the way of this initiative, as Westheimer and Kahne admit.

If civic education matters, so too does community organizing. As the famous settlement house activist, Jane Addams, understood so well during the Progressive Era, there has to be an effort to create spaces in which ordinary citizens can be introduced to creative public problem solving. There was a realist argument to much of Addams's work: many citizens, after all, come to politics only when some sort of problem is thrown their way in their local communities (a place where they can *see* and *feel* politics, so to speak). At these moments, there is great potential in widening citizens' perspectives on politics and participation. In his chapter, Benjamin Shepard discusses a few case studies of urban areas that have successfully used local civic work and community organizing to reconnect citizens to more traditional forms of political engagement—including recent struggles, some of them quite heated, over the preservation of community gardens. Through community organizing, citizens are led back to a more diverse and multilayered form of political participation. They get to see why politics matter, thus building a pathway into the long-term commitment of active citizenship.

Building on Shepard's argument, Peter Levine takes note of an advantage that we have over the progressives that came before us—namely, new technologies that can potentially enhance public deliberation and civic education. This is especially important considering that many citizens no longer live in the dense urban areas of yesteryear. When the Internet and World Wide Web originally emerged, there was great enthusiasm that they could become tools for citizens to come together and deliberate about public matters. Of course, the same was said for television in the 1950s, and now as the hype has died down, the civic and political results of the Internet have been mixed—much of it being used for people to explore entertaining hobbies and find like-minded people rather than discuss important issues with their fellow citizens. Levine makes clear that the original hype of the Internet has proven to be a house of cards. The Internet will *not ensure* more public deliberation. Nonetheless, he shows how citizens have used it for certain civic projects and argues in favor of an on-line "commons" that could ensure more civic and political uses of the Internet in the future. If nurtured more intelligently, the Internet might be able to serve as something of a public sphere where citizens can be exposed to new ideas and share their political thinking with others. But this requires care and initiative on the part of reformers to make sure that the Internet is conceived and crafted as a democratic medium rather than just a space for commercial entertainment.

Clearly, there are numerous ways to reengage citizens in political participation and deliberative democracy. Progressives today must find new and creative means to make politics touch ordinary citizens' lives. Without doing this, removing barriers becomes meaningless. If there are no *positive* ways in which citizens can engage in politics, getting rid of impediments only allows citizens to enter a barren world, the sort of barren world that American politics has become for many citizens today.

MAKING THE SYSTEM MORE RESPONSIVE

Ever since the 2000 election, Lani Guinier—the "godmother" of proportional representation and the victim of Bill Clinton's slipperiness when it came to appointees—has been receiving more invitations to appear on television shows, speak at conferences, and publish articles. Suddenly the idea of proportional representation—a reform that seemed so out of touch with the mainstream that it lost Guinier a federal appointment—appears not so much insane as provocative. Ever since Al Gore won the popular vote but lost the election (partially due to Nader's independent run), the ideas of proportional representation and instant run-off voting have been rehabilitated. Americans are increasingly interested in the possibility that voting could express not simply a choice for the candidate most likely to win but also of more interesting candidates more in synch with their political views.

We argue in this part that for engaged and deliberative citizens to select representatives of their choice effectively—and to keep government responsive and accountable—alternative voting mechanisms are necessary. The lead chapter in this part, by Robert Richie, Steven Hill, and Caleb Kleppner, looks at how such alternative voting systems affect voter participation, political representation, and public policy making. Their chapter examines alternatives to contemporary redistricting methods—a pressing current issue—by exploring the range of proportional representation and semiproportional voting systems for legislative elections, including the option of instant run-off voting for elections with a single winner. These authors contend that such reforms are not only essential for providing fair representation of political minorities (i.e., minor parties, women, and racial and ethnic minorities) but will also help increase voter participation. Moreover, they argue, such reforms are now more viable, given the anomalous past election.

Of course, for citizens to know about a wider variety of political choices, they must hear from a wider variety of political candidates. With this in mind, Jamin Raskin argues for opening up political debates to those who fall outside America's traditional two parties. He shows why the Commission on Presidential Debates (CPD) has stood against this idea and why this organization's arguments are constitutionally suspect at best. Currently, the rules that determine who can participate in candidate debates virtually exclude third-party candidates. There is a classic catch-22 operating here, for if a candidate does not have a chance to participate in debates and be heard by the people, how can he or she be expected to obtain the interest of a significant portion of the electorate? Short of having substantial amounts of money—which, again, precludes most progressive candidates—only a mass grassroots social movement could produce the conditions for such a candidate to qualify. Raskin argues that third-party candidates can invigorate democratic discussion and debate on policy and potentially draw more voters into political participation and deliberation. He calls for legal action to assure this, as well as the participation of civil society organizations like the League of Women Voters.

Another way of getting new voices into electoral politics is for citizens themselves to initiate and vote on legislation. Originally conceived as a means of "direct legislation" by populists and progressives at the turn of the century, the initiative and referendum have become hot topics of debate today. David Broder recently called for their abolition—arguing that the invasion of big money into the process of initiating legislation has ruined the original hope of contemporary progressives. Galen Nelson argues, instead, that progressives must try to inject deliberative democratic principles back into citizen legislation. That is, instead of citizens remaining passive while millionaires fund whimsical forms of legislation, progressives must find ways to educate citizens about pending legislation. Nelson calls for opening up knowledge about spending on initiatives so that citizens can make informed judgments about the ways in which economic influence works on direct legislation (this could be especially effective since directly regulating money has failed historically for constitutional reasons). The initiative and referendum provide ample opportunities for citizens to reengage in political debate and make high-stake political judgments. Nelson argues that Broder and others are throwing the baby out with the bathwater, that instead of pushing citizens out of direct legislation, progressives should invite them back in—albeit while protecting constitutional principles and showing how citizen deliberation serves a key political function in a democracy.

For the American political system to be truly representative of its citizens, it needs to be reformed. Citizens must sense that their vote "counts," and this requires us to rethink the way voting operates today, as Richie and his colleagues point out. We close this section with reflections on the Electoral College. This constitutional provision was originally intended to protect states that had lower populations from being bowled over, so to speak, by states with larger populations. Today, the Electoral College faces enormous animosity among many Americans. Joel Lefkowitz explains why the system was constructed and how it might be reformed today, without threatening less populous states.

THE BIGGER PICTURE: ENRICHING OUR DEMOCRATIC IMAGINATION

With so many different reform initiatives being presented, it could become easy for the reader to miss the bigger picture. Of course, our intention is to stay focused on the bigger picture while also paying attention to details. And staying within the world of details here, we should note that all of these reform initiatives take a great deal of energy and require different initiatives all at once. For instance, take Jamin Raskin's proposal for a more inclusive presidential debate. It requires legal action, reforms at the political level concerning the use of the media for public purposes, and the efforts of civil society organizations like the League of Women Voters. All of these things must work in concert. As Mark Schmitt points out, campaign finance reform requires not just legislators but also ordinary citizens pressing for a fairer system within their own states. And the crucial role foundations play in shaping the reform terrain, by providing funding to particular initiatives and organizations that then have greater capacity and legitimacy to carry out certain reform efforts, is another important factor to consider in assessing reform strategies and outcomes over time (though we pay only cursory attention to it here). As with other reforms, the improvement of democratic participation requires multifaceted initiatives.

The authors in this collection are not pie-in-the-sky reformers. None of us believes that these reforms will be instituted overnight (in fact, some of them might never be adopted). We also do not believe that there is a magic bullet—one way of doing reform—that will solve all of our problems. Hence, we recognize our own diversity and take it as a sign of strength rather than weakness. Some of the authors (and even the editors) disagree on some substantive issues here: For instance, some of us believe that Nader was right in running for office in the last election; others of us believe he should have waited for political reforms like instant runoff voting in order not to damage the status of progressivism in America. Some of us emphasize legal reform, while others believe it more important to build institutions that touch ordinary citizens' lives. Some of us are more worried about opening up political debate to far right views; others believe this is simply the necessary consequence of democratic reform. These conflicts and differences, though, represent strengths, not weaknesses, since a diverse movement is a strong movement.

With this said, it is necessary to remember here that even where there is conflict, the authors of these chapters remain committed to the idea that democracy requires a great deal of attention and reform from progressives. It requires that we remain open-minded and test the consequences of reform in the often murky world of political reality. It requires that we stay tough-minded and realistic about the possibilities of accomplishing reform—as Lincoln Mitchell points out in one of our closing chapters. Perhaps most of all, it requires that we strengthen our democratic imagination. The real reason that American democracy has fallen into disrepair is that we have failed to think beyond our present political arrangements. If progressives can show how the system can better reflect a wide variety of voices and opinions and how this requires us to think beyond the present, then we can remember the important lesson taught by the great thinker and reformer of the Progressive Era, John Dewey: The cure for the ailments of democracy is more democracy. The 2000 presidential election debacle has provided an opening for reformers to expand the boundaries of democracy. If we can successfully capitalize upon this window of opportunity, what we call here *democracy's moment*, the 21st century may just turn out to be a more progressive one than the previous two.

2

History as Hope: The Legacy of the Progressive Era and the Future of Political Reform in America

KEVIN MATTSON

> Democracy is more than the absence of czars, more than freedom, more than equal opportunity. It is a way of life, a use of freedom, an embrace of opportunity. . . . A nation of uncritical drifters can change only the form of tyranny, for like Christian's sword, democracy is a weapon in the hands of those who have the courage and the skill to wield it; in all others it is a rusty piece of junk.
>
> —Walter Lippmann, *Drift and Mastery* (Lippmann 1985 [1914], 16)

Eras in American history pass away, but their residuals evoke strong memories within the contemporary American mind-set. Think 1930s, and most Americans remember not only the Depression but also labor struggles and the growth of the welfare state through FDR's leadership. Think 1960s, and most recall a heightened Cold War in Vietnam and the rise of protests as well as ensuing racial conflict. Today, it seems that the Progressive Era, traditionally seen as stretching from the 1890s to America's entry into World War I in 1917, is getting more attention from both political scientists and historians. For good reason, scholars and journalists see the Progressive Era as a time of massive political and social reform. Some believe there might be something worthwhile to be learned and applied to the present (see Hamby in Milkis and Mileur 1999; Dionne 1996; Levine 2000; and Putnam 2000).

Intellectuals during the Progressive Era saw a need for a "usable past," a term used most evocatively by "Young American" social critics like Van Wyck Brooks and Lewis Mumford. As Mumford himself put it, "Establishing its own special relations with its past, each generation creates anew what lies behind it, as well as what looms in front; and instead of being victimized by those forces which are uppermost at the moment, it gains the ability to select the qualities which it values and by exercising them it rectifies its own infirmities and weaknesses" (Mumford in Blake 1990, 296–97). Mumford and others believed that the past could shed light for those trying to improve their present conditions. This hope energized numerous scholars during the Progressive Era. Charles Beard, for instance, believed that an interpretation of the origins of the American Constitution could help explain the political corruption of his own time. Vernon Parrington traced out a lineage of democratic social thought that traveled through history and could inspire contemporary reformers. James Harvey Robinson coined the term "new history" and argued that historical inquiry could "help us understand ourselves and our fellows and the problems and prospects of mankind" (Robinson 1912, 17). History became for Progressive Era scholars and intellectuals a source of critical insight about the present.

The idea that history can teach lessons about today's political predicaments seems best applied to the Progressive Era itself—a period that holds remarkable parallels with our own. After all, the Progressive Era was dominated by a fear of special interests and the idea that "business corrupts politics" (McCormick 1981). More importantly in the context of this book, numerous reform initiatives—including campaign finance reform—arose around these themes. Though many historians doubt that Progressivism was a coherent movement, there seems at least one strain of reform that focused on ridding the American political system of corruption and creating a more vibrant democracy. Some reformers within this tradition believed in building a "new state," one that could displace older forms of corruption while nurturing more vigorous forms of civic participation among ordinary citizens (Follett 1998). Engaged intellectuals created a political philosophy that could explain the spirit behind reform initiatives. Two core principles—pragmatism and democracy—guided much political thought during this time. As a historian engaged in contemporary democratic reform, I believe that these Progressive Era developments—a reaction against corruption in politics, a faith in democracy building, and a pragmatic orientation to reform—provide us with a helpful orientation for the present.

CORRUPTION: THE ENEMY OF DEMOCRACY

The Progressive Era followed on the heels of the Gilded Age—a time of massive corporate consolidation. Robber Barons like Andrew Carnegie and John O. Rockefeller built colossal business empires, all the while looking for favors from government. The railroads—the most evocative symbol of national business consolidation at the time—especially benefited from the federal government's beneficence, receiving cheap public land often in return for payoffs to elected officials. Americans might have feared political corruption ever since the founding of this republic, but now middle-class citizens grew more aware of the ways in which corruption actually worked. For instance, numerous legislative investigations at the turn of the century exposed how corporations directly influenced political decision making. During the late 1890s and early 1900s, "muckraking" journalists started to reveal shady deals to a growing reading public. Henry Demarest Lloyd, for example, described how Rockefeller climbed to economic power and political influence (the details were not pretty); Lincoln Steffens documented the way city governments fell prey to business interests. Working on the assumption that if the public knew about these things something would be done, these journalists helped galvanize moral outrage and a sense that enlightened reform was the answer.

The origins of progressive reform were local. City leaders were first to take the lead in reform. Tom Johnson, the colorful mayor of Cleveland, Ohio, showed how a strong leader could stand up to special interests. The muckraker Lincoln Steffens called Johnson "the best governor of the best-governed city in the United States" (quoted in Mattson 1998, 33). Johnson was especially concerned with the power and influence of local streetcar companies (often as corrupt as the national railroads). The solution, as he saw it, was to municipalize the streetcar system, making it into a public entity incapable of pursuing private influence through city government. While engaging in this reform, he made sure to talk with citizens during his famous "tent meetings" throughout the city. Fearing political corruption, he endorsed the use of the referendum as a means to ensure citizen approval of public policy, even when it meant that his own policies lost.

Other city leaders followed the example of Cleveland and eventually reform initiatives reached the state level. From 1905 to 1906, many states, in the words of Richard McCormick, passed important laws "explicitly designed to curtail illicit business influence in politics. These included measures regulating legislative lobbying, prohibiting corporate campaign contributions, and outlawing the acceptance of free transportation passes by public officials" (McCormick 1981, 266). Wisconsin, which became a beacon of Progressivism, experimented with the direct primary—driving special interests out of the internal operation of political parties. As Governor Robert La Follette explained, this reform would "emancipate the legislature from all subserviency to the corporations." The progressive governor of New York, Charles Evan Hughes, concurred (McCormick 1981, 267). Numerous other state legislatures battled corruption in the name of a "public interest."

Political reform reached the national level in the presidency of Theodore Roosevelt. Roosevelt began his career as a local reformer in New York City, cleaning up its police force. From there, it was on to the governorship of

New York, then eventually the vice presidency, all the while building a reputation as a progressive politician. When he became president due to an assassin's bullet in 1901, Roosevelt, like Tom Johnson, made clear that he would stand up to the special interests. When J. P. Morgan, the Robber Baron financier, tried to talk Roosevelt into looking the other way as he consolidated his economic power and broke the law in the process, Roosevelt told him in no uncertain terms that the presidency could not be bought (Cooper 1983, 83). Roosevelt then went on to regulate corporate special interests—by passing pure food and drug laws and strengthening the Interstate Commerce Commission. He believed a more powerful federal government was necessary to combat the corrupting influence of special interests.

After winning election in a landslide and holding the presidency for four years, Roosevelt took a break from national politics in 1908. But he quickly returned in 1912, only to find that the Republican Party did not want his brand of progressive politics. Roosevelt chose to run for the presidency on a third-party platform—the Progressive Party. As Roosevelt saw it, Progressivism and the causes of social and political reform could gain enough of a constituency to ensure victory for a third party. John Cooper argues that Roosevelt "hoped that the two parties might be on the verge of breaking up over the issues of progressivism, as the Whigs and Democrats had broken up over slavery" (Cooper 1983, 160). Though Roosevelt lost the election, he won 27.4 percent of the vote in 1912, beating out the Republican Party incumbent, William Taft. Roosevelt had drawn a coalition of reformers into the Progressive Party. What his independent run for presidency showed was the popularity of reform during the Progressive Era.

THE NECESSITY OF DEMOCRACY

Roosevelt symbolized not simply the popularity of Progressive Era reform but its underbelly as well. After all, Roosevelt left behind the legacy of centralized power and the "imperial presidency" (so coined by another progressive historian, Arthur Schlesinger Jr.). Roosevelt's personal machismo (enhanced by his war hero status) and top-down leadership qualities represented an antidemocratic tendency within Progressivism. Numerous historians have pointed out that some progressive reformers put far too much faith in bureaucracy and the rule of experts (see for instance, Wiebe 1980). Many wanted to build up stronger government in order to combat special interests but failed to understand that this might marginalize ordinary citizens from public life. Indeed, ridding political parties of corruption seems to have also weakened their participatory element. Ironically, the political party was one of the few venues for popular participation (i.e., parades and other gatherings) for numerous citizens (McGerr 1986). Thus, progressive reform, though intending to rid politics of corruption, sometimes ridded it of citizen participation.

This is why Theodore Roosevelt's endorsement of settlement houses and other local, democratic initiatives is so important. A Progressive Party poster from 1912 depicted Roosevelt shaking hands with Jane Addams, the founder of Hull House in Chicago. For the previous twenty-two years, Addams had focused her energy on building a neighborhood settlement where new immigrant citizens could join with middle-class women like herself in order to upgrade local civic conditions. Through numerous initiatives, such as holding lectures on critical issues and organizing citizens to get roads paved and other local conditions improved, Addams saw herself building democracy at the neighborhood level and initiated, in the process, the modern tradition of community organizing. In the process, she tried to take on a local ward boss (someone who, Addams admitted, had done a great deal of good for the neighborhood, albeit through corrupt means). From her perspective, settlement house workers "pledged to devote themselves to the duties of good citizenship and to the arousing of the social energies which too largely lie dormant in every neighborhood given over to industrialism" (Addams 1960, 100). Addams believed that local initiatives had to link up with national policies—hence her endorsement of the Progressive Party—but she remained a *local* activist. She also argued that women needed the right to vote in order to create a more inclusive democratic system (the Progressive Party made female suffrage a plank). Addams and Roosevelt's handshake on the Progressive Party's poster signified a hope that democratic practice could actually replace older forms of political corruption—that local democratic initiatives went hand in hand with progressive state building. As Herbert Croly, a leading Progressive Era intellectual who inspired Roosevelt's political thinking, explained, "The great object of progressives must always be to create a vital relation between progressivism and popular political education" (Croly 1914, 145).

Most important in this context was the social centers movement. Originating in Rochester, New York, in 1907, this movement organized to use public schools after hours for deliberative meetings between citizens about pressing issues of the day. Social centers organizers moved beyond the settlement house's reliance on private philanthropy, arguing that their work was important enough to warrant public tax support. In social centers, citizens were free to discuss and deliberate on everything from local to national issues. Often, they would invite politicians to discuss their policies with citizens. One alderman who accepted such an invitation explained, "If every member of the common council and every other public servant had frequently such opportunities as this to come before the people whom he is supposed to represent, and discuss with them the things in which he is supposed to represent them it would mean that we would have a better representation of the people's interest and a more intelligent government" (quoted in Mattson 1998, 57). Social centers activists saw local deliberation as a key means of repairing American democracy and replacing older forms of corruption. Not surprisingly, Theodore Roosevelt endorsed the movement during his 1912 struggle for the presidency, arguing that the social center could become the "Senate of the people" (Mattson 1998, 66).

This democratic tendency within Progressivism came to fullest fruition in the proliferation of the initiative and referendum during the Progressive Era. Through these processes, citizens themselves could initiate legislation. One of the original spokespeople for the initiative and referendum, J. W. Sullivan, a political thinker active with the American Federation of Labor (AFL), argued, "The obligatory Referendum makes of the entire citizenship a deliberative body in perpetual session" (Sullivan 1892, 20). Many progressives were drawn to the initiative and referendum solely as a means to circumvent corrupt politicians. But these measures held a more profound democratic promise since they could encourage citizens to deliberate about how they were to vote on legislation. Action and education would merge in this process. Indeed, many social centers activists believed they were building the means by which citizens could deliberate about such decisions. What all of this shows is that some progressives believed bottom-up and citizen-based initiatives could help end corruption in politics.

REFORM AS PUBLIC PHILOSOPHY: PRAGMATISM AND DEMOCRACY

Another reason the Progressive Era appeals today is because there was so much interesting intellectual fermentation surrounding reform at the time. If ever a period was associated with the dawn of modern culture and social thought, it was most definitely the turn of the century. The popularization of Darwinism and other scientific developments encouraged educated citizens to raise questions about religious faith. There seemed a certain "end of American innocence" as one historian described the turn of the century (May 1964). This was a time when earlier foundations of thought and intellectual inquiry started to fall into disarray, a period when the religious certitude of the Victorian Era gave way to secularism. While some despaired about the loss of religion and certitude, many intellectuals saw an opening and opportunity, embarking on a search for new (a term that proliferated at the time) foundations for modern society and politics.

The most important figure in this context was certainly William James, the philosopher brother of the novelist Henry. As one historian tells the story, William James personally struggled at the turn of the century with the cold hard facts that modern science revealed and the loss of religious certitude. Indeed, he went through a profound depression, feeling debilitated and lost amidst his own intellectual confusion (see Cotkin 1990). As he pondered the methods employed by scientists, he became convinced that absolute truth and conviction were things of the past. The world was too "pluralistic" (James's term) to impose a single meaning upon it. As he pledged himself to becoming a public philosopher while teaching at Harvard University, he tried to convince his fellow Americans they could no longer cling to age-old doctrines. Instead, knowledge and truth were now defined as partial and tentative. This was perhaps the most important teaching of what James called pragmatism. He explained, "We have to live today by what truth we can get today, and be ready tomorrow to call it falsehood" (James 1978, 107). Nor could philosophers or citizens remain passive about knowledge; they must go into the world to experiment and learn from active engagement. James expounded, "Truth happens to an idea. . . . Truth is *made* . . . in the course of experience" (James 1978, 97, 104). James believed certitude was gone for good, but there remained the possibilities of engaged experimentation and open-mindedness.

James had an enormous influence on progressive reformers and other intellectuals at the time, including perhaps the most important philosopher and activist of the Progressive Era, John Dewey. At the turn of the century, Dewey was shedding an idealist framework for pragmatism. Before discovering James, Dewey had made an idealist commitment to the principle of democracy, that is, he believed democracy was a universally credible value that transcended the need for empirical testing (like other 19th-century religious beliefs). As the historian Robert Westbrook illustrates, Dewey thought democracy was an ethical good, one that ensured the fullest possible self-realization of all citizens (Westbrook 1991, 40–41, 77). When he embraced James's pragmatism, the ideal of democracy remained though God was taken out of the picture. Dewey now embraced "critical inquiry and testing" (Westbrook 1991, 141) and the idea that "knowledge . . . involves active use of the environment" (White 1976, 138). No longer could a philosopher believe there was any hope of achieving absolute truth; instead, there was only open-ended experimentation within a democratic community. While at the University of Chicago, he embraced the activities of Jane Addams at Hull House, lecturing there frequently. Dewey saw at Hull House the sort of democratic, community-based experimentation that would stand at the core of his political theory. In many ways, Addams's work represented Dewey's philosophical ideas put into practice during the Progressive Era.

The open-endedness that Dewey and James counseled made an impact on numerous reformers. Progressive Era reformers threw off the certitude of 19th-century evangelical reformers. Though these modern reformers embraced commitment, they also learned from the testing and experimental qualities of pragmatism. The spirit behind reform became more *modern* during the Progressive Era—that is, it became more tentative and open-ended. For many activists, reform was no longer to be an imposition of preordained values but an opening up of opportunities for other citizens to act democratically. For instance, social centers ensured citizens *only* the possibilities of open-ended deliberation; what citizens *did* within these deliberations depended on their own initiative.

The reformer Frederic Howe best represented this strain in Progressive Era reform. Howe grew up in a Presbyterian household within a small Pennsylvania town and then attended Johns Hopkins University. He worked at a settlement house and then as an aide to Mayor Tom Johnson, finally joining the social centers movement. Thus, Howe was right in the midst of the Progressive Era reform discussed here. When he recounted his life in a cunningly entitled book, *The Confessions of a Reformer*, he wrote it around the central process of "unlearning." Unlike previous evangelical reformers, Howe put his own motivation to scrutiny, openly discussing the "evangelistic morality [that] became bone of my bone, flesh of my flesh" (Howe 1967, 17). Howe explained that the experiences of the modern city challenged this preconceived, evangelical morality. For instance, by exploring saloons, he saw the benefits they offered working people and thus rejected the temperance movement he might have otherwise embraced. By engaging in dialogue with new immigrants, he saw how their values and customs served them well; therefore, he rejected nativism. As Howe explained it, this process of "unlearning" his moralistic inheritance was a prerequisite to becoming a good reformer who was capable of working with people different from him. That is perhaps why he believed that all progressive reform needed to have a deliberative element—the sort that settlement houses and social centers practiced. Howe lived the life of pragmatism outlined by William James and John Dewey. By opening his mind toward new experience, he made clear that effective reform demanded acceptance of a "pluralistic universe," rather than preconceived morality. Of course, Howe was one of many reformers and thus exceptional. Nonetheless, the loss of certitude at the turn of the century made a definite impact on Progressive Era reform as a whole.

CONCLUSION: IS THERE A USABLE PAST?

So what do these historical lessons teach us today? The strain of Progressivism that I am drawing out here certainly makes clear that money can corrupt political processes and, more importantly, that something can be done about this problem. The presidency of Roosevelt provides another crucial lesson: that well-intentioned attempts at making politics less corrupt can also take on antidemocratic tendencies. Those who organized settlement houses and social centers understood that political reform must incorporate citizen participation lest it become technocratic or authoritarian. Thinkers like John Dewey and activists like Frederic Howe teach us another important lesson that reform must be open-ended, always testing its assumptions in the world of reality.

Many historians have criticized the work of Progressive Era reformers. Some argue that Progressive Era reformers were limited by the strictures of their middle-class worlds (see Hofstadter 1955 and Crunden 1984). Some on the left suggest that reformers did little to change the inequalities and injustices of corporate capitalism (see Lustig 1982). Admittedly, I am emphasizing one strain within a bigger rubric of Progressivism. I do this because, though I am a historian, I am also concerned with contemporary democratic reform and believe that there is a "usable past" that activists today can learn from and from which they can even draw a certain amount of hope. Nonetheless, history provides us no solace or faith for our present conditions. The historian Arthur Schlesinger once talked about "cycles of history," pointing out that periods of liberal reform often followed times of social gluttony (as the Progressive Era followed the Gilded Age and the New Deal followed the Jazz Age of the 1920s). I draw no such hope from history. Reform depends too much upon the energy and initiative of reformers themselves, not upon some mythical change in history.

With this warning in mind, I do think the democratic reform that Progressive Era reformers committed themselves to provides us with an important vision of politics, one that is committed to civic participation while remaining open-ended and finite. These reformers made clear that social justice, democratic participation, and political inclusion (i.e., Addams's arguments for woman's suffrage) must be joined together. Like those who came before them, contemporary reformers must make connections between different goals. That is, getting money out of politics will not necessarily work unless we, at the same time, create new civic forums where citizens can learn about politics and become engaged in local projects. For these reasons, the past teaches us to think both pragmatically and broadly about the bigger ramifications of reform within the history of American democracy.

It is obvious that much has changed since the Progressive Era. For instance, Progressive Era reformers could allude to a "public interest" without as many problems as we have today. In our current world of political discourse, the idea of "special interests" has become so broad as to become almost meaningless. When we consider that the lobby of handicapped citizens is seen as similar to the lobbying power of corporations—both are, after all, "special interests" in current parlance—we realize how much our world has changed from that of the Progressive Era. Just as importantly, the power of money has become more insidious than it was during the Progressive Era. Indeed, money now threatens progressive reforms like the initiative and referendum, reforms initially intended to get money out of politics. With the rise of a powerful mass media, citizens seem more passive and cynical about the possibilities of political change, even though they often complain about corruption like those in the past did.

None of this means that we must abandon the importance of the history discussed here. Things are more complex today, for sure. Nonetheless, the reform tradition traced out here—one that focuses on corruption and the revival of democracy—seems more needed today than ever before. We still need to work to get money out of politics and to build a more inclusive political system (in terms of both people and diverse political viewpoints, the way the Progressive Party tried in 1912). The history discussed here does not provide us with a road map for the future but it shows that reformers before us struggled for democracy with the sort of intelligence and thoughtfulness that we need today.

Part Two

Eliminating Barriers
to Political Participation

Tearing Down Walls

RONALD HAYDUK AND KEVIN MATTSON

Almost everyone would agree that low levels of voter turnout and political participation constitute one of the biggest problems facing American democracy. But *why* there is such a low level of participation produces debate. Social scientists continue to argue about which factors carry the lion's share of responsibility. Many political scientists focus on the social characteristics and attitudes of nonvoters, showing that these citizens tend to have lower levels of education and income, are younger and disproportionately people of color (Campbell et al. 1960; Verba and Nie 1977, 1992). This approach sheds a great deal of light on our problems. But we believe it more effective to examine *institutional mechanisms and arrangements that can be changed through democratic reform*. That is what the authors in this section have set out to do.

Many scholars have already started down this constructive path. Some have focused on changes in the nature of political party system: the relative decline of the parties, the degree of competition between them and the limited range and character of the parties and candidates, the rise of obstacles to ballot access, the increased costs of campaigns and the role of money in elections, and the impacts of cash-intensive media and the use of new campaign technologies (Schattschneider 1960; Burnham 1965; Kleppner 1982; Ware 1988; Wattenberg 1990; McChesney 1999). Others have examined restrictive legal and administrative obstacles that inhibit participation: rules such as poll taxes, literacy tests, residency requirements, and voter registration procedures (Wolfinger and Rosenstone 1980; Powell 1986; Jackman 1987; Piven and Cloward 2000; Keyssar 2000).

Drawing on both of these approaches, the authors in this part discuss the historical genesis of particular election rules and procedures and the ways they continue to shape what Schattschneider refers to as the "scope and bias" of American political participation. In this vein, for instance,

27

Hayduk describes how political elites at the turn of the century promulgated restrictive rules that narrowed possibilities for electoral participation by low-income voters, as well as by third parties and insurgent candidates. The imposition of literacy tests, restrictive voter registration laws, poll taxes, grandfather clauses, and election administrative procedures effectively disenfranchised poor and minority voters. Richard Winger focuses on how the rise of ballot access obstacles snuffed out a vibrant third-party tradition. Taken together over time, these electoral changes narrowed the electoral universe: they created a class- and race-skewed electorate and eroded the capacity of third parties to act as political mobilizers of disenfranchised groups. Both Hayduk and Winger show how these barriers still exist today and help to make clear why voter participation is so low in America. They also make clear that certain reforms can actually combat these problems.

Mark Schmitt then rounds out this part by discussing what can be done to remove another major barrier to political participation—namely, the exorbitant cost of running for elected office. Drawing upon his vast experience in creating campaign finance legislation, Schmitt outlines the history behind the campaign finance struggle that continues at the national level and in a dozen states. He emphasizes what sort of reforms will not work and why, and then sets out his own modest proposal for getting money out of politics.

3

The Weight of History: Election Reform during the Progressive Era and Today

RONALD HAYDUK

In politics as in everything else it makes a great difference whose game we play. The rules of the game determine the requirements for success.

—E. E. Schattschneider, *The Semisovereign People* (1960, 47)

Why were so many Americans, in different places and at different times, denied the right to vote? How could Americans have thought of themselves as democratic while they possessed such a restricted franchise? Most fundamentally, perhaps, how, why and when did the laws governing suffrage change?

—Alexander Keyssar, *The Right to Vote: The Contested History of Democracy in the United States* (2000, xvi–xvii)

There has always been considerable debate and political conflict over the rules and procedures that govern how elections are conducted. For good reason too, since shaping the rules of the game often influences electoral outcomes. If you can manipulate election practices, you can determine the winners and losers. For example, imposition of various restrictions on the franchise, such as poll taxes and literacy tests, severely constrict voter turnout, particularly of poor and minority constituencies. Conversely, providing greater access to voting, such as through Election Day registration, produces higher turnout. Because the stakes can be high, the fights over these electoral changes can be bitter; they are almost always partisan (Keyssar 2000).

One of the obvious lessons of the 2000 elections is how much election practices matter. The presidential limbo the country was mired in revealed that election rules and practices vary greatly and can affect patterns of voter participation and political outcomes. The imbroglio in Florida cast a spotlight on the structures, personnel, procedures, and technologies used to administer elections, highlighting how these elements of the American political system can either disenfranchise eligible voters, or, on the other hand, can facilitate voter participation.

Moreover, the recent presidential election—and previous struggles over electoral arrangements—starkly exposed the political motives and interests of the contenders who fought bitterly over various election procedures. While scholars have debated the degree to which election rules can affect the participation of particular constituents, politicians seem confident that the rules can shape the outcomes of elections, as evidenced in the pitched battles they wage over election law and practice. Not only do they frequently split along party lines to support or oppose electoral changes that can have far-reaching effects (such as campaign finance, ballot access, and proportional representation: see below), but also many politicians readily admit that partisan considerations lie at the heart of such conflict over the rules and procedures governing electoral processes. The machinery that governs elections—literally and figuratively—has been the object of partisan conflict long before the debacle in Florida, precisely because parts of the electoral system have the potential of determining political fortunes. Long before "hanging chads" and "butterfly ballots" became household words, elected officials sparred over the minutia of elections. Indeed, such dynamics are abundantly evident in political debate over the sixteen hundred pieces of election reforms bills that have been proposed (or passed) since the 2000 elections alone (see Center for Policy Alternatives at www.cfpa.org; National Conference of State Legislators at www.ncsl.org/programs/legman/elect/taskfc/database.htm).

Progressive Era reformers successfully enacted measures aimed at cleaning up "corrupt elections," particularly targeting "machine politics." Ironically, while many reform advocates were well intentioned and passed important measures that expanded democracy, some ended up establishing electoral rules and mechanisms that posed substantial barriers to voting. The establishment of restrictive voter registration procedures and partisan election boards are examples of such electoral reforms. These electoral laws and institutions have been subject to political manipulation and continue to disenfranchise millions of otherwise eligible voters today. (On the recent elections, see, for example, CalTech-MIT Voting Technology Project 2001; Roth 2001; Woods and Hancock 2001; Traugott 2001; House Committee on the Judiciary 2001; Barstow and Van Natta Jr. 2001; U.S. Commission on Civil Rights 2001; Lichtman 2001; Brady, Buchler, Jarvis, and McNulty September 2001; General Accounting Office October 2001; The National Commission on Federal Election Reform August 2001; Fagan 2000.) Yet it is often in hindsight or in periods of crisis, however, that the full impacts of such electoral arrangements can be known. Thus, these electoral laws and agencies have come under renewed attack by contemporary democracy advocates.

CONTESTED TERRAIN: VOTER REGISTRATION AND ELECTION ADMINISTRATION

While voter registration procedures have been liberalized, particularly with the passage of the National Voter Registration Act of 1993 (popularly known as motor voter), they still operate to significantly limit voter participation. Scholars have shown that voter registration helps account for much of America's low voter participation. Moreover, nonvoters are disproportionately low-income and minority groups (Wolfinger and Rosenstone 1980; Powell 1986; Rosenstone and Hansen 1993; Piven and Cloward 2000). Requiring voter registration makes voting a two-step process: one must first register to vote up to thirty days before actually casting a ballot. Thus, before voter interest peaks, millions of eligible citizens are effectively disenfranchised. Similarly, in our highly mobile society, where nearly 20 percent of the population moves every year and more than 30 percent moves every two years, voters often find themselves unregistered at their current address (Squire, Wolfinger, and Glass 1987; U.S. Bureau of the Census at www.census.gov/population). About a third of all Americans of voting age are unregistered: over fifty million were not registered on November 7, 2000. While there are a numerous reasons for this, primary are restrictive election policies and bureaucratic hurdles. More importantly, reformers argue, we can actually do something to boost voter participation and therefore make the electorate more representative of the population as a whole and thus politicians more responsive and accountable. Effective voter registration reform—such as Election Day registration (discussed below)—could help make the electoral system more democratic.

Similarly, although election administration has improved in parts of the country, it has been moderate at best. The conduct of elections, overall, remains highly deficient. What became public knowledge with Florida was hitherto a well-kept secret of election officials and observers: that in nearly every election across the country, millions of would-be voters are routinely turned away from poll sites or have their ballots rejected because of bureaucratic snafus. Numerous problems at poll sites frequently continue to mar elections. As was made all too clear in Florida, particular election practices can disenfranchise eligible citizens at any stage: before an election, on Election Day, and during vote certification. This is especially true with regard to low-income groups, minorities, people with disabilities, first-time voters, and older citizens, who are disproportionately among the nonvoting population.

A multitude of factors is to blame. Sometimes eligible voters' names do not appear on the voter registration rolls because of their own missteps or because their registration applications were not properly processed by election officials. Of course, it is the latter types of problems that particularly work to undermine voter confidence in our electoral system. Sometimes, registration applications are not properly and timely transmitted to an election board by another government agency—such as a department of motor vehicles or by some other agency where a voter registered. With disturbing frequency, voters' names are improperly removed (or "purged") from the voter rolls. Furthermore, many would-be voters are discouraged by long lines at the polls, caused by insufficient staffing, a paucity of working voting machines, or a lack of necessary voting materials (such as affidavit or provisional ballots). Poll workers sometimes provide voters with incorrect answers and information, or even illegally ask for identification or otherwise intimidate prospective voters. After an election, poll workers might lose ballots or misread voting machine counts. And different voting technologies can have disenfranchising and discriminatory effects, such as when a ballot counting machine (for example, an optical scanner) fails to recognize a voter's "intent." Again, this is an area that contemporary democracy reformers believe can be readily remedied. Therefore, contemporary reform advocates have set their sights on doing away with these aspects of our electoral system (among others discussed within this volume) that were set up over a hundred years ago.

FROM SECURITY TO ACCESS: THE HISTORICAL ROOTS OF ELECTION RULES AND ADMINISTRATION

The historical trajectory and legacy of the inauguration of voter registration procedures and the establishment of boards of elections are critical in order to understand how they operate and function today. Voter registration and election administration embody a tension inherent in their twin mission: to ensure security against vote fraud and to provide access to the ballot. Striking a balance between these mandates is not easily maintained, particularly in the context of partisan conflict where election practices can become a means to achieving particular ends.

Election fraud, which lies at the heart of the rationale for registration rules and boards of elections, explains many of these rules and administrative structures. Charges of fraud justified the imposition of restrictive voter registration procedures, led to changes in electoral laws and state constitutions, and resulted in the establishment of bipartisan election administration. Allegations of rampant election fraud during decades around the turn of the century were the main justification for these electoral changes. Indeed, the bipartisan structure of boards of elections was founded on the notion that each party will check and balance the other and thereby ensure a fair process (Harris 1934). Today fear of fraud continues to be the most frequently stated reason for opposing liberalizing electoral reform and dispensing with restrictive board of election practices.

This fearful response is flawed. The stated mission of deterring election fraud—like voter registration procedures and bipartisan boards of elections—is largely a product of the rhetoric of elites who had economic and political interests at stake in electoral contests. While election fraud certainly did occur (and may still), evidence suggests that such charges appear to be wildly overblown (Allen and Allen 1981; Argersinger 1985–1986; Keyssar 2000). Whether by design or default, charges of fraud instead served to justify the institutionalization of a host of restrictive procedures that continue to have significant disenfranchising consequences, especially of lower strata groups. The charges of fraud served to justify and perpetuate a more insidious form of "fraud," that is, administrative disenfranchisement of eligible voters.

Registration laws spread across the nation beginning after the Civil War, but particularly between 1890 and 1910 (Harris 1929: it should be noted that Harris's account is flawed but remains the most thorough treatment of this subject.) These registration laws have been characterized as "weak" or "strong" systems (Converse 1972, 283; Kleppner 1982, 60). "Weak" systems, which were established during the earlier period, involved legislation that commissioned election officials to draw up lists of names of residents eligible to vote within their districts. This was done on the basis of their familiarity with their precincts or on the basis of door-to-door canvassing. The vote was thus restricted to those names. To a large extent, however, the burden for registration still remained with the state.

During the 1890s "stronger" types of voter registration systems replaced "weaker" ones that had been used in most states and were introduced in some states that previously had none. The key feature of these changes was the introduction of a personal registration requirement, which shifted the burden of establishing eligibility from the state to the individual (Converse 1974). Moreover, stiff residency requirements were added, from several months to over a year. Over time these general features became more uniform and institutionalized throughout the states.

Many of these laws were initially enacted in most older states in the North, with the law applied only to large cities (Harris 1929). Moreover, some states imposed registration requirements statewide, while others applied one type of requirement to cities and a less stringent one to nonurban areas. States with these "mixed registration systems" often amended their statutes, usually to raise or lower the city size limits. A few states pursued a gradualist approach, first requiring personal registration in the largest cities and then successively extending coverage to smaller-sized cities. In most states, the personal registration requirement put into place near the turn of the century was the final stage in the evolution of its system from "weak" to "strong." The new more stringent registration requirement replaced either a loosely administered nonpersonal system or the complete absence of any registration (Kleppner and Baker 1980, 207; see also Kleppner 1987 and Harris 1929).

At this time, newly established election boards inaugurated restrictive voter registration procedures, hoping to deter fraud and eliminate corruption from the election process. As Joseph Harris explained, "In general, special boards of election were created in the larger cities during the period from 1880 until 1910. These special boards were set up as a device to bring about election reform" (Harris 1934, 19). Like registration, boards of elections were initially only applied to the largest cities but were extended statewide over time. Increasingly, elections officials employed restrictive and disenfranchising election practices, especially toward particular groups such as new immigrants and blacks. And, as the electorate shrank, such practices became more routine.

THE REFORMERS: CONFLICTED MOTIVES AND RESULTS

Perhaps nothing characterizes the Progressive Era of the turn of the 19th century and today's progressives better than the impulse to reform. Many progressives attacked corruption in government—particularly by urban political machines—and sought to make government more efficient and economical. By "throwing the rascals out," progressives hoped to "clean up" government and inject a strong dose of "democracy." They held that "good government" was possible by rationalizing and democratizing politics. To achieve these ends, early progressives inaugurated a broad range of reforms—including important electoral changes—that have had significant and lasting impacts on our electoral system.

While the previous chapter discussed a democratic tendency within Progressivism, there is another strain that demands attention here. One group of Progressive Era reformers tended to be more conservative in their attempt to overthrow the power of urban political machines, regimes that often had the loyal following of ethnic immigrant working-class voters (even when corrupt). In fact, many such progressives held a nativist animus that led to electoral changes that adversely affected working-class immigrant groups. Restrictive voter registration procedures and bipartisan boards of elections were among these. These disenfranchising measures were enacted throughout most parts of the country. Restrictive residency requirements for voting and cumbersome registration procedures effectively barred poor and working-class citizens from participating in elections.

The charge of fraud—so prevalent among this more conservative group of reformers—is also integral to an explanation of why turnout declined precipitously around the turn of the century. From 1830 to 1900 turnout ranged from 70 to 80 percent, as compared to 49 percent in 1924. Some scholars contend that much of the precipitous decline in the rate of voter turnout was illusory (Converse 1972, 1974; Rusk 1970, 1974; Campbell et al. 1960). These scholars argue that the high turnout throughout much of the 19th century was mainly an artifact of a large number of fraudulently cast ballots. They maintain that apparent turnout decline resulted from the adoption and enforcement of legal and institutional reforms including voter registration laws and bipartisan boards of elections. They hold these changes reduced control over the electoral process by the parties themselves and "machines" in particular, and increased regulation and control by "bipartisan" elections officials. Thus, the apparent decline in turnout resulted largely because reform measures reduced the numbers of fraudulent or coerced ballots cast. As evidence they correlate the introduction of reforms and decline in turnout and note variations in registration and voting requirements (such as residency requirements, poll taxes, closing dates for registration, etc.) that correlate with differences in state turnout levels.

But other scholars have criticized these assumptions and produced compelling counterevidence. Burnham (1974a, b), for example, argues that allegations of electoral fraud reflected elite motivations and interests of those who inaugurated and implemented them. Kleppner (1980) argues that although allegations of fraud abound, there are only a handful of concrete cases that have become "classics" partly because they were referred to so frequently in the contemporary "reform" literature: "What is most impressive about that literature is how few (and *not* how many) concrete instances it cited. It did not pile case upon case to build to a conclusion, but used specific examples only as illustrations of the general— and taken for granted—principle that 'corruption' pervaded the electoral (and political) system" (Kleppner 1982, 59). Kleppner acknowledges that fraud certainly existed, but we should not assume the frequently cited "notorious cases" were but the tip of the iceberg (much as the image of the all-powerful "machine" has been mythologized). He argues that fraud was more "episodic than routine, not sufficiently widespread to account for a general inflation of the turnout rate of as much as 5 to 8 percent, and certainly not supported by any underlying ethos of corruption. . . . [If] routine and extensive vote fraud was unlikely, then it is equally unlikely that the general decline in turnout after 1896 could be attributed to procedural changes that eliminated it" (Kleppner 1982, 59–60). Kleppner cites other factors (like the decline of party competition) for the drop-off in turnout.

Perhaps most revealing is that charges of fraud—and the laws they helped create—reflected a nativistic animus aimed at the new urban immigrants who were tied to party machines, which some reformers reviled (Allen and Allen 1981; Argersinger 1985–1986). Most fraud allegations originated within Republican Party organizations, oppositional factions within Democratic Party ranks, or upper-class reform movements, who charged dominant regimes (generally Democratic Party machines) with fraudulent activities. The most frequent charges came during the years of the heaviest immigration (1870s through the 1920s). Much writing was "openly condescending, moralistic, and prejudiced toward the new arrivals. . . . The literature on election fraud, in sum, corresponded roughly with the years of the mugwump-progressive reform movements and can be seen as a manifestation of the middle and upper-class reform of these years" (Allen and Allen 1981, 172–74).

These studies show that charges originated in muckraking magazines (such as *Harper's Weekly, Outlook, McClure's, Century,* and *Forum*) whose writers were native born, white, Protestant, middle- and upper-class progressive reformers. The accounts were largely anecdotal and based on accounts of highly motivated observers and participants. Most accounts were not written by "disinterested" observers, but rather by people who were engaged in reform activity. Indeed, authors of this strain of reform literature (including the influential work of Joseph Harris and his affiliates, which included the Brookings Institute and the National Municipal League, that funded his studies), were very active in the movement to reform election procedures. "Not to say he [Harris] distorted consciously the record, but marshaled evidence to make the best case for his point of view" (Kleppner 1987, 168). Nevertheless, this perspective has been generalized from these anecdotes and substantially incorporated into the scholarship on the subject.

Debate at the time over the merits and consequences of voter registration procedures and boards of elections, however, was pointed and revealing. For example, Judge George W. McCrary, U.S. Circuit Court judge and former member of the House of Representatives and chairman of the Committee on Elections, argued:

A question of great practical importance and of some difficulty has of late been much discussed in the courts, and conflicting views have been expressed. It is this: Is an act which denies the right to vote to all persons not registered on or before a fixed day prior to the day of election and which makes no provision for registration after the time limited, so onerous and unreasonable as to be justly regarded an impairment of the constitutional right to vote? (McCrary 1887, 59)

Clearly, the disenfranchising consequences of these new more restrictive laws were not lost on those who were on either side of these debates.

Indeed, changes in election law reflected distinct partisan considerations. Scholars have documented the patterns of political actors who promoted and opposed such electoral rule changes (McCormick 1981; McGerr 1986; Piven and Cloward 1988). Richard L. McCormick (1981) describes how Republicans sought to impose a more stringent registration law for New York City, for example, while maintaining a weak or nonexistent registration law for the rest of the state. Conversely, Democrats sought a less stringent law for New York City or a uniform statewide registration law. (See also Harris 1929.) Richard P. McCormick documents a similar pattern in New Jersey, concluding: "The significant fact is, however, that all but a conspicuous few of the scores of laws that were passed [during 1870s–1900] were intended for no other purpose than to insure the supremacy of the temporarily dominant party" (McCormick 1953, 163). It was common for Republicans to pass a restrictive registration law, and then, when Democrats took over control of a state's legislature, for them to repeal it. Moreover, McCormick argues that in creating and controlling the election boards "the party controlling the municipality could be fairly well assured of having complete control of the registration and election machinery" (McCormick 1953, 163). Indeed, Republicans and reformers won the day by firmly ensconcing such measures not just in statutes but in states' constitutions.

One of the earliest studies that documented the disenfranchising impacts of registration and administrative procedures was conducted by Charles Merriam and Harold Gosnell (1924). They and their team of researchers documented that "legal and administrative obstacles" contributed to nonvoting in the 1923 mayoral election in Chicago (garnering information from interviewing 6,000 voters, 300 "experts," and census data). They observed that the manner in which elections are conducted can contribute to nonvoting, even while they attributed greater weight to other factors. They found that registration and other administrative obstacles kept 13 percent of the eligible electorate from the polls. The legal and administrative obstacles to voting they found included "insufficient legal residence, fear of loss of business or wages, congestion at the polls, poor location of polling booth, and fear of disclosure of age. . . . A common characteristic of all of these five reasons for not voting is that they are based, in part at least, upon some defect of the election system which could be remedied either by changing the law or its administration" (1924, 78). Merriam and Gosnell described how even though the election law prescribed particular parameters for the administration of elections, these were not always complied with and could result in nonvoting. For example, the law stated that a voting precinct should contain "as nearly practicable" up to 400 voters, but some precincts contained 500–600 voters, and "it is quite obvious that the congestion at the polls in the working-class precincts early in the morning kept a considerable number from voting." Similarly, poll site locations are to be "the most public and convenient places that can be found in each precinct," but some "were located in barber shops, pool rooms, basements, garages, and other places to which sensitive women hesitated to go." Moreover, "the complaints regarding voting facilities were found more largely among the colored, the German, the Polish, and Russian non-voters . . . , and in poor neighborhoods" (1924, 96–98).

Furthermore, the study found that the motives of the dominant party organization (Democrat) and election workers appear to have been at work in many of these instances. "By far the greatest number of cases of intimidation were found in the colored settlement that had recently sprung up in the Ghetto district. The Democratic Party organization in this district was strongly entrenched and resented the influx of colored Republican voters. Consequently the party workers used various devices to persuade the Negroes not to vote. The Democratic workers made application to have the names of registered Negroes erased. The Negroes were then sent 'suspect' notices which they had to answer in person before the Election Commissioners" (Merriam and Gosnell 1924, 107–8). Consequently, they concluded that "not only did the residency requirements, the voting hours, and the registration system keep many people from voting, but the failure of the local boards to perform their tasks efficiently had a depressing effect upon the number voting."

Thus, the interests of those who won these political struggles are embedded in the electoral arrangements and these institutions. Moreover, the trajectory of restrictive voter registration procedures and practices of boards of elections continues to operate today. In the name of protecting against election fraud and reforming corrupt political machines, elite political interests successfully established an election system—whether by design or default—that perpetrated restrictive electoral practices and thus political disenfranchisement. The political biases of the past continue to haunt the contemporary electoral system through the development of these legal rules and institutions. There appears good historical reason to believe electoral changes have helped depress turnout, especially of low-income and minority groups.

THAT WAS THEN, THIS IS NOW—AND
NOT A WHOLE LOT HAS CHANGED

Contemporary political actors continue to benefit from such arrangements. The trajectory of these earlier reforms left their imprint on electoral processes and are still intact. Contemporary voter registration procedures and practices of boards of elections continue to have significant impacts in constricting participation. Moreover, if the establishment of registration barriers was not accidental, neither is their persistence. Contemporary dominant political parties and politicians have deliberately sustained these barriers for similar motives. Although there have been important successes in reforming the electoral system—particularly toppling of the most egregious features of the southern electoral system, the expansion of the electorate to include eighteen-year-olds, and the passage and initial implementation of the National Voter Registration Act—efforts to liberalize the system have been repeatedly turned back at the national, state, and local levels.

The fraud bugaboo still serves as the major justification for blocking contemporary reforms, particularly voter registration laws and practices (Piven and Cloward 2000; Advancement Project 2001a, b). Since the 1960s, opposition to legislation that would ease voter registration procedures and election administration—whether at the federal or state level—has come from Republicans, "conservatives," and incumbents more generally. In their view, though the electoral system has shortcomings, they are relatively minor compared to the potential problem of increased fraud that current reforms would produce.

But Florida has provided contemporary democracy reform advocates with a new opening. Efforts to change voter registration procedures have generally been championed by a variety of voting rights and civic organizations and "liberal" Democrats. These advocates of reform indict the American political system as not being sufficiently representative and democratic, and they place part of the blame on what they characterize as our overly restrictive registration system and antiquated election administration. They aim, in part, to increase turnout in electoral contests, especially among minority groups and the poor who, since the postwar period, traditionally have very low rates of voting turnout and who generally support Democrats. They contend that an enlarged electorate would potentially lead to different candidates and policies and would invigorate democratic practice more broadly.

Despite this sort of opposition, some of the most onerous electoral laws and rules—poll taxes, literacy tests, and restrictive registration procedures—have been eliminated or liberalized on the premise that they tend to fetter voting, particularly for lower-income and minority citizens.

Changing the rules, many scholars and reform advocates thought, would lead to increased participation. Yet, voter registration and turnout has remained low or continued to decline. Attempts to explain the ineffectiveness of rule liberalization on voter participation has been termed the "puzzle of participation" (Brody 1978), and this apparent discrepancy has generated much debate in political science.

While several factors certainly contribute to low rates of registration and turnout, we need to dig deeper. Just as the patchwork of election law varies between states and contributes to differential levels of registration and turnout, the *process* of implementing electoral law is highly variable—even within states—and can produce distinctly different outcomes. The way reforms have been implemented may have rendered them ineffective. Practically speaking, discretionary administrative actions and/or noncompliance can void even well-conceived laws and executive directives. Making voter registration possible by mail does not in itself put registration forms in the hands of voters, nor does mandating that government agencies expand registration opportunities.

Studies in public administration and policy analysis demonstrate how distinct patterns of implementing law produce variable impacts. Throughout American history, state and local officials have undermined national programs (i.e., during the Depression, southern officials distributed public goods intended for all only to the white population). Some have suggested that discretionary administrative practices in implementing law often reveal political considerations at their roots (Pressman and Wildavsky 1973; Sabatier and Mazmanian 1983). Such dynamics can have important impacts, especially in the context of devolution of federal power and oversight.

Elections are especially susceptible to partisan dynamics because of their decentralized structure and potential to affect the balance of political power. Because the administration of elections in most of the United States is decentralized with effectively little or no federal or state oversight, there is considerable latitude for discretionary actions by state and local boards of elections. Reform of the laws governing the franchise has largely not been accompanied by the necessary and concomitant changes in the bureaucratic structures that administer elections. For instance, elections officials could institute programs that provide for wide distribution of registration forms—and in places some administrators in fact did. (Knack 1995; Piven and Cloward 2000). Such examples, however, have been few and far between. In the main, boards of elections tend to reflect the influence of dominant political actors, especially incumbents (Gosnell and Smolka 1976, 118–22; Piven and Cloward 1988, 195–200).

Partisan politics clearly plays a role in the way electoral rules are written and administered. Election officials, whether local, county, or state-level, are closely tied to and dependent upon dominant politicians. In most places, election boards are staffed by political appointees of the two major parties. Dominant political actors of *both parties* have incumbency interests in maintaining a stable and constricted electorate and party system; they mutually resist outsiders, whether as new and unpredictable voters or as insurgent candidates (Schattschneider 1960; Shefter 1994). Dominant politicians wield tremendous influence over employees of election boards even in "nonpartisan" electoral systems (Hayduk 1996). Thus, given the leeway election officials have in implementing electoral law, their practices often reflect political relations. Even the most sacrosanct and insulated election procedures and agencies can become the focus of sharp partisan conflict, particularly when elections are close and contested.

Several studies of voter registration reform expose the power of local elections officials. For example, the League of Women Voters conducted a study that documented the administrative practices of elections officials in 257 communities in 47 states during the fall of 1971. The League of Women Voters found that election administration in the United States was generally "inefficient," often "obstructive" to efforts to increase participation, and that "millions" were disenfranchised by the practices of boards of elections. Similarly, the National Municipal League conducted a study of election reform across the United States in the early 1970s concluding, "legal expansion of the electorate can be administratively blunted . . . when that is the intention of local administrators[. This] demonstrates the important relationship between administrative procedures and electoral participation" (1974). They pointed to examples where election officials played a clear role in disenfranchising particular groups, especially blacks and youth. The disenfranchisement of blacks and poor whites in the South through the use of literacy tests and restrictive voter registration procedures provides ample evidence of how election officials can implement election laws in exclusionary ways (Key 1949; Kousser 1974).

Scholars of elections have also shown that election administration can have important impacts on voter participation and electoral outcomes:

> There are many administrative decisions affecting the outcome of elections (including voter turnout) which can be made by election administrators. The usual practice is to have policy determined by a bipartisan board controlled by the major political party in the county or the state. This practice has permitted a substantial advantage to accrue to the majority party, in particular, and to the incumbents of both parties with respect to party primary elections. . . . If the dominant political party thinks that it can gain by getting more people to register, there will be a great effort to establish decentralized registration locations, appoint deputy registrars, widely advertise registration activity, and concentrate such activity in geographic areas

where the party stands to gain the most. On the other hand, if the dominant party thinks that increased registration may weaken its plurality by admitting large numbers of persons who are expected to vote with the opposition, it will be reluctant to encourage registration, will react against proposals to increase registration opportunity, may limit the number of deputy registrars, or establish time-consuming procedures which tend to discourage both workers and prospective registrants. (Gosnell with Smolka 1976, 118–22)

Following the Florida election fiasco, there is now a plethora of information on practices of contemporary election administration. More recently, several studies show how differing electoral practices and technologies can have significant electoral impacts. (See, for example, CalTech/MIT 2001; Roth 2001; Woods and Hancock 2001; and Traugott 2001, from a joint project of the American Political Science Association, the American Psychological Association, and the Consortium of Social Science Associations at www.apsanet.org/new/briefing.cfm; Brady, Buchler, Jarvis, and McNulty 2001; U.S. Commission on Civil Rights 2001.)

PROSPECTS FOR THE FUTURE

The flaws in our electoral system exposed by the Florida debacle made the most technologically advanced and richest nation in human history the laughing stock of the world. Not surprisingly, a plethora of reform measures have been proposed at the federal, state, and local levels. By some estimates, over 1,600 election-related bills have been introduced, with perhaps only 200 proposing substantial reform to our election rules and institutions (Center for Policy Alternatives, www.cfpa.org). Few have actually passed. (See Election Reform Information Project, October 2001.)

Some of these bills propose that bipartisan commissions study potential reforms. These bills primarily focus on improving the efficiency of election administration and machinery through increased funding (whether by the federal government or by state governments). Other proposals aim to establish uniform standards and procedures in election administration that ensure the integrity of casting and counting ballots. Professional organizations that represent elections officials—including the National Association of State Election Directors (NASED), the National Association of Secretaries of State (NASS), the National Conference of State Legislatures (NCSL), and the National Association of County Recorders, Elections Officials, and Clerks (NACRC)—have also established task forces to examine potential reforms. Twenty-nine states have proposed similar studies and task forces ("Democracy Dispatches," Number 4, June 25, 2001, Demos: A Network for Ideas and Action, www.demos-usa.org). A number of private organizations have set up prestigious commissions to examine elections and recommend reforms, including the National Commission on Federal Election Reform headed by former Presidents Carter and Ford (and managed by the Century Foundation); the Constitution Project's Forum on Election Reform; academic institutions, such as MIT and CalTech; and a broad range of voting rights and civic groups.

The kinds of reform proposals percolating up vary, particularly at the state level. Many reforms involve upgrading election machinery and developing uniform voting standards in time for upcoming elections. Others go beyond this by arguing for independent or nonpartisan professionals to oversee and administer elections rather than the political parties, politicians, and their appointees who staff most election boards today. Some reformers call for establishing a holiday for Election Day, extending voting over a two-day period (possibly a weekend or part of a weekend and a weekday), making it possible to register and vote on Election Day, vote by mail, or over the Internet. Still others call for expanding the franchise to felons or to noncitizens. These reformers argue that there are currently over four million primarily African American and other people of color that are denied voting rights, even after serving their sentences; and some twelve to fifteen million legal permanent residents are similarly without the vote, though they are subject to all laws and taxation (Manza et al. 2001; see also the Sentencing Project and the Advancement Project Web sites). These reformers believe democracy is diminished not just by poor voter turnout, but also by the exclusion of minorities and the powerless. They argue that far-reaching reforms could increase electoral competition, make the parties more responsive and accountable to the electorate, and invigorate our democracy.

Many reformers point to a wide range of innovative election laws and programs that already exist in several states that have proven successful in expanding voter participation and democracy. Election Day voter registration, for example, exists in six states (Maine, New Hampshire, Wisconsin, Minnesota, Idaho, and Wyoming). Voting by mail is used effectively in Oregon and Washington; early voting programs are used in Texas; expanded use of absentee voting has been implemented in several states; motor voter is in effect in forty-six states since 1995–1996; and Internet voting has been used in Arizona.

Such electoral reforms provide easier access to the franchise and thus enhance possibilities for marginal voters to participate, which in turn encourage challengers to run and stimulate competition or effective appeals further drawing voters into the active electorate, and so on. States with Election Day voter registration, for example, continue to have the highest turnout; states that permit mail elections and early voting also show an increase in voter participation. Not surprisingly, many of these states have more progressive social policies reflecting the demands of newly included minorities and the previously disenfranchised (Hill and Leighley 1992).

Dominant and incumbent politicians of all leanings, who were elected by a constricted electorate, are cool to such broader reforms. They often see new voters as a threat (see the Mitchell chapter in this volume). Elected and elections officials often resist changes not just because of incumbency interests but due to bureaucratic inertia. Once again, these elected and elections officials—and other conservative groups—point to potential voter fraud to justify the status quo. (For example, see Voting Integrity Project at www.votingintegrity.org.) In fact, some not only oppose easing registration and voting processes but also propose "reforms" that call for greater safeguards to the ballot, which are tantamount to establishing even more restrictive measures.

CONCLUSION

The events in Florida obviously change things. The already existing democracy movement got a shot in the arm and grew in size and breadth. The democracy renewal movement is now larger and more diverse than in any time since the civil rights era. Multiracial coalitions of old-time predominantly white civic organizations (such as the League of Women Voters) are teaming up with mobilized African American and other communities of color organizations. Together, these groups provide hope for real change rather than the simple act of upgrading voting machines. Indeed, many such groups—including labor unions—are developing a broader democracy agenda that incorporates linking electoral reforms to issues of economic and social justice. This mobilization could prove powerful and significant, if it can expand over the next several years. Although there is a broad mobilization to expand the franchise and further democratize America's electoral system, there is at the same time, forces working to thwart such efforts. Florida created an opening to expand democracy in the United States; it remains to be seen if it will usher in democracy's moment.

4

More Choice Please! Why U.S. Ballot Access Laws Are Discriminatory and How Independent Parties and Candidates Challenge Them

RICHARD WINGER

It is working well by having a Republican Party and a Democratic Party. I don't think North Carolina having the most restrictive ballot access rule is a bad thing.

—Representative Leo Daughtry,
North Carolina House Republican leader, June 5, 2001

BALLOT ACCESS AND DEMOCRACY

The United States has the most discriminatory ballot access laws of any democratic nation. The vast majority of free nations provide equal ballot access procedures for all parties and candidates. For instance, in the United Kingdom, each candidate for the House of Commons must submit ten signatures and a fee of 500 pounds. The requirement is the same for every candidate. By contrast, every state in the United States makes general election ballot access automatic for Democratic and Republican Party nominees, but many states provide that nominees of other parties must submit tens of thousands of signatures on petitions. These petitions sometimes must be notarized. Sometimes the signatures must be gathered in a short period of time and submitted a year before the election. Sometimes they cannot be signed by voters who intend to vote in a Democratic or Republican primary. Almost always, the signatures are checked, and names are invalidated if the handwriting is illegible or if the address shown on the petition does not match the address for that voter on the registration rolls.

Thus, petitions are often invalidated, and the nominees of minor parties, and independent candidates, fail to appear on the ballot. Essentially, some voters are denied a choice. At the November 2000 election, for example, Ralph Nader supporters were disenfranchised totally in North Carolina,

South Dakota, and Oklahoma, and Nader supporters in Georgia, Idaho, Wyoming, and Indiana were forced to cast a write-in vote in order to vote for Nader. Also in November 2000, supporters of Harry Browne, the Libertarian presidential nominee, were completely disenfranchised in Arizona, while Buchanan supporters were forced to use write-in procedures in Michigan.

Some feel that laws that keep minor-party and independent candidates off the ballot do not matter, since, they assume, minor-party and independent candidates never get elected anyway. This assumption is wrong. In the course of the 20th century, voters sent numerous independent and third-party candidates to federal office and to state houses. Minor-party or independent candidates for governor won sixteen times, five of which were in the 1990s. Twelve times since 1914, the year popular election of senators began, voters sent third-party and independent candidates to the U.S. Senate, and nineteen times to the House of Representatives. Minor-party and independent candidates have frequently also been elected to state legislatures. In the 2000 election alone, five minor-party candidates (who were not jointly the nominees of any major party) were elected to state legislatures.

But these victories for third-party and independent candidates have come despite the onerous ballot access obstacles erected by state legislatures. Restrictive state ballot access laws have been *encouraged* by the U.S. Supreme Court. A quick look back into history helps elucidate how this came to be. Indeed, as we shall see, the United States previously had much more open ballot access laws that did not pose such problems for third parties and independent candidates.

BALLOT ACCESS IN U.S. HISTORY

Until 1888, there were no government-printed ballots in the United States. Voters were free to prepare their own ballots, though most voters simply used the ballot provided by a political party. Ballots printed by political parties only named that particular party's candidates, but a voter using a party-printed ballot was free to cross out names he didn't like and substitute others. Before government-printed ballots existed, it was impossible for governments to prevent voters from voting for anyone they wished. Once the government started printing ballots, it could prevent voters from voting for certain candidates. Sometimes the government gained total control over the voter by even abolishing write-in space on the ballot or by refusing to tally any write-in votes.

Beginning in 1892 and especially after 1896, however, states began to impose more onerous requirements on third parties. In part, this was in response to several strong third-party movements—such as the populist People's Party—that not only challenged the two major parties, but actually won offices at the federal level and in many states and localities. Similarly, direct primaries replaced party conventions as the mechanism to select candidates. In response, state legislators created more restrictive barriers to their potential opponents. From 1910 to 1920 many states passed legislation that raised the bar higher for third-party and independent candidates.

Once the government started printing ballots in the 1880s and 1890s—replacing party-printed ballots—third parties and independents began to experience greater difficulties obtaining ballot status and votes. This reform, often referred to as the "Australian Ballot," was pressed by reformers who sought to dislodge party control over elections. Ironically, minor parties themselves also were proponents of the move to have the government print ballots, thus alleviating them of the burden to distribute ballots where they had no political base. The government would now be mandated to carry the names of all candidates.

In the early years, few state legislatures used their power to write laws that kept minor parties and independent candidates off the ballot. By 1920, every state except Georgia and South Carolina had some type of government-printed ballots. Still, the median petition requirement to place a new party on the ballot that year was only eight-hundredths of 1 percent of the electorate. Thus, in 1924, independent Progressive presidential candidate Robert La Follette was able to get on the ballot of all states except Louisiana, even though he didn't decide to run until June.

The harshest laws have been passed since 1969. As recently as 1948, *thirty-one* of the forty-eight states permitted a minor-party presidential candidate to get on the ballot with a procedure that required 1,000 or fewer supporters. Thirteen states did not require any petitions, or other numerical requirements, for a minor-party presidential candidate to get on the ballot. Instead, the candidate or the party simply made a request. Another eighteen states required a petition or a meeting but demanded 1,000 or fewer signatures or attendees. By contrast, in 2000, instead of thirty states with a numerical requirement of 1,000 or fewer, there were only twelve such states.

Between 1931 and 1951, fifteen states drastically increased ballot access hurdles. Ohio, for example, increased the independent candidate petition from 1 percent of the last gubernatorial vote, to 7 percent; also presidential candidates could no longer use the independent petition method. After 1951, the only method open to new party or independent presidential candidates to get on the Ohio ballot was to circulate the new party petition, which required signatures equal to 15 percent of the last gubernatorial vote. Write-in votes were also banned. By 1968, a new party or independent presidential candidate needed 433,100 signatures to get on the Ohio general election ballot. Although Ohio had kept all minor-party and independent presidential candidates off its ballot for the years 1952–1964, no group or candidate had ever brought a lawsuit against the post-1951 ballot access laws, until 1968.

In 1967, Alabama Governor George Wallace decided to run for president as an independent. In some states, he created a new party; in other states he ran as an independent. Between September 1967 and September 1968, he got on the ballot of every state except Ohio. On July 29, 1968, he sued Ohio, alleging that its ballot access laws violated the First and Fourteenth Amendments. The three-judge U.S. District Court agreed with Wallace that the Ohio laws were unconstitutional, but it refused to put him on the ballot, saying that he should have filed the lawsuit earlier. It did order the state to print write-in space on ballots and to count write-in votes for president.

INCREASED RESTRICTIONS TO BALLOT ACCESS: BLAME THE U.S. SUPREME COURT

State legislatures have the authority to write all ballot access laws—even for federal elections—and since 1971 state legislatures have passed more severe ballot access laws. These laws are largely due to encouragement legislators receive from the U.S. Supreme Court. Though the Constitution includes the Fourteenth Amendment, which proclaims that "no state shall deny to any person within its jurisdiction the equal protection of the laws," the U.S. Supreme Court has approved state ballot access laws that discriminate against voters who wish to support parties other than the Democratic and Republican Parties. Thus, the role of the Supreme Court helps us understand the severity of ballot access in the United States over time.

Although the Supreme Court had been more lenient toward third-party and independent candidates prior to 1971 (particularly in 1968), crucial appointments made by President Nixon after Chief Justice Warren and Abe Fortas resigned allowed a majority of justices to form on the Court that opened the flood gates to bad state laws. This majority has held hostile attitudes toward minor-party and independent candidates and the voters who support them. The Court's rulings since 1971 have sent a clear message to state legislators: restricting ballot access is legal.

The consequences are that Americans who are activists or members of minor parties, or who prefer to vote for the candidates of a minor party, are treated as second-class citizens. In certain states, such voters are barred from serving as local elections officials, based on their party membership. In certain states these voters cannot register as members of their parties, even though their Democratic or Republican neighbors are free to register as they wish. Sometimes minor-party and independent candidates are barred from government-sponsored debates, or barred from even attempting to qualify for public campaign funds. Worst of all, minor-party voters are not permitted to vote for the candidate of their choice in all but a handful of states.

It is this majority of U.S. Supreme Court justices that have ruled that the U.S. Constitution permits unequal treatment of voters and candidates who aren't Republicans or Democrats. On numerous occasions, the Court has approved of discriminatory policies toward minor-party and independent candidates and voters. On other occasions, the Court had a chance to stop these policies but refused to do so. Apparently, the Court has misunderstood how minor parties and independent candidates have historically not only always been present in American politics but have also made significant contributions to public debate and policy. Or it may be that they understand this history all too well and are opposed to such challenges to the two dominant parties and their allies.

It is hard to overemphasize the role this hostile majority on the U.S. Supreme Court has played in thwarting candidacies of third parties and independent campaigns. Again, history is a good teacher. The Court's role became evident as early as 1970, during a case where the Socialist Workers Party filed lawsuits challenging the number of signatures required in four states. The Socialist Labor Party was a coplaintiff in the Ohio case; it had also been a coplaintiff with Wallace in *Williams v. Rhodes*. The lower courts had to take some sort of action on the 1970 cases in time for the November 1970 election, but they were puzzled as to what the Supreme Court wanted them to do. In *Williams v. Rhodes*, the Supreme Court had struck down all of the Ohio ballot access laws. This included the independent candidate petition requirement of 7 percent of the last gubernatorial vote, which applied to all offices except president. Since the U.S. Supreme Court had struck down a 7 percent petition, it would have been reasonable for the lower courts to strike down somewhat similar petitions in other states. However, only the U.S. District Court in Ohio struck down any of the challenged laws. The court in California ducked the issue, saying the case had been filed too late in the election year to be decided. The court in Massachusetts refused injunctive relief but postponed the decision on the law's constitutionality until 1972. The court in Georgia upheld the state law in 1970.

Meanwhile, in 1970, the Socialist Workers and Socialist Labor Parties had sued New York, not over the 12,000-signature requirement for statewide minor-party and independent candidate petitions (12,000 was only one-seventh of 1 percent of the number of registered voters), but against the requirement that the petition include fifty signatures from sixty-one of the state's sixty-two counties. The case was called *Socialist Workers Party v. Rockefeller.* The three-judge U.S. District Court invalidated the law on June 18, 1970. This was not surprising, since the case seemed to mirror the Supreme Court's 1969 Illinois ruling, *Moore v. Ogilvie.* However, since New York permits "fusion," and since major-party candidates in New York sometimes create new "political parties" in order to give themselves additional lines on the voting machines, the decision opened a ballot access stampede. Republican and Democratic candidates alike rushed to complete petitions under newly created party labels, nominating themselves multiple times, with such "parties" as the "Conservation Party," the "Civil Service-Independent Party," and the "Independent Alliance." The county distribution requirement had been eliminated, so it was possible to complete such statewide petitions entirely in New York City and its densely populated suburbs. With no distribution requirement, it was fairly easy to get 12,000 signatures. It seemed there would be so many parties on the 1970 ballot the voting machines would be unable to handle them all.

The Supreme Court, in response to an emergency request from the state, stayed the order of the U.S. District Court on July 11. However, on October 12, after the dust had settled and it was apparent that voting machines could in fact accommodate all the petitions, the Court dissolved the stay. It also voted not to hear New York's appeal. However, three of the justices voted to hear the New York case, suggesting that they were alarmed by the potential ballot-crowding and were perhaps ready to reverse *Moore v. Ogilvie.* The three justices were Burger, Stewart, and Harlan. Harlan and Stewart had opposed the *Moore* decision, and Burger was casting his first vote on a ballot access matter. The decision not to hear the case had the legal effect of affirming the decision of the lower court, since at the time, the Supreme Court had no choice but to either hear constitutional cases or affirm them with no hearing.

On October 26, 1970, the Supreme Court agreed to hear the Georgia ballot access case brought by the Socialist Workers Party. It is likely that, as of that date, a new majority on the Court had already resolved to accept a new ballot access appeal and to uphold some states' ballot access laws to forestall an avalanche of new litigation around the next presidential election. All members of the Court were surely concerned that New York had narrowly avoided the nightmare of an overly crowded ballot. The Georgia case was the only ballot access case in which either side was asking for U.S. Supreme Court review. The Socialist Workers Party had not appealed its California case, and its Massachusetts case was still in the lower court. Ohio did not appeal its loss until January 14, 1971 (the Court accepted Ohio's appeal on March 29, but a few months later the legislature lowered the petition requirements substantially, so Ohio dropped its appeal).

A Bad Precedent: *Jenness v. Fortson*

The Georgia case, *Jenness v. Fortson*, was argued on March 1, 1971, and it proved to be disastrous for minor parties. The Georgia law required the Socialist Workers Party 1970 candidate for governor of Georgia, Linda Jenness, to obtain 88,175 signatures, which was 5 percent of the number of registered voters as of 1968. The state pointed out that the 5 percent petition requirement had been successfully used both in 1966 and in 1968. The Socialist Workers Party arguments were too extreme to be convincing. The party representatives pointed out that Democrats and Republicans could gain a place on the primary ballot with no petition (they only had to pay a fee). Therefore, the lawyers reasoned, a requirement for other parties to go hunting for signatures violated Equal Protection. Of course, the state countered this by saying that Democrats and Republicans had the burden of winning a primary, in order to advance to the general election ballot. The state mentioned that twelve individuals had sought the gubernatorial nomination of either major party in 1970 and suggested that Linda Jenness must be unaware of how much work it was to win a primary.

The Court also suggested that petitioning in other states where there were more restrictions was more difficult than in Georgia. However, one of the alleged restrictions, a law in New York saying no one could sign a petition unless he or she had been registered at the preceding general election, had already been held unconstitutional in 1970 in *Socialist Workers Party v. Rockefeller*. This was the same decision that the U.S. Supreme Court had affirmed a few months earlier. Hence, that restriction was no longer in effect and should not have been cited as an example of an existing law. Another example, a Rhode Island law barring petition signers from voting in a primary for two years, was to be held unconstitutional by a U.S. District Court in 1972. All of the other examples listing restrictive practices in other states were to be repealed during the 1970s.

The *Jenness* decision said, "The 5% figure is, to be sure, apparently somewhat higher than the percentage of support required to be shown in many States." But this was misleading. Georgia and the Socialist Workers Party had jointly prepared an appendix, listing the ballot access requirements of all the states, which was part of the case record. Georgia had the toughest requirement in the nation for third parties. Arkansas had a petition signed by 7 percent of the last vote cast for governor, a number that, following the 1970 election, was only 4.4 percent of the number of registered voters as of 1972. Ohio had no valid law at the moment, but in a few months it was to pass a 1 percent (of the last vote cast) procedure for new parties, and an independent candidate procedure of only 5,000 signatures (which was only one-eighth of 1 percent of the number of registered voters). All the other states had minor-party procedures that were equal to, or less than, 5 percent of the last vote cast. The median requirement (using the state's easier method for ballot access, either independent candidate or new party methods) of the fifty states for the 1970 election was one-third of 1 percent. The U.S. Supreme Court was dishonest when it described Georgia's requirement as "apparently somewhat higher than . . . in many States," since it was actually the toughest in the nation.

Completely lacking in the *Jenness* decision is any rationale for why the state needed to have such a high petition requirement. But the most disastrous aspect of the *Jenness* decision was that it approved how Georgia defined a "party" as an organization, which had polled 20 percent of the vote for president (in the entire United States) or 20 percent for governor of Georgia. Because the Court mentioned this and seemed to find no fault with it, lower courts ever since have interpreted the *Jenness* decision to approve of a 20 percent vote test definition of "political party." As a result, no federal Court of final jurisdiction has ever invalidated any state's definition of "political party," no matter how onerous it was. A 1984 U.S. District Court in Colorado struck down that state's definition of "party," a group that polled 10 percent for governor. But the 10th Circuit reversed the District Court and upheld the law.

The implications of *Jenness*—a unanimous decision—are disturbing. The decision made it constitutional for any state to raise its petition procedures to 5 percent of the registered voters and require multiple petitions for each candidate. Such petitions could not be circulated until after the group had chosen its candidates, which meant that they would need to choose their candidates in the year before the election. Also, such procedures could be required for all organizations that had not polled 20 percent of the vote at the last election for president (in the entire nation) or governor. If every state were to exercise its right to make these changes, a new party or an independent candidate for president in 2000 would have needed 8,230,958 valid signatures to appear on the ballot in all states and the District of Columbia. The existing requirements were too tough even for Ralph Nader to get on the ballot in all states in 2000; he missed qualifying in seven states. The *Jenness* decision allowed the states to require sixteen times as many signatures as were actually required in 2000. If the states were to implement *Jenness* rules to a tee, it is likely that every state would have had a Bush–Gore ballot monopoly in 2000 and that 4 percent of voters who ended up voting for someone else would have been disenfranchised. Georgia itself voluntarily lowered its statewide petitions from 5 percent of the registered voters to 1 percent in 1986; no state currently requires a petition signed by as many as 5 percent of the registered voters. But, if any state desired to, it could.

Throughout the 1970s, sympathy for minor parties and independent candidates on the U.S. Supreme Court continued to be in short supply. In 1972, the Court summarily affirmed three-judge District Court opinions from Ohio and Kentucky, upholding March petition deadlines for minor party and independent candidate ballot access. Again, although the news media barely noticed these decisions, the implications were shocking. Numerous important new political parties had been formed in the United States during an election year. The Republican Party had been formed on July 6, 1854, and had gone on to win a plurality in the U.S. House of Representatives that same year. If a law had existed back in 1854 requiring new parties to have completed petitions bearing thousands of names by March of an election year, the Republican Party would have been barred from the ballot in the very year it took control of the House. Other important parties or candidacies that were formed after March of election years were the 1912 Progressive "Bull Moose" Party (which placed second in that year's presidential election), the 1924 La Follette Progressive candidacy, and the Strom Thurmond "States Rights" candidacy in 1948. Notwithstanding all that history, in 1973 the Supreme Court summarily affirmed yet another decision upholding a March petition deadline. The Supreme Court's hostile rulings on petitioning procedures, from 1971 through 1975, encouraged state legislatures to increase ballot access requirements. Six states made them substantially more difficult in 1971; four in 1973; two in 1974; and two again in 1975.

One Step Forward

Fortunately, in 1983, the Supreme Court took a surprise step forward on ballot access. It struck down Ohio's March petition deadline for independent presidential candidates. The vote was 5–4. The decision was written by Justice Stevens. The dissenters were Justices White, Powell, O'Connor, and Rehnquist. This case, *Anderson v. Celebrezze*, had been brought by independent presidential candidate John B. Anderson in 1980. He had not declared his independent candidacy until April 23. By then, he had already missed the petition deadlines in five states. He had sued all five states, and had won all these lawsuits in U.S. District Courts. After the election, the 6th Circuit had reversed his Ohio victory. The Supreme Court restored his Ohio victory, and established a national precedent that early petition deadlines for independent presidential candidates are unconstitutional. It was unclear if the precedent extended to independent candidates for office other than president. It was also unclear if it extended to petition deadlines for new parties.

Stevens said that since the major parties, ever since 1956, had chosen their presidential candidates at national conventions held in July and August, it denied Equal Protection to force other groups to make a decision about whom to run before July or August. He also pointed out that, according to historians, early petition deadlines actually cause more party factionalism than late deadlines. Since a faction must bolt an existing party quite early if it hopes to have a chance of forming a viable third party, early signature deadlines ironically encouraged the breaking apart of parties.

Two Steps Back

Minor parties thought that perhaps the court was now friendlier on other ballot access matters, since it had acted favorably toward independent presidential deadlines. They were quickly disappointed. A few weeks after *Anderson v. Celebrezze* was decided, the Court refused to hear a case from Oklahoma, against the law removing any party from the ballot if it had not polled 10 percent for the office at the top of the ticket (president or governor). The consequences of being removed from the Oklahoma ballot were severe. Such a party could not regain its place on the ballot unless it submitted a new petition signed by 5 percent of the last vote cast. For 1982 the petition requirement was 57,486 signatures. And when a party was removed from the ballot, all its registered members lost their right to remain registered in that party; the state reclassified them as independents, regardless of their wishes. At the same time, the Court refused to hear a Louisiana case where the state would not print a party label on the ballot next to the names of any candidates, unless those candidates were members of a qualified party. "Qualified party" was a group that had 5 percent registration membership, or that had polled 5 percent of the presidential vote at the last election. Plaintiffs showed that no party, other than the Democrats or Republicans, had ever had registration membership of 5 percent or more in any state. Even the Republican Party had not attained 5 percent registration in Louisiana until 1979. The Court refused to hear the case, as it shifted rightward with Reagan appointments.

Then, the year Bill Clinton would become president the U.S. Supreme Court made a decision that undermined the century-old judicial understanding that a voter is free to vote for anyone, via write-in space on ballots. The Court ruled that nothing in the Constitution guarantees the right of voters to cast a write-in vote. It upheld Hawaii laws, which didn't permit write-in voting. Nevada, South Dakota, Oklahoma, and Louisiana also banned all write-in votes. The vote was 6–3. The case, *Burdick v. Takushi*, contradicted the opinions of twenty state Supreme Courts, which had, as long ago as 1892, stated that no government had the power to forbid a voter from voting for anyone he or she wished. While ballot access could be limited, write-in space was always required by courts, to preserve the voter's freedom of choice. Federal courts had also been ruling in favor of write-in space. Ohio, Delaware, Kansas, and Indiana had restored write-in space to their ballots because of federal court actions, during the period 1968–1990. Write-ins were meaningful, since write-in candidates had been elected at general elections to Congress in 1918, 1930, 1946, 1954, 1958, 1980, and 1982. But due to *Burdick*, no voter in Oklahoma was physically able to vote for Nader in November 2000 since the state disallowed write-ins. Though such a denial appears scandalous, it receives little commentary.

PRECARIOUS ASSUMPTIONS OF THE COURT

There are clues in a case called *Timmons v. Twin Cities Area New Party* as to the attitudes of conservative justices like Scalia and Rehnquist toward minor parties. Though not about ballot access, *Timmons* deals with the First Amendment's association rights of political parties. The specific question is whether two parties have a constitutional right to jointly nominate the same candidate. The Court ruled 6–3 that states are free to ban this practice, which is usually termed "fusion." This was a big blow to third-party challenges. Scalia did not write separately in the case, but at oral argument, he stated his opinion that New York State has a "three-party system." From the context of his remarks, it was evident that he felt New York was disadvantaged by its "three-party system." Chief Justice Rehnquist's opinion in the same case says, "The States' interest permits reasonable election regulations that may, in practice, favor the traditional two-party system, and that temper the destabilizing effects of party-splintering and excessive factionalism. The Constitution permits the Minnesota Legislature to decide that political stability is best served through a healthy two-party system."

It is clear that Rehnquist and Scalia believe that vigorous minor parties are bad for society. They argue for an ill-defined "two-party system." Most political scientists agree that a two-party system is inevitable in any system that does not use proportional representation. If a nation does not use proportional representation, being "for" or "against" a two-party system, is like being "for" or "against" gravity.

But animus toward third parties fails to recognize the important role they can play even within a predominantly two-party system. Minor parties, and independent candidacies, help the two-party system to work better. The chief virtue of a two-party system is that, if one of the major parties becomes corrupt or incompetent, another party of comparable size is standing ready to take over at the next election. Two-party systems fail if one of the major parties becomes too powerful. Such an occurrence happened in the United States between 1860 and 1910, when the Republican Party won eleven out of thirteen presidential elections. The Democrats only got back into the White House because, in 1912, the new Progressive ("Bull Moose") Party was formed, splitting the Republican vote. Similarly, there was much talk of a Republican "lock on the Electoral College" in the late 1980s. It appeared that there were so many resolutely conservative states, with large numbers of electoral votes, that the Republican Party could never be defeated in a presidential election. But Ross Perot's independent candidacy in 1992 changed the arithmetic, giving the Democrats a chance at the White House and restoring balance to the two-party system.

Justice Scalia does not understand the term "two-party system," because he thinks New York State has a "three-party system." Presumably he thinks the three major parties of New York State are the Conservative, Republican, and Democratic Parties. The Conservative Party has, for most of its forty-year history, polled between 5 percent and 10 percent of the vote for its nominees, who, for the most part, have also been the Republican nominees, enjoying the support of both parties via "fusion." No political scientist would consider the Conservative Party of New York to be a major party. No member of the Conservative Party of New York has ever been elected to federal or state office, except for Congressman William Carney between 1978 and 1984. Although James Buckley was elected to the U.S. Senate on the Conservative Party's line in 1970, and although Buckley defeated the Republican and Democratic nominees in that election, he was not himself a registered member of the Conservative Party. He was a registered Republican, and when he took his seat in the Senate, he became part of the Republican caucus. When he ran for reelection in 1976, he ran as the joint nominee of both the Republican and Conservative Parties. In thirty-eight years of its existence, it managed to elect one of its members to any state or federal office. It is not a "major party." New York State, like every other state, has a two-party system.

Justices Rehnquist and Scalia fear the instability of third parties. But the fear is unfounded. Political scientists usually find instability in nations that use a parliamentary system combined with proportional representation. In those systems, governments "fall" because there is no independently elected chief executive with a fixed term, and the national leader is dependent on continuous support from a coalition of several parties. This system is entirely different from the system mandated by the Constitution of the United States, which provides for an independent chief executive whose term of office is fixed. A misunderstanding of basic concepts about political parties dominates the thinking of some, if not most, Supreme Court justices. As a result, minor-party and independent activists, candidates, and voters are treated badly and denied equality at the voting booth.

GLIMMERS OF HOPE: BALLOT ACCESS REFORM ACTIVITY AND THE 2000 ELECTION

For the last fifteen years, the nation's most active minor parties and ballot access reform activists have generally worked with each other to persuade state legislatures to ease the ballot access laws. Minor-party activists who are concerned about ballot access laws formed the Coalition for Free and Open Elections in 1985. The Coalition, also known as COFOE, coordinates lobbying activity and disseminates useful information for reformers through a newsletter, *Ballot Access News* (which can be seen on the Web at www.ballot-access.org). A host of democracy reform organizations have also take up the ballot access cause, including the American Civil Liberties Union, the Brennan Center for Justice, the Appleseed Foundation, the Center for Voting and Democracy, the Center for Constitutional Rights, and some state units of Common Cause and the League of Women Voters.

Activists who work for fairer ballot access laws have had some success by working to persuade state legislators to ease ballot access laws. Lobbying tactics have worked best in states with moderately severe laws; but it has not seemed to work in the states with the most severe laws. Sixteen state legislatures have been persuaded to ease their ballot access laws during the last fifteen years (Arizona, Colorado, Connecticut, Hawaii, Idaho, Iowa, Kansas, Maine, Maryland, Missouri, Montana, Nevada, New York, South Dakota, Virginia, and Wyoming). The improvements made in these states have been significant. Yet, in the states with the worst ballot access laws, where, for example, more than 25,000 signatures are required for new-party ballot access, only once has a legislature ever voluntarily lowered the requirement to a number smaller than 25,000 (Oregon in 1993).

Another tactic that has worked to ease ballot access restrictions is through the use of voter initiatives and referendums (see Galen Nelson's chapter in this book). Twice, ballot access reformers have managed to arrange a vote of the people of a particular state to determine whether the ballot access laws should be eased or not. In Massachusetts, a 1990 initiative asked voters to decide if the petition requirements should be reduced from about 40,000 signatures for statewide office, to about 10,000. A debate ensued in the mass media, and ballot access reformers won with 51.6 percent of the vote. Interestingly, the major newspapers called for a "Yes" vote, but network television stations editorialized for a "No" vote. Then, in 1998, the voters of Florida voted 65 percent in favor of revising the state constitution to provide that ballot access requirements should be the same for all candidates, regardless of their party. This wiped out mandatory petition requirements (for statewide office other than president) of 240,000 requirements, which had been upheld by courts repeatedly. Reformers have sought such an initiative in Oklahoma, where voters couldn't vote for Nader in 2000, but found trouble in raising enough money to pay petition circulators to get the initiative on the ballot. It would take 100,000 valid signatures gathered in three months. Minor parties have also turned to Congress for help, but with similar disappointing results.

Congressman John Conyers (D-Michigan) introduced a bill in 1985 (and again in 1987 and 1989) to outlaw restrictive ballot access requirements for federal elections. The same bill was later introduced by Congressman Tim Penny (D-Minnesota), and, after he left Congress, by Congressman Ron Paul (R-Texas). In 1998, Paul successfully offered his bill as an amendment to a campaign finance bill, forcing every member of the U.S. House of Representatives to vote on it. The same bill was introduced in 2001, called the "Voter Freedom Act," which has been endorsed by the Green, Libertarian, and Reform Parties. It remains to be seen whether it will be acted upon.

Finally, activists for more equal ballot access laws have turned again to the courts. Ironically, the Supreme Court may have recently given minor parties and independent candidates a boost by striking down two state laws related to term limits for members of Congress. An Arkansas law, barring candidates from the ballot if they had already served three terms in Congress, was invalidated in 1995 (the law had provided that anyone could still be a write-in candidate). A Missouri law, labeling incumbent members of Congress and incumbent state legislators who had not worked for a U.S. constitutional amendment to impose term limits on members of Congress, was invalidated in 2001. The Missouri label was "Disregarded voters' instructions on Term Limits." The 1995 decision was 5–4, but the 2001 decision was unanimous. Justice Stevens wrote both opinions, which were called *U.S. Term Limits v. Thornton*, and *Cook v. Gralike*. The basis for both decisions was not the First or Fourteenth Amendment. Instead, it was Article One of the original U.S. Constitution, which contains the qualifications for anyone to be a member of Congress. The Court said that the states are powerless to add to the qualifications listed in the Constitution. It also said the states are powerless to discriminate against a class of candidates for Congress. Whether the U.S. Supreme Court intends that to apply to minor-party and independent candidates is an unanswered question. Probably some members of the Court do not intend to apply the principle to minor-party or independent candidates, but others do.

During 2001, activists tried very hard to persuade state legislatures to improve ballot access laws, but virtually all of these attempts failed. Reform bills in 2001 were defeated in Alabama, Arizona, Connecticut, Georgia, Kentucky, Maine, Nebraska, North Carolina, North Dakota, West Virginia, and Wyoming. However, bills to improve ballot access did pass in Oregon, South Dakota, and Washington. Although 2001 was been a disappointing year for ballot access reform in the state legislatures, state COFOE groups were hoping to get bills introduced in the latter half of 2001 in Illinois, Michigan, and Pennsylvania.

CONCLUSION

It is possible that the Supreme Court's famous evening decision of December 12, 2000, now known as *Bush v. Gore,* will help minor-party and independent candidates with their ballot access problems. The Court said that states must treat each voter "with equal dignity." Already, one court, the 9th Circuit, has cited *Bush v. Gore* to prevent a government from discriminating against Republican voters relative to Democratic voters. The case involved a school board election in the Northern Mariana Islands and is called *Charfauros v. Board of Elections.* The local election board had disqualified several voters who were Republicans just prior to an election, but had not disqualified any challenged voters who were Democrats until after the election. The election was so close, if these actions had not been taken, the results would have been different. The 9th Circuit upheld the lower court, which had reversed the results of the election.

Whether minor-party and independent voters will eventually be able to win cases using *Bush v. Gore* remains to be seen. What should be clear is that choice matters for democracy—the sort of choice that can only be ensured through open ballot access. Without this sort of reform, American democracy will be weakened.

5

Freeing Politics from the Grip of Money: The Limits of Campaign Finance Reform and the Need for a New Approach

MARK SCHMITT

For a moment recently, the United States seemed ready to confront the distortion of its politics by money. Campaign finance reform became a political issue in the 2000 elections, and one major party nominee (Vice President Gore) even proposed full public financing for congressional elections. In July 2000, President Clinton signed a campaign finance reform bill, a trifling bit of legislation but, nevertheless, the first to reach the White House in almost a quarter-century. The McCain–Feingold legislation to eliminate soft money came within a hairsbreadth of passing both houses of Congress.

Further, a popular movement for reform finally emerged to back up the voices of Washington-based professional advocates who represented no one. Whether it was "Granny D," the ninety-year-old with the improbable 19th-century New Hampshire accent who walked from California to Capitol Hill in support of reform, or the several hundred thousand citizens who signed petitions to put reform on the ballot in five states, or the numerous statewide coalitions that have formed around the issue, it seems that ordinary citizens—not professional advocates or experts—have become committed to transforming American democracy.

Campaign finance reform has also come to be a powerful organizing principle for a larger progressive political movement. It brings together environmentalists, advocates of labor rights at home and abroad, organizers of low-income communities, liberal religious groups, public health professionals, and others who share a belief that they are bound together in defeat by the influence of moneyed interests on the democratic process. Whether or not campaign finance reform ever achieves its own goals, the not-so-simple act of bringing together a diverse grassroots, progressive political force is an achievement in itself.

At the same time, though, the problem this movement set out to solve suddenly got worse. It is not just that $3 billion was raised and spent for candidates, parties, and interests, nor that the legislative obstacles to reform have become almost infinite in number and cleverness. (This is written just after the House leadership forced reformers to vote down the rule under which the bill would be considered, stalling further progress.) Nor is it that voters in Missouri and Oregon turned down ballot initiatives for full public financing of state campaigns, ending a string of victories for that approach.

Of greater concern is that money in politics took a whole new form, one that challenges not just our political will but our wisdom. Vast amounts of political money now move outside the boundaries of both the existing system of regulation and the broader reach of the McCain–Feingold bill. Gloomy as it may sound, we no longer know whether even the most ambitious solutions will *work.*

Campaign finance reformers now find themselves in the position of police officers who have been trying to bash down the door of a house full of fugitives, only to discover, at just the moment the barricaded door is about to give way, the house has gone silent. Their targets have slipped out back and into the surrounding forest. In this case, the forest is the zone of unregulated, big-dollar spending, of which party soft money—the unregulated donations given to political parties—is just the underbrush.

THE RISE OF OUTSIDE MONEY
AND THE LIMITS OF REFORM

There are three paths through which unlimited outside money enters and influences elections. Of these, political party soft money is merely the best known. Party soft money was created deliberately by the Federal Election Commission (FEC) in the early 1980s, in the hope of strengthening parties. By allowing parties to ignore normal contribution limits and even take money from corporations and labor unions, it was assumed that, as long as funds were used exclusively for "party-building" activities unconnected to federal elections, American democracy would be strengthened. This stricture was always a bit of a fiction, but it was not until 1995 that either party realized that soft money funds could be used for television ads. Since that moment of revelation, party soft money has exploded, reaching about half a billion dollars last year—more than that spent by all candidates for the White House and both houses of Congress combined as recently as 1992.

There is nothing good to be said for soft money: It has brought the million-dollar contribution and the corporate contribution, both long forbidden, back to politics. And rather than strengthening parties, the rise of soft money has coincided with a period in which the parties, especially at the state and community level, are as weak as they have ever been on every dimension except fund-raising. It seems fair to surmise that when the parties became banks, they ceased to function as political parties.

The McCain–Feingold legislation would eliminate party soft money by subjecting all gifts to parties to the existing hard money limits. This is worth doing, and might even revitalize the parties by making them find something else to do, but it would not eliminate large or corporate contributions from campaigns. That's because the same trick that allows political parties to use soft money for campaign television ads is available to any independent committee. Virtually all the ads that end with lines like "Call Sam Jones and ask him why he's such a tax-loving liberal" are funded by independent committees. The point of "Call Sam Jones" is not to force the poor tax-loving liberal to disconnect his phone. It is to evade the Supreme Court's absurd "magic words" test for what constitutes a campaign ad, under which, unless the ad said, "vote against Jones," it would be considered just a benign statement about taxes.

Two years ago, these independently funded false issue ads were fairly isolated. They constituted a disturbing trend but seemed less important compared to both soft money and regulated contributions. But in 2000, outside groups spent more than the Republican Party itself in support of Republican House candidates. The attempt at a voluntary ban on soft money between New York Senate rivals Hillary Rodham Clinton and Rick Lazio foundered on the candidates' inability—or refusal—to restrain spending by outside groups. And in a number of other Senate races, notably Montana's, outside groups were the primary messengers on both sides.

Recognizing the limited value of banning only *party* soft money, the McCain–Feingold bill would try to bring much of this outside spending under a regulatory umbrella based on content and timing. To slow campaign ads disguised as nonpartisan discussions of issues, any ad that mentions a candidate for office and is broadcast during the sixty days preceding an election would be considered a campaign expenditure. It would thus be subject to limits or, in another version of the bill, a requirement that the source of money be revealed. *If* such a tight restriction (not just disclosure) were to become law and survive review in the courts (a big "if," since proponents of a restriction on speech based on content, which might infringe on legitimate speech about issues, will have to prove that it is narrowly drawn to achieve a compelling government interest), an issue ad ban would shut down the "Call Sam Jones" ads funded by big contributions. But even that would hardly be the end of the story. For one thing, plenty of spending takes place before the sixty-day window would open: The issue-ad campaign that effectively sealed the 1996 election for Clinton went on the air fifteen months before the vote.

And there is also a third path of big-money spending that would not, and could not, be restricted by any version of McCain–Feingold, or any other law. That is the true issue ad, the one that doesn't need to mention a candidate at all. In the current political world, which is often more about issues than we realize, politicians and consultants know that "control of the issue environment" is the most valuable asset a campaign can possess. Prescription drug coverage, Social Security, reproductive rights—it was only by making these the key issues in the 2000 campaign that Democrats won Senate and House seats and the popular vote for president. But none of this was accidental. *Money*, spent wisely, created this favorable issue environment for Democrats. A targeted effort to remind a small group of swing voters (moderately conservative, pro-choice women in a few states) that reproductive rights were at risk—even without naming names—was surely every bit as effective as an ad attacking Bush. Former California Governor Pete Wilson figured out a long time ago that an easy way to create a big-money slush fund is to run a ballot initiative on a popular issue like crime side-by-side with a statewide campaign for office based on the same themes (see Galen Nelson's chapter in this collection for more on this). *Any issue campaign that amplifies a candidate's campaign message is likely to significantly benefit that campaign.*

Much of this spending is unreported, but by one estimate, progressive groups spent about $68 million on such issue messages (Lux 2000). Conservative groups spent much more, though less effectively. If soft money were banned, and false issue advocacy effectively restricted, it is easy to foresee that a great deal more money could move into this third zone of unrestricted, unrestrictable spending.

Civil libertarians and critics of reform will argue that there is nothing evil about most of this spending, that it is constitutionally protected speech, and that it is part of a robust democratic debate. And they will be right. Completely divorcing money from politics is not a meaningful goal in a capitalist country with a First Amendment. While not abandoning the quest to make elections fairer and money less decisive, reformers will have to recognize that the campaign finance system—that is, the regulated system of contributions to candidates and to the party's hard money committees—is embedded deeply in a rich and complex world of political speech, all or most of which is dependent on money in some way, and also strongly protected by spirit and the letter of the First Amendment.

THE LIMITATIONS OF A
QUARANTINE MODEL OF REFORM

Nonetheless, the traditional approach to campaign finance reform has rested on the hope that campaign speech and spending can be walled off from the rest of our market-driven, inherently unequal society. Traditional campaign finance reform is best understood as a quest to define a zone in which the equality necessary to democracy can be quarantined from the contagion of the unequal distribution of wealth and economic power in that larger world. Within the quarantine, democracy would be somewhat protected from capitalism. Reformers seek to build a wall around *candidates* and to some extent around *legislation*, rather like the seventy-five-foot perimeter around polling places within which electioneering is prohibited. Within the zone, the requirements of political equality must take priority over free expression.

While reformers disagree, sometimes bitterly and self-destructively, about what should be permitted within the regulated zone, they share the basic approach of the quarantine. That is, they believe it possible to set rules for the "campaign finance system" as if it were self-contained. And as they see the system fail—for instance, as outside money penetrates the regulated zone—they see the cure in similar terms: find the loopholes and close them off. Former Senator Bill Bradley (for whom I worked on this issue) used to say that "money in politics is like ants in the kitchen: If you don't close *all* the holes, they'll keep getting in." But what if that can't be done? What if there is no wall at all, just a "sea of holes" (the sort in the Beatles movie, *Yellow Submarine*)? What happens to reform if closing off soft money simply pushes big money into independent issue ads, and closing off independent issue ads simply pushes the money into ads intended to "shape the issue environment"?

Reforms that don't take into account the other ways that money can influence politics are not simply ineffectual. They risk making things worse in two ways. First, by pushing money out of the controlled system, reforms can have the very opposite effect of that intended. In particular, reforms meant to reduce the size of contributions, if they push money into the uncontrolled system, can result instead in greater influence by a few large donors. When Oregon experimented briefly with $100 contribution limits in 1994–1996, the effect was not the intended one of nurturing a new breed of candidates who raised all their money from ordinary folks earning $11 an hour. Instead, independent expenditures, which were not restricted, took the place of direct campaign spending, with the unintended consequence that larger, rather than smaller, contributions determined elections.

The second risk in the quarantine model of reform is that pushing money into the unregulated zone will divorce candidates from the messages of their own campaigns, since the legal definition of independent spending generally involves a demonstrable absence of coordination with the candidate. Alan Ehrenhalt, writing in the magazine *Governing*, described the extreme case, Wisconsin, where two main clusters of interest groups—the teachers' union, joined by some lesser allies from the labor movement, and the state business and industry association—dominate the battle for control of the legislature. In several key races, these two groups outspent *both* candidates, dominating the airwaves and voters' awareness. Candidates wake up in the morning to radio ads describing them as heroes or villains, proclaiming them champions of one cause or another—ads that neither they nor their opponents have approved. The chief lobbyist for the business group mocks Ehrenhalt's concern: "It's interesting," he says, "that the candidates seem to think the campaigns belong to them" (Ehrenhalt 2000, 20).

Campaigns certainly don't belong exclusively to candidates, as the New York branch of the National Abortion Rights Action League correctly pointed out in refusing to be bound by Hillary Clinton and Rick Lazio's "deal" to forswear outside spending. Every voice, especially those that represent large numbers of citizens, has a right to be heard. But it is healthiest for democracy if candidates are the primary voice in their own campaigns. This allows voters to hold them accountable for their promises if elected, and it encourages candidates to build a broad base of support instead of depending on a single interest group. Candidates should have the greatest flexibility to make themselves heard, followed by parties (which also have to build broad coalitions), and finally individual interests, whether single-issue groups or corporate entities. Instead, we have a system that places the strictest controls on candidates, to be followed (if soft money is banned) by parties, but the loosest restriction on outside groups. We limit candidate fund-raising in order to reduce the influence of narrow interests on candidates and officeholders. But by doing so within an environment of unrestricted political speech, we risk letting those same narrow interests not just influence campaigns but dominate them, much as they do in Wisconsin.

The dangers of the quarantine model of reform raise questions about just how effective a single reform such as the McCain–Feingold ban on soft money will be. McCain–Feingold cannot be the end of the matter; it must be followed by a serious effort to craft a comprehensive approach. And that comprehensive approach must not rest on the illusion that politics can be sealed off from money. It must work within an environment of unlimited spending.

There is an alternative that is gaining adherents: voluntary full public financing, under which participating candidates agree to accept a predetermined amount of public funds and virtually no private money. But while full public financing appears to be an absolute solution—a complete replacement of a system of private influence-peddling with one of equal allotments of public money—it presents problems of its own if it simply extends the quarantine model and ignores the problem of outside money.

Vermont, for example, enacted such a program for its statewide campaigns, but the Democratic governor who signed the bill backed out of a promise to participate himself, citing fears that he would be unable to respond to anticipated independent spending or issue ads that would support his opponent. In other words, he could not trust the quarantine. The circumstances were peculiar to Vermont; other states that have passed full public funding try to give participating candidates matching funds to respond to independent spending against them. But the matching system asks state ethics officials to make, on a moment's notice, the distinction between ads intended to support or hurt candidates and those merely expressing opinions on issues—the same distinction that has vexed the Federal Election Commission and courts for years. As the American Civil Liberties Union has pointed out, this gives an unelected state official a disturbing level of power to decide whether a certain ad or statement should be offset by public funds for the opposition. (In Vermont, for example, much of the attack on the governor was led by forces opposed to gay rights and his approval of same-sex domestic partnerships. Under a matching system, if an ad mentioned the governor, he might get money to respond, but an anti-gay ad attacking the bill he signed would go unanswered, even if it had a similar impact.)

Full public financing is an extraordinarily promising system, not least because its clarity attracts voters whose eyes glaze over at the scholastic moral distinctions among various types of money—PAC money, soft money, bundled money, hard money, coordinated money—in the traditional approach to campaign finance reform. Full public financing recognizes that all private money is potentially corrupting and the only reliable solution to corruption or potential corruption is to replace private money with funds that are raised and distributed through democratic and publicly accountable means. Full public financing also has the chance to dramatically change the culture of politics, bringing forward community-based or ideologically motivated candidates who would never have considered running and even giving them a chance to win.

But there is a problem with full public financing that is not shared by partial public financing systems. It is that full public financing is also an extreme form of the quarantine model of reform. It asks candidates voluntarily to bind themselves to exactly equal and fixed spending, but in doing so, it places a very high premium on any tactic that can get around that agreement to give a candidate or a cause a slight edge. It is virtually a mathematical certainty about the quarantine model: any reform that attempts to equalize all the variables in campaign spending, but leaves one out, will give decisive power to that variable that is left open. In this case, equalizing candidate spending and party spending but inevitably leaving the independent spending of interest groups alone risks giving those groups more power, not less, in deciding elections and greater leverage on elected officials. To make full public financing work, policy makers will have to find a way to close or offset every other avenue of spending.

TOWARD AN EFFECTIVE REFORM

The recognition that campaign spending is inseparable from other political speech is typically part of an argument against reform, some version of the standard reactionary argument that it would either be futile, or lead to something even worse than the status quo. But this is an unjustified surrender. The status quo is unacceptable: it is impossible today for all but a few people even to consider seeking public office, and large donors have far greater voice than they had even in the Watergate era. And while there is no perfect solution, it ought to be possible to make things less bad.

If McCain–Feingold passes, there must be a solution that can operate effectively within a context of unlimited outside political spending. This calls for an approach different from the quarantine model, but in the end it is an approach that is more likely to work, to survive constitutional challenge, and to coexist with the First Amendment and the principle of free expression.

The problem of money in politics is not just about money. It is about communication. The right question is not "How do we get money out of politics?" but rather "How can we make sure that all candidates and parties can communicate with voters, and voters communicate among themselves and back to elected officials, without giving excessive power to those who can pay for that communication?" Framed this way, the problem of money in politics becomes the fact that there is a wall between candidates (along with the larger number of civic-minded people who would be candidates if they could imagine raising the money) and the voters they need to reach. In the case of a reasonably competitive House seat, the wall is roughly a million dollars high. (For instance, only one new House member who won a reasonably competitive seat spent less than a million.) That wall consists mainly of the cost of paid television advertising, still the principal means by which candidates communicate with voters. For Senate candidates, or for those facing well-known or well-financed opponents, the wall is much higher.

Under current rules, there are three ways to be heard over that wall. The official, legally recognized way is to build a staircase of bricks to the top of the wall, accepting no more than one brick ($1,000) from any one person. To be heard over a million-dollar wall means finding at least a thousand individuals (in reality, more like 3,000) willing to contribute. The advantage is that no donor can be said to have given so much that the candidate would owe his or her success to that donor. But the downside is that most candidates can't even think of raising money from that many people. The exceptions are incumbents, candidates who have deep connections among relatively well-off people (such as friends from an Ivy League college or colleagues at a law firm), and those who have the support of a national fund-raising network like the National Rifle Association or EMILY's List for women candidates.

A second way over the wall is to bring your own ladder. Self-financed candidates such as Senators Jon Corzine, Mark Dayton, and John Edwards face no limit on what they can contribute to their own campaigns. Courts have held that such candidates can't corrupt themselves with their own money, a theory that interestingly matches a familiar election slogan for these candidates: "He's too rich to be bought." These candidates are no longer anomalies: exactly half of the Democratic senators who defeated Republican incumbents in the last two election cycles were self-financed, and more than one hundred congressmen and senators are millionaires.

The third way over the wall is to cheat. In this case, cheating means violating the spirit (though usually not the letter) of the law by raising or spending money through the unrestricted outside channels—soft money or issue ad committees. The consequences are as described above: huge contributions, direct corporate contributions, a far greater potential for corruption than we have had in the past, and a divide between candidates and their own campaigns. Yet many candidates cannot be heard at all by either of the first two methods, and all the incentives in the current system encourage candidates to cheat, especially if they think their opponents will.

Reform should turn these incentives on their head. Since it cannot hope to close off every possibility of cheating, it should instead encourage participation in the aboveground system as much as it discourages evasion. There are four ways that procedural changes could make it easier for candidates to get over the metaphorical wall and be heard, without cheating:

1. *Lower the wall.* Money matters so much more than it should in politics because candidates reach voters mainly through television. They are forced to compete with car companies and beer companies for the right to pay broadcasters tens of thousands of dollars to reach voters for

thirty seconds. Yet the public owns the airwaves, lends it to broadcast-ers, and has the right to set the terms on which broadcasters borrow them. Reserving just a tiny sliver of the public resource that each broadcaster is granted and setting it aside for purposes of democracy in the form of a broadcast time bank for candidates would significantly lower the cost of being heard. Free television and radio time has long been ancillary to campaign finance reform (although it was dropped from the McCain–Feingold bill several years ago). It should move to the center. The Alliance for Better Campaigns in 2000 joined state ac-tivists and academic institutions to persuade local broadcasters to com-ply, with only limited success. But the Senate, in one of the few positive changes to McCain–Feingold, passed an amendment putting some teeth into the long-standing requirement that candidates be able to buy airtime when they want it, at the lowest possible commercial rate.

2. *Create a path around the wall.* The era in which paid television is the main channel of political information did not end with the emergence of In-ternet politics in 2000, as James Fallows wrote recently, but the end may be in sight (Fallows 2000). If politics were ever to become less de-pendent on such an outrageously expensive and limited medium, one that rewards the short, sharp, visual attack and discourages subtlety and deliberation, money would matter much less and ideas would matter more. In the meantime, well-designed Internet projects, such as the Democracy Network (DNet), can create a space for candidates to be heard where they stand on equal footing, where they can say as much or as little as they want, where they can initiate debates and even en-gage directly with voters. There may or may not be a role for govern-ment in creating this space, but it will be worth the effort now to model the kind of communication system that will work best for politics when the television era finally wanes (for more on this point, see Peter Levine's chapter in this collection).

3. *Make small contributions count for more.* Imagine how much easier it would be to get over a million-dollar wall if every small contribution counted for much more? What if every $250 gift were really a much larger contribution? That's the case under New York City's law, passed in 1998, which provides four dollars in government money for every dollar raised in small contributions. As a result, the donor who can give $250 has almost the same value to a candidate as the donor who can give $1,250. A similar approach would involve tax credits for small contributions. In Minnesota, a full tax credit for contributions of $100 or less has the effect of giving every citizen $100 with which to rein-force his or her political views. (Such tax credits would leave out the poorest citizens unless, as in Minnesota, they are refundable to families who do not otherwise owe taxes.) Rather than banning large contribu-

tions, these approaches would increase the incentives to candidates to seek out small contributors.

Full public financing, or "Clean Money Reform," extends this concept even further. Under this system, a certain number of very small contributions triggers a fixed amount of money sufficient to fund an average campaign. In Maine, for example, candidates who collect enough $5 contributions to show a base of support receive public funds as long as they agree to raise and spend no more money. In 2000, about one-third of legislative candidates participated in the system, more Republicans than Democrats. If it works in larger races that include television advertising, this system has the potential to make private money all but irrelevant to political success and allow candidates to compete on their ideas. But it remains an experiment. Much depends on the integrity of the voluntary limits, which are, for outside money, zero. If the limits fail—that is, if candidates pretend to participate in the system but actually bring in outside money or issue ads—no candidate will be willing to risk being bound by such an all-or-nothing system. New York City's system has overall spending limits for participating candidates as well, but they are relatively high, and if candidates evade the limits, it does not bring down the whole system in the way that evasion jeopardizes full public financing.

4. *Allow candidates to raise more through the legal system.* For *some* candidates, the freedom to raise contributions from individuals larger than the current $1,000 limit would be a boost to their ability to be heard. Contributions of $3,000 or even $5,000 are not so large that the contributor would automatically have a corrupting leverage on an elected official, and they are unquestionably preferable to the million-dollar corporate contributions that come in today through soft money and outside funds. Obviously this would concentrate the influence of money in the hands of an even smaller group than today. But realistically, as long as there is private money in politics, it will come from the small percentage of the population that has discretionary cash and a deeper interest in politics. Most of those who can give $1,000 could also give $3,000, but most of us can't, or don't, give either amount.

Passage of an amendment raising the individual contribution limit to $2,000 led several reform groups to withdraw their support of McCain–Feingold. But perhaps this is shortsighted. Consider an analogy from the tax system: In 1960, the top income tax rate in the United States was, on paper, 90 percent. Yet, as Harvard law professor Stanley Surrey pointed out at the time, even the wealthiest paid nothing close to that rate, and many paid no tax at all. The 90 percent tax was too easy to evade and the incentives to evade it were too great. We were "dipping deeply into great incomes with a sieve," he wrote. Similarly, today we are dipping deeply into big political contributions with a sieve.

It took decades, but eventually liberals saw that a system of lower but meaningful rates, coupled with fewer opportunities and fewer rewards for evasion, would be more progressive than one with high, but meaningless, tax rates. We should look at the $1,000 and $25,000 limits in the same way: a higher limit that people actually adhered to would be preferable, by any standard, to what is now a meaningless stricture. Raising hard money limits is emphatically not a solution in itself, and is of no value to many candidates. Coupled with a soft money ban and New York City–style public financing (as proposed by the Committee for Economic Development last year), it will significantly shift the balance of power from the unregulated, outside world of political money back to the regulated sphere.

CONCLUSION

The alternatives I have outlined here, coupled with a soft money ban and improved disclosure, would not eliminate money from politics but would make money less decisive in political choices. They would reduce the incentives to cheat and the rewards for evasion. Best of all, they would do so by opening up the system to candidates and ideas rather than attempting to close it down. They will not be uncontroversial, in part because elected officials have a stake in maintaining a limits-based system that has significant barriers to entry. But opponents won't have much to say. This approach presents no constitutional problems, no problems of implementation, no difficult choices between the requirements of free expression and those of political equality. And finally, it is at least something different from the approach reformers have pursued, with little to show for it, for a quarter-century.

Part Three

Engaging Citizens

Building Citizens

RONALD HAYDUK AND KEVIN MATTSON

As part two showed, removing barriers is crucial for allowing citizens to enter the public world. But what happens once they enter this world? Will there be places where they can learn about politics and educate themselves about the public good? We believe that this is a crucial question for democratic reformers to examine. And so the authors in this section go about explaining how we can nurture the fine arts of citizenship—deliberation, political education, and active engagement in public life.

R. Claire Snyder opens this part by examining what democratic political theory has to teach us about the concept of public deliberation. In many ways, all of the reforms discussed in this part aim to create a more deliberative democracy—one where citizens educate themselves and one another about political matters. Snyder shows that a great deal of thinking has gone into this concept. She also makes clear that there are organizations that have tried to make good on the often abstract lessons of political theorists. Often this is harder than it might at first seem, especially considering just how alienated many citizens have become from public life. Nonetheless, Snyder stresses the important relation between healthy public discussion and a healthy democracy.

Joel Westheimer and Joseph Kahne argue that schools can play a crucial role in preparing young people for public deliberation and democratic citizenship. Nonetheless, the authors also make clear that a great deal cuts against this aim today. Americans want their schools to turn out young people ready for the challenges of a new economy, not necessarily for the demands of public-minded and active citizenship. While recognizing this, the authors focus on a key experiment in democratic schooling, showing how teachers can provide young people with the ability to learn democratic skills like debating public policy and examining public problems with the aim of improving the quality of our collective lives. This sort of democratic schooling, as Westheimer and Kahne point out, is crucial for enlivening our democracy.

Moving beyond young people, Benjamin Shepard focuses his attention on adult citizens. He believes that community organizing—the sort pioneered by Jane Addams during the Progressive Era and by community garden activists of today—can introduce citizens to democratic responsibilities. Shepard points out that people often have to feel that politics affects their everyday lives; often, this takes the form of small things like a dangerous intersection in their community or a lack of public space. When democratic community organizers enter the picture, they can help show citizens what can be done to improve these things. In the process, they open up the world of public life—that is the art of working together with different people, a skill that is central to democracy's operation.

Finally, in closing this part, Peter Levine examines the possibility that the Internet might enhance public deliberation. He is rightfully suspicious of those who fall prey to technological determinism and argue that the Internet will automatically make us more informed and more deliberative citizens. He shows why this is not the case. But he does not give up on the possibility that the Internet's lateral communication between citizens can create some new democratic possibilities. In arguing for an "on-line commons," though, he makes clear that reformers will have to combat some of the more pernicious forms of communication that have shaped up on the Internet over the last few years. As with so much else, the Internet demands conscious and intelligent reform if it is to become a place that is favorable toward democratic education.

6

Democratic Theory and the Case for Public Deliberation

R. CLAIRE SNYDER

We hold these truths to be self-evident, that all men are created equal, that they are endowed by their Creator with certain unalienable rights, that among these are Life, Liberty, and the pursuit of Happiness. That to secure these rights, *Governments are instituted among Men, deriving their just powers from the consent of the governed.*

—Thomas Jefferson, *The Declaration of Independence* (1776) (emphasis added)

It is for us, the living, . . . to be here dedicated to the great task remaining before us—that . . . *government of the people, by the people, for the people,* shall not perish from this earth.

—Abraham Lincoln, *The Gettysburg Address* (1863) (emphasis added)

If the legitimacy of American democracy depends upon the *consent* of the governed, then the current state of politics should be cause for concern. Consider the following: A very large number of American citizens do not actively give their consent to government because they do not participate in the political process. Only 51 percent of voting-age Americans went to the polls in the 2000 presidential election, compared to 63 percent in 1960. In the 1996 presidential election, less than half of voting-age Americans went to the polls (49 percent), the lowest turnout since 1924. In fact, "another percentage point [lower] would have pushed us back to 1824." Congressional races fare even worse; the self-proclaimed "Republican revolution" of 1994 was authorized by only 38 percent of eligible voters (Tolchin 1999, 4). Four years later, turnout rates dropped to 36 percent, the lowest point since 1942 (Boggs 2000, 3). Worst of all, vitally important presidential primaries have attracted as few as 5 percent of voting-age Americans

(Tolchin 1999, 4). Naturally, other forms of political participation have declined as well. For example, "Americans were roughly half as likely to work for a political party or attend a political rally or speech in the 1990s as in the 1970s" (Putnam 2000, 41).

Second, American citizens cannot be said to consent if they do not have a clear sense of what is happening in the political realm. While relatively stable for the last fifty years, "political knowledge levels are, in many instances, depressingly low," particularly among "women, African Americans, the poor and the young" (Delli Carpini and Keeter 1996, 269, 271). Moreover, "as the amount of detail requested increases and as less visible institutions or processes are asked about, the percentage of the public able to correctly answer questions declines" (72). Newspaper reading has declined markedly, especially among the young (113). While in 1966, 60 percent of first-year college students thought "keeping up to date with political affairs" was "essential" or "very important," in 2000 only 28 percent thought so—"the lowest percentage" since the freshman year survey began and particularly striking in a presidential election year (Bennett and Bennett 2001, 296).

Furthermore, most people rely on the mass media for information, an industry owned and dominated by a few large corporations. Our country's 25,000 media sources, including daily newspapers, magazines, broadcast stations, books, and movies, are controlled by only *twenty* large corporations. With corporate mergers, the number keeps shrinking. For example, in 1981 only twenty corporations controlled most of our nation's 11,000 magazines; by 1988 that number had shrunk to *three* (Barber [1995] 1996a, 124; Delli Carpini and Keeter 1996, 113). Driven by the profit motive, these privately owned mass media corporations naturally focus on making money rather than on educating citizens about public affairs (Barber [1995] 1996a). That's their purpose. Yet consequently, "social issues of real consequence end up being ignored or trivialized, while popular attention" gets diverted by "media-generated" dramas—like O. J. Simpson, Elian Gonzalez, and Chandra Levy. While events such as these can generate productive discussions of social issues among citizens, overall they divert attention from important decisions that are being made simultaneously without the knowledge or input of American citizens (Boggs 2000, 4).

This lack of political engagement is disheartening for democrats, but does it tell us anything about the legitimacy of our current political system? After all, if citizens are *choosing* not to engage in politics because they trust their representatives to act on their behalf, then the legitimacy of government is not an issue. However, that is not the case. In fact, most American citizens no longer trust their own government. In the late 1990s, only 25 percent of people said "they trusted the federal government to do the right thing most of the time," compared to 75 percent in 1964 (Boggs 2000, 3; Nye 1997, 1; Putnam 2000, 47). Similarly, in 1966, 66 percent of

Americans "*rejected* the view that 'the people running the country don't really care what happens to you,'" whereas in 1997, 57 percent "*endorsed* that same view" (Putnam 2000, 47).

Alternatively, if citizens are *choosing* not to engage in politics because they are satisfied with the status quo, then the legitimacy of government is also not an issue. However, again, this is not the case. In fact, far from satisfied, many citizens report feeling *angry* about being "pushed out of the political system by a professional political class of powerful lobbyists, incumbent politicians, campaign managers—and a media elite" (Mathews [1994] 1999, 12). A 1992 Gallup poll found that 76 percent of people say they are "'dissatisfied' with the 'way the political process is working in this country'; and . . . 81 percent were 'dissatisfied with the success of the nation in taking care of its poor and needy'" (Tolchin 1999, 10–11). A 1995 Harris poll found that nearly two-thirds of voters "feel government is corrupt," three-quarters believe that "special interest groups have too much control" over government, and 83 percent "feel frustrated" with "the political situation in the country" (Tolchin 1999, 11). Clearly political disengagement does not correlate with a sense of satisfaction with the status quo.

POPULAR SOVEREIGNTY: ARE CITIZENS IN CONTROL?

If American government is supposed to be "government of the people, by the people, and for the people," then the current situation should trouble us. After all, the widespread alienation from, lack of trust in, and dissatisfaction with government discussed above means that American citizens do not believe that elected officials are governing in accordance with the interests of the people. "Since 1964, for example, the number of Americans who feel that the government is run by a few big interests looking out only for themselves has more than doubled (to 76 percent)" (Orren 1997, 81).

Just as important, with such a large disconnection between citizens and government, it is no surprise that citizens feel that they do not have control over the forces that govern their lives. Michael Sandel argues that such feelings underwrote the support of American citizens for dismantling "big government," which was seen as "disempowering citizens and undermining community," an effort that began in 1980 with the election of Ronald Reagan (Sandel 1996, 312)—one that George W. Bush continues to pursue (although with no mandate from the people). Both men ran on a platform that "pledged to 'reemphasize those vital communities like the family, the neighborhood, [and] the workplace' that reside 'between government and the individual,' and to encourage the 'rebirth of citizen activity in neighborhoods and cities across the land.'" Both proposed shifting power "from the federal government to states and localities" in order to "restore people's control over their lives by locating power closer to home" (312).

In the case of Reagan, people were hopeful. During his first term, public confidence rose to pre-Watergate levels. However, the "Reagan Revolution" did little to give control back to citizens (for the same reasons that the Bush administration will not):

> In the end Reagan's presidency did little to alter the conditions underlying the discontent. *He governed more as a market conservative than as a civic conservative. The less fettered capitalism he favored did nothing to repair the moral fabric of families, neighborhoods, or communities.* The "New Federalism" he proposed was not adopted, and in any case did not address the disempowerment that local communities—and even nations —now confronted as they struggled to contend with global economic forces beyond their control. (Sandel 1996, 315, emphasis added)

Indeed, by the end of Reagan's first term, the decline in confidence quickly resumed—and continued through the reign of the first George Bush—which indicates that citizens soon came to realize that simply dismantling government would not restore popular sovereignty.

In fact, dismantling government gave control over the public agenda not to citizens, but to large corporations. That is to say, while civic discontent authorized the attack on large concentrations of political power institutionalized in "big government," it not only did nothing to contest large concentrations of corporate power but also in fact destroyed the only institutions strong enough to reign in "big business" (Boggs 2000, 10–11; Sandel 1996; Barber [1995] 1996a). Furthermore, with few constraints large corporations have been able to "colonize" the public sphere and significantly influence the public agenda through campaign contributions and lobbying (Boggs 2000, 10–11), as well as through the pop culture ideology of "McWorld" (Barber [1995] 1996a). Faced with the unconstrained power of corporations, the cultural hegemony of consumer capitalism, the media-proclaimed inevitability of globalization, and the scarcity of "space for genuine participation," "a definite majority of Americans has come to feel justifiably enough, that it is almost completely powerless" over the forces that govern their lives. Consequently, many people have opted to "retreat from politics" in order to pursue "privatized lifestyles" (Boggs 2000, 13).

The unfettered triumph of consumer capitalism has exacerbated the individualistic strand of American culture and seriously eroded the connections between individuals within civil society—what Robert Putnam refers to as "social capital." As Putnam has documented, in every single category American citizens are less engaged with each other than they were forty years ago. While "nearly half of all Americans in the 1960s invested some time each week in clubs and local associations," in the 1990s "less than one-quarter" did (Putnam 2000, 62). In fact, "between 1973 and 1994 the number of Americans who attended even one public meeting on town or school affairs in the previous year was cut by 40 percent" (42). While all forms of social activity have decreased, Putnam notes that "strikingly, the forms of participation that have withered most noticeably reflect organized activities at the community level" (44). Moreover, "the fraction of the American public utterly uninvolved in any . . . civic activities rose by nearly one-third" since the 1970s. Participation has declined in almost every type of political, civic, and social activity.

While individualism certainly has its merits, it also undermines the ability of ordinary citizens to address the problems they care about. For example, in a recent study by the Harwood Institute, citizens repeatedly pinpointed a wide range of problems that can only be solved collectively, since they are rooted in the structure of our contemporary political economy. During focus group interviews people expressed concern about rising levels of poverty and the widening gap between the "haves and the have-nots"—what one woman referred to as our "hour-glass society" (Harwood 2000, 10). They complained about corporate indifference to and exploitation of working people (12). They noted that "the more Americans move around to follow jobs, the more everyone's sense of community is weakened" (13). They saw "corporations and businesses as increasingly remote, and narrowly focused, wielding a kind of undue and unwanted influence that is utterly changing what we as a nation value" (11). "People talked about values which, having long served to motivate and shape America—the values of competition, of control, and of material success—now have become supercharged . . . as if fed on vast quantities of steroids" (17). While people could only envision individualistic approaches to solving these problems—a further illustration of how entrenched individualism has become—clearly the problems cited above are systemically produced and thus cannot be adequately addressed via the personal choices of individuals.

THE NEED FOR PUBLIC DELIBERATION

Some political theorists argue that a well-functioning democracy requires a certain amount of deliberation among citizens for a number of reasons. First, we need public deliberation in order to create political legitimacy. According to the liberal political tradition, legitimate government requires the consent of the governed. But given the situation just outlined, how can we be sure that our government really has the full consent of the governed? Moreover, theorists of deliberation stress that legitimacy must not be assumed or taken for granted. Instead, it must be consistently reestablished through the process of "free and unconstrained public deliberation of all about matters of common concern. Thus a public sphere of deliberation about matters of mutual concern is essential to the legitimacy of democratic institutions" (Benhabib 1996, 68). Informed consent requires active dialogue.

The question of legitimacy has practical as well as philosophical consequences. That is to say, people are less likely to respect laws and policies that they feel are simply imposed upon them whether by the legislature or the courts. Consider the Vietnam protests, the massive resistance to court-ordered busing, and the never-ending attacks on *Roe v. Wade*. Such examples illustrate that people will not simply accept political decisions with which they disagree when they have no say in the decision-making process. Conversely, people are much more likely to accept unpleasant political compromises—such as managed health care or tax increases—when they participate in making those hard decisions. Indeed many argue that the Clinton health care plan failed (at least in part) because it was formulated with very little public discussion.

Second, we need public deliberation in order to create connections within our increasingly diverse citizenry, thus countering the fragmentation of communities that has helped reduce American citizens to self-interested individuals. Importantly, we cannot simply revive community in its 1830s or 1950s form, given that we are now a profoundly multicultural, heterogeneous society. Instead we must figure out how to create new civic bonds across difference. By coming together to deliberate about issues of common concern, a diversity of individuals in a particular community can meet each other and hopefully forms bonds that will enable them to work effectively together to help solve public problems.

Deliberation is particularly important because given the significant moral disagreement that characterizes the American public in the age of the "culture wars" (Hunter 1991)—disagreements that are all too often exacerbated by sensationalistic media coverage—citizens can easily become suspicious of the motivations of those with whom they disagree. This is especially likely given that many people never have the opportunity to talk with diverse others about controversial issues. The suspicion and misunderstanding generated by a widespread lack of communication help to reinforce the broadly accepted idea that American citizens are too diverse to ever be able to agree on anything. By creating a public space in which those with different views can talk face-to-face in a focused way, public deliberation might increase understanding—or at least civility—in the face of disagreement.

Third, we need public deliberation in order to have popular sovereignty. Once people come together as a community, they will need to deliberate in order to decide what to do, given that not all will agree. "The core idea [of deliberative democracy] is simple: when citizens or their representatives disagree morally, they should continue to reason together to reach mutually acceptable decisions" (Gutmann and Thompson 1996, 1). And since disagreement is the necessary by-product of a free society—as James Madison pointed out in *Federalist* 10—we will always need deliberation. While deliberative process is no panacea, its aim is to make controversial decisions in a way that does not completely alienate those who disagree with the outcome. Besides, since "political decisions are collectively binding," shouldn't they "be justifiable, as far as possible, to everyone bound by them" (Gutmann and Thompson 1996, 13)?

Fourth, greater levels of public deliberation can play a role in educating citizens about important public affairs and teach them new ways of thinking about political issues. To start, the practice of deliberation has been shown to increase knowledge among participants (Button and Mattson 1999, 620–21). This is important because "knowledge is both an important political resource in its own right and a facilitator of other forms of political and thus, indirectly, socioeconomic power" (Delli Carpini and Keeter 1996, 1). Moreover, many Americans "hate" politics because they are turned off by the partisan sniping of politicians and the "false choices" presented by party ideologues (Dionne 1991). In coming together to deliberate, people might learn that a large degree of common ground exists on a wide variety of issues, despite what political elites and the corporate-owned media want us to believe. Indeed, the 2000 presidential election illustrates this point: Voters were evenly divided between two candidates who ran as centrists and who seemed to be—quite deceptively as it turns out—almost identical on the issues.

Finally, greater levels of public deliberation could help reconnect American citizens to the political process. Exit interviews with people who have engaged in deliberative forums reveal that participants plan to become more involved in politics, specifically mentioning a variety of different activities "from more dedicated newspaper reading, to fund-raising for candidates . . . , to starting discussion groups and supporting civic classes in schools" (Button and Mattson 1999, 621). And since higher levels of knowledge do in fact correlate with higher levels of political participation (Delli Carpini and Keeter 1996, 6–7) these plans will probably be more than just good intentions. Despite some significant barriers to popular sovereignty—including a constricted set of policy options presented by our current political parties, the corrupting influence of money in politics, and the seriously compromised 2000 presidential election—citizens still have the power to vote politicians out of office. If more citizens were to get involved, perhaps we would no longer have politicians who run on one platform and govern on another.

PUBLIC DELIBERATION IN THEORY:
PHILOSOPHICAL AND COMMUNITARIAN APPROACHES

What does deliberation entail? There are two major approaches to public deliberation among political theorists: the philosophical and the communitarian. The philosophical approach is most fully articulated by Jürgen Habermas, who began his theory of deliberation with a historical study of the "bourgeois public sphere," which originated within early liberal societies, like the United States, during the 18th and early 19th centuries. Distinct from both the government and the market economy, the "public sphere" constituted a realm of discourse in which individuals came together as a public to reason together about issues of common concern. The "public sphere" encompassed conversations that occurred in a wide array of actual places, such as local pubs, coffeehouses, and salons, as well as the larger society-wide discussions made possible by the emergence of print culture during the 18th century (Habermas 1989, 27). Although restricted at the time to white property-owning (bourgeois) men, Habermas argues that the "public sphere" existed as the realm in which the people made public use of their reason and "the authority of the better argument could assert itself against that of social hierarchy" (36–37). However, as the market economy gained prominence in liberal societies, the distinction between the "public sphere" and the market economy "dissolved" and the "public sphere" unfortunately lost its "political function" as the locus of public deliberation about the common good (140).

Habermas's larger philosophical project attempts to recover and reconfigure the emancipatory potential of the bourgeois public sphere. With his emphasis on the "people's public use of their reason," Habermas builds directly on the legacy of Immanuel Kant, who argued that men are capable of governing themselves because they have the capacity for reason. More specifically, the capacity for "practical reason" makes it possible for men to construct universal moral laws in accordance with the *categorical imperative*, which states "act only on the maxim through which you can at the same time will that it should become a universal law" (1956, 88). Consequently, man "is subject only to laws which are made by himself and yet are universal," defined as impartial and equally binding on all (100).

Kant bases his conception of human dignity upon this capacity for normative reason: "Now I say that man, and in general every rational being, *exists* as an end in himself, *not merely as a means* for arbitrary use by this or that will" (Kant 1956, 94). Consequently, you must "treat humanity, whether in your own person or in the person of any other, never simply as a means, but always at the same time as an end" (96). Treating other people as ends implies that we should "consult them, . . . offer them explanations, and . . . give them a chance to object to actions that affect them" (Chambers 1996, 4). Thus, Kant builds his theory of self-government upon a foundation of humanist principles, including civil liberties, political equality, and human dignity.

Building directly on the Kantian legacy, Habermas maintains the emphasis on rational self-government but shifts the rational process from the mind of the individual subject (monologism) to the intersubjective realm of deliberative conversation among a plurality of individuals (dialogism). More specifically, Habermas agrees with Kant that valid norms and laws must accord with the "principle of universalization," a standard met when "*all* affected can accept the consequences and the side effects its *general* observance can be anticipated to have for the satisfaction of *everyone's* interests (and these consequences are preferred to those of known alternative possibilities for regulation)" (Habermas 1990, 65). However, unlike Kant, Habermas insists that whether or not a norm is universalizable can only be determined through the *actual practice* of deliberation among citizens: "Only those norms can claim to be valid that meet (or could meet) with the approval of all affected in their capacity *as participants in practical discourse*" (Habermas 1990, 66). In other words, "'rather than ascribing as valid to all others any maxim that I can will to be a universal law, I must submit my maxim to all others for purposes of discursively testing its claim to universality. The emphasis shifts from what each can will without contradiction to be a general law, to what all can will in agreement to be a universal norm.' This version of the universality principle does in fact entail the idea of a cooperative process of argumentation" (Habermas 1990, 67).

Habermas argues that through rational deliberation, a diversity of individuals can come to an agreement about which laws and policies are most valid based on the force of the better argument. This implies several things. First, it implies that citizens should make political judgments by assessing the rationality of arguments presented, rather than on the basis of selfish interests or with their emotions or in accordance with nonrational religious beliefs. Second, it implies that the better argument would in fact be recognized as such by all participants in the conversation—or at least all the rational ones. Third, if all people must be included in the process of deliberation, then the conversation can never be finally concluded, as new people are constantly arriving. Thus, as Kant argued two hundred years ago, no generation may be forever restricted by the understandings of its ancestors or bound by their traditions—a sentiment also expressed by both Thomas Paine and Abraham Lincoln.

Benjamin R. Barber, whose work poses an alternative and more communitarian approach to deliberation, criticizes Habermas and others for failing to distinguish between philosophical discourse and pragmatic public judgment. Citizens are not prepared to engage in the level of discourse that meets the standards of "rational-critical discussion"—nor should they want to. However, this does not mean that citizens cannot engage in public deliberation.

According to Barber, the type of judgment required by democratic politics arises out of a public process that requires a citizen not to construct philosophical arguments, but rather to debate her ideas "with her fellow citizens, run them through the courts, offer them as a program for a political party, try them out in the press, reformulate them as a legislative initiative, experiment with them in local, state, and federal forums, and, in every other way possible, subject them to the civic scrutiny and public activity of the community to which she belongs" (1988, 199). Thus, in the communitarian approach to deliberation, citizens might make arguments and evaluate competing claims using a wide array of different standards, including not only philosophical argumentation, but also religious beliefs, moral intuitions, personal experience, and common sense.

While dispensing with the "universal" standards of dialogical reason complicates the process of agreement, citizens remain unified by focusing on a shared problem and the pragmatic need for common action. While many modes of discourse come together in the public arena, the goal of public deliberation for communitarians is not to reach an agreement about which is the better argument, but rather to find common ground for action by making a normative judgment among a variety of viable arguments, weighing the pros and cons of each. The question is not philosophical but pragmatic: "What shall we do when something has to be done that affects us all, we wish to be reasonable, yet we disagree on means and ends and are without independent grounds for making the choice" (Barber 1996b, 349)? "Since all citizens are trying to adjudicate conflicts or make decisions or get along with neighbors or pay for common services, and since it is finally common action that concerns them, they show little interest in truth or certainty or the epistemological status of moral propositions" (1988, 8). Citizens worry more about the *consequences* of various decisions for the community and its members than they do about philosophical justifications.

Finally, while the attempt to ground deliberation on a foundation of universalist Kantian principles is appealing, Barber insists that this desire for security actually impinges upon the democratic ideal of popular sovereignty by constraining the will of the people. Opposing all ideals that claim immutability, Barber goes so far as to argue that even the U.S. Constitution must not be treated as a sacred text, but rather as the political creation of "we the people" at a particular historical moment. In other words, the Constitution remains authoritative only so long as citizens continue to endorse its principles. Moreover, the ostensibly sacred principles of the Constitution must be reinterpreted by each generation—"Is advertising to count as speech? How about child pornography? Are slaves property?"— rather than ossified in light of some notion of "original intent" (1996b, 352). "In a democracy," he tells us, "living popular will is always trump" (356).

Despite the appeal of Barber's communitarian approach, however, his valorization of radical popular sovereignty raises a serious philosophical question for those committed to democratic government: What if the people involved in deliberation endorse antidemocratic policies, like white supremacy, the subordination of women, or legalized discrimination against homosexuals? Speaking for the philosophical school, Seyla Benhabib addresses this concern directly, insisting that universal principles like civil liberties, basic equality, and human dignity should never be called into question by a deliberative public because these principles form the necessary prerequisite for democratic deliberation. She emphasizes that while the philosophical approach to deliberation allows citizens to *interpret* principles like freedom of speech and equal rights for their own generation, such principles cannot be legitimately revoked by the majority; they exist as inalienable human rights not subject to community approval (Benhabib 1996, 78). In opposition to communitarianism, Benhabib argues that a rich humanistic approach to deliberation rooted in the Kantian tradition gives decision-making power back to citizens, while also maintaining a commitment to universal principles that prevents questions like "are slaves property?" from ever being answered in the affirmative. However, while Benhabib defends the philosophical methodology, one could certainly imagine a communitarian approach to deliberation contained within the bounds set by the U.S. Constitution.

PUBLIC DELIBERATION IN PRACTICE: "NATIONAL ISSUES FORUMS" AND "STUDY CIRCLES RESOURCE CENTER"

These intellectual discussions help illuminate the deliberative process, but the actual practice of public deliberation is not strictly academic. All across the country, citizens are regularly engaging in public deliberation in forums convened by a wide array of different organizations. Two important players in the field of deliberative democracy are National Issues Forums (NIF)—a national network of civic and educational organizations that facilitates "non-partisan discussions about timely public policy issues based on the tradition of the early American town meetings"—and the

Study Circles Resource Center (SCRC)—"a private, nonprofit, nonpartisan foundation which is dedicated to advancing deliberative democracy and improving the quality of public life in the United States." Both organizations endorse a vision of public deliberation that addresses the paradoxical reality that despite the fact that we live in prosperous democratic times, we often feel alienated from the political process, disengaged from civic life, and disconnected from one another. My discussion of the way in which actual citizens deliberate draws on the methodologies developed by these two groups.

As opposed to academic approaches to deliberation, the methods deployed by both NIF and SCRC arise not out of theory, but rather out of the actual *practice* of deliberation. Each group publishes booklets that communities across the country use to jumpstart their deliberations about a shared problem, such as "money and politics" or "racism and race relations." The NIF booklets "frame" the issue at hand in terms of three or four broad "choices" that research shows will resonate with ordinary citizens. Each "choice" highlights its consequences for things that citizens generally value, each includes key "strategic facts" that citizens must know in order to make an informed decision, and each presents a list of pros and cons that must be carefully considered. The SCRC takes a similar approach, but its booklets divide the deliberation into four segments: an introduction to the topic, defining the nature of the problem, determining alternative approaches to addressing the problem, and hammering out a plan for action. Both organizations hope to present issues in a way that will allow citizens to work through their differences of opinion, "while discouraging the usual debates in which people lash out with simplistic arguments" (Mathews [1994] 1999, 223). Even if citizens do not reach common ground in the end, at least they will hopefully have a better understanding of not only the issue at hand, but also of the reasons why people of goodwill sometimes disagree (Mathews [1994] 1999).

In terms of the two academic approaches to deliberation outlined above, the methods presented by NIF and SCRC most closely resemble the communitarian approach. That is to say, their approach to deliberation asks ordinary citizens to reflect on their own experiences, values, and beliefs in conversation with diverse others about how to address a shared public problem. Thus, like the communitarian approach, this process allows for a wide array of different modes of argumentation, ways of knowing, and standards for judgment. The process aims at finding common ground for action; it is not a philosophical search for the better argument.

As a practical model of deliberation meant to be used by ordinary citizens in contemporary America, both NIF and SCRC recognize that while it is important to give reasons for your claims and back assertions up with evidence, less educated or less articulate folks might have valid beliefs and intuitions but lack the intellectual or rhetorical skills to convince others via "rational" academic-style arguments. Consequently, at the beginning of a forum or a study circle, participants are encouraged to share their personal experiences concerning the issue on the table. If the session progresses correctly, the experiences, intuitions, and gut reactions of citizens are brought to the fore and reflected upon by the group as a whole. This process recognizes that gut feelings are not always irrational or invalid or random. Instead, commonsense understandings often express an intuitive grasp of an important issue (Chambers 1996, 6).

At the same time, however, "intuition" and "common sense" can also constitute prejudice and bigotry, and in that case, deliberation is even more important because it forces people to reflect on their values and opinions. "Deliberative dialogue is especially important when political issues draw out feelings about those who are different, feelings based on unwarranted stereotypes." In fact, studies of NIF reveal that "one way people might get beyond stereotypes and the conflicts they generate is through the common work of making choices about practical issues—rather than focusing on the differences *per se*" (Mathews [1994] 1999, 240). As one NIF forum participant put it, "What you need is a redneck like me and a black fireman over there to come together and talk about crime, and realize that the other person is not so bad. We'll . . . leave talking to each other" ([1994] 1999, 221).

CONCLUSION: WHAT USE IS PUBLIC DELIBERATION TODAY?

Given the current structure of American government, some people wonder why citizens should bother deliberating. After all, no institutional mechanism currently exists that connects public deliberation to the legislative process. Moreover, according to a recent study, including elected officials in deliberative forums with citizens does not work very well. First, in almost every instance, in the face of an elected official, citizens quickly assumed a passive, deferential posture, even when organizers had deliberately made efforts to prevent that from happening (Button and Mattson 1999). Second, in none of the cases studied could researchers find "any evidence of deliberation having any measurable effect on public policy," not even "a pledge to vote differently in the future" (630). In fact, in one case people became "bitter and cynical" and "visibly upset" when they realized that their deliberations would have no impact on government (630).

While reforming our political system so that citizens play a key role in setting the normative direction for public policy and so that elected officials are held accountable to the people remains a goal for which to work, increased levels of public deliberation can still make a positive difference even in the absence of such changes. Because deliberation leads to increased levels of political knowledge, it can help citizens make more informed choices when they go to the polls and express more thoughtful opinions to pollsters. In fact, since most politicians do in fact care about public opinion polls (perhaps too much so today), we could improve those polls by bringing a representative sample of people together to deliberate before questioning them, an innovative approach pioneered by Jim Fishkin. If deliberative polling were "employed in a general election, at the beginning of the primary season, or before a referendum, then the recommending force of the public's considered judgments, broadcast on national television, might well make a difference to the outcome" (Fishkin 1995, 169–70). Deliberation might pose as one means to improve the current problems surrounding the initiative and referendum (see Galen Nelson's chapter in this collection).

But in the end, we need increased levels of public deliberation within communities to help make American culture more democratic, a vitally important factor in the political socialization of young people. After all, Putnam attributes the deterioration of social capital to generational change, so the culture in which a young person comes of age makes a critical difference. As discussed above, deliberation could provide a variety of benefits, including the creation of legitimacy, community building, popular sovereignty, greater civic engagement, and political participation. We will never be able to move beyond a political system that simply adjudicates between conflicting interests with no regard for the common good, unless we create the necessary prerequisite for government aimed at the common good: an engaged citizenry with a coherent vision for the future. The first step toward political reform is convincing citizens that they should care. Hopefully, stimulating dialogue across difference can play a role in creating a more democratic public—one that can talk through its differences, create a shared yet pluralistic public life, and become a self-governing community for the 21st century.

7

Educating for Democracy

JOEL WESTHEIMER AND JOSEPH KAHNE

The purpose of education is not just for kids to have choices, but for kids to act on their knowledge, to create structures and to change and transform structures so that the world is a better place for everybody.

—A teacher at C. Wright Mills Academic Middle School
(All names and places have been changed for this chapter.)

It is often said that today's youth will be called on to solve tomorrow's problems. Schools provide essential preparation for this task. Despite this rhetoric, curriculum that considers the nature of social problems and ways youth might respond as citizens rarely gets center stage. Rather than focusing on ways youth might participate through democratic institutions to foster a better society, curricular discussions focus on the acquisition of academic and vocational skills. To the extent that the democratic purposes of education are raised, educators emphasize conveying knowledge regarding U.S. history and government structures, on opportunities for community service, and on exercises where students simulate the operations of various public institutions such as courts and legislatures. Occasionally, reformers focus on eliciting student input about the design and implementation of a curriculum or on better aligning curriculum materials with students' lived experiences (Wigginton 1986; Wood, 1992). When students conduct oral histories of community members, for example, they fulfill an ideal of democratic education by showing that academic disciplines like history and English have relevance to issues in their own lives and the lives of their community.

These matters are all worthy of attention, but they differ in fundamental ways from efforts to prepare students to improve society. Ever-declining civic commitments and a growing sense of alienation and disaffection among American citizens make this task all the more urgent. In this chapter, we consider what it might mean to move preparation for membership in a more *participatory* democracy to the center of a school's educational agenda, while never suggesting the need to supplant representative political institutions. In framing our discussion of education for participatory democracy—that is, education that fosters youth's ability to work collectively toward a better society—we examine a school designed to promote participatory democracy, a school unabashed in its commitment to fostering the attitudes, skills, and knowledge required to engage and act on important social issues. C. Wright Mills Middle School seemed to us to offer such a model, doubtless one among many alternatives.

We recognize that some find this orientation romantic and that other goals are also of great importance. Given the fundamental significance of these democratic goals, however, we believe this alternative agenda warrants careful attention in order to understand its potential, its risks, and the complexities associated with its pursuit.

VOICES FROM THE PAST: PROMOTING CRITICAL ANALYSIS, CIVIC PARTICIPATION, AND ACTION

The age-old idea that education needed to orient itself to the challenges of democracy heightened during the Progressive Era. John Dewey led the charge that a democratic education required students participating in the community life of the school. As he explained, the school needed to become "an institution in which the child is, for the time, to live—to be a member of community life in which he feels that he participates and to which he contributes" (Dewey quoted in Westbrook 1991, 106). This democratic and more participatory educational approach would nurture, so Dewey believed, citizens capable of taking on the responsibilities of democratic self-governance.

In the second and third decades of the 20th century, conceptions of democratic education rooted in commitments to improving society through collective action, many inspired by Dewey, achieved a wide hearing among educators. Known as "social reconstructionists," these reformers emphasized teaching students to be active participants in a democratic civic community, able to envision, articulate, and act on conceptions of a better world.

Some, such as Harold Rugg, focused on critical analysis of major social issues and institutions. He wanted students to examine "Problems of the 'market' and its historical development," "How the press developed its influence at various times in our growth," and "The history of labor problems; movements for the increase of cooperation between capital and labor; problems of wages, hours, living conditions" (1996 [1921], 47).

Rugg developed a series of textbooks and learning materials that sold more than one million copies during the 1930s. The goal of this series, and of the social reconstructionists more generally, was to engage students in the analysis of major institutions and social issues so that social problems, causes, and ways to respond could be identified. The series of textbooks sold well until the start of World War II when nationalist sentiments made critiques of American society unpopular. Rugg's texts became a lightning rod for the rising anti-Communist power in politics (Fine 1995; Kliebard 1995).

A second group of curriculum theorists and educational reformers were attracted to experience-based approaches that emphasized projects tied to social needs. "As the purposeful act is thus the typical unit of the worthy life in a democratic society," wrote William Kilpatrick in 1918, "so also should it be made the typical unit of school procedure" (323). These educators believed that experiential activities could transform students' political and social orientation toward fighting injustice. Their focus bridged their concern for the coarse individualism of the 1920s and the social dislocation of the 1930s with their desire to create "miniature communities" through which students learned the value of working together to identify and respond to problems they confronted (Dewey [1900] 1956). This focus on communal undertakings tied to social needs led many Progressive Era educators to promote what they called the "core curriculum" (see Faunce and Bossing 1951; Alberty 1953). The "core" was designed to place multidisciplinary analysis and action regarding social problems and themes from social life at the heart of students' school experience. It was a common feature of many schools participating in the Progressive Education Association's (PEA's) Eight-Year Study, for example. Students in the thirty schools that took part in this study commonly spent between two and three hours a day in core classes initiating projects where they examined and responded to major issues facing both individuals and their community. For instance, they studied and initiated programs of environmental improvement; did work with the elderly, orphans, and infants; and examined safety issues in the home and community (Giles, McCutchen, and Zechiel 1942).

Then as now, many of those who endorsed "progressive," experience-based curriculum downplayed the importance of analysis, critique, and action related to social institutions and the pursuit of social justice. Then as now, many progressive educators, particularly those who emphasized a child-centered approach, attended to students' individual interests and needs without engaging students in critical analysis of social issues. What made this period unique was its critical mass of leading educators who believed that "by manipulating the school curriculum they could ultimately change the world" (Cremin 1988, 187).

Those focused on reconstructing society to make it more democratic found a leader in George S. Counts who, at the 1932 meeting of the Progressive Education Association, delivered a speech "Dare Progressive Education be Progressive?" which became the book *Dare the School Build a New Social Order?* He argued that progressive education had "elaborated no theory of social welfare" (1932, 258), that "it must emancipate itself from the influence of class" (259), and that "it cannot place its trust in a child-centered school" (259). In short, he argued that if progress was the goal of progressive education, then progressive educators needed to be explicit about what progress required. Writing during the Great Depression, he was highly critical of our economic and social norms of competition, selfishness, individualism, and inattention to human suffering. He wanted educators to do more than engage students in analysis of these issues. He wanted them to "engage in the positive task of creating a new tradition in American life" (262). As he put it, "the word [indoctrination] does not frighten me" (263).

The speech had enormous impact. Discussions scheduled for the rest of the convention were replaced by informal discussions of Counts's challenge, and the PEA leaders and members continued to discuss these matters in detail in committee meetings and through their publications (see Graham 1967, 66–67). Counts's argument and reactions to it provide a helpful frame for discussing the educational implications of concern for participatory democracy, particularly in relation to the creation of democratic communities that focus explicitly on matters of social betterment.

For some, Counts's writing was a much appreciated wake-up call. It led educators like Paul Hanna (1932) to recommend redesigned teacher education programs that could address this agenda. Indeed, even educators like Dewey and Bode who did not endorse Counts's call for indoctrination, fearing that it mistakenly implied that there were fixed truths that could be transmitted to students, often did support Counts's critique of the educational system. Dewey praised Counts for "arousing teachers to think more about existing conditions, and in exposing the kind and amount of indoctrination for a reactionary social order that goes on in the schools" (Dewey cited in Graham 1967, 14).

Writing in a similar vein, Boyd Bode supported Counts's general critique that progressive educators needed a direction, but not his program of indoctrination. In *Progressive Education at the Crossroads*, he wrote, "If progressive education is to fulfill its promise, it must become consciously representative of a distinctive [democratic] way of life" (1938, 5). He argued, as we do in this chapter, that educators must aim at creating a communal mode of life that reflects democratic sensibilities and social analysis— collective undertakings and the creation of common bonds are not sufficient. This democratic orientation could, he argued, provide direction and norms for school communities without requiring indoctrination.

If those committed to democratic communitarian goals had strong allies, however, they also had fierce critics. Some doubted that social improvement should guide educational policy. Moreover, as noted above,
many educators who were attracted to experiential project-based activities rejected Counts's proposal. They preferred child-centered goals such
as creativity and individual freedom. Elizabeth Moos (1932) reflected the
mood of many members of the PEA when she argued that the focus on the
child rather than on society was most appropriate for elementary schools:
"During these years, foundation for emotional and spiritual growth is
laid, and this work must not be subordinated to any particular social situation" (264). Many educators also worried that the emphasis on radical
politics might marginalize the PEA by limiting the support of teachers
and administrators (Cremin 1961, 262). Carlton Washburne (president of
the PEA in 1940–1942), for example, argued against disseminating the report of Counts's Committee on Economic and Social Problems in 1933, believing that the report might stir "up a feeling on the part of many people
who are at the present time overly sensitive that the association has gone
radical" (in Graham 1967, 69). These tensions both in the PEA and among
progressive educators generally were never resolved. To the extent that a
working consensus was achieved, it came through invoking the goal of
"democracy as a way of life," something the different factions within progressive education could support. This support, however, seemed as
much a function of the goal's vague nature as of a meaningful consensus
(Graham 1967). The contradictions within this set of goals often reemerge
in contemporary experiments in democratic schooling.

C. WRIGHT MILLS
ACADEMIC MIDDLE SCHOOL

On a crowded, bustling side street in a Latino community sits C. Wright
Mills Academic Middle School. In 1984, the school, located in the heart of
a major North American city, closed and reopened under a court-ordered
consent decree with an almost entirely new staff and the goal of attracting
a diverse student population. Currently, Mills enrolls a student body that
is 38 percent Spanish-surnamed, 20 percent "other" white, 14 percent
Chinese, 9 percent African American, and 6 percent Filipino. Once
counted among the poorest performing schools in the district, Mills now
boasts high attendance rates, high performance on standardized tests,
and numerous awards.

Following the consent decree restructuring, the new Mills faculty created a series of mission statements and learning objectives. In many ways,
their mission is progressive, but not unique. The school "seeks to develop

the whole child academically, socially, and emotionally." The faculty use
a "student-centered approach" that develops "self-esteem." They maintain "high academic expectations" recognizing that students "bring a rich
diversity of cultures, experiences, languages, and learning styles that can
be developed and shared in [the] school setting."

The Mills tenets, however, also include less typical commitments to improving society. The faculty want students to "think critically about what
they are learning, draw appropriate conclusions, and discover what is relevant to their lives." Students will "carry out complex projects involving
predictions, research, analysis, and evaluation" and they will do so in
"contexts relevant to their education and to their lives." They will learn to
"work individually and cooperatively," taking responsibility for "their
own lives and actions and for the well being of both the local and global
community." (For an in-depth discussion of Mills, how its teachers work
collectively, professional development activities at the school, and its governance structure, see Westheimer 1998, chapter 3.)

Like the Progressive Era educators discussed above, the teachers at
C. Wright Mills aim to instill in students hope for a more just society
and equip them with the tools to pursue that hope. As one teacher explained:

> I'd like to see them have an awareness of what makes the world, in their eyes,
> a good place and a set of skills that allows them to act on their vision. I'd like
> [students to understand] the need for individuals and groups to act collec-
> tively to make the world a good place.

Social Studies and Project-Based Curricular Goals

The curricular approach taken at Mills, similar to that taken by pioneer-
ing progressive schools, is to emphasize what the Mills staff call transdisciplinary projects aimed at social needs and to couple these with academic
analysis of the social and institutional context. These projects and related
analysis comprise a substantial portion of students' work at the school. Indeed, a group of four subject area teachers designing the year's curriculum are more likely to begin with learning objectives linked to their goal
of preparing responsive citizens and then think of ways to make links to
academic material than the other way around. The challenge for this
school and others with a democratic mission is to structure curriculum activities that advance these goals while simultaneously supporting systematic and sequential development of disciplinary knowledge.

In an effort to link the curriculum to the school's mission, teachers decided early on to base their transdisciplinary curriculum in the social studies. To make clear the importance of their discussions, teachers provided

links to students' present-day realities. Mills's "Learning Challenges," for example, reflect the faculty's belief in the power of interdisciplinary experiences and hands-on, purposeful activities to achieve these ends. These learning challenges bring students and faculty at Mills together in interdisciplinary groups to study problems of social consequence.

In many schools, interdisciplinary curriculum revolves around themes. Elementary school students might study dinosaurs through stories, art, and science. Middle school students might carry the theme of "cities" through each of the subject areas. The learning challenge is structured differently. It begins with a prompting challenge that requires investigation and response—how to respond to hunger or homelessness in the community, for example. The subject areas are then employed in answering the prompting challenge. As Bernard Farges (who worked extensively with Mills faculty crafting the learning challenges curricula) explains, the educational purpose shifts from the learning objective to *learning from the objective*. Students work in groups on pieces of a larger project, make presentations on their findings, and take actions with respect to their ongoing commitments to the community. At Mills, the commitment to democratic education means that each challenge that is selected (between six and ten each year) revolves around an issue of social significance.

"Addressing Violence in Our Everyday Lives" was a challenge for an eighth grade group that began with the question: "How can you empower yourself and your peers to address the violence in your life and in society in a positive way?" The two-week challenge began with five days of regular core academic classes that provided students with the background knowledge and skills they would need for week two. Students then broke into groups focused on one of five "subchallenges." The first, led by the social studies teacher, assessed violence in the media. Students watched television and movies, chronicling observations and statistics about what they saw. They interviewed experts in an effort to critically analyze media portrayals of violence. They asked questions like "When you sit down in front of the television, you're doing the watching, but who's really in control, you or the show?" and "Does the media show violence as it really is?" Based on their analysis, students formulated, wrote, and revised action recommendations for their peers.

A second group dealt with the problem of gang violence. The language arts teachers engaged students in readings, discussion, and written exercises that examined the causes and impact of gang membership. A group led by a physical education teacher who voluntarily joined this particular family's challenge activities examined violence in sports. They asked how society has condoned and encouraged violence in sports. The math teacher explored the economic costs of violence in their city. After researching the statistics on the costs of different violent activities, students were required to develop solutions to urban violence. Finally, the science teacher led a group that explored violence in families. They talked about the myths and realities of rape, sexual abuse, and domestic violence. They assembled a survival guide with tips and community resources for other teenagers and created a public service announcement that they distributed on video.

For each "subchallenge" project, students were required to complete learning logs, oral and visual presentations, a substantive written product, and an evaluation of their group's cooperative work process. As would be expected, the curriculum appears to have affected youth in different ways. For one student, the two weeks spoke to personal issues: "I had never dared to talk about all of these things [how violence affects me] before this week. It made me realize how much violence is in my life." Another student was more focused on the imperative of action: "I hope that by talking about some of these things in the classroom, we'll be more able to speak out in the streets about these problems." Though these sentiments were commonly expressed, they were not universal. Many were drawn more to the excitement generated by the experiential nature of the projects than by the emphasis on critical politics:

> It was fun. Like well, it was a lot of hard work because you had to do a lot of research, calling up people. . . . We did all the things on our own. And you know, it wasn't like sitting in class and listening to the teachers talk. It was just like doing things on our own.

Moreover, students did not select this school because of its focus on social issues; they were attracted by the "high [academic] standards," because, "the teachers really want you to learn," and because "the school is safe and teachers are nice." Not all students were ready or interested in engaging in sustained analysis of social issues.

On the other hand, many were. The opportunity elicited energy that would have otherwise been dormant. When asked about the learning challenge on violence in their community, for example, one student responded: "We did a poster on violence that had a slogan: If you don't like a gun in your face, look back to your roots and your race." He went on to explain that learning about the Aztecs can help Latino gang members understand their condition, namely that "they're all killing each other for a color . . . we're trying to say just look back to your roots and it shows that you guys are all the same [all descendents] from Latins and also we're all just people."

A Project-Based Curriculum

If the desire and capacity to respond to social needs are prerequisites for a more participatory democracy, young people need to have experiences that develop this orientation and foster these abilities. In addition to traditional academic discipline-based goals, preparation for participatory democracy requires that youth develop a "spirit of service" and the civic skills needed for effective civic action. Making speeches, writing memos, facilitating and participating in group discussions, organizing community events, and mobilizing fellow community members are examples of skills required for effective participation in a civic democracy. Such opportunities are rare in traditional classrooms, which focus primarily on the academic performance of individual students. Indeed, an extensive review of the literature (Berman 1997) reveals that social studies texts rarely emphasize the importance of or skills connected with civic participation, that teachers rarely engage students in such activities, and that students tend to view participation in their community and school as unrelated to their status as a "good" citizen (also see Dynneson and Gross 1991). In contrast, both teachers at Mills and social reconstructionists during the Progressive Era pursued this democratic agenda by making projects connected with social needs a central component of their curriculum.

For example, in one learning challenge we observed at Mills, "The Garden Against Hunger," students produced a brochure showing sites of soup kitchens in their neighborhood, wrote to parents and leaders of city agencies inviting them to attend a fund-raiser, and published a newsletter. They created computer databases to share information with other groups, parents, and members of city agencies and chose sites for brochure distribution. Finally, they made presentations to parents and representatives from city agencies, homeless organizations, local media, and members of the local community.

These learning challenges modeled for students the importance of civic participation and required that students employ the skills needed to engage such tasks. This emphasis is reminiscent of early reforms during the Progressive Era that engaged youth in projects of social significance to make schools "a genuine form of active community life, instead of a place set apart to learn lessons" (Dewey [1900] 1956, 14).

A Social Studies–Based Curriculum

Mills orients both its overall curriculum and its transdisciplinary projects around social studies. Nationally, the trend is in the opposite direction. Increasingly, mandated tests and other school policies emphasize math, science, and literacy skills rather than social studies. New York State public schools' new curriculum standards, for example, specify achievement standards across three areas—math, language arts, and science—omitting social studies entirely. Social studies, for the

New York State Board of Education and others, provide topics, as needed, in the service of acquiring skills in these other three disciplines, but is not viewed as a primary concern. At Mills, in contrast, disciplinary learning is used in the service of social studies, that is in the service of projects, themes, and objectives of social interest and consequence. Thus, interdisciplinary learning challenges focused on the environment, political elections, food production and distribution, and violence in the community.

In an effort to make students aware that the social issues being studied were not simply matters for abstract speculation, the curriculum consistently linked topics to contemporary issues and their personal experiences. In a literature class, for example, students read a biography of a Native American woman and discussed historical oppression—the treatment of native peoples by the U.S. government. Teachers used this as a springboard to examine contemporary and controversial examples of oppression and injustice in their city. A science class studied the environmental impact of European colonization of the Americas and also explored recent environmental damage from an underreported oil spill off a nearby coast.

EDUCATION FOR PARTICIPATORY DEMOCRACY: TWO CHALLENGES

1. *Development of Academic Skills.* Although we argue for emphasizing links between academic work and civic priorities, we also recognize that many educators' hesitation to endorse civic education stems from the concern that this focus distracts them from their most fundamental task—development of academic skills. We believe such concerns are warranted. Some experiential activities and projects that aim primarily at social development may neglect academic priorities. A math teacher at Mills, for example, described his frustration with trying to tie sophisticated understandings of math concepts to project-based activities:

> Some interdisciplinary projects are great and can be a good way to learn. But it's not the best way for all curriculum. Math always ends up accommodating the other subjects, statistics one day, land area the next. . . . A student like Tom ends up doing algebra on the side. It's fine, but are they learning? They're learning math in a way . . . but mainly social skills, how to keep on task, issues of tolerance, research skills. That's fine, but pressure's on me to get the math through; I won't get through all I have planned this year because of Challenge Week, Ocean Week,

Awareness Month. . . . All these things take away, [and] how it takes away bothers me.

Similarly, Dewey (1931) worried that the projects undertaken as part of the "project method" were often "too trivial to be educative" (86) and that the learning that results is often of "a merely technical sort, not a genuine carrying forward of theoretical knowledge" (87).

Designing curriculum similar to Mills's learning challenges that enable sequential development of disciplinary knowledge is enormously difficult. Often, teachers may not have the time, commitment, or insight necessary to implement this kind of curriculum. This concern parallels contemporary discussions of "hands-on" math and science education where educators worry that the focus on experience may undermine attention to the formal and theoretical aspects of the disciplines (Driver et al. 1994; Varelas 1996).

To note this risk, however, is not to concede the case. The same math teacher quoted earlier went on to say:

> I like [the interdisciplinary projects] because it gives me a chance to see how students do all around, like Lisa [a science teacher] and I were just talking, you get a broader range on each student. . . . So I can't NOT do challenge week. Instead, I have to say, how else can I do it? Maybe I'll do probability.

This parallels Dewey's (1931) perspective on the project method:

> The defect is not inherent. It is possible to find problems and projects that come within the scope and capacities of the experience of the learner and which have a sufficiently long span so that they raise new questions, introduce new and related undertakings, and create a demand for fresh knowledge. (86)

Similarly, Deborah Meier (1995), George Wood (1992), and reformers who advocate whole language approaches and constructivism have demonstrated that curriculum that promotes the development of disciplinary knowledge through methods consistent with democratic priorities can be successfully implemented in contemporary schools (see also Fine [1995] for discussion on the unnecessary division between teaching the "basics" and teaching democratic values). Indeed, Mills was a popular school primarily because of its reputation for high academic standards, and students consistently performed in the top 20 percent of the district on standardized tests.

2. *Education or Indoctrination.* If a group of visitors walked down the hall at Mills prior to the recent California election, they would have seen walls covered with a variety of posters. Some of these posters simply communicated information:

PROPOSITION 204—THE CLEAN WATER ACT
Pro: More water in residential and agricultural areas.
Con: Increase in water costs and taxes.

WHAT IS PROPOSITION 210, THE MINIMUM WAGE?
Currently the minimum wage is $4.25/hour. Proposition 210 would raise the minimum wage to $5.00/hour as of March 1, 1997 and to $5.75/hour as of March 1, 1998.

Other posters, however, presented clear positions on issues of social and political significance:

YES TO PROPOSITION 204: Safe, Clean, Reliable Water Act. Encourage safe drinking water.

NO ON PROPOSITION 209: 209 Will take away affirmative action and with it the chance for everyone to go to school.

DANA MARTIN FOR THE HOUSE OF REPRESENTATIVES: She is Pro-Choice! She Supports Affirmative Action!

Although most educators and parents agree that the ability to analyze and form opinions on issues is an important part of students' education, the specifics of curriculum and pedagogy that aim to accomplish this goal are far more controversial. When a social studies teacher in a school in Oregon taught a unit on the history of environmentalism, some parents and school board members objected asserting that the unit was indoctrinating children to be antilogging and proenvironment. Oregon board members, along with officials of several other districts and states, also banned the Dr. Seuss book *The Lorax,* which depicts a factory rapidly chopping down all the trees to make a popular (but useless) product, because of similar concerns. Similarly, opponents of New York City's proposed "Rainbow Curriculum" argued that the section on prejudice was not to be part of the school curriculum because it contained a passage encouraging tolerance for homosexuals. The conflict ended with not only the exclusion of the passage, but also the resignation of the chancellor of the New York City schools.

When does teaching become indoctrination? How can schools teach students to be critical thinkers when it comes to matters of social policy while maintaining a judicious balance of alternative perspectives? What happens when students examine current issues and explore paths to improving society that conflict with mainstream or parental values? At Mills, for example, some parents and administrators had misgivings about the signs in the hallways described earlier that advocate particular candidates or positions. Before addressing these questions, it is worth noting that the Mills faculty as well as educators of the Progressive Era share two approaches to meaningful explorations of important social issues and that these approaches are themselves the subject of serious debate.

First, both linked their discussion and analysis of important issues to action. Both groups believed in challenging the prevailing culture of inaction and passivity with respect to issues of social significance and saw action as essential to the workings of a participatory democracy. The primary value of this action lies not in the service it provides, these educators argue, but in the opportunity it offers students to develop skills related to participatory democracy and in the social, participatory orientation it models. This perspective was well articulated by a Mills student who, when asked about the learning challenges, told us:

> It teaches us how important it is to have social responsibility, like telling people about what's happening in the world, like the teachers are doing for us, and we're going to do it for the community.

Second, both the Mills faculty and the progressives worked to ensure that students were exposed to—and could understand—a range of alternative perspectives. A democracy cannot function meaningfully without informed and critical analysis of issues and social problems. Although it is common for social studies teachers and others to engage students in exercises where they must differentiate between "facts" and "opinions," rarely are these discussions linked to participation and action. At Mills, for instance, information and perspectives on the legislative issues described earlier are not simply learned, but are communicated to the school community.

Moreover, the ability to discern fact from opinion is developed through explicit challenges to widespread cultural assumptions rather than through reexamination of historical issues, which, by virtue of time, have become unassailable. Whereas many teachers demonstrate to students the potential tyranny of opinion over facts in landmark historical controversies (ill-informed legislative decisions based on the idea that black Americans could not be as intelligent as their white counterparts, for example), both Mills teachers and the progressives understood that to develop the capacity for critical analysis, students need to examine issues for which their own perspectives and positions could be challenged. That there are not, as of yet, clear "answers" (widespread cultural agreement) to the questions raised specifically makes those issues useful. Whether gay men should be allowed to serve in the U.S. military becomes a more useful issue for discussion and critique than whether African American men should be allowed to serve. The former forces difficult analysis and consideration of a variety of viewpoints, while the latter, piggybacking on already established widespread agreement, fails to do so.

Progressive educators may correctly recognize that students must have experiences engaging controversial issues, but this does not mean that they have worked out strategies for doing so that are consistent with both democratic sensibilities and parental concerns. The tensions raised by the approaches to teaching critical analysis and linking learning to action described above are many; educators' pursuit of such goals through curriculum is fraught with complications. At their base, these "complications" arise because the rhetoric of participatory democracy is being taken seriously and enacted. The prevailing culture of inaction and passivity with respect to issues of social significance is being explicitly and overtly challenged. The hesitancy of many educators to engage critically and then act on controversial issues, however, has a rational basis.

First, while the actions students take in conjunction with the Mills learning challenges may be beneficial, others may be inappropriate. In a well-functioning democracy, citizens act when they find issues compelling and after gathering sufficient information. Frequently, students will not find all issues worthy of civic action or will not achieve the level of clarity regarding an issue that would make actions appropriate. Moreover, teachers must have a certain degree of control over their curriculum. Many kinds of actions such as attending a protest or working with a community organization, that would be appropriate for citizens, may not be structured in ways that enable a teacher to be sure a given action will be safe or educationally valuable. Thus, while experiences at Mills demonstrate the substantial educational potential of civic action as part of students' curriculum, there are reasons to temper blanket support of this practice.

Second, the broad consensus that teachers should help students think critically does not mean pursuit of this goal is straightforward. The consensus regarding critical thinking generally vanishes when the possibility arises that students will articulate conclusions that differ from mainstream or parental values. Critical thinking is commonly understood to be the use of reason in reaching judgments, while indoctrination is a process whereby ideologically committed instructors constrain reason in an effort to lead students to particular conclusions (Siegel 1988). The problem with this formulation is that it assumes a "neutral" ground exists. More exactly, this perspective obscures the ways the dominant culture and ideology are embedded in allegedly neutral reasoning.

Many critics of the kind of curriculum employed by Mills teachers and used during the Progressive Era argue that these educators indoctrinate. They charge, for example, that the social reconstructionists' curriculum emphasizes liberal or left-wing critiques of immigration policy, environmental policy, and the capitalist system. In one sense, these concerns have an empirical basis. No Mills students, for example, engaged in a community action project that would be considered politically conservative. Mills teachers, in fact, often struggled with this tension. A "debate" on immigration was retitled a "panel" on immigration after teachers grew concerned that the invited participants did not represent a broad spectrum of perspectives. These concerns lead many educators, including many at Mills, to respond that they aim to be "value free" by presenting "all sides" of a given controversial subject.

This stance, however, fails to resolve the problem and encounters resistance from both the left and the right. A variety of conservative groups, for example, criticize "critical thinking" because they feel it "means teaching children to empty themselves of their own values (transmitted from parents, church, and culture)" (Simonds 1994, 15). They argue that such curriculum, far from being "value-free," often reflects a form of indoctrination toward "relativistic" and "secular-humanist" values.

On the other hand, social reconstructionists and modern-day criticalists (McLaren and Pruyn 1996) argue that claims of "value neutrality" often function to obscure the mainstream values (the importance of individual autonomy and the efficacy of market incentives, for example) in which they are embedded. Educators may strive to tell "both sides of the story." They may seek balance or neutrality and hope students will then be free to form their own ideas about issues. But, as George Counts wrote in 1932, "neutrality with respect to the great issues that agitate society . . . is practically tantamount to giving support to the most powerful forces engaged in the contest" (263). False notions of neutrality, Counts argued, can constrain critical thinking by failing to make visible those "social forces" hidden by familiarity. It was this concern that led Dewey, who criticized other aspects of Counts's vision, to praise him nonetheless for making visible the "kind and amount of indoctrination for a reactionary social order that goes on in the schools" (cited in Graham 1967, 14).

Furthermore, because the media and the broader culture disproportionately reflect particular interests and perspectives and obscure others, there is no level playing field on which students can discuss issues. Educators must therefore help students consider the interests and power relations embedded in various perspectives—a formidable task. Such concerns motivated Harold Rugg's curricular focus on the ways various powerful groups shaped the development of institutions that in turn helped shape society. This concern was also evident in Mills's learning challenges where study of "gang violence and ways to prevent it" led students to consider how society might condone and encourage violence through sports and the media. One teacher explained his stance on "value neutrality" this way:

> What I'd like students to have is an open mind to things that are different from what they've experienced and an eagerness to find out about it. Not a lack of prejudice necessarily, but an awareness of where their prejudices lie.

In sum, critical thinking in relation to political issues requires attention to situated ideas—ideas in the context of power relations and cultural norms. Students must learn how to respond to social problems and also how certain problems come to the fore while others remain unnamed. They must learn to evaluate legislative proposals and also the social and political dynamics that favor one proposal over another.

CONCLUSION

Reinvigorating the American political system requires that our youngest citizens regain a sense of civic commitment and a belief that they have the capacity to work with others to improve society. A clear vision exists for education that promotes participation and action as well as a keen appreciation of the obstacles educators pursuing this vision face. On the one hand, the importance of this task, and the thought and care with which Mills's teachers and students pursue it, is inspiring. We have found other institutions and more individual teachers who have taken up Mills's example. But in whole, the social reconstructionists' stance probably invites more controversy than efforts to validate students' experiences and interests or efforts to simulate the operations of courts and legislatures. Nonetheless, in our opinion, the approach of Mills is more exciting. The social reconstructionists, unlike many of their progressive colleagues, provide a vision that aims directly at preparing youth to improve society.

On the other hand, it is doubtful that a significant number of teachers, let alone schools or districts, will pursue this goal. Not only are the talents and commitments necessary to pursue these priorities formidable, but also the incentives to bypass these goals are significant. The curricular agenda described earlier breeds controversy, and controversy is not something schools handle well. In part, this is because they are governed democratically. Ironically, the civic community (parents and community members) that governs schools often sanctions those who implement curriculum that engages the contentious issues a civic community should face. Administrators also work to avoid controversy. When a science class studying levels of radon at Mills discovered levels above the recommended standard, the school district leaders grew concerned, not primarily with the levels of radon, but with the potential controversy and political pressures such findings might promote.

The policies and practices of teachers, schools, and districts can promote or constrain the degree to which students acquire the knowledge, skills, and attitudes necessary to function effectively as citizens in a democracy. The social reconstructionists and their modern-day colleagues at Mills and elsewhere may lack sufficient answers to important questions, and many roadblocks may constrain implementation of their vision, but they do provide a vision for a school curriculum that encourages participation, critical analysis, and action—pedagogical prerequisites for democracy and citizenship. These educators offer not only a vision of education for action, but also important strategies for getting there.

8

Community as a Source for Democratic Politics

BENJAMIN SHEPARD

There is no limit to the liberal expansion and confirmation of . . . personal intellectual endowment which may proceed from the flow of social intelligence when that circulates by word of mouth from one to another in the communications of the local community. . . . But that intelligence is dormant and its communications are broken, inarticulate and faint until it possesses the local community as its medium.

—John Dewey (1927, 219)

Without some sort of local community where citizens can act together, there can be no democracy. Without a space where people have common interests and goals, it is difficult to imagine the process of citizens linking their needs to mechanisms for political participation and reform. As such, democracy renewal must be considered within a broader framework of community development and organizing. Only when citizens are organized and mobilized can communities create the kind of pressure needed to buttress reform initiatives; only when citizens are organized can we consider ourselves living democratically.

A century ago, Tocqueville postulated that American democracy thrives because it balances three aspects of national life: government, the market, and civil society. If any one of these three sectors overwhelmed the other, Tocqueville suggested, democracy is imperiled. Ideally, each sector performs a separate function: The government creates laws and manages problems, the market provides jobs and choice, while civil society provides space where people come together to build community. Civil society can be understood as the mechanism that creates links between neighbors and their route between public policy and private enterprise. The local institutions of civil society—community organizations like union halls, parks, and churches—serve as the places where citizens learn civic skills crucial to democracy. As John Dewey explained, in his classic work *The Public and Its Problems*, "Democracy must begin at home, and its home is the neighborly community" (Dewey 1927, 213).

As most of us know, civil society is suffering within contemporary America. Powerful economic forces increasingly dominate government processes and threaten civic spaces. Affordable housing is cut back, community gardens are bulldozed, and community centers are sold off (see Shepard 2001). Driving these phenomena is the powerful collusion between global capital, big real estate, and unrepresentative governments. Against these relationships, grassroots civic groups fight an uphill battle. This is why the reconstitution of communities through a variety of different civic institutions is so important today. Without attempts at community building, democracy will continue to be under threat (Shepard and Hayduk 2002).

Of course, I am not pining for the communities of yore—tightly knit and homogeneous neighborhoods based on closed-minded traditions. If that sort of community ever existed, it is certainly gone now. Nonetheless, some sort of elemental community life must be in place for democracy to operate well. As someone who has been involved in numerous community struggles over the year, I have personally witnessed how the building of community can bring together diverse actors in meaningful ways. I have seen how "innocent" community work—the building of a public park or a community garden, for instance—can often take a distinct political turn and come to serve an educational function about the way power works. In this chapter, I will show how this has historically been the case and why it is still so today. The examples I draw upon in this chapter are admittedly limited; nonetheless, I believe they teach us important lessons about how citizens have reconnected to politics via local communities. Democracy reformers have a great deal to learn from such experiments.

THE ORIGINS OF COMMUNITY IN THE SETTLEMENT HOUSE MOVEMENT

Jane Addams, the founder of Hull House (see the Mattson chapter in this volume), described her goal as interpreting "democracy in social terms." Addams was one of the first to see how building community could lead citizens to realize a wider public and civic life where they could become citizens.

The first and most basic step in the process Addams tried to nourish at Hull House was to alleviate the harshness of her residents' lives. To this end, Hull House organized activities and services including a day nursery, kindergarten, clubs for kids, and vocational classes. These Settlement

House workers focused on immediate needs—nursing the sick, washing newborn babies, providing meals and shelter—before asking anything else of residents. Political involvement would have to wait until basic needs were addressed. Once met, Hull House residents were expected to organize, "to develop whatever of social life its neighborhood may afford, to focus and give form to that life" (Addams [1910] 1998, 86). From meeting basic needs, the next step was improving civic and cultural life. Thus, Addams set up a museum where local neighbors could display their own work (i.e., clothes and other crafts made by new immigrants); she held lecture series on the humanities where professors from local universities participated in rigorous discussions. These activities would ensure that the neighborhood nurtured a civic life beyond meeting basic material needs.

Addams also taught her residents to see the needs of the neighborhood as a whole, to produce data for legislation, and use citizen influence to achieve it (Addams [1910] 1998, 86). Beginning by exposing widespread sweatshop conditions on Halsted Street in Chicago, where Hull House was located, Addams and her residents successfully lobbied for fair labor legislation in Illinois and helped President Theodore Roosevelt to pass child care legislation. By creating spaces where people could know each other and build neighborhood ties, the Settlement House cultivated communities where "democracy [could] endure" (Sidel 1998, xxiii). Hull House also helped to create spaces where citizens could learn together and become actively engaged in politics.

Over the hundred years since it began, the Settlement House framework of placing people in housing, providing services, and getting them involved in neighborhood activities has become a standard model for housing providers and community organizers around the country (see Cyler 2001). For instance, New York's Housing Works, an organization that locates affordable housing, regularly organizes busloads of their residents for trips up to Albany to lobby for issues ranging from housing to reform of the Rockefeller Drug Laws in New York, but only after these citizens have been housed and primary needs addressed. The wisdom of the Settlement House movement is that it understood this. And Housing Works is but one example of the still thriving housing and tenant organizing movement building on their roots in the Settlement House movement.

BEYOND SETTLEMENTS: THE CHICAGO AREA PROJECT AND DEBATES ABOUT COMMUNITY

In fact, the tradition begun by Hull House passed itself down to other organizers within Chicago. In 1932, Clifford Shaw founded the Chicago Area Project (CAP) to help neighborhood members organize against crime and delinquency through the creation of webs of interaction among neighborhood residents. The goal was to encourage both neighborhood delinquents and leaders to participate within community life (Shaw 1939; Schlossman et al. 1984). Like Addams before him, Shaw's model of democracy renewal began with community organizing. His approach was to incorporate delinquents into the core of existing communities rather than marginalize them. They were reformed by being organized into the community.

Today, a handful of the original CAP staffers who worked during the 1930s remain. These CAP staffers witnessed the full utility of neighborhood organizing during a period in our history when the question of democracy in America was truly in peril. Shaw effectively mobilized the human resources of neighborhoods. His view was that delinquency was an "area problem" associated with industrialization and things like crime, poverty, disease, suicide, and family instability (Short 1972, xxvii). While other strategies failed, the CAP answer then was to enlist the participation of "local people, ordinary people." Shaw reasoned that if delinquency was a problem of specific areas, the solution lay in "community organization" by neighborhood residents in such areas (xxvi). "That's when the area project sprung to life from Shaw's brain," Ray Raymond, an eighty-five-year-old CAP veteran, recalled in a personal interview.

The Chicago Area Project grew out of a response to the social ills plaguing Chicago's waves of Irish, German, Italian, Polish, and African American immigrants. Shaw believed that neighborhoods needed to form community committees. The idea was to make the neighborhood "conscious of the problem of delinquency, collectively interested in the welfare of its children, and active in promotion programs for such improvements of the community environment." CAP emphasized four components: 1) neighborhood autonomy, 2) utilization of those with established positions of local leadership, 3) maximum involvement of existing neighborhood institutions, and 4) participation of those living in the community (Schlossman et al. 1984, 1).

Shaw put great effort into aligning his organizers with existing South Chicago local institutions. The aim for CAP was to gain entry into community social life and thereby contact with neighborhood juveniles and their gangs. He gained the sponsorship of St. Michael's, a South Side church, by subsidizing a youth program the church could not afford on its own. St. Michael's Club for Boys spurred the creation of the Russell Square Community Committee, the first of Shaw's initial three pilot projects (Schlossman et al. 1984, 6–7,10–11). In doing this community organizing, Area Project staffers concentrated on building ties among neighborhood members, emphasizing the cohesive nature of personal connections among residents. Neighborhoods were the center of all CAP organizing efforts. Henry McKay, Shaw's assistant, described neighborhoods as "areas of participation" (Bennett 1981, 171). And through participation in neighborhood affairs citizens gained a sense of ownership, which in turn led to political participation and calls for reform.

An early staffer for the Area Project was a University of Chicago–trained sociologist named Saul Alinsky. He began his career as a community organizer in Chicago's Back of the Yards neighborhoods in the 1930s (Bennett 1981, 215). The association was short-lived. While Shaw maintained a very low-key disposition, Alinsky often put himself at the center of his campaigns (Bennett 1981, 216). Alinsky left (or was fired as the story goes) in 1940. Conceptions of community and politics lay at the core of the split. Both Alinsky and Shaw believed that the cornerstone of good organizing involved understanding and respect for "community traditions" (Alinsky 1969, 76). Where they differed was in strategy. While CAP functioned around the concept of "primary community" or neighborhood personal relationships, Alinsky viewed community as place of values and interests that needed to be defended through mobilization and conflict tactics—two principles that lie at the center of politics (132). Alinsky organized around "secondary community, many different areas." Shaw, a much less political man, advocated the virtues of interconnectedness among neighborhood members to combat social problems. Shaw did not talk about achieving power (Bennett 1981, 216).

As primary communities have shifted, so have notions of community organizing. Today, the flexible CAP umbrella model containing autonomous project groups remains a popular, effective organizational structure for grassroots groups. But so too does Alinsky's argument that local community organizing must eventually confront existing political institutions and challenge the power structure. If anything, community organizers have recognized the need to press citizens to become more connected to political change as they become members of a local community.

FROM DELINQUENCY TO GARDENS: CONNECTING THE LOCAL COMMUNITY TO POLITICS

Over the next thirty years, the Shaw and Alinsky organizing models continued to form the basis of community organizing and renewal projects from coast to coast. The neighborhood organizing approach became increasingly necessary as the federal role in urban areas receded during the Reagan/Bush years. Due to devolution (transfer of power from federal to state authority), a new generation of organizers began to take stock of what existed within their neighborhoods. Instead of focusing on what was missing, they took inventory of neighborhood resources: from a bank to a vacant lot to public transportation, to cultural, institutional, and even intellectual assets such as universities and hospitals (Herbert 2001). The new "assets-based" approach to community development offered countless possibilities.

At its best, this tradition of community organizing has even interacted with national public policy. Take the Community Reinvestment Act (CRA). While the CRA, which forces banks to end discrimination in lending and to create loans in low-income areas, had been in place for years, it was rarely implemented. During the 1980s and 1990s, local community organizers worked within existing civic institutions in order to highlight the problem of redlining and local neglect of the CRA. Community groups such as the Chicago Woodstock Institute and the Northwest Bronx Community and Clergy Coalition (NWBCCC), one of the community organizations that had fought for passage of the CRA in 1977, created pressure, which forced the law to be fully implemented.

The NWBCCC provides a good case in how such groups have used innovative tactics and local civic institutions to achieve this goal. In 1995, the House Banking Committee passed a bill that exempted 88 percent of banks and lender from the CRA's provisions. The NWBCCC moved to counter this development and threat to their constituency. Their phone calls to try to meet with their senator and the House Banking Committee chair, Al D'Amato, were not returned. So, coalition members took another tact: they rented a bus for neighborhood members and armed with banners and fliers explaining their mission, they headed up to a swanky Park Avenue building where Senator D'Amato's girlfriend lived. The very next day, D'Amato made a return the call to the NWBCCC, complaining about the coalition's tactics, but also agreeing to meet with them. That fall, CRA was preserved, with support from D'Amato (see Groarke and Moss 2002).

Without redlining, an economic pulse returned to many low-income neighborhoods from South Central Los Angeles to the Bronx. The result was an incredible economic resurgence in cities across the country (Herbert 2001). The democratic reforms intended by the CRA could only thrive once community organizers got involved to force the issue. The result of this organizing is a model of bottom-up community redevelopment that helps enhance the practices of the national government that pertain to social justice.

Another recent movement that has connected local community activities to politics has been the community gardens movement. To a large extent the garden movement builds on generations of community organizing. Garden activists organize neighborhood artists and residents, who learn to work with each other through tilling the earth and community in much the same fashion that CAP organized neighborhood area project groups. While Clifford Shaw helped reform delinquents by working to incorporate them back into communities, garden activists teach local kids to plant seeds and learn about the urban environment, within community. Just as Jane Addams encouraged Hull House residents to get involved in creative arts, the garden movement uses garden as spaces for theater. Community gardens often become places for neighborhood members to meet, share a space, work on a common project, and plant the seeds of community together. These are spaces for people to be introduced, to be creative, to solve problems, and to discuss issues of mutual interest. Yet, like many public spaces in the era of globalization, they are under attack.

HOW COMMUNITY GARDENS
BECAME POLITICS IN NEW YORK CITY

In January 2000, members of the More Gardens Coalition welcomed guests for a teach-in in a community garden on East 7th Street. The subject at hand was resisting the destruction of La Esperanza, a community garden in Manhattan's Lower East Side. Over the previous weeks, the twenty-two-year-old garden, named for hope, had come to symbolize the tensions between privatization at the center of globalization and the civic need for public spaces open to all. Despite its history as a community center for picnics, refuge for children, and parties, Mayor Giuliani's office sold La Esperanza to developer Donald Capoccia back in August 1999— a man who had just happened to donate some $50,000 to the mayor's electoral campaigns and acquired the garden site from the city without any fair bidding process. Giuliani claimed that Capoccia planned to construct "low-income housing" on the site, and that garden supporters were "not living in the real world" (Chivers 2000). In reality, the seventy-nine apartments Capoccia slated to build are "80/20 housing"—80 percent market-rate, luxury apartments, with a token 20 percent set aside for low-income tenants.

To place the struggle for La Esperanza in context, we have to go back to May 1999. "Nueva York Necesita Jardines Communitarios" (New York Needs Community Gardens) stickers could be found throughout the Lower East Side; an international public space group took over an avenue in the neighborhood for a street party entitled "Reclaim the Streets and Build a Garden"; and some fifty garden activists were arrested for committing civil disobedience to prevent the planned auction of some 125 community gardens. In the end, local pop culture celebrity Bette Midler helped to purchase and preserve the gardens. The garden movement had become a force to be reckoned with—already reconnecting local citizens to political protest.

In response, Mayor Giuliani changed tactics. In a new strategy, the city began selling off individual gardens, perhaps one or a small group at a time, but not enough to draw citywide attention along the lines of the May auction. All the while, the general public believed all the city gardens had been saved. Yet, the city continued to put more Lower East Side community gardens up for auction. Then in December 2000, developers ripped the wall off the back of the Esperanza garden, preparing to bulldoze. The scene was a vivid reminder of the way Capoccia had bulldozed the Chico Menendez Garden two days after Christmas back in 1997. Activists, community members, and friends of Esperanza were determined to prevent the same thing from happening again. Neighborhood members started organizing.

Garden advocates sought an injunction to save Esperanza after its sale. Little came of it. By mid-November, Alicia, the original gardener who had planted the seeds of Esperanza back in 1977, received a letter from Capoccia, stating construction would start on the land behind the garden within the week. Having traversed every legal and policy channel they knew of, the activists sought other solutions for their struggle against the bulldozers. In Puerto Rican folklore, the Coqui, a species of frog, has long been known to successfully vanquish larger adversaries. Esperanza could use the same sort of patron and mythology. Garden activists built a giant steel and canvas version of the Coqui for the garden. The ten-foot-tall frog faced the street, drawing crowds of sympathizers to the cause of the garden (and serving as an exemplar of public and community art). Activists could spend the night inside the structure, equipped with telephone lines, a heater, and materials to lock themselves down to the Coqui if bulldozers were to roll in early in the morning.

To add a sense of urgency, state Attorney General Elliot Spitzer was filing papers calling for an injunction barring the destruction of all gardens that morning. No injunction could go into effect until 2 P.M. that afternoon at the earliest, but if activists could stall the police and bulldozers all morning, there was a chance the garden could be saved. Some activists locked themselves to the surrounding fence with bicycle locks around their necks, another group locked themselves to a 45-foot-high steel tower of a sunflower and tripods. Five activists locked themselves inside the Coqui.

Police swarmed the front of the garden, while a bulldozer loomed in the distance to the back of the garden. The activists were locked inside. The police moved in, tearing down the fence in front of the garden, sawing off the chain of an activist who had locked herself to it. While protestors were being arrested, Giuliani played to the usual debate that the city has to decide between housing or gardens. Garden activist spokespeople retorted that with thousands of vacant lots and dilapidated buildings to rebuild in the five boroughs, there is room for both gardens and housing. A Giuliani spokesman would claim that Capoccia's contributions had nothing to do with him winning city development contracts for the Esperanza site. But it was clear from all of this that community activists could no longer simply protest and use a variety of cultural means to do so; instead, they needed to engage in politics. The More Gardens Coalition, which organized the Esperanza resistance campaign, successfully constructed a multicultural coalition, mobilizing activists from all over the city. Yet, this was not enough to match the deep pockets of New York's real estate industry and their influence on New York's political culture.

As long as the attorney general's yemporary restraining order prevented further bulldozing, many took a breather from the garden fight. But no real policy solution was emerging. Meetings were held in a nearby community center that had ironically been sold to another developer that could be taken over at any time. Calls to representatives had gone unreturned. The city council refused to even put pending garden legislation to a vote. Therefore, community organizers decided to create a ballot referendum to save the gardens. Language in Municipal Home Rule Law, section 38 of the City Charter, offered a route to curtail the power of elected officials by amending the City Charter. This would take collecting 60,000 signatures within the next two months, which amounted to 10 percent of the votes cast for the governor in the last election, getting them certified, but since usually half of the signatures get thrown out, activists strove to collect another 60,000 and file them with the city. (See the Nelson and Winger chapters in this volume for more on this process.)

The challenges to such a strategy were inordinate. In the first place, community organizers needed to create a public language that had teeth and was agreeable to those whose emotions were running high. While garden activists had always just agreed that they wanted to keep the gardens as they were, there was little consensus about what a permanent administrative solution would look like. Forsaking idealism for winnable solutions required a great deal of this group of community organizers. While many had hoped for more community control of the parks, case law suggested the best route for success was to draft language that would call for the gardens to be moved under the control of the New York City Parks Department. After much haggling, the group agreed to this strategy. The referendum language called for the following amendments to the city charter: "Notwithstanding the provisions of this charter, no community garden space may be sold, leased, exchanged or otherwise disposed of except with the approval of the Department of Parks and Recreation." The next step was to collect signatures with apartment numbers on them and countless other bits of electoral minutia. As this chapter is being written, countless activists are outside at the

Puerto Rican Day parade collecting signatures for the referendum. Community activists are also using other institutions of civil society to find signatures, such as local community-based housing groups, labor unions, civil liberties organizations, and numerous activist organizations. As of today, we have some twenty-six days to collect the first round of 60,000 signatures, half of which will be thrown out.

"From the very beginning we've known that getting it on the ballot is a dream, and that's what we're trying to do," explained organizer Mark Read in a personal interview. Short of that, probably the most important part of the campaign is to create a dialogue about the role of gardens and public space in urban centers. Activists recognize that the city needs both affordable housing and green space. The New York Attorney General's office has brokered deals that satisfy the needs of both developers so housing can be built and gardens preserved. Yet, Mayor Giuliani has refused to sign the agreements (Lobbia 2001). The mayor has refused any dialogue with organizers; in his refusal there is a deep betrayal of democracy. In the efforts of community organizers, we see a hope that local efforts and community initiatives can actually have an impact on political institutions. The conflict between these two visions will prove crucial to the future of democratic reform in America.

CONCLUSION

The previous three cases outline methods for organizing communities to participate in democracy renewal. In the case of the Settlement House movement, immigrants needed a home and sense of community before they could contribute to reform efforts. Jane Addams understood this. In the case of the Chicago Area Project, Clifford Shaw was able to keep delinquents out of jails by incorporating them into the life of the neighborhood, while Saul Alinsky tried to push this effort in a political direction in order to challenge local power structures. The efforts of CAP helped organize a model that would become a cornerstone of programs of LBJ's War on Poverty. In the third case, we witnessed the challenges of community building. Not only do citizens have the difficult challenge of maintaining public space (in this case community gardens) in the face of privatization, they must also challenge the way political power works. In the process, they learn the important lessons of democracy—that the health of local communities relies upon the political initiative of its members.

Communities need to create civil society organizations in order to facilitate communication and democratic activity. This is the hard but necessary work of democracy. Most importantly, when citizens organize locally, they can create connections to the wider political world—even if that connection might very well be antagonistic (something Alinsky understood so well). In the context of this book, it is crucial to understand that only when politics "touches home" will most people enter into the political realm. We must understand this and create more places where this can actually happen. Without this sort of initiative, the promise of democracy remains simply that—a vague promise.

9

Can the Internet Rescue Democracy?
Toward an On-line Commons

PETER LEVINE

American democracy is marred by low levels of participation. Poor and poorly educated people are especially unlikely to vote, which means that powerful officials can safely ignore their interests. Meanwhile, even citizens who do vote, join political associations, and give money to political causes often cannot find satisfying ways to participate.

A large literature now suggests that the Internet is a cure for these ills. As Tracy Westen writes, "To the extent that democracy needs saving, the new generation of interactive digital communications technologies [has] arrived—just in time to help" (Westen 1998, 56). Enthusiasts believe that computer networks will make various forms of political participation more convenient, thus increasing participation. For example, we will be able to vote from home or make financial contributions with the click of a mouse. At the same time, information will be readily available, so citizens will possess the knowledge they need to participate effectively. Faced with an informed and powerful citizenry, various elites will grudgingly allow more public participation. Among other innovations, we may see frequent on-line referenda. Citizens may deliberate en masse, creating a kind of ongoing national town meeting. As a result, some argue, the public will make wise decisions without much need for mediating institutions such as newspapers, legislatures, parties—maybe even governments.

In essence, some political thinkers suggest the Internet will give citizens greater control over the decisions that governments have traditionally made. Howard Rheingold, an early and influential observer, calls the Internet "the great equalizer," because it changes "the balance of power between citizens and power barons" (quoted in Bimber 1998, 138). Computer networks may even render legislatures, constitutional courts, and other governmental bodies irrelevant, permitting direct rule by "the people." Lawrence Grossman puts the case forcefully when he writes:

> Today's telecommunications technology may make it possible for our political system to return to the roots of Western democracy as it was practiced in the city-states of ancient Greece. Tomorrow's telecommunications technology almost certainly will. . . . The electronic republic cannot be as intimate or as deliberative as the face-to-face discussions and showing of hands in the ancient Athenians' open-air assemblies. But it is likely to extend government decision making from the few in the center of power to the many on the outside who may wish to participate. (Grossman 1996, 33, 49)

Many analysts have criticized such predictions by invoking the "digital divide." They demonstrate that disadvantaged people are much less likely than privileged ones to use the Internet—especially from home, where citizens can most easily participate in politics. Income, education, race, and disability all have strong, independent effects on the likelihood that Americans use the Internet. Although more disadvantaged people are going online each year, the divide remains large. For example, in 2000, 41.5 percent of American households were connected to the Internet, but the rate was half that among single-parent African American families in central cities. Only about a fifth of disabled citizens were using the Internet (U.S. Census Bureau 2000b, xv, 6, xvi).

The digital divide is obviously an important issue, but I want to go beyond it in this chapter. Even if *all* citizens could use the Internet from home, computer networks would still not improve our democracy by giving citizens more or better control over decisions traditionally made by governments. However, the Internet does have a different kind of democratic potential if we handle it right. In this chapter, I first criticize the main assumptions of the standard optimistic view, and then offer an alternative.

MYTH #1: CONVENIENCE
IS THE KEY TO PARTICIPATION

According to the Census Bureau, "Of the 40 million people who reported that they registered, but did not vote in the 1998 election, about one-third reported that they did not vote because they were too busy or had conflicting work or school schedules" (U.S. Census 2000a, 11). This statistic implies that turnout would increase if citizens did not have to travel to a polling place during limited hours on Election Day. Likewise, Robert Putnam notes that "I don't have enough time" is the most common reason Americans give for not volunteering in their communities (Putnam 2000, 189).

Clearly, the Internet can make political and civic participation more convenient and less time-consuming by bringing certain activities right into people's homes. An organization called Hands On Atlanta provides "flexible volunteer opportunities" for people who simply enter information about their interests and availability on a Web page. And citizens who were excited by Senator John McCain's 2000 Republican Primary victory in New Hampshire were able to contribute money through his Web page; he raised $10,000 *per hour* online before the South Carolina primary (Fose 2000).

But it is important not to exaggerate the value of convenience. For instance, making a political contribution has never been difficult for people who have the money to give; the barrier for most of us is financial. Besides, John McCain did not *win* the South Carolina primary because the Internet allowed him to collect contributions quickly; he was still outspent and defeated.

Likewise, a lack of time is not a major reason for the decline in our civic connectedness. The busiest people are generally the most avid volunteers. People who feel tied to their communities have always found opportunities—and incurred obligations—to volunteer locally. But these ties have diminished, and most categories of Americans (including retirees and other nonworkers) are now less involved in their communities than they used to be (Putnam 2000, 191, 203). Therefore, reducing the time it takes people to identify volunteer opportunities is unlikely to raise the level of participation by much. Building social and emotional connections to communities is more important. And here the Internet may have just the opposite effect by insulating us from the kinds of people whom we could serve face-to-face.

Finally, what keeps citizens from voting is not the inconvenience of casting a ballot. Even if we allowed citizens to vote instantaneously from home, most would not be able to choose a candidate, either because they would lack relevant knowledge or because the choices would be unappealing (Delli Carpini and Keeter 1996). However, it is relatively easy for people with high social status to obtain political information, because they already read the newspaper for business and entertainment purposes and attend meetings at which politics is discussed. Also, the leading candidates tend to cater to their interests. Therefore, voting correlates with income and educational levels (Rosenstone and Hansen 1993, 14).

The group that the Census Bureau identified—registered voters who said that they did not vote because they were "too busy"—amounted to just 15.25 percent of adults. This group was more male, better educated, and more white than other registered nonvoters. (They were even more privileged compared to nonregistered adults.) Thus allowing them to vote from home might raise turnout a bit, but it would also increase the proportion of voters who were wealthy, college-educated, white men.

If knowledge is an important resource whose scarcity keeps people from participating, then it follows that as we increase the intellectual demands on voters, we will see lower turnout—especially from those who do not have much money or education. Thus a system of frequent referenda is likely to produce much lower turnout than one in which citizens are asked to make occasional decisions about the general direction for their community. Participants in on-line referenda will be a privileged minority, even if everyone has Internet access at home. And this governing elite, unlike today's elected representatives, will have no obligation to deliberate before they make decisions.

MYTH #2: WE NEED
MORE INFORMATION

The last section suggests that more people would participate in politics and civic life if they had better access to information. If this theory is right, then the Internet might boost participation by providing free and accessible information. Access to the Internet might even facilitate more *direct* democracy. Citizens could prepare themselves to participate in referenda by "surfing" the World Wide Web to gather relevant facts.

Indeed, the Internet now puts more information in people's homes than ever before, but this is just a continuation of long-term trends that have brought data increasingly within everyone's reach. Throughout the 20th century, educational levels climbed upward; thousands of libraries, bookstores, and colleges were built; and millions of books and periodicals were written and read. Yet there was no payoff in political participation. Indeed, turnout declined from about two-thirds of the adult population in the 1950s and 1960s (when most African Americans still could not vote) to less than half by the end of the century (Bimber 1998, 140–41).

We do need information before we can vote or take other political action. We need to know which positions to adopt and which candidates and organizations come the closest to supporting our views. Such information is available on the Internet (although it is mixed up with much *mis*information that requires skill to detect). However, facts are not scarce. Long before we had personal computers in our homes, there was already far too much information at the local library and newsstand for us to process.

Thus we ought to ask: What makes people *interested* enough in complex issues that they gather facts and try to interpret and apply what they learn? In other words, what makes citizens turn *available information* into *applied knowledge*? If you think of yourself as an individual trying to pursue personal goals through political action, then it is not worth your time to collect enough information to vote. Moreover, you will not have enough conscious or definable interests to give you a personal stake in most of the issues that the government considers important, so your conscious self-interest will not guide your voting. And no one will make a personalized appeal to persuade you to participate, because you are just 1 of 100 million voters.

The whole situation changes if you are an avid member of a group. Whether it is a political organization, an ethnic association, a sports league, or a gardening club, its welfare will sooner or later be affected by government decisions. If it has many members, then they may see a clear effect from lobbying, protesting, and voting together. When the members convene, they may persuade one another about political issues and convince one another to participate. Statistics show that group members are much better informed about politics, more likely to have been asked to vote, and more likely to discuss issues than nonmembers (even comparing people of the same educational and economic background: see Levine 2000, 93–94 for more detail). Because of a group's clout, politicians and other important officials will appeal to its membership for support. This matters because people who are asked to participate in politics often comply, but most people are never asked (Verba et al. 1995, 135, 150). Above all, group members often feel a "we-ness" that gives them a clear sense of interests, ideals, and obligations, compared to what they would feel as individuals.

If group membership is the key to political participation, then the Internet may provide billions of Web pages full of data without raising the turnout rate by one person. The relevant question will be: What kinds of groups and collective activities does the Internet promote? People who participate in typical on-line activities (such as email among friends, chat rooms, game-playing, and file-sharing) sometimes initiate political discussions and organize political actions. However, the participants tend to be distributed across jurisdictions, which makes political organizing difficult. Also, it is a simple matter to exit an on-line forum when the talk unexpectedly turns political, whereas one cannot easily walk away from a card table or march out of a union hall. So there may be less pressure to think about politics on the Internet than there is in traditional associations.

A parallel argument can be made against those who think that a lack of information is what causes Americans to vote *unwisely*. Robert McChesney, for instance, believes that his fellow citizens would support more progressive policies if only they understood how badly corporations misbehave. Unfortunately, citizens are denied the information they need by the few powerful media companies that determine what news gets through to the public. "Long-term issues, like racism or suburban sprawl, tend to fall by the wayside," McChesney thinks, while the media "tend to accept the elite position as revealed truth" on matters such as "the innate right of the United States to invade another country or the equation of private property and the pursuit of profit with democracy" (McChesney 1999, 50). McChesney argues that the Internet would have a progressive influence, except that it is being dominated by the same companies that control traditional media.

I read the mainstream, commercial press, and I see articles almost every day about the very issues that McChesney thinks are overlooked. Journalists actually cover some "progressive" issues more than many of their readers would like them to; for instance, most whites apparently think that "too much attention" is paid to "race and racial issues" (Morin 2001). And more information is available about the misbehavior of corporations than one could read in a lifetime. So mass-media corporations are not preventing us from acquiring facts. The problems are (1) a lack of persuasive *arguments* for progressive positions, and (2) a dearth of large and effective organizations that can motivate people to act against corporate interests.

MYTH #3: THE INTERNET IS
A MASSIVE TOWN MEETING

Perhaps the democratic promise of the Internet lies not in its vast array of facts, but in its many egalitarian *discussions* of public issues. By talking online, citizens may acquire the motivation, knowledge, and even the wisdom they need to participate in politics. Indeed, deliberation is an essential element of any democracy. When discussions go well, citizens encounter alternative perspectives, articulate their goals and priorities in ways that appeal to others, sharpen their sense of realistic options and necessary trade-offs, abandon support for indefensible positions, and develop mutual respect that allows them to coexist and cooperate even when they disagree.

A great deal of deliberation can be found on the Internet. However, Marshall van Alstyne and Erik Brynjolfsson have drawn attention to an important problem. They argue that if most people want to expose themselves to diverse views, then the Internet is a wonderful tool because it makes an almost infinite range of ideas and perspectives available. But if people want—and are able to find—material that is tailored to their own initial values and interests, then they will naturally "balkanize," creating many separate communities or conversations that are not in mutual contact. The Internet encourages balkanization, because it increases the universe of available material and also provides efficient tools for selection, such as search engines and filters (Van Alstyne and Brynjolfsson 1997).

Van Alstyne and Brynjolfsson do not argue that people actually prefer to see only a narrow range of material. They note that if we are generalists with a taste for diversity, then the Internet will promote deliberation. According to a survey taken in 2000, 67 percent of Americans considered it important to obtain "general news that gives you general information about important events that are happening," whereas just 28 percent preferred to see "news that is mostly about your interests and what's important to you." These statistics suggest that most of us at least understand the value of a broad outlook. However, citizens may satisfy their desire for general news by glancing at headlines, while actually deliberating about much narrower issues. Besides, the same survey found that young people, men, and poorly educated people were relatively unlikely to care about general news, which implies that these groups may opt out of public deliberations (Pew Research Center 2000).

More generally, the trend in American culture is away from diverse, multipurpose organizations (such as unions, national churches, and strong geographical communities), toward single-interest associations with narrow niches. Dennis Thompson says that he has scanned the Internet and found: "Hikers to Free our Parks, National Whistleblower Union, Citizens against Daylight Savings Time, Citizens for Finnish-American Power, the U.S. Committee to Support the Revolution in Peru, and the Anarchists Anti-Defamation League" (Thompson 1999, 37). But as Andrew Shapiro notes, "you'd be hard pressed" to find a group "committed to the General Common Good" (1999, 113).

Meanwhile, the Internet provides few effective ways for people to put their case to others who are not initially disposed to listen. Shapiro argues that Web users are unlike visitors to a physical space, because they do "not have to hear the civil rights marcher, take a leaflet from the striking worker, or see the unwashed homeless person. Their world [can] be cleansed of all interactions save those they explicitly [choose]" (1999, 136). A similar logic suggests that the Internet may increase intellectual *stratification* as experts are able to talk only among themselves and ignore the rest of the public.

Cass Sunstein, a political and legal theorist who has done much to advance our understanding of deliberation, summarizes the disadvantages of balkanization in his book *Republic.com* (2001). Among other problems, balkanized groups tend to move toward the views of their own most radical members. Members of such groups do not understand other perspectives or learn how to relate to people who are different. Not realizing that some thoughtful citizens disagree with them, they assume that the government is corrupt when it takes contrary positions. And they constantly reinforce their own beliefs—even completely false ones—without ever being challenged. For instance, many people who are opposed to gun control have encountered the following quotation more than once online: "This year will go down in history! For the first time, a civilized nation has full gun registration! Our streets will be safer, our police more efficient, and the world will follow our lead into the future!" On numerous Web sites, this quote is attributed to Adolf Hitler, who is supposed to have extolled gun control in the *Berlin Daily* on April 15, 1935 (Page 3 Article 2). Everything about this alleged statement is false, including the implication that the Nazi government imposed gun control. But only Second Amendment purists are likely to encounter it, and their faith is never challenged (for a small sample of this, see www.urbanlegends.com/politics/hitler_gun_control.html).

MYTH #4: DEMOCRACY WILL FLOURISH
WHEN THE "POWER BROKERS" ARE GONE

What Andrew Shapiro calls the "Control Revolution" implies, among other things, a shift of power away from the leaders of formal organizations and toward individuals who have computers on their desks. As Grossman writes, "The big losers . . . are the traditional institutions that have served as the main intermediaries between government and its citizens—the political parties, labor unions, civic associations, even the commentators and correspondents in the mainstream press" (Grossman 1996, 16).

The Control Revolution implies some advantages for democracy, because even highly democratic organizations usually concentrate power in their professional staffs, steering committees, and elected leaders. In other words, they reflect Robert Michels's "iron law of oligarchy" (1915). In the 1960s, proponents of *participatory* democracy looked for alternative models that were more voluntary, individualistic, consensual, loose, and egalitarian than traditional parties and interest groups. Jane Mansbridge has analyzed the "unwritten rules" that governed these "free schools, food co-ops, law communes, women's centers, hotlines, and health clinics." Their norms included "face-to-face, consensual decision making and the elimination of all internal distinctions that could encourage or legitimate authority" (1983, vii, 21). College towns, especially along the Pacific Coast, were hotbeds for such experimentation. The same communities then played a crucial role in the development of personal computers and networks. Manuel Castells argues that the global, postindustrial "network society" arose in part out of "a sprawling computer counterculture" that was one of the "aftershocks of the 1960s' movements in their most libertarian/utopian version." "If the first industrial revolution was British," Castells writes, "the first information technology revolution was American, with a Californian inclination" (2000, I, 49, 61). It embodied the spirit of Berkeley, California, circa 1968.

The Internet contributes to the general crisis of authority that has weakened traditional leaders, from politicians to clergypeople and educators (Poster 1995). For example, membership organizations can now perform many of their functions (such as meetings, elections, fund-raising, and publishing) online, which means that their members can leave with the click of a mouse and find other groups that are less restrictive. Heads of organizations must therefore avoid imposing rules and dues on their members, whenever possible. The Internet also spells trouble for newspaper publishers and editors, who once exercised a lot of control over the content of the news; now citizens can search for any combination of stories they want. And computer networks undermine the authority of religious leaders, because individuals can search the Web for religious thoughts that appeal to them—any time of the day or night (Brinton 2001).

Finally, the World Wide Web further undercuts our already weak political parties, because now anyone can cheaply produce the on-line equivalent of a campaign flyer. The operator of www.voterepublican.net, for example, is a completely independent citizen who says, "If my site was run by the Republican National Committee, they'd be saying, 'Do this' or, 'Don't say that.' I wanted to be involved promoting Republican conservatives. But I didn't have time to get involved with the parties" (quoted in Wayne 2000). His site could potentially be as popular as the official www.rnc.org, yet the party would have no control over its content. A Web page could even be devoted to lambasting the party that it ostensibly supported. The publisher of a liberal feminist political site based in Texas predicts that "these sites will increase democracy in the long run," because "you don't have tightly scripted campaigns as the sole voice. You will have independent citizens voicing their opinions in a way they couldn't before" (Wayne 2000).

The "power brokers" are indeed in trouble, but before we jump to the conclusion that their demise will be good for democracy, we should consider a few problems. First, corporate managers are not threatened in the same way that the leaders of unions, parties, religious bodies, and newspapers are. There is a lot of chatter about companies' new enthusiasm for decentralization and "empowered" employees (Nye in Kamarck and Nye 1999, 9–10). To some extent, there has been a real shift of authority in the workplace, thanks to the increased bargaining power of highly skilled workers in the "knowledge economy." However, the people who clean bathrooms and prepare chickens still work at the bottom of powerful hierarchies. For them, the decline of unions and parties is a loss, not a gain. Besides, to a considerable extent, companies are simply using new strategies to maximize profits. When their employees' interests conflict with their bottom line, top managers will make the ultimate decisions (which means that they really retain power).

Second, strong, organized nonprofit organizations would be missed if they disappeared from civil society, because they provide avenues for upward mobility. In the past, some rank-and-file industrial workers acquired real power by rising to union leadership positions. Some Catholic immigrant boys gained political influence by becoming bishops or cardinals. And quite a few people climbed out of poverty into political office with the assistance of parties. None of these paths to power was ever easy or fair, but at least there were many of them. In a society with only one category of powerful leaders—business executives—most people will have no hope of acquiring authority.

Third, citizens benefit from disciplined organizations that impose rules and make demands. Loose, voluntary groups cannot overcome pervasive collective-action problems that are especially damaging to disadvantaged citizens. For instance, poor individuals often do not give money to support political causes, because they reasonably believe that most of their neighbors will not contribute, and therefore their own donations would make no difference. But a powerful, disciplined organization such as a church or a civil rights organization can impose dues and use the money for political action. Similarly, an individual worker cannot force her company to raise wages, but a union can—precisely because it can compel all its members to stop working once it has called a strike (Levine 2001b).

Finally, voting and other forms of democratic participation depend on exactly the kind of organizations that Howard Rheingold and others think will be rendered obsolete by the Internet: ethnic and fraternal organizations, unions, activist churches, and political parties. Steven Rosenstone and John Mark Hansen have convincingly attributed more than half of the decline in voter turnout to a decrease in "mobilization," by which they mean the kind of persuading and organizing work that these organizations perform (1993, 31).

THE INTERNET AS COMMONS

So far, I have raised doubts about the thesis that the Internet will give citizens more or better power over their government. These doubts should not discourage anyone from experimenting with on-line deliberation or political organizing, but I believe that they will be swimming against the tide. On the other hand, no one today believes that a democratic government (whether direct or representative) should monopolize power. Private organizations and individuals ought to be free to pursue their own diverse interests. Besides, it is possible to generate free *public* goods and resources without relying on the state. There is a word for a system of social organization that does not rely on competition and private ownership, nor on laws and taxes. Such an organization is a "commons."

A classic example is a field of grass, either outside a medieval village or in the center of a New England town, on which every citizen is entitled to graze privately owned cattle (Ostrom 1990; Taylor 1987). Although this kind of commons benefits a market economy, the land itself is held as public property and never sold. Moreover, in a classic commons, laws and governments are remote; most management is handled by the partici-pants themselves. Thus a commons is attractive—at least at face value—because it avoids both competition and coercion while encouraging broad participation. It gives people opportunities to perform the very satisfying kind of "public work" that comes from producing a good that is available to all (Boyte and Kari 1996).

Unfortunately, well-known problems beset any traditional commons. On a public field that is open for grazing, each person may be tempted to put more cattle than the pasture can bear if everyone acts the same way. Although they are all harmed by the consequent deterioration of their shared property, as individuals they gain more from the free fodder than they lose as the field goes slowly to ruin. One person might be distressed by the state of the commons and consider limiting her own use of it. But even if she decides not to put her cow on the field, the grass will still turn to mud because of other people's overuse, and she will have passed up free food. Since everyone faces the same dilemma, the pasture is doomed.

This "Tragedy of the Commons," as Garrett Hardin called it, seems to imply that any valuable asset must be managed either by enforcing strict laws (the governmental approach) or by dividing the good among prop-erty holders who have incentives to preserve their private shares (the market approach) (Hardin 1968). The idea of a pure commons is said to be naïve. But the Internet and other new electronic media have an unusual capacity to overcome collective-action problems (Barbook 1998; Moglen 1999). For one thing, "overgrazing" is much less likely when an asset is digitized. If I put a document or computer code on the Internet, it does not matter how many other people copy it for their own use; the file remains unharmed and ready for countless more appropriations. Consequently, I have much less reason to worry about other people's selfish behavior (the "free-rider" problem) than I would in a classic commons.

Another typical barrier to maintaining a commons is simply finding and coordinating a large enough cadre of volunteers to provide the hard, skilled labor that is always necessary. Again, this problem is mitigated by the Internet. For one thing, we are relatively likely to volunteer if selfish behavior cannot ruin our work. So, for example, certain programmers spend a lot of time improving the technical details of HTML, the free lan-guage for designing Web pages, without worrying that HTML may be de-stroyed through overuse. More importantly, the Internet makes communi-cations cheap and efficient, thereby allowing just a few enthusiasts out of the world's six billion people to identify one another and to collaborate at low cost. An enormous amount of invaluable labor has thus been donated by programmers who have designed the protocols, computer languages, and norms that govern email, file-sharing, the design of Web pages, and most of the basic functions of the Internet. Efforts to explain *why* these people are willing to bear so many free-riders miss the point; the volunteers are rare (and often eccentric) exceptions to normal human behavior. But it only takes a tiny percentage of the population to keep the electronic commons going.

So consider the Internet circa 1993. Beneath the sight of most users, computers exchanged information using protocols that were no one's intellectual property. Each computer or length of wire belonged to someone, but the system had been designed to be "interoperable," meaning that equipment could easily be substituted and messages could travel freely across the whole network. If someone tried to block a packet of data or charge for its passage, it would automatically find a different route.

At a more visible level, most people used free software for sending email, transferring files, and browsing the Web. The code for these programs was disclosed ("open source") and subject to improvement by anyone. Meanwhile, most Web sites, discussion forums, and emails were contributions of free material, ranging in value from pirated pornography to original research, art, and literature. There was widespread copying of good ideas for Web-page designs and discussion groups. Imitation was easy because Web pages were literally open-source documents that used accessible and replicable code.

Thus, the Internet was *open* in much the same way that the Boston Commons is accessible to the whole community, and it was full of *resources* (from the data on Web pages to the protocols governing email) that could be used by anyone at no cost. In these respects, it was quite close to a large-scale commons.

Two caveats are in order. First, the cyber-commons was never pure. Governments, universities, and industries had contributed to its development and continued to own and manage its elements. Nonetheless, market and state institutions coexisted with a powerful set of resources that were unowned and available to all. Second, a commons is not necessarily democratic: indeed, the two most famous examples came from medieval England and puritan New England, neither of which gave the vote to all citizens. A commons can even *threaten* democracy by undermining the public's ability to regulate the social world. Compare the traditional telephone network (which was centralized, corporate, and proprietary) with the email system (which is a good example of a commons). The telephone network is often described as undemocratic, because tremendous power belonged to the people who owned the lines and switches. They had the capacity to eavesdrop on any conversation or even to cut off citizens for speaking in a way they disliked. However, the American telephone network was also eminently regulable, being owned by a few companies that were clearly subject to U.S. law. Therefore, when Congress and the federal courts created rights to privacy and nondiscrimination, these rights were enforced. Often, the mere threat of public opposition caused telephone companies to act in acceptable ways. By contrast, the government would have difficulty guaranteeing the privacy of emails, because no one can be held responsible for the passage of an electronic data-package across switches and lines that belong to hundreds of separate parties in several countries.

Nevertheless, a commons can serve some of the same values as a democracy: especially equality, participation, and freedom. And within a democratic society, a commons can provide resources (such as skills, information, and social networks) for disadvantaged citizens. It seems at least plausible that voluntary, collaborative work on the Internet teaches skills and habits that potentially transfer to politics. Thus a cyber-commons could perform some of the crucial democratic tasks that were traditionally handled by formal organizations. In his day, Alexis de Tocqueville attributed the vitality of our democracy to citizens' work in building the 19th-century "commons": free, local, public assets such as hospitals, churches, parks, seminaries, and schools (Tocqueville 1954, II, 114). Today the Internet is a promising venue for such public work.

Consider, for example, work that young Hmong and Latino people are doing today in St. Paul, Minnesota, as part of a project organized by the Jane Addams School for Democracy. They are building a database of the community's "learning resources": everything from formal classes at the high school to an elderly Mexican immigrant in a retirement home who is willing to teach traditional Indian medicine. Soon citizens will be able to visit a computer in the public library, enter a word that describes their interests, and see the local learning resources displayed on a map. The information on the map will be a free public good. The process of gathering information is already building local trust, skills, and networks. And because the map is stored in digital form, it can be widely disseminated at low cost; therefore, the project is not heavily reliant on support from formal organizations or the government. The participants justly claim that they are building a "St. Paul Information *Commons*," and their work has considerable democratic potential (Levine 2001b).

THE COMMONS UNDER THREAT

The English medieval commons gradually vanished as the lord of each manor asserted property rights and evicted the peasants so that he could graze his sheep for profit. There is often money to be made from privatizing a common resource—if one can get away with it. Following this pattern, much of the global Internet commons has been privatized since the early 1990s. For instance, many people looked at early Web pages by using Mosaic, which was free, open-source software. But the Netscape Corporation borrowed Mosaic's technology, developed a new version that was incompatible with it, and copyrighted its version as Navigator (Bollier 2001, 51–52). Now most people browse the Internet using such proprietary software.

On a much wider scale, Microsoft™ has adopted a policy of "embrace, extend, and extinguish" toward open-source software. The company adopts free and publicly accessible programs, adds wrinkles that allow it to copyright a new version of the program, and then makes only the copyrighted version compatible with its other products, such as Windows. It has used this strategy to undermine HTML; Java, the versatile programming language; and multimedia applications such as RealAudio and QuickTime (Bollier 2001, 52).

Although the Justice Department sued Microsoft™ partly for this reason, the federal government has sometimes abetted the new enclosure movement. An example is the Digital Millennium Copyright Act of 1998, which prohibits copying information that is protected by a technological measure, even if individuals have a right to see that information. For instance, citizens are allowed (under the fair use doctrine) to broadcast snippets of music or film for critical purposes. But making a good copy of a movie from a digital video disk (DVD) would require defeating technological barriers, and this has become a criminal act. Copying part of a movie and inserting it into another film—even for a school project, even for the purposes of parody—is illegal (Benkler 2000, 571). Furthermore, people can now be prosecuted for making or selling products or services that are used to circumvent technological protections, even if the devices in question are used to view (and not to copy) material that people have a right to see. At least one person is in jail for designing software that could be used to commit copyright violation (Lessig 2001).

Meanwhile, private companies have won patents for Internet business methods (for instance, Amazon.com's "1-click" method of paying for products), which means that the "look and feel" of their sites has become private property that cannot be copied (Bollier 2001, 58). Companies are also trying to control the Internet more broadly by steering people to their own Web sites and by preventing certain kinds of hostile sites from attracting audiences. When a citizen searches for "McDonalds™," the McDonalds™ Company wants to make sure that she only finds its site—not pictures of a family with the same name or (worse) a vegetarian, pro-labor, or anti-American site that might use the word "McDonald's™" in its text, its links, or its domain name. When companies sue outsiders for using their trademarks in Web pages, they sometimes lose on First

Amendment grounds. But corporations tend to prevail before the non-governmental organization that distributes domain names, ICANN, which decides who should have the most desirable addresses. Moreover, companies are able to purchase favorable treatment from many of the leading search engines (Cohen 2001, 18–23).

The enclosure of the commons is troubling because it means that ordinary people cannot collaborate to produce public goods online without running afoul of property claims. Too much of the Internet is now being managed by companies that pursue their own economic interests that are not publicly accountable. Constitutional values are undermined, because almost no part of the Internet now qualifies as a "public space" in which free speech would enjoy the strongest protection (see Cohen 2001). People who use private Internet service providers and Microsoft™ Explorer to look at corporate Web pages are visiting private property in which their constitutional rights are limited.

Unless we intervene forcefully at this stage, it is likely that most people will use the Internet in the following way within a few years. They will receive high-speed video and email service from a massive corporation such as AOL Time Warner or Microsoft™ that also has holdings in various entertainment and news companies. This corporation will require them to go online through some kind of portal with a proprietary search engine and a few prominent links. Both the links and the search engine will direct customers, whenever possible, to sites owned by the Internet service provider. Most of this material will be slick, multimedia programming created by paid professionals for large audiences—without the participation of ordinary citizens. Since there will be some competition among service providers, they may decide that they should permit customers to view low-budget, free material as well. But they will do their best to downplay such offerings, since only their own sites will generate advertising and sales revenue. According to the Center for Digital Democracy, the top four "digital media properties (AOL Time Warner, Microsoft™, Yahoo, and Lycos) . . . attract more visitors than the next 14 combined. And the top 10 companies (which include NBC, Disney™, and Amazon) attract more visitors than the rest of the top 50 combined. The traffic patterns of today's Web, in other words, are much closer to those of network television in the 1960s than to those of the Internet in the early 1990s" (Chester 2001).

Under these conditions, citizens who try to operate their own sites for democratic purposes will become increasingly discouraged, since few visitors will be able to find their work and will be legally barred from using the patented production techniques employed on commercial sites. Thus the Internet will begin to look like the next generation of cable television instead of a decentralized, participatory medium. Most nonprofit sites will be as marginal as public-access television stations today.

BUILDING THE COMMONS

Preventing this calamity requires three important steps. First, the federal government must impose statutes and regulations to preserve the openness of the Internet. How best to achieve that goal is a complex matter beyond the scope of this chapter, but some promising strategies include:

- preventing Internet service providers from discriminating among Web sites and search engines and not allowing them to impose any particular portal or software on their customers;
- separating Internet service providers from the producers of news, information, and entertainment;
- requiring Microsoft™ (and any other software company that attains monopolistic control of a particular field) to publish its software in a form readable by human beings so that it can be imitated and modified within the limits of intellectual property law;
- reducing the scope of intellectual property, especially companies' ability to *patent* software and business methods; and
- making federal grants to support the development of open-source software, public protocols, and noncommercial search engines.

As long as the federal government uses traditional antitrust arguments to regulate companies such as Microsoft™, its interventions will probably be too moderate. The main problem is not the potential of monopolies to lower the quality and raise the cost of consumer goods. The main issue is that our democracy requires a commons to release the civic energy of its citizens.

Meanwhile, the government and foundations must support the creation of attractive, exciting, free material that can be disseminated online. Documents, data, and images can be produced at low cost, but the really valuable ingredients of the cyber-commons would include whole libraries and museums translated into digital form, information-rich maps, massive databases (e.g., of pollution statistics or candidate profiles), and exciting multimedia presentations. Such offerings are expensive, and if their owners pass the costs on to consumers, then many people will not be able to afford access. In their *Digital Promise* report, Lawrence Grossman and Newton Minow recommend auctioning the broadcast spectrum to generate revenues that would fund free on-line material (Grossman and Minow 2001).

Third, we need networks of human beings who are committed to the idea of a commons and who can share skills, experience, and even software. The young people who are building the St. Paul Information Commons are working more or less alone, so they must invent all their own models and strategies. If they belonged to a broader movement, then they would benefit from many economies of scale—not to mention mutual support and encouragement. Indeed, networks have begun to grow up among groups that maintain nonprofit community portals and that try to use the Internet to build civic bonds. But it would be beneficial to broaden these networks and to bring them together into one fairly cohesive force devoted to commons-style work. That is the purpose of a new institution, the Public Telecommunications Service, an organization that I am presently helping to form.

Today there is no groundswell of popular support for legislation or regulation that would support the commons. As long as issues such as software patents pit a small cadre of Washington-based activists against industry lobbyists and lawyers, the latter will always win. But citizens who actually use the Internet for civic purposes will sooner or later encounter concrete, practical problems that will motivate them to support appropriate reforms. For instance, volunteers who try to map the assets of their communities can initially manage perfectly well using the hardware and software of today's Internet. But when they try to build larger and more elaborate projects, they will find that commercial search engines do not lead people to their sites and that privacy concerns keep residents from listing themselves as "community assets." Volunteers will not be able to afford to advertise or to buy the necessary equipment to serve a larger audience. They may even find themselves in competition with companies that offer databases of "community assets" without including a full range of informal, nonprofit resources (Levine 2001a). Faced with these problems, they will join a constituency for the cyber-commons.

CONCLUSION

The fact that the Internet can work as a commons hardly guarantees that American democracy will flourish. It is not clear that even a vibrant commons could serve the functions of political mobilization and socialization that ordinary people need before they can influence public policy. Nor will the Internet *necessarily* operate as a commons; in fact, the odds favor an increasingly privatized and commercialized cyberspace. Nevertheless, one of the most promising strategies for democratic renewal today is to try to keep the Internet a publicly accessible space in which citizens create and share free public goods.

Part Four

Making the System
More Responsive

Making the System More Responsive

RONALD HAYDUK AND KEVIN MATTSON

Al Gore won the popular vote but lost the electoral vote in the 2000 election. At the same time, some progressives debated if they should throw their weight behind Ralph Nader and the Green Party, fearing that the result might be what it became—a Bush victory. Because of these events, discussion about reforming the Electoral College and the way we select representatives has been gaining greater public attention. These national events have popularized reforms like instant runoff voting and proportional representation. The authors in this section argue for such alternative voting schemes as well as opening up political debates to third-party candidates, making more effective use of the initiative and referendum, and reforming the Electoral College. All of these reforms aim to make the political system more responsive to citizens.

Robert Richie, Steven Hill, and Caleb Kleppner address the possibilities for alternative voting methods to allow third parties and independent candidates into the electoral system. The authors show how various voting schemes have made a difference where currently used and what potential they hold if expanded into other jurisdictions. At the time of this writing there is legislation pending in twelve states and in Congress that would institute some form of instant runoff voting; some states and municipalities are also considering proportional representation in hope that this will bring more citizens to the voting booths.

Galen Nelson then examines a legacy from the Progressive Era— namely, the initiative and referendum, a reform that intended for citizens to initiate and vote on legislation. Nelson notes that the wealthy have taken advantage of this reform, but he argues that it can still be made responsive to the will of an informed public. Without the sense of political efficacy that this reform could potentially provide, we might see further declines in democratic participation. After all, representatives will pay greater attention to a citizenry that is able to make its preferences about specific policy matters known. Nelson shows how progressives can reclaim this reform from the clutches of powerful moneyed interests and use it as a tool for a different kind of politics.

Jamin Raskin takes on another democratic reform that could make the political system more representative and responsive—opening candidate debates to a wider variety of candidates. As he points out, the current rules established by the two major parties that determine who can participate in public debates essentially exclude third-party candidates. Given the prohibitive cost of running campaigns and gaining media access, third-party and independent candidates are doomed to obscurity. Without the possibility of such independent voices being heard, progressive movements will continue to be marginalized and progressive politics will remain elusive. Raskin therefore argues for reforming this exclusionary system and allowing third-party candidates to enter public debate.

Joel Lefkowitz ends this part in a shorter piece on the Electoral College. While proposals to reform the Electoral College are not new, they are now gaining greater public attention and are seriously being discussed in several state houses. Lefkowitz takes us back to the constitutional period to remind us that this institution was not only the subject of substantial debate, but also that several mechanisms were seriously discussed about how to select the chief of the executive branch. Partisan politics were evident in these debates and various schemes. And the likely differential consequences of the various mechanisms to select the president were plainly acknowledged. Lefkowitz gives us insight into these founding dynamics, how the Electoral College was used for partisan manipulation over time, and how it retains political advantages for particular states and parties. He concludes with discussion of viable reform possibilities.

10

Instant Runoff Voting and Full Representation: Keys to Fulfilling Democracy's Promise

ROBERT RICHIE, STEVEN HILL, AND CALEB KLEPPNER

Election reform, including proportional representation, is not primarily about electoral rules. It is not simply about getting more people of color and women into office, although that would be an important incidental benefit. It is about transforming how power itself is exercised and shared.

It is about opening up a different kind of political conversation, as elections become forums for voters to express their ideas and choose their representatives. It is about giving citizens their due.

—Lani Guinier, Foreword, *Whose Vote Counts*
(Robert Richie and Steven Hill 2001)

It had been decades since the White House and Capitol Hill were so tightly contested. In the November 2000 elections the presidential polls were close right up to Election Day, producing the most competitive race in a generation. Control of both the House and Senate, and even many state legislatures, hung by the threads of a handful of cliffhanger races. Yet more than 100 million American adults abstained from voting (Heilprin 2000). Disproportionately young, poor, less educated, and of color, they provide stark evidence that we are becoming a postelectoral democracy— one where many civil institutions are strong and rights reasonably well-protected, but where elections fail to inspire or mobilize.

There is no single solution for fulfilling democracy's promise. But a fundamental precondition for real reform is that voters have viable choices reflecting our full political, racial, and general diversity. More choice in the political spectrum is not simply about bringing consumer values to the public realm but instead about deepening our democracy. Behind every new viable candidacy stands the potential of a political movement: one that can mobilize a community of concern, articulate its interests, and give it a stake in elections and government. Suppressing such candidacies smothers participation, silencing voices whose story never reaches the broader public.

Elections in the United States are largely held under "winner-take-all" rules, where a viable candidate must by definition be all things to at least half the people. The process of assembling a winning coalition is hardly a neat exercise of candidates finding and supporting issues with the strong support of each significant group backing their candidacy; rather, it is a sausage factory of hashing and mashing and slicing and dicing that ultimately leaves many people without champions of their concerns. Winner-take-all elections leave most voters bunkered down in safe, one-party districts and underrepresent women and political, racial, and ethnic minorities, as well as "orphaned" Democratic and Republican voters living in the wrong districts. With few practical options under current rules, most voters are stuck with the unpalatable options of either voting against the perceived "greater evil," or staying at home.

It doesn't have to be this way. Indeed, many democracies around the world, and in certain places in the United States, already provide a better range of choices. In presidential elections, they hold runoff elections that require winners to develop broader support even as they facilitate a diverse range of candidacies—and the movements and participation they encourage—in the initial round of voting. To elect legislatures, they use proportional representation systems that elect more diverse representatives for like-minded groupings of voters from across the political spectrum in proportion to their numbers. Proportional representation systems make every voter important, not just those fortunate few living in the handful of states and districts that are competitive in our system. These voters not only have more meaningful choices between the major parties, but also *within* those parties and among smaller parties to their left, right, and center.

Does all this matter? Reforming electoral rules can seem secondary to pressing concerns like universal health care, a living wage, a humane criminal justice system, protection of ecosystems, or greater income equity within and among nations. It would be impractical to drop everything else to work solely on electoral reforms. On the other hand, it would be equally impractical to miss a real opportunity to open up electoral politics through replacing winner-take-all rules. Meaningful electoral reform may be necessary for achieving these policy goals because it will liberate social change activists to organize electorally, generate new candidacies, and win a seat at the legislative table where policy is made. Under the winner-take-all system, proponents of change often are effectively excluded from political debate and representation.

INSTANT RUNOFF VOTING
TO ELECT THE PRESIDENT

In 2000 a debate raged for months among progressives over whether Green Party presidential candidate Ralph Nader was a savior or a spoiler. But neither argument satisfied because both were partly right—and both partly wrong. The progressives who chose Nader instead of Democrat Al Gore in New Hampshire and Florida—two states where the Nader vote was far greater than Republican George Bush's margin of victory—really did help elect Bush, with clear consequences for progressive constituencies such as people of color, feminists, workers, and environmentalists. Yet without Nader in the campaign, the progressive critique of the Clinton–Gore administration would have been unheard in the general elections, and centrist Democrats would have been able to bury progressive politics even deeper.

The very need for a debate over the Nader candidacy reveals a serious flaw in our antiquated plurality voting system—a system in which voters have a single vote and the candidate with the most votes win. Given that the top vote-getter wins even if opposed by more than half of the voters, it follows that voting for your favorite candidate can split the majority and directly lead to the election of your least favorite candidate. The result is either the suppression of a candidacy or the fracturing of an electoral majority. Providing a fair range of choices while ensuring majority rule is a basic requirement of democracy, but our system fails on this count.

Runoff elections are one well-known means of addressing the problem of split votes among candidates allowing rule by a nonmajority. Under runoff laws, a candidate must reach a certain threshold of support—typically a majority of 50 percent, plus one—before being declared the winner. If no candidate reaches that threshold, then a second election is held between the top two candidates. Most presidential elections around the world use runoffs (LeDuc, Niemi, and Norris 1996), as do many mayoral races and primaries in the United States. But because they require two separate elections, runoffs add costs to taxpayers, exacerbate campaign finance inequities, and often result in large changes in turnout between the two rounds of election.

The British, Australians, and Irish have turned to a simpler solution: instant runoff voting (IRV). Although sharing our tradition of electing candidates by plurality, they have adopted IRV for nearly all of their most important elections. Ireland elects its president by IRV; indeed in 1990 its first woman president, Mary Robinson, would have lost under plurality rules. Popular Labour Party maverick Ken Livingstone was denied his party's nomination by party bosses in London's first mayoral election in

2000 (Startin 2001), but IRV made it natural for him to launch an ultimately successful independent candidacy without fear of the spoiler impact. The Australian legislature has been elected by IRV for decades, establishing a stable multiparty range of choices (Reilly 1997).

IRV simulates a runoff election, but in a single round of voting. At the polls, people vote for their favorite candidate, then indicate on the same ballot their "runoff" choices by ranking candidates 1, 2, 3, and so on. If a candidate receives a majority of first choices, the election is over. If not, the candidate with the fewest votes is eliminated, and a runoff round of counting occurs. In this round, your ballot counts for your top-ranked candidate still in the race—the first choice of most voters and the second choice of supporters of the eliminated candidate. Eliminated candidates thus are no longer "spoilers." Rounds of counting continue until there is a majority winner. IRV essentially reproduces what would take place in a series of runoff elections, but all in one election.

Imagine the 2000 presidential race with IRV. Those Nader supporters who were concerned about George Bush could have ranked Nader first and Gore second. Suppose Bush won 45 percent of first choices in a key state, Gore 44 percent, Nader 9 percent, and the rest 2 percent. Under current nonmajority rules, Bush wins despite opposition from 55 percent of voters (and 53 percent clearly identified as liberal or progressive). But with instant runoff voting, Nader's supporters would have propelled Gore above 50 percent and a victory. Rather than contributing to Gore's defeat, Nader could have helped stop Bush, even while influencing what issues were debated and delivering an important message to Gore.

Of course, IRV isn't only for liberals. In 2000 it might have encouraged John McCain to ride his Straight Talk Express over to the Reform Party, and helped Republicans "spoiled" by Libertarians in key congressional races. In past years it could have boosted Ross Perot. IRV has no ideological bias, as has been proven by its shifting partisan impact in eight decades of parliamentary elections in Australia. Its virtue for all sides is that it gives all voters the incentive to vote for their favorite candidate and ensures that, at the end of the day, the true majority rules.

States can implement IRV right now for all federal elections, including the presidential race, without changing the U.S. Constitution or a single federal law. Alaskans will do just that in 2004 if they pass a pro-IRV ballot measure on Alaska's November 2002 ballot. Legislation to implement IRV for federal offices has also passed one house of the New Mexico legislature and gained the support in Vermont of the governor, a third of the state senate, and leading civic groups like the League of Women Voters, Common Cause, and Grange. Eleven other states and the U.S. Congress introduced IRV legislation in 2001. IRV has proven to be a particularly winning argument when a major party is confronted with an actual or potential spoiler, as has been the case for Republicans in Alaska and Democrats in New Mexico. Campaign finance reform advocates like Common Cause, Public Campaign, and US PIRG also are drawn to IRV, as it would eliminate any spoiler difficulties associated with multicandidate races. With IRV, "clean money" candidates could run from across the spectrum without splitting the vote and producing winners with a low percentage of the vote.

In the short term, cities with traditional runoff elections appear to be the easiest targets for IRV campaigns. In July 2001, the San Francisco Board of Supervisors voted 10–1 to place on the March 2002 ballot a charter amendment to implement IRV for all citywide elections, including mayor and district attorney, and for the Board of Supervisors. The city currently uses November elections followed by December runoff elections for these races, with resulting high costs for the candidates and the city. Turnout often drops precipitously, particularly in even-year elections when the first round takes place at the same time as the presidential and congressional elections.

The Berkeley, California, city council has voted in favor of IRV and requested the city manager to draft a charter amendment for placement on an upcoming ballot. In Austin, Texas, a charter commission has recommended replacing two-round runoffs with IRV, and supporters are gearing up for a May 2002 campaign, either via petition or the council. Voters in Santa Clara County, California; Vancouver, Washington; and San Leandro, California, recently approved ballot measures to make IRV an explicit option in their charters. Other cities are contemplating establishing a similar option, while Oakland, California, is preparing to use IRV to fill its city council vacancies.

FULL REPRESENTATION FOR ALL

For all of its promise, instant runoff voting remains *majoritarian*, providing little hope for minorities—a term that includes "orphaned" major-party voters living in the wrong districts who have as little hope of winning political representation as minor-party candidates everywhere. Fair and full representation in government demands proportional representation, as used in most established democracies. Proportional representation or, as has more meaning in the context of American politics, full representation, is based on the principle that any grouping of like-minded voters should win legislative seats in proportion to its share of the popular vote. Whereas the winner-take-all principle awards 100 percent of the representation to a 50.1 percent majority (or as low as a 34 percent plurality in a three-candidate race), full representation allows voters in a minority to win their fair share of representation.

How does this work? A typical system of winner-take-all divides voters into "one-seat districts," each district represented by one person. With full representation, voters in a constituency instead have several representatives: ten one-seat districts might, for example, be combined into a single ten-seat district. A party or grouping of voters that wins 10 percent of the popular vote in this district, then, would win one of the ten seats; a party or slate of candidates with 30 percent of votes would win three seats, and so on. There are different varieties of proportional voting systems in use in the United States and other nations, both partisan and nonpartisan, and the details of different systems matter, but all of them provide "full representation." Achieving the principle of full representation is fundamental to having a truly inclusive, unifying and more participatory democracy.

Full representation would have a dramatic impact on voter choice and representation of women and racial minorities in our congressional elections. Under current winner-take-all rules, few House elections are competitive. In both 1998 and 2000, more than 98 percent of incumbents were reelected, and fewer than one in ten races were won by less than 10 percent victory margins—the traditional definition of a competitive race. Most congressional districts are inherently noncompetitive due to the lopsided balance of voters within the district clearly tilting toward one party. The effects of campaign inequities, incumbency, or other factors are secondary to the effects of these partisan districts. Such imbalances are unsurprising given the power given to party leaders and incumbents in redistricting. Most districts have been purposely drawn during the redistricting process to make them "safe" for one party or the other. Quite simply legislators use redistricting as a means to choose their constituents before their constituents have a chance to choose them.

Winner-take-all elections make it extremely rare for racial minorities to win in white-majority districts. Only two black members of Congress, Julia Carson of Indiana and J. C. Watts of Oklahoma, initially were elected from districts that were majority-white. But the House of Representatives, with its scattering of black, Asian, and Latino officials, makes the U.S. Senate look like an exclusive private club. No states are majority-black or majority-Latino and, with race still a powerful role in American politics, it is no surprise that none of our 100 Senators or fifty governors is black or Latino.

Full representation would break open one-party monopolies and give women, political independents, and racial minorities, as well as orphaned Democrats and Republicans living in the wrong districts, realistic chances to run and win all across the country. Most people could support their favorite candidates and political parties no matter where they lived, and often could help elect them. In 2000 the fight for control of the House of Representatives would have been a national election, rather than the piecemeal, sound bite–driven campaigns that took place in the shrinking number of swing districts scattered across the nation. For some Americans, control of the House of Representatives is more important than the presidency, but the only way most of them can affect that control is by mailing a check to a candidate in a tight race halfway across the country.

The redistricting process underway in 2001–2002 underscores the importance of how majorities are secured through crafting district lines. In a moment of candor, the primary architect of the 1991–1992 redistricting plan for Texas admitted that the process "is not one of kindness, it is not one of sharing. It is a power grab" (Sheffner 1997; Anderson and Richie 1998). A North Carolina state senator was even more blunt: "We are in the business of rigging elections" (Hoeffel 1998). Although past redistricting has never been fair, the combination of the narrowly divided U.S. House and new redistricting technologies has raised the stakes. Politicians and their consultants now have at their disposal extremely sophisticated computer technology, combined with the latest census, demographic, and polling data, to precisely gerrymander their districts.

Ironically, "gerrymandering" has come to be associated more with the use of redistricting to empower racial minorities than its much more prevalent use to protect incumbents and gain partisan advantage. In the early 1990s, racial minorities experienced remarkable gains in legislative representation due to amendments to the Voting Rights Act that required certain states and localities to create opportunities for such minorities to elect candidates of their choice. The result was many more electoral districts drawn with majorities of racial and ethnic minorities and, in turn, a leap in representation of people of color in legislatures. In the U.S. House, for example, the number of black and Latino members rose from thirty-five in 1990 to fifty-five in 1992.

But in a series of recent rulings against so-called racial gerrymandering, starting with its 1993 ruling in *Shaw v. Reno*, the Supreme Court has made it much harder to establish such districts. The result is almost certain to be a halt in the rise in elected black legislators, if not a decrease, unless we turn to full representation systems. Unlike majoritarian systems, full representation is specifically designed to represent both the majority and minority. By building from a fundamental principle of equality and political fairness, full representation could provide lasting security to voting rights of racial minorities—just as the universal nature of Social Security protects cuts that would hurt low-income seniors. Combining adjoining one-seat districts into bigger districts with three to five representatives elected by full representation would almost certainly increase the number of African Americans elected to the U.S. House in states such as Alabama, Arkansas, Louisiana, Mississippi, North and South Carolina, and Virginia—and represent far more white voters currently residing in the "wrong" districts, and avoid redistricting disputes as well.

In addition to winning a fair share of seats, racial minorities with full representation systems would have greater opportunities to negotiate for influence because they could "swing" among parties. When South Africa used a party-based proportional representation system in its first all-race elections in 1994, the two leading parties—the African National Congress and the National Party—ran multiracial slates with messages of inclusion. When New Zealand had its first proportional representation election in 1996, the first Asian citizen was elected, and Pacific Islanders and indigenous Maoris tripled their representation. A Maori-backed party formed a coalition government with the governing party—a party whose relationship with Maoris had been analogous to Republicans' post-1960 relationship with American blacks, but that accommodated the party's concerns.

Full representation also would provide a means to increase the number of women elected to office. In state legislative elections, women win seats in significantly higher percentages in multiseat districts, even when using winner-take-all methods, than in one-seat districts. With multiseat districts, women are more likely to run and voters are more likely to seek gender balance when there is more than one seat to fill. Because full representation systems expand options all the more, they give women additional leverage to force the major parties to support more women candidates. In 1994, a threat by women supporters from the major parties in Sweden to form a new women's party led to women winning 41 percent of seats to their national legislature after the major parties made a commitment to recruit more women candidates. Germany, Italy, and New Zealand are among a growing number of democracies that use systems with a mix of winner-take-all districts and party list proportional representation seats. It is instructive that women in all three countries often are more than twice as likely to win seats elected by proportional representation than in one-seat districts.

IT REALLY DID HAPPEN IN AMERICA . . .

The potential of full representation in the United States can be glimpsed through two case studies: five "choice voting" elections to the New York City council during the Fiorello La Guardia era and a century of "cumulative voting" elections to the Illinois state House of Representatives. In the first half of the 20th century, full representation had much support and relative success, particularly at a city level. The Proportional Representation League had the active support of such Progressive Era luminaries as League of Women Voters founder Carrie Chapman Catt, U.S. Senator Paul Douglas, women's leader Jane Addams, city reformers Richard Childs and Tom Johnson, union leader A. Philip Randolph, and writers Charles Beard and Walter Lippmann. Two dozen cities ultimately adopted the choice voting method of full representation (also called "single transferable vote," "preference voting," and "the Hare system"), including Cincinnati, Cleveland, Kalamazoo, Sacramento, and Worcester. Several other major cities came very close to adopting the system and with a quicker means to count ballots and greater tolerance of minorities, choice voting might have become the dominant means of electing local government (Barber 2000).

The most significant victory for reform backers was in New York City. With the backing of Mayor Fiorello La Guardia and the tacit support of President Franklin Roosevelt, voters in 1936 overwhelmingly approved the adoption of choice voting to elect members of its city council in the wake of scandals involving Tammany Hall. Its impact was immediate. In 1935, the last election under winner-take-all rules in single-seat districts, the Democrats won 66.5 percent of the popular vote but captured a disproportional 95.3 percent of the seats on city council. In 1937, in the first election under choice voting, Democrats won only half the seats with about half of the votes—their fair share—and machine Democrats lost control of the council due to reform Democrats choosing to caucus with members of the four other parties that won seats, including the American Labor Party and La Guardia's Fusion Party.

In each of the five elections with choice voting, at least four political parties won seats. Democrats regained control, but still faced a vigorous, multifaceted opposition. Attendance at council meetings soared, and the first black candidates (including future congressman Adam Clayton Powell) were elected. The population's tolerance for diversity had its limits, however, and the election of two members of the Communist Party created an opening for the major party establishment to join together and use "redbait" tactics to repeal choice voting in a 1947 referendum over the objections of groups like the NAACP, League of Women Voters, and progressive labor unions (Zeller and Bone 1948). In 1949, in the first election since the repeal, the old political order was immediately restored: Democrats won a disproportionate 96 percent (twenty-four of twenty-five) of city council seats, even though they had a far smaller percentage of the popular vote. Despite lingering support reflected by a 1965 petition drive to restore choice voting that was chaired by Franklin Roosevelt Jr. and U.S. Senators Robert Kennedy and Jacob Javits, the city council has never again come close to approaching its vibrancy under choice voting.

Illinois's history with cumulative voting goes back even further in American voting system reform history. Around 1870, the state of Illinois adopted cumulative voting for electing its House of Representatives.

Joseph Medill, editor of the *Chicago Tribune*, persuaded delegates at a constitutional convention to adopt cumulative voting to lessen polarization in the state between the Confederacy-leaning south and Union-leaning north.

In a three-seat district with cumulative voting, any constituency with close to 25 percent of the vote is nearly certain to win representation. In Illinois this meant two-party representation in nearly all three-seat districts, as the second biggest party nearly always had at least 20 percent of the vote in even the most one-sided districts. The lower threshold also opened the door for political independents, women, and people of color. Under its current single-seat districts system, Illinois has become a state politically balkanized along regional lines, with Democrats representing urban areas and Republicans representing the down-state areas. But under cumulative voting and three-seat districts, Democratic strongholds like Chicago elected a few Republicans as well as Democrats, and conservative suburbs and rural areas elected a few Democrats along with Republicans. Both major parties had a direct interest in serving the entire state. Political independents within the major parties were successful everywhere. Former Representative Harold Katz described the legislature as "a symphony, with not just two instruments playing, but a number of different instruments going at all times."

Recurring themes heard in Illinois include ones that resonate deeply when applied to current concerns about national politics:

- *Filling out the spectrum.* In a two-party system, the parties are supposed to be "big tents." But winner-take-all leaves whole swathes of the electorate without strong representation—be it Catholics who are both prolife and prolabor, union members opposed to gun control, or reform-minded independents drawn to John McCain. In contrast, Illinois's districts typically had three representatives from distinct parts of the political spectrum: two representing liberal and moderate wings of the majority party and one from that area's minority party. Political minorities in office included Chicago Republicans concerned with urban issues and independent reformers like Harold Washington willing to take on local machines.
- *Less regional polarization.* Contrary to their reputation, single-seat districts don't necessarily represent geographic interests very well. Across the nation, for example, Republicans represent most rural districts, while Democrats represent nearly all urban districts despite both areas almost always having significant numbers of the minority party. When only one side represents a region, policy for that area is subject to the whims of the majority party in each state and in Congress. Cities can suffer under Republican legislatures who don't have

members representing urban areas, but also can suffer under Democrats too quick to accept the local status quo. Setting wilderness policy in the Rockies is far more problematic when the region's conservative majority can deprive wilderness and environmental backers of representation. Illinois's legislature today suffers from regional divides, but it was different with three-seat districts. The loss of full representation has undercut bipartisan support for key policies and greatly exacerbated urban/suburban divisions. Chicago has been a big loser in equitable funding of public schools, for example.

• *Less partisan rancor.* The impeachment of President Bill Clinton was only the most pronounced example of the bitter partisanship that reigns in Washington. Nearly every major legislative initiative seems calculated for political advantage. Voices of compromise are vanishing, in part because of the growing homogeneity of representation in districts that lean clearly toward one party or the other. Yet in Illinois, former Republican Congressman John Porter has written that with full representation "we operated in a less partisan environment because both parties represented the entire state." Former state Representative Giddy Dyer said that under Illinois's current single-seat districts "now we see an absolute partisan approach to government. It's gamesmanship, how can we beat the other one? Each party views the other one as an enemy. That lack of civility began when we did away with cumulative voting." One political analyst observed, "You had far more people getting elected in the middle. Now we have lost a lot of moderates in the Illinois Assembly, and I think that's a big loss for the state" (Center for Voting and Democracy 1998).

• *More minority representation, less representation of big money.* Cumulative voting also resulted in much better representation of African American and women candidates in Illinois over the course of the century than the winner-take-all state Senate elections (Everson 1992; Center for Voting and Democracy 2001). It encouraged more grassroots campaigns where money was less of a factor, and more independent candidacies that could buck the local machine because only 25 percent of the vote was needed to win a seat. Full representation plans would not do away with the problems of inequities in campaign finance, but it would give important new opportunities to lesser-funded and grassroots candidates with strong support among constituency groups that can turn out voters without a lot of cash.

Illinois's system of cumulative voting in three-seat districts was in place for 110 years, until it was repealed in a 1980 Reagan-era populist "cutback" amendment that opportunistically promised to reduce the size and costs of the House by a third after the House had passed for itself a pay increase. But in 2001 a high-profile task force headed by former Republican Governor Jim Edgar and former Democratic Congressman Abner Mikva recommended restoring cumulative voting. The report from that task force published by the Institute for Government and Public Affairs stated that cumulative voting tends to "generate richer deliberations and statewide consensus among all legislators since both parties would be represented in all parts of the state" (Institute for Government and Public Affairs at the University of Illinois 2001; Parsons, 2001). Mikva, who got his political start in Chicago with cumulative voting, has observed that it "helped us synthesize some of our differences, made us realize that even though we were different from the downstaters, different from the suburbanites, we had a lot in common that held us together as a single state" (Center for Voting and Democracy 1998).

While full representation certainly can be recognized as a fundamental challenge to the status quo, the current "drive to revive" cumulative voting in Illinois shows how obstacles can be overcome when people are familiar with the system. The Edgar–Mikva report in 2001 generated significant media coverage and attention to the case for reform. Legislation to restore cumulative voting has had hearings, and leading players are exploring a state initiative. Both Chicago daily newspapers have opined in favor of its return. Nationally, Congress probably won't order states to elect House members by full representation tomorrow, but it has the constitutional power to do so. More realistically, it could adopt legislation like the States' Choice of Voting Systems Act that was sponsored in 1999 by Representative Mel Watt. Attracting bipartisan support at a hearing, the bill sought to return to states the option of using multiseat districts to elect their congressional delegations.

BUILDING A MOVEMENT FOR FAIR ELECTIONS

For voting system reform advocates, it can seem like the best of the times or the worst of times. On the one hand, few nations are in need of the benefits of reform as much as the United States. The infamous election administration breakdowns in Florida in 2000 have opened people's eyes toward our creaking electoral machinery and antiquated rules. Our voter turnout is among the world's lowest: in 2002, turnout among eligible voters is sure to again dip well below 40 percent A nation largely of immigrants, the increasingly complex racial and ethnic diversity in the United States cries out for modification of the distortions of winner-take-all elections. The relative strength of the American women's movement is poorly reflected in Congress. The desire by a majority of Americans for a national third party is in stark contrast to the paucity of viable third-party and independent candidacies. The nation's vast number of elections—there are estimated to be a half million elected offices in the United States—would seem to create great opportunities to introduce reform at some level of government.

Yet these same factors create barriers as well. Rather than broadening their reform agenda, the Florida aftermath has narrowed some potential reformers' scope to only fixing voting machines and improving election administration. Low voter turnout means that potential supporters of reform aren't at the polls to support it. Racial and ethnic diversity means that the white majority can feel threatened by the potential electoral success of racial minorities. The absence of elected third-party representatives means that the multiparty argument for full representation appears abstract: minor parties are not visibly deprived of many seats due to their absence in legislatures, a catch-22. The nation's many overlapping and competing levels of government muddy citizens' perceptions of what difference full representation would make.

A 1996 campaign for full representation in San Francisco perhaps best illustrates both the strengths and the weaknesses of the movement. An elections task force established by the voters in 1994 had recommended that choice voting be placed on the ballot as an alternative to the at-large system then in place. Choice voting won endorsements from key organizations, including the San Francisco Democratic Party and the chair and key activists of the San Francisco Republican Party, the Green Party and Libertarian Party, NOW, the Police Officers Association, Mexican American Legal Defense and Education Fund (MALDEF); the largest labor unions and the most influential city organizations representing communities of color, the gay/lesbian community, housing and tenant advocates, and seniors. The campaign also gained the support of prominent individuals like Mayor Willie Brown, the United Farm Workers' Dolores Huerta, Jesse Jackson, and the district attorney, as well as key newspapers.

The campaign had a moderate volunteer base that distributed over 50,000 palm cards door-to-door, and allied organizations distributed another 20,000 cards to targeted neighborhoods. In addition, more than 20,000 pieces of campaign literature were directly mailed to targeted audiences, supportive ballot statements were solicited from endorsing organizations, a letters to the editor and op-ed campaign was launched, and 2000 "Vote Yes on Prop H" signs were posted throughout the city. But choice voting won only 44 percent. The many supportive organizations did not view it as central to their primary mission and typically did not donate significant funds or turn out volunteers. Given the lack of financial resources for an educational campaign via the electronic media, the three-month campaign proved to be too short to convey a new idea like choice voting to a majority of San Francisco voters—

especially in the middle of the presidential campaign and California's controversial Proposition 209 vote on affirmative action. The complexity of the ballot-count for choice voting did not help, but, as in most American cities, nonpartisan elections don't allow other simpler, party-based forms of full representation. The major newspaper opposed the measure. Finally, San Francisco voters had another reform alternative—going to a more familiar single-seat district system, which won a majority of the vote.

Voting system reformers' current strategy is predicated on the belief that instant runoff voting has immediate opportunities for adoption through legislatures and ballot measures, while the best immediate avenue for full representation generally is through Voting Rights Act litigation. The most dramatic recent example of the impact of full representation in a voting rights case comes from Amarillo, Texas. In May 2000, Amarillo used cumulative voting for the first time to elect members of its school board as a means to settle a voting rights lawsuit involving MALDEF, League of United Latin American Citizens (LULAC), and the NAACP. Blacks and Latinos in Amarillo together make up a quarter of the city's population, but no black or Latino candidate had won a seat on the school board in decades. Cumulative voting had an immediate impact. With strong support in their respective communities, both a black candidate and a Latino candidate won seats, voter turnout more than doubled over the previous school board election, and all parties in the voting rights settlement expressed satisfaction with the new system (Hill and Richie 2001).

With more such success stories of full representation systems used in the United States, a broad nonpartisan coalition will be better equipped to compare them favorably to our deeply flawed winner-take-all methods. The elements of the proreform coalition are coming together. National groups recently endorsing full representation include the Sierra Club, US PIRG, Alliance for Democracy, and NOW. After a two-year study, the ACLU in 2001 came out in favor of lifting all statutory barriers to full representation and adopting it where appropriate. State affiliates of Common Cause and the League of Women Voters support IRV legislation, and the League is conducting a national study of voting system reform. The NAACP and other civil rights groups are actively exploring full representation as a means to preserve minority representation in the upcoming round of redistricting.

The 2000 presidential and congressional races highlighted the need to reform our voting system, from top to bottom—starting with election administration and voting machines, but continuing with our appalling low rates of voter registration, low voter turnout, underrepresentation of our rich diversity, shrinking number of competitive congressional races, the poor quality of campaigns, bitter partisan divides and exploding amounts of campaign cash. Full representation voting methods and instant runoff voting address these democratic maladies in profound and unique ways that require it to be part of the democracy reformers' toolkit. Given the potential to win their adoption, we fervently hope the legacy of the 2000 election is further growth in the electoral reform coalition, rather than growing resignation and declining participation in a postelectoral democracy.

11

Putting Democracy Back into the Initiative and Referendum

GALEN NELSON

I have the choice of buying a $2 million painting and looking at it on the wall . . . or I could spend $2 million and have a chance of saving the last 5% of California redwood forests.

—Millionaire Hal Arbit, Patron of the 1990 "Forests Forever" initiative (quoted in Shultz 1996, 22) (emphasis added)

In 1997 Microsoft cofounder and billionaire Paul Allen, who had recently purchased the Seattle Seahawks football team, decided he wanted Washington State taxpayers to help fund some of the cost of a new stadium. Rather than waging a lengthy lobbying campaign in the Washington legislature, Allen spent over $6 million to gather signatures and campaign for a ballot initiative that would fund the stadium. After the state demanded he spend an additional $4 million to fund a special election for the measure, Allen earned a high return on his initiative investment. Voters approved the stadium construction measure by 51 percent. Allen had single-handedly funded an effort to qualify and pass an initiative purely for his self-interest.

Increasingly, critics of the ballot measure point to these events and complain that barriers to participation are too high—even for well-organized citizen groups—and that it has become an exclusive tool for wealthy, special interests. Initiative campaigns like Allen's stadium measure feed into this sentiment. The relatively rapid shift toward higher cost, "Astroturf" ballot campaigns, with their misleading advertisements that leave voters guessing prompts the question: What can be done to recapture the grassroots spirit of the initiative and referendum and the optimistic vision of direct democracy so prevalent during the Progressive Era?

In the short term, reformers could help restore some integrity to the process by more carefully and comprehensively disclosing the money

159

behind the measures. For a range of reasons, voters depend more heavily on interest groups' endorsements, both financial and substantive, when evaluating a ballot measure. Unfortunately, weak and inconsistent initiative donor disclosure laws shield those who attempt to buy laws at the ballot and distort the ballot measure process. In the wake of the electoral voting irregularities in Florida in the recent presidential election, Americans are more aware of the need to bring our democratic infrastructure into the 21st century. The reform community and concerned voters should also take this unique opportunity and momentum to reexamine, evaluate, and reform the ballot measure process.

A BRIEF HISTORY OF DIRECT DEMOCRACY

For over 100 years, voters have exercised their right to circulate petitions and place laws directly on ballots through the initiative process and have gathered signatures in order to repeal laws passed by their elected state legislators by referendum. Initiatives and referenda, collectively known as direct democracy or direct legislation, grew out of the populist and progressive movements of the late 19th and early 20th centuries. Alarmed by the growing power of the entrenched mining and railroad industries, populist reformers originally advocated the initiative and referenda, along with other reforms. Progressive Era reformers, also alarmed at political corruption, followed suit. Theodore Roosevelt, an early booster of direct democracy, argued that initiatives complimented legislative lawmaking: "I believe in the Initiative and Referendum, which should be used not to destroy representative government, but to correct it whenever it becomes misrepresentative" (Web site of the Initiative and Referendum Institute, www.iandrinstitute.org).

The initiative and referendum process expanded most rapidly throughout the western states where populist sentiments ran deep. In the eastern and southern states, there was much more resistance from an entrenched political party apparatus.

Over the years, ballot measures have often accurately reflected the most pressing popular concerns in their jurisdictions, and their use has been a barometer of popular discontent with elected officials and bipartisan consensus, both local and national. Today, voters in twenty-four states and the District of Columbia are empowered with two forms of direct democracy, citizen-initiated ballot measures and legislative referenda, which may be used to address concerns long neglected by state legislatures and to overturn laws passed by the same. The process is far from perfect. Ballot titles, the short descriptions voters read in the polling booth that encapsulate an initiative, are often misleading. A lack of contribution limits and weak donor disclosure laws leaves the process vulnerable to the corrosive effect of special interest dollars. Many argue that creating laws via initiative lacks the deliberative qualities of legislative lawmaking (see Broder 2000). Other critics are concerned that the initiative process threatens minority rights. With all of these structural flaws in mind, direct democracy can still empower citizens with a check against unresponsive state legislatures and foster a deeper understanding of democratic politics. Furthermore, it is difficult to imagine voters ever repealing the initiative and referendum process. Like it or not, it seems that the process is here to stay.

The popularity and use of the process has grown tremendously in recent years. As elected bodies have become more and more polarized, deal making and compromise have given way to gridlock. Rather suddenly, Americans are passing more and more laws via initiative. Perhaps more importantly, ballot proponents are forcing the public to wrestle with a whole set of issues largely ignored by legislatures and the media. Despite the growing influence of direct democracy and the millions of dollars spent supporting and opposing ballot measures each year, initiative campaign funding remains largely underregulated.

While state and national campaign finance reform groups have done a commendable job tracking money in state and federal *candidate* campaigns, little has been done to systematically disclose initiative donor information. This enormous campaign finance disclosure blind spot, coupled with other structural weaknesses in the initiative process, deserves reformers' immediate attention. While the spotlight shines brightly on the voting irregularities in Florida during the 2000 election, reformers should not forget the ballot measure process among the broad array of democratic structures deserving of an overhaul.

WHY TRACK CONTRIBUTIONS
TO BALLOT CAMPAIGNS?

Consider the scope and reach of the ballot measure process. Qualitatively, voters encountered a wide range of ballot measure issues in 2000 often breaking new policy ground or overturning court decisions across a range of issues including abortion rights, animal rights, campaign finance reform, corporate regulation, education, environmental protection, gay civil rights, gun control, health care reform, labor issues, physician assisted suicide, tax reform, and more. In 1994, a nonpresidential election year, initiative proponents circulated just over 200 petitions and slightly over half (104) qualified for the ballot. In 1998, the next off-year election, proponents circulated over 260 measures; 130 qualified for the ballot. In 1996, a presidential election year, ballot measure proponents circulated over 450 petitions; over 90 qualified. In 2000, another presidential election year, nearly 500 petitions were circulated and about 130 measures qualified for ballots around the country. Ballot initiative use in odd-numbered years has also increased (I & R Institute Web site. See www.iandrinstitute.org. "I & R Usage").

Politicians, both state and national, often "run with" ballot measures throughout the course of their campaigns in order to link themselves with popular issues. In 1994, then California Governor Pete Wilson endorsed Proposition 187, a measure that denied social services to illegal aliens, during his campaign for reelection. While stumping in Colorado in 1996, presidential candidate Robert Dole asked voters to support Amendment 17, a so-called parental rights measure supported by religious right political groups. In 1998, organized labor launched a minimum wage measure in Washington State. In that same election, state Democratic candidates enjoyed great success. Many political observers believe the minimum wage measure significantly boosted voter turnout among labor union rank-and-file members and other voters sympathetic to the Democratic platform.

Advocacy organizations and political strategists, cognizant of the unique public relations platform ballot measures provide, often launch identical measures in multiple states to mobilize their supporters or to affect dialogue about national policy. The term limits, drug reform, and campaign finance reform movements have used this strategy effectively. Ballot proponents often use initiatives to drive a wedge between their political opponents (e.g., anti-abortion and anti-gay ballot measures). Finally, groups may exploit the unique way in which ballot measures pit a voting majority against the courts to force the judicial branch to reconsider a controversial issue. Initiated measures addressing social services provided to illegal aliens, gay civil rights, and the medical use of marijuana have all been the subjects of Supreme Court decisions over the last decade.

Ballot measures also allow well-organized or well-financed groups to exert considerable control over policy debates in state legislatures simply by threatening to launch an initiative campaign. In 2000, a coalition of health care reformers in Massachusetts organized a petition drive to place a "patients bill of rights" measure on the ballot. Seeing the writing on the wall, the legislature passed a similar law that met many of the health care reformers' demands before the initiative reached the ballot.

Despite the grassroots, populist origins of the ballot measure process, initiative campaigns are increasingly costly. A survey of recently gathered initiative donor data comprising eight states in the 2000 election found nearly 58 percent of contributions to initiative campaigns were made in quantities of $50,000 or more (BISC Foundation, www.ballot.org. See "Ballot Funding Database." I should make clear that I helped organize this survey.). Still, most researchers agree that overwhelming spending does not guarantee success in the initiative arena. Well-organized citizen groups of modest means have enjoyed success at the ballot while wealthy interests often fall short trying to win a "yes" campaign. In *The Populist Paradox*, Elizabeth Gerber notes that "citizen groups are much more successful at modifying policy through the direct legislation process [whereas] economic groups are more successful at blocking measures through opposition spending" (Gerber 1999, 119). Still, heavy spending on the "no" side of an initiative campaign continues to be one of the best predictors of initiative outcomes. In the survey of twenty-one initiative battles, we found that when the "no" campaign outspent the "yes" side by more than a two to one margin, all but three "no" campaigns were successful.

In 1998 alone, issue committees spent $400 million supporting or opposing ballot measures. By comparison, the national Republican and Democratic Parties raised only $193 million in "soft money." With the largest population in the Union, California leads in ballot measure spending. In 1998, issue committees spent nearly $250 million on twelve primary and general election ballot measures in California—a figure more than twice that amount spent on legislative races. In Colorado, a state with one-eighth the population of California, ballot measure spending topped $10 million in 1998. Even in sparsely populated Montana, opponents of Initiative 122, which would have required tougher water treatment standards in mine operations, spent nearly $9 per vote in 1998 to defeat the measure (Smith 2001). In 2000, health maintenance organizations and insurance companies teamed up to defeat a health care reform measure in Massachusetts outspending proponents 30 to 1 (BISC Foundation, www.ballot.org. See "Ballot Spending Watch.").

Ironically, candidate campaign finance reform (recently defeated) in Congress may increase the need for better initiative donor disclosure laws in the states. If Congress passes campaign finance reform that restricts or eliminates "soft money" contributions to political parties and increases limits on "hard money" contributions to candidates, some wealthy donors may attempt to buy influence through other means. Some ideological donors may begin to seek "donation shelters" outside the traditional candidate and party political apparatus. Since they have no contribution limits, ballot measures, along with independent expenditures and issue advocacy, may provide one such safe haven.

INITIATIVE CAMPAIGN
FINANCE REFORM HISTORY

Efforts to regulate ballot campaign contributions are not new. But legislative efforts to limit ballot contributions have largely been limited by the courts. Following the Watergate scandal, California voters approved Proposition 9, the Political Reform Act, which limited contributions to ballot measure campaigns. The California Supreme Court struck down the measure two years later (Smith 2001). Ever since the Supreme Court's 1976 landmark *Buckley v. Valeo* decision, which equated political contributions with protected speech under the First Amendment, reformers have tried to carve out constitutional remedies to restrict contributions to ballot campaigns.

More recently, voters in Montana approved Initiative 125 on the 1996 ballot, a bold effort to ban corporate contributions to ballot campaigns while allowing corporations to fund political speech through a segregated fund. In arguing for the ban, reform advocates cited a 1990 Supreme Court ruling that recognized that states may act to limit "the corrosive effects of immense aggregations of wealth that are accumulated with the help of the corporate form and that have little or no correlation to the public's support for the corporation's political ideas." That ruling, *Austin v. Michigan Chamber of Commerce*, 494 U.S. 652 (1990), upheld limits on corporate independent expenditures in candidate elections (posted at www.iandrinstitute.org. See "I & R Legal" legal cases). Nonetheless, the Montana Chamber of Commerce, the Montana Mining Association, and other business interests successfully challenged Initiative 125 in a divided 2–1 ruling in the 9th Circuit panel. Reform advocates represented by the National Voting Rights Institute are presently planning an appeal.

In a related decision, efforts to regulate paid signature gathering were dealt a serious blow in the 1999 *Buckley v. American Constitutional Law Foundation* case. The state of Colorado, in an effort to prevent fraud and preserve the integrity of the electoral process, passed legislation requiring that (1) petition circulators who verify the signatures of petition signers must be registered electors; (2) petition circulators must wear identification badges; and (3) proponents of an initiative must file reports disclosing the amounts paid to circulators and the identity of petition circulators. The U.S. Supreme Court struck down Colorado's regulations and restrictions on their initiative process as "undue hindrances to political conversations and the exchange of ideas," according to Justice Ruth Bader Ginsburg who wrote for the majority.

While legislative and initiated efforts to limit ballot campaign contributions wind their way through the court system, democratic reformers should focus their efforts on improving ballot measure campaign contribution disclosure laws. With the courts effectively standing in the way of initiative contribution limits, better disclosure laws can help voters make more informed decisions about the critical issues they face in the polling booth each election.

Most national candidate campaign finance reform groups, while generally supportive of reforming initiative campaign finance laws, have not made the issue a priority for a variety of reasons. Many have left the issue to their state affiliates; others cite resource limitations or the seemingly insurmountable legal barriers. The Public Interest Research Groups (PIRGs), perhaps the most ardent supporters of the ballot measure process, believe that contributions to initiative campaigns from for-profit corporations should be banned. Some reformers advocate the use of public money to ensure that both sides of an initiative campaign are adequately funded. However, efforts to provide public funds to ballot measure proponents have been found unconstitutional by the California Supreme Court (*Stanson v. Mott*, 17 Cal. 3d 206, 1976).

INITIATIVE DONOR DISCLOSURE: CHALLENGES AND OPPORTUNITIES

Given the difficult legal hurdles to limiting initiative campaign contributions, providing voters with better donor disclosure information may be our best and most immediate path for reform. Furthermore, voters tend to rely heavily on endorsements from groups and individuals they know and trust when evaluating a ballot question since other cues, like partisanship and voting history, are absent (Gerber 1999). Perhaps more broadly, an informed citizenry is an essential ingredient in any democracy. More and better quality initiative donor data will help voters make more informed decisions *and* teach important lessons about how interest groups, individuals, and political parties exert their influence in our democracy.

Unfortunately, initiative donor disclosure laws are shamefully inadequate. In fact, less than half of the states with the initiative process offer a sufficiently robust initiative donor database to the public and the media. Those that do often post donor data after the election on scanned forms that are difficult to access and read.

In the 2000 election, BISC Foundation tracked contributions to ballot measure campaigns in a handful of states (Arizona, Colorado, Massachusetts, Maine, Missouri, Oregon, and Washington) in partnership with the National Institute on Money in State Politics (NIMSP). Our goal was to make initiative donor data available to voters prior to the election in an easy to use, on-line donor database at www.ballotfunding.org. We knew that we were navigating uncharted territory; state and national reform groups have tracked candidate contributions for years but documenting donations to ballot measures presents a whole set of new challenges.

First, initiative campaign finance disclosure laws in the twenty-four states with the ballot measure process vary widely. Donor and committee disclosure reports and schedules are not standardized across state lines. State disclosure agencies are frequently understaffed and underfunded. Ballot measure committees (those organizations formed to collect contributions for direct democracy battles) can avoid tough monitoring, since disclosure laws are generally weaker for them than for candidates. In Arizona, for example, a ballot committee is not required to declare which initiative it is supporting. Furthermore, ballot committees often support more than one initiative, which makes tracking how contributions are apportioned more difficult.

State-level donor disclosure agencies are generally required to follow a schedule by which they release candidate and initiative donor data to the public in either paper or electronic format. Unfortunately, initiative donor data are often made available by state reporting agencies later than promised (oftentimes after the election) and in formats that varied widely in type and quality. Part of the problem is that money spent on state-level political activity is reported later than money spent on federal races. By the time state contributions are reported, state election officials are swamped with entering federal donor data. States that release data in electronic format are not much faster but are improving slowly—thanks in part to pressure from groups like BISCF, NIMSP, and the California Voter Foundation.

Ballot committees disband and reconvene frequently and tend to change their name after initiatives are assigned numbers or letters (the "Good Schools Committee" becomes the "Yes on 5" committee). To make matters worse, ballot committee names, unlike candidate committee names, are often not intuitively linked with the initiative they were formed to support or oppose. In 2000, the Arizona issue committee "Not With The People's Money" was a tobacco industry–funded group opposed to an initiative that would have increased cigarette taxes to fund health care. In Maine, the "Coalition To Save Small Woodlands" was organized to defeat a forest protection measure. Furthermore, issue committees often receive large contributions from political action committees in other states with less stringent donor disclosure laws, further complicating transparent disclosure. Finally, some issue committees file paperwork, yet never raise or contribute money to any ballot campaign.

In the wake of the voting irregularities in Florida in the 2000 presidential election, the climate is ripe for electoral and democratic reforms. The campaign finance reform community should help lead the way in fighting for stronger initiative donor disclosure laws. There are some concrete steps reformers can take now in order to provide comprehensive, transparent funding data to voters, journalists, and opinion leaders.

- Recognize good practices—Some states, including Oregon and Washington, have developed commendable initiative donor disclosure practices and should be recognized for their efforts. Other states are farther behind and need our help. State disclosure agencies can only provide voters with initiative donor information to the extent to which they are allowed under the law. Sadly, in the course of our research, we learned that state disclosure agency staff seldom communicate across state lines. The Money in State Ballot Measures project will work with other organizations to develop model guidelines for initiative disclosure and recognize those states that are leading the way.
- Learn and lobby—Learn about ballot initiative campaign finance disclosure laws in your state then ask your state legislator to support stronger legislation.
- Educate yourself and others—Tap into our initiative donor data at www.ballotfunding.org and urge your family, friends, and coworkers to do the same. Ask your local newspaper to site our research so that more voters will have access to ballot funding information.
- Broaden the base—If you are involved in a state or national electoral or campaign finance reform organization, urge them to adopt a position on initiative campaign finance reform issues including better disclosure and contribution limits.

While initiative campaign finance laws deserve our attention and resources, advocates should also consider a wider range of structural improvements that could deeply strengthen the initiative process. Below, I have outlined just some of the concerns that legislators, citizen groups, academics, and political practitioners have with the initiative process. Following each concern is a list of possible reform solutions. Some of the proposed reforms listed below are controversial. Far from being a precise prescription for reform, these proposals are meant to stimulate discussion and spur debate.

Citizen Participation Is Low/Too Many Measures on the Ballot

In elections with both candidates and citizen initiatives on the same ballot, there is often a certain amount of voter "drop-off." That is, while most voters tend to choose major candidates at the top of the ballot, a certain number skip voting for or against "down ballot" initiatives or candidates on the same ballot. This phenomenon is especially common when there are many initiatives on the same ballot. "Drop-off" may be caused by a range of factors including voters' lack of information about ballot measures, lengthy and confusing ballot titles, or simply voter fatigue. To make matters worse, some ballot measures appear on primary or special election ballots when voter turnout is already low. Following are some simple remedies.

First, urge state agencies with jurisdiction over the initiative process (usually the Secretary of State's office) to sponsor publicly funded debates or forums on ballot measures in partnership with major media outlets and newspapers. Good government groups, like the League of Women Voters, already sponsor candidate debates. Why not introduce voters to ballot measures with a spirited debate between advocates and opponents in order to encourage greater interest, deeper understanding, and participation? Ballot measure debates could be Web cast and transcripts could be reproduced in newspapers.

Some have argued that the number of initiatives on any one ballot should be limited. Mississippi limits the number of ballot measures in any one calendar year to five. This might help alleviate voter fatigue and promote greater debate and dialog about qualifying ballot measures. Finally, initiatives could be limited to general election ballots only when voter turnout is higher. This would prevent a small number of voters from changing public policy. Alternatively, some states require that, beyond winning a simple majority, votes cast on an initiative must equal a percentage of the total votes cast in the election (35 percent in Nebraska, 30 percent in Massachusetts, and 40 percent in Mississippi).

Initiatives Are Highly Inflexible/Prone to Legal Challenges

Once ballot measures are drafted and signature gathering begun, there are few opportunities to offer amendments, correct mistakes, or make improvements. Errors are often revealed during the petition circulation period, and each year, the courts find a handful of ballot measures unconstitutional. These problems threaten to imperil both voter confidence in ballot measure process and, perhaps more importantly, the independence of the judicial branch. After all, voters tend to question the impartiality of judges who overturn popularly approved measures. Both problems could be avoided with a better system of precirculation, expedited judicial review. Voters will be less likely offended if ballot measures are found unconstitutional and tossed off the ballot before an election.

Only Florida requires the state Supreme Court to review the constitutionality of all ballot proposals. There is some debate on this score. Some scholars argue that ballot measures should be subject to a higher standard of judicial review since the process lacks the deliberative quality of the legislative lawmaking. Others argue that the election provides the greatest check against the excesses of the initiative process; historically, voters have approved roughly 40 percent of all ballot measures. On balance, some type of preelection judicial review seems wise.

Only eleven of the twenty-four ballot measure states require ballot petition language to undergo a preelection judicial review; in all but four of those states, the review is advisory only. Greater use of the indirect initiative might also improve the quality of ballot language and preserve citizen control over the process while introducing a greater degree of the deliberative quality common to legislative lawmaking. Indirect initiatives are a form of the ballot measure process used only in Alaska, Massachusetts, Ohio, and Wyoming that allow legislators an opportunity to debate the merits of an initiative and offer amendments to the proponents. Some variations of this process allow proponents to make necessary changes to their own ballot measure.

Ballot Titles Are Often Misleading

Many voters and critics of the initiative process complain that ballot measure titles are confusing and often misleading. In every initiative state except Washington, initiative proponents either write or exert considerable control over the content of summaries that appear on their petitions and the official ballot. Clearly, this arrangement invites deception since proponents will want to portray their measure in the best light possible. In Colorado, a drafting board prepares a caption and summary with input from the proponent. Public hearings are held. Any registered voter may challenge the ballot title. Colorado's initiative law directs the title setting board, consisting of the secretary of state, the attorney general, and the director of the Office of Legislative Legal Services, to consider the potential public confusion caused by misleading titles and to avoid titles in which the general understanding of the effect of a "yes" or "no" vote will be unclear. In other words, Colorado's initiative summary and title setting laws are generally quite fair and help ensure an accurate ballot title. The Colorado ballot title setting model is worth exporting to other initiative states.

These are but some of the changes reform advocates should consider to improve and strengthen the ballot measure process. None of them try to remove money from the process (since any such action would probably be deemed immediately unconstitutional). Instead, these reforms attempt to make it easier for citizens to initiate and understand direct legislation.

CONCLUSION

The initiative process turned 100 in 1998 with the centennial anniversary of the adoption of the initiative process initiative in South Dakota. While the process remains very popular, polling suggests that voters support

Nelson

substantial reforms including mandatory precirculation judicial review and reducing the role of money in initiative campaigns (Initiative and Referendum Institute 1998: "National Opinion Survey Conducted on Behalf of the Initiative and Referendum Institute," posted at www.iandrinstitute.org. See "I & R Resources," polling). With the Florida election experience still fresh in the minds of most Americans, reformers should seize this opportunity to press for a whole range of democratic reforms outlined in this collection. Given its increasing use and broad influence, the tools of direct democracy seem just as worthy of our attention as democratic reformers.

12

The Debate Gerrymander and America's Electoral-Industrial Complex

JAMIN RASKIN

> If there is any fixed star in our constitutional constellation, it is that no official, high or petty, can prescribe what shall be orthodox in politics.
>
> —Supreme Court Justice Robert Houghwout Jackson,
> *West Virginia State Board of Education v. Barnette* (1943)

Democracy requires debate. Abraham Lincoln, who spoke poetically of "government of the people, by the people, and for the people," showed us that debate is the lifeblood of democratic government and politics. As a candidate for U.S. Senate in Illinois in 1858 from a newly emerging third party, he met Democrat Stephen Douglas in eight raucous debates before active audiences of partisans who cheered and jeered the candidates (Holzer 1993). The fact that Lincoln lost the election to Douglas did not render his campaign futile or the debates a waste of the public's time. On the contrary, Lincoln captured the White House two years later based on his extraordinary debate performance and the pro-Union, delicately anti-slavery philosophy he espoused while clashing with Douglas.

If the conditions of debate are any measure of the health and vitality of democracy, it is a signal of the erosion of American democracy that debates today are closed spectacles carefully scripted by the state or major-party elites and private corporations. Because of the pervasive practice of self-appointed governmental and corporate debate managers excluding third-party, independent, and maverick candidates from candidate debates, the principal function of debates is neither to educate the public on how politics works nor to force confrontations on major issues of the day but rather to establish the collusive "two-party system" as America's official political ideology. When compared to debate practices in almost every other democratic nation on earth (such as Mexico where all six presidential candidates debated in 2000), our incumbent "two-party system" produces one of the least democratic and most lethargic electoral discourses on earth.

The pervasive practice of what I call "debate gerrymandering" has been sanctioned by the operation of both law and naked power. In *Arkansas Educational Television Commission v. Forbes*, 118 S. Ct. 1633 (1998), the Supreme Court upheld the state of Arkansas's exclusion, in 1992, of Ralph Forbes, a conservative independent congressional candidate, from a televised debate between his Democratic and Republican rivals on the state-run and taxpayer-financed cable TV channel. The state's decision to close its debate to one candidate in a three-way race not only trampled his free speech rights and effectively endorsed his opponents before the public but also sharply restricted the scope of political discussion. This intervention almost certainly changed the photo-finish outcome of the race and drained democratic legitimacy from the election.

The majority decision in *Forbes* reflected the Supreme Court's embrace of the "two-party system" and the integration of plutocracy and the dubious science of polling into constitutional law. The high court's indulgence of Arkansas's self-fulfilling prophecy about Forbes's "viability" kept it from seeing how the state's decision to sponsor debates for two entrenched parties violated fundamental free speech and Equal Protection values. Government has no rightful power to predict winners and losers in a democratic election, pasting merit badges or scarlet letters on candidates, much less to award everyone's tax dollars and television air time to two candidates against their opponents. Government manipulation of public debate is an assault on the very idea of democratic elections and free public discourse. Moreover, under the Qualifications Clause, a state government has no power to interfere substantively with the people's election of their own representatives to the United States Congress.

The Supreme Court's defense of government debate gerrymandering in congressional elections has emboldened the Commission on Presidential Debates (CPD) to continue on its mission of marginalizing third-party presidential candidates with inscrutable judgments about their "viability." The CPD was launched in 1987 by the Democratic and Republican National Committees as an explicitly "bipartisan" private organization to sponsor "general election presidential and vice-presidential debates . . . by the national Republican and Democratic Committees between their respective nominees" (Raskin 1999). Cochaired by Frank Fahrenkopf Jr. and Paul Kirk Jr., the former chairmen of the RNC and DNC, the CPD is funded to the tune of millions of dollars a year by large private corporations like Philip Morris, RJ Reynolds, Dow Chemical, and Anheuser-Busch, which in 2000 ponied up $550,000 and won the right to sponsor the final Bush–Gore debate in the hometown of its corporate headquarters, St. Louis, Missouri.

In a rational world, televised debates run by two political parties for their own benefit and financed by corporate America would be seen to violate the Federal Election Campaign Act (FECA), which prohibits corporate contributions and spending in federal campaigns. When corporations promote the Republican and Democratic presidential candidates by paying for four 90-minute debates between them and exclude their opponents, these debates become illegal corporate contributions. The purpose of FECA is to build a wall of separation between private corporations and public elections, but here the corporations get to finance and promote their favored candidates through gerrymandered debates.

When the CPD locked Reform Party candidate Ross Perot out of its 1996 debate on the grounds that, under its *nonexhaustive* eleven-part viability test, he had no "realistic chance" to win, it provoked complaints to the Federal Election Commission (FEC). A detailed complaint by Perot '96 nearly produced a watershed victory for multiparty democracy when the FEC's General Counsel in 1998 recommended to the FEC that it fine the Commission on Presidential Debates for its unlawful corporate-subsidized debate exclusion and for operating as an unregistered and illegal political committee on behalf of the major parties. But the CPD was able to fall back on the parallel bipartisan lock-up of the FEC—three Republican commissioners and three Democratic commissioners, who promptly voted to reject the findings and recommendations of their own General Counsel.

Reeling from its close brush with justice and the widespread criticism of its absurd viability test, the CPD in 2000 introduced a new but equally arbitrary rule that invited only those presidential candidates to debate who stood at 15 percent in public opinion polls. This new rule *tripled* the federal statutory requirement of 5 percent in the popular vote to qualify for federal funding in presidential elections. It worked effectively to exclude the Green Party's presidential nominee Ralph Nader, who was hovering between 6 percent and 9 percent in the polls. When Nader appeared at the first presidential debate in Boston with a ticket to join the audience given to him by a Boston University student, the CPD dispatched a team of security officers and state policemen to block his path, making its vision of robust political debate perfectly clear.

To break the cycle of bipartisan debate gerrymandering in 2004, we need to confront the intellectually lazy claims about America's "two-party system" and find a way to usher in debates based on fair and viewpoint-neutral participation criteria. Though some might argue for reforming the CPD, I believe our presidential debates require the creation of an independent people's debate commission outside the control of any political parties or corporations. The challenge is for America's civil society organizations—the League of Women Voters (which was ousted by the CPD), unions, universities, and foundations—to stand up and take back our presidential elections from what can only be described as America's new electoral-industrial complex. Otherwise we will be like the helpless citizens Simon and Garfunkel sang about in "Mrs. Robinson" who were "sitting on a sofa on a Sunday afternoon, going to the candidates' debate. Laugh about it, shout about it: When you've got to choose, every way you look at it you lose."

THE RISE OF A NONPUBLIC POLITICAL FORUM: THE OUTRAGEOUS CASE OF *FORBES v. AETN*

America has no two-party system in a constitutional sense. The Constitution does not mention political parties, much less a two-party system, much less two specific parties. The First Amendment gives citizens the right to speak and participate in politics without regard to ideology. Equal Protection forbids interference with the right to vote and discrimination against minority political groups. Any formal effort to entrench two particular parties, in essence to give them a kind of title of nobility against their competitors, violates basic constitutional values.

It is one thing to predict, as a political science hypothesis, that in a representative democracy with winner-take-all elections, the electorate will over time divide into two political camps. This empirical claim may or may not be true but it is very different from a normative constitutional claim that the two leading parties today should be able to confer upon themselves public advantages to entrench themselves. By analogy, it is one thing to observe that, in an empirical sense that the United States is a majority-Christian nation and quite another to conclude that the government may establish Christianity as the official religion of the nation. We should treat the First Amendment and Equal Protection as erecting an anti-Establishment principle in the field of political expression and electoral competition. This empirical claim may or may not be true but it is very different from a normative constitutional claim that the two leading parties are entitled to confer upon themselves selective public advantages.

To respect the sovereignty of the people, the government must be scrupulously careful not to endorse one or two political parties against all others by tampering with the process of political debate. It must remain neutral and stand aside when the people are forming their political will. Indeed, we can define democracy as the system in which the government is not permitted to regulate or manipulate the sovereignty of the people over the continuing reconstitution of their political leadership. Rather, democracy requires free and open deliberation. In elections, the government must serve as an umpire or referee by enforcing agreed-upon rules but never interfering with the course of play itself by pre-judging the outcome.

In the *Forbes* case, the state of Arkansas departed from a position of electoral neutrality. A dogged and passionate right-wing candidate, Forbes had irritated the Arkansas Republican establishment for years because his maverick campaigns, built on antichoice, antitax, anti-affirmative action hard-right Christian rhetoric, struck a chord with conservatives. In 1990, he ran for lieutenant governor and captured 46.8 percent of the vote in a three-way primary race for the Republican Party nomination, defeating two rivals, only to lose in the runoff against a candidate backed by the party Establishment. But in the first round Forbes captured a majority of the vote in fifteen of the sixteen counties in his home congressional district. He had become a force to be reckoned with, and when the U.S. House seat in the Third District opened up in 1992, he declared for Congress as an independent. He knocked on doors through the summer, sweating his way across the rural district to collect more than 6,000 signatures, earning a ballot position next to Republican Tim Hutchison and Democrat John Van Winkle.

In the sprawling mountains of Arkansas, television plays a key role in elections. So it was significant when AETN, the state agency operating five public TV stations, decided to sponsor televised debates in Arkansas's four House districts. There were nine U.S. House candidates in 1992: four Democrats, four Republicans, and one Independent—namely, Forbes. AETN invited all but Forbes to debate. He only found out about the debate by accident from AETN's promotional newspaper ads with photographs of his rivals under the headline: "Do you know your candidates?" When Forbes asked to be included, AETN said it was going to "stick with the major candidates" instead. On the evening of the debate, Forbes showed up but was turned away after being told the station would rather show "reruns of St. Elsewhere" than include him.

Forbes sued *pro se*. He gave his First Amendment case the irresistible caption *Forbes v. The Arrogant Orwellian Bureaucrats of the AETN; The Crooked Lying Politicians; and The Special Interests*. He won in the Eighth Circuit Court of Appeals, where Chief Judge Richard Arnold found for the court that the televised debate was a "limited public forum," which means public property opened up by the government for specific speech purposes. In such a forum, a speaker may not be excluded unless the government shows a compelling reason (*Forbes v. Arkansas Educational Television Commission*, 522 U.S. 666 [1998]). As a balloted candidate, Forbes naturally belonged to the class of speakers invited to the forum and Arkansas lacked compelling reason to exclude him. The "government cannot, simply by its own ipse dixit, define a class of speakers so as to exclude a person who would naturally be expected to be a member of the class on no basis other than party affiliation" (*Forbes v. Arkansas Educational Television Commission* 522 U.S. 666 [1998]). AETN's final rationale for excluding Forbes—its standardless judgment about his "viability"—violated the First Amendment because his political viability was a "judgment to be made by the people of the Third Congressional District, not by officials of the government in charge of channels of communication." AETN appealed to the Supreme Court, urging it to treat its debate not as a limited public forum but as a form of private journalism. On this theory, AETN did nothing more unlawful than omit mention of Forbes from a private news report about the campaign.

By a vote of 6–3, the Supreme Court reversed the Eighth Circuit and upheld AETN's closed debate. Writing for the majority, Justice Anthony Kennedy started sensibly by rejecting AETN's extreme claim that the First Amendment should protect the government channel against the citizen rather than vice versa. The First Amendment must apply when government media sponsor candidate debates, Justice Kennedy wrote, because such debates are designed as "a forum for political speech by candidates" and "candidate debates are of exceptional significance in the electoral process" (*Forbes v. Arkansas*, 523 U.S. at 676 [1998]). At this point, Forbes's case should have been clinched because the First Amendment forbids government to practice "viewpoint discrimination" in any kind of public forum. To silence political candidates on the grounds that they are not "viable"—that is, they are likely to lose—is plainly to discriminate against them based on their (allegedly) unpopular viewpoints.

But Justice Kennedy did not see things this way. He rejected the Eighth Circuit's sound conclusion that the debate was a limited public forum. Squinting hard, he wrote that AETN "did not make its debate generally available to candidates for Arkansas' Third Congressional District seat," but rather "reserved eligibility for participation in the debate to candidates for the Third Congressional District seat (as opposed to some other seat). At that point . . . [AETN] made candidate-by-candidate determinations as to which of the eligible candidates would participate in the debate. . . . Thus, the debate was a nonpublic forum" (*Arkansas Educational Television Commission v. Forbes*, 523 U.S. 666, 680 [1998]).

A "nonpublic forum"—an amazing oxymoron—is one to which government opens only to *certain* people for specific purposes. In a nonpublic forum, a government can make any "reasonable" exclusions as long as they are not viewpoint-based. But in fact, AETN did not "reserve eligibility for participation in the debate to candidates for the Third Congressional District seat." It simply invited two of the candidates and rejected the third based on the fact that he was neither Democrat nor Republican. The freewheeling "candidate-by-candidate determination" method that

Justice Kennedy invokes as proof that the debate was a nonpublic forum was *itself* the essential violation of Forbes's First Amendment rights. For there were no viewpoint-neutral standards used in making these selections: not whether the candidates were balloted, not whether they had run for office before or how well they performed. Had there been a standard based on past electoral performance (itself dubious), Forbes would have made the grade, having drawn more than 46 percent of the statewide vote in his run for attorney general in the Republican primaries just two years before. But it was, of course, critical to the partisan selection process that no actual standards be defined.

Having accepted the potential legitimacy of candidate-by-candidate exclusions, Justice Kennedy proceeded to present a dangerously weakened version of the viewpoint-neutrality doctrine by swallowing the logic of "viability" without even a second look. He simply cited, in conclusory fashion, the trial jury's finding that Forbes's exclusion was not based on "objections or opposition to his views," and quoted approvingly AETN's executive director, who testified Forbes's views had "absolutely" no role in the decision to exclude him from the debate. She further testified Forbes was excluded because (1) "the Arkansas voters did not consider him a serious candidate"; (2) "the news organizations also did not consider him a serious candidate"; (3) "the Associated Press and a national election result reporting service did not plan to run his name in results on election night"; (4) Forbes "apparently had little, if any financial support, failing to report campaign finances to the Secretary of state's office or to the Federal Election Commission"; and (5) "there [was] no 'Forbes for Congress' campaign headquarters other than his house." It is, in short, beyond dispute that Forbes was excluded not because of his viewpoint but because he had generated no appreciable public interest (*Arkansas Educational Television Commission v. Forbes*, 523 U.S. 666, 682 [1998]).

This argument, framed to make Forbes seem ridiculous, is a house of cards that collapses at the slightest touch. Not only are all of the conclusions about how the voters and the media regarded Forbes rank speculation, but they are wholly irrelevant. The rights of candidates and speakers in public fora do not depend on their being backed by any specific percentage of the population or the press pool or on having raised this or that amount of money. Forbes's modest fund-raising, itself more than the fund-raising by two Republican congressional candidates in Arkansas who were invited to debate, cannot constitutionally be used against him, which is why the Court has invalidated poll taxes and high candidate filing fees, efforts to institutionalize a rule of wealth in politics. As for the fact that Forbes's headquarters was in his house, the same was true of John F. Kennedy's presidential run in 1960 where his home in Hyannisport was the campaign headquarters.

Justice Kennedy misunderstood the doctrine of viewpoint discrimination. The trial jury's factual finding that Forbes's exclusion was not based on "objections or opposition to his views" cannot control the legal question of whether his exclusion was viewpoint-based. The test of First Amendment viewpoint neutrality is an *objective* test that focuses on the nature of a governmental classification that treats two classes of speakers differently. It is not a *subjective* test that focuses on the intentions or motivations of specific government actors in suppressing someone's speech. Subjective animus may be *evidence* of objective viewpoint discrimination, and often is, but it is not a necessary factual predicate in order for it to exist as a matter of law.

In *Rosenberger v. Rectors and Visitors of University of Virginia*, 515 U.S. 819, 831–32 (1995), a decision Justice Kennedy himself wrote, the Court struck down the University of Virginia's practice of reimbursing the publishing costs of all student-run periodicals except those religiously identified. Although there was no allegation of animosity toward religious students in the case, the Court found that religiously motivated expression provided a distinctive viewpoint that could not be blocked out from public consideration. The university bore no malice toward religion, but when it declined to give the same speech privileges to religious student publications as it did to the secular ones, the Court struck its policy as viewpoint-discriminatory.

The whole purpose and effect of excluding Forbes's appearance as a candidate was to block out presentation of a political viewpoint deemed unpopular by a candidate deemed unpopular. This is essentially viewpoint discrimination. The fact that AETN would also have excluded unpopular candidates of the left does not rescue the policy. As Justice Kennedy wrote in *Rosenberger*: "The dissent's declaration that debate is not skewed so long as multiple voices are silenced is simply wrong; the debate is skewed in multiple ways."

THE ELECTORAL-INDUSTRIAL COMPLEX: HOW THE COMMISSION ON PRESIDENTIAL DEBATES MANIPULATES PRESIDENTIAL ELECTIONS

In presidential elections, the gatekeeper is not an unaccountable bureaucracy but an unaccountable private corporation: the Commission on Presidential Debates (CPD). Set up by the DNC and the RNC in 1987, funded lavishly by large corporations, its five Democratic commissioners and five Republicans operate aggressively in the interests of the two parties.

In 1988, when the CPD displaced the League of Women Voters and took over the George Bush–Michael Dukakis debates, the League of Women

Voters boycotted the event. "The League of Women Voters is withdrawing its sponsorship of the presidential debates scheduled for mid-October because the demands of the two campaign organizations would perpetrate a fraud on the American people," League President Nancy M. Newman told the press on October 3, 1998. "It has become clear to us that the candidates' organizations aim to add debate to their list of campaign-trail charades devoid of substance, spontaneity and having to answer tough questions. The League has no intention of becoming an accessory to the hoodwinking of the American Public" (Raskin 1999).

In 1992, the CPD instinctively sought to exclude Ross Perot from the debate between President Bush and Bill Clinton. But the Bush campaign pushed for Perot, and the Clinton campaign agreed. Ironically, Perot was invited not because the CPD thought it was right but because both candidates ultimately thought it would be to their advantage. (It turned out Clinton, not Bush, was right about that.) Having had this chance to debate Bush and Clinton in 1992, Perot won a smashing 19 percent of the popular vote and helped increase turnout by a remarkable 12 million votes. When he ran again in 1996 he not only had much broader name recognition and ballot status in fifty states and the District of Columbia but also had been given $30 million in public funding based on his 1996 performance. Everyone simply assumed that the CPD would have to permit him to debate again.

But the CPD had other plans. It solemnly, and unlawfully, announced that Clinton and Dole would be invited because they were "the respective nominees of the two major parties." As for Perot, the CPD consulted a mushy eleven-factor test to conclude unanimously that Perot was not "electable" and therefore ineligible to debate. The commissioners reported that among the factors they considered were "the professional opinions of the Washington bureau chiefs of major newspapers, news magazines, and broadcast networks"; "the opinions of a comparable group of professional campaign managers and pollsters not then employed by candidates under consideration"; "published views of prominent political commentators"; and "the findings of significant public opinion polls conducted by national polling and news organizations" (Raskin 1999).

Perot went to federal court in the District of Columbia to enjoin the debates, complaining that the CPD's decision-making process was arbitrary and violated the FEC's rules requiring debate sponsors to use only "preestablished objective criteria" in determining which candidates may participate and forbidding them to "use nomination by a particular party" as "the sole objective criterion" (Raskin 1999). Yet, citing the Federal Election Campaign Act's requirement that injured parties go to the FEC first to exhaust their administrative remedies, the federal courts refused to enjoin the CPD's exclusionary debates. Judge Hogan recognized the candidate's "frustration" and "perhaps unfairness in the process" but opined that "the complaint should be with Congress and the statutory framework established for the FEC to operate" (*Perot 96 v. Federal Election Commission*, 97 F. 3d 553 [D.C. Cir. 1996]).

Ironically, the real decision to exclude Perot in 1996—as to include him in 1992—was a strategic one made secretly by his rivals. The published proceedings of a postelection conference at the Harvard Kennedy School's Institute of Politics tell the whole story. George Stephanopoulos, then senior adviser to the president, said in reference to the Dole–Kemp campaign's bargaining position when the two parties negotiated the debates: "They didn't have leverage going into the negotiations. They were behind, they needed to make sure Perot wasn't in it. As long as we would agree to Perot not being in it we would get everything else we wanted going in. We got our time frame, we got our length, we got our moderator" (Harvard University Institute of Politics 1997, 171). Tony Fabrizio, the Dole/Kemp pollster, followed up with: "and the fact of the matter is, you got the number of dates." He added later: "George made very good observations about the positions we walked into the negotiations" (Harvard University Institute of Politics 1997, 171). Stephanopoulos even pointed out that the Democrats themselves had no reason to want Perot in the debate: "we didn't want [people] to pay attention. The debates were a metaphor for the campaign. We wanted the debates to be a nonevent" (Harvard University Institute of Politics 1997, 162).

The CPD did not act as an impartial debate sponsor but as a "political committee" that cut deals with Democrats and Republicans. The CPD's secret agreement to exclude Perot turned the 1996 debates into millions of dollars of free television time purchased for the Clinton and Dole campaigns by the CPD's commercial sponsors. The CPD's corporate benefactors, like Philip Morris, Anheuser-Busch, Dun & Bradstreet, and Lucent Technologies, had found one more giant loophole for funneling money to the Democrats and Republicans.

Nothing was heard from the FEC until 1998, long after the election was over, but the first official reaction was nothing short of astonishing. Lawrence Noble, the general counsel, issued a thirty-seven-page report agreeing with Perot '96 that there was "reason to believe" that the corporate contributions to the CPD were illegal and that the CPD itself was acting as an unregistered and illegal "political committee." He proposed an investigation and series of subpoenas to determine what exactly took place when the CPD voted to exclude Perot by bending to the wishes of the Clinton and Dole campaigns.

True to form, however, when Noble gave his report to the all-Democrat and Republican commissioners, they voted unanimously to override his analysis and recommendations. They found "no reason to believe" that the CPD had "violated the law by sponsoring the 1996 presidential debates or by failing to register and report as a political committee" (FEC Statement of Reasons MURs 4481 and 4473, February 24, 1998). The FEC's statement was classic Doublespeak: "The pool of experts used by CPD consisted of top level academics and other professionals experienced in evaluating and assessing political candidates. By basing its evaluation of candidates upon the judgment of these experts, CPD took an objective approach in determining candidate viability" (FEC Statement of Reasons MURs 4481 and 4473, February 24, 1998). Without any further analysis, the FEC found that "viability" itself is an objective criterion for selecting debate participants, that poll results are also valid, and that the amount of money a candidate has available to him or her "is certainly an objective factor which can be legitimately used by a sponsoring organization" (FEC Statement of Reasons MURs 4481 and 4473, February 24, 1998). There the matter has rested.

THE 2000 PRESIDENTIAL ELECTION AND
THE ANHEUSER-BUSCH–GORE DEBATES

Although the bipartisan CPD was rescued in the nick of time by the bipartisan FEC in 1996, the CPD's managers realized that their soggy eleven-part test gave the game away and invited political trouble. So on January 6, 2000, the CPD released a new standard that required presidential candidates to have "a level of support of at least 15% of the national electorate as determined by five selected national public opinion polling organizations, using the average of those organizations' most recent publicly-reported results at the time of determination" (CPD Web site, www. debates.org). The new standard was undoubtedly easier to understand, but no less arbitrary or unfair. The use of preference polling for these purposes is deeply suspect since it asks a basically irrelevant question: Who do you support before the debate has taken place? The relevant issue is: Who would you like to see debate in order to make up your mind as to whom to vote for? Ironically, the American people, for whom the CPD claims to speak, reject the 15 percent preference rule. Some 51 percent of the people told the NBC News and Wall Street Journal poll that they believed third-party candidates should *not* have to meet the CPD's 15 percent requirement (Appleseed Project on Electoral Reform 2000).

But if the CPD was determined to use polling, it could defensibly have chosen 5 percent as the level of necessary support since that is the national electoral showing a presidential candidate must have in the popular vote in order to have his party qualify for public financing in the next election.

Yet the CPD tripled this federal statutory figure in a way certain to reduce the chances of third parties qualifying. The 15 percent figure raises the bar absurdly high. A candidate who stands at a disqualifying 14 percent in the polls commands the allegiance of more than 17 million voters, who are structurally disregarded by the debate managers.

In 2000, the major third-party candidate was the Green Party nominee Ralph Nader, who ran a populist campaign focused on the dangers of excessive corporate power. Nader would have clearly benefited from debating Bush and Gore, but he hovered between 6 percent and 9 percent in the polls in the summer and fall and thus fell short of the CPD's threshold. In Boston, after appearing at a raucous rally at Harvard Law School, Nader showed up at the first debate at the University of Massachusetts but was met by a security force that threatened him with arrest if he did not leave the premises. Thousands of people protested his exclusion, and Nader might have blown the doors off the system of debate exclusion by submitting to arrest, but it was not to be. Although his campaign focused on the closed debates as a metaphor for corporate-controlled democracy, the lack of vivid images of *democracy under arrest* undercut Nader's ability to galvanize public sentiment. He never recovered from the defeat of being left standing out in the cold. In federal court in Boston, Nader attacked the FEC's rule authorizing private corporations to sponsor debates as outside of its granted authority under the Federal Election Campaign Act. But the Court's decision in *Forbes* and the FEC's rejection of the Perot suit in 1996 had set the table and the First Circuit Court of Appeals easily upheld the system of debate gerrymandering.

WHAT'S WRONG WITH DEBATE GERRYMANDERING? THE "VIABILITY" FALLACY

Whether it is of a "public" or "private" character, debate gerrymandering depends on two essential arguments. The first, purportedly self-evident, is that only "viable" candidates should be allowed to debate and the second is that, without the viability screen, we would suffer an impossible "cacophony" of political voices rendering debates all sound and fury. Both of these arguments are demonstrably specious and deeply at odds with our constitutional values.

Viability means that the candidate is perceived to be popular and a good prospect for winning; nonviability means the candidate is unpopular and unlikely to win. But the First Amendment protects equally the political speech of *popular* citizens with mainstream views and *unpopular* citizens with minority views. In *Texas v. Johnson*, the Supreme Court upheld the right of political outsiders to burn the American flag. The majority explained, "If there is a bedrock principle underlying the First Amendment, it is that the government may not prohibit the expression of an idea simply because society finds the idea itself offensive or disagreeable" (*Texas v. Johnson*, 491 U.S. 397, 414 [1989]).

A state-controlled "viability" screen violates the Qualifications Clause, the First Amendment, and Equal Protection. In our democracy, state government has no rightful power to predict winners or losers in an election, especially a federal one, much less publicize its predictions to voters and selectively favor chosen candidates with free television time. If the government cannot add the words "abandoned term limits pledge" or "not viable" or "likely winner" next to candidates' names on the ballot, it should not be able to send such messages during the campaign.

The citizenry must decide which candidates are "electable" by *electing them* and the government's role is to guarantee fair process and secure counting of the ballots. If the people, through their government, decide that a publicly sponsored debate is necessary for enlightenment of the electorate, then the government must find an equal place for *all* ballot-qualified candidates. By picking and choosing "viable" candidates, the government usurps the role of the electorate. Indeed, it is likely that, if Forbes had been invited to the debate the AETN held, his participation would have changed the outcome of the race. The razor-thin Republican victor, Tim Hutchinson, received 125,295 votes or 50.2 percent of the total, compared to Democrat John VanWinkle, who received 117,775, or 47.2 percent (all numbers come from *Statistics of the Presidential and Congressional Election of November 3, 1992*, Office of Clerk, U.S. House of Representatives, www.clerkweb.house.gov/elections/1992/92stat.htm). Meanwhile, Forbes captured 6,329 votes, or 2.5 percent. If Forbes, a strong conservative with proven vote-getting power, had been allowed to debate and had converted just one out of every fifteen of Hutchinson's eventual voters, the election would have gone to the Democrat Van Winkle. The government's closed debate probably elected Congressman Hutchison.

The "viability" test is clearly a pretext for excluding third-party and independent candidates because it is never applied to Democrats or Republicans, no matter how novice or incompetent they are. In Arkansas in 1992, the AETN excluded Forbes but invited the thirty-one-year-old Republican candidate in the neighboring First Congressional District, one of the most Democratic districts in the country that had not elected a Republican since 1868, despite the fact that he had never collected a single vote and was outspent 11–1. In the very similar Second District, the AETN invited a hapless Republican who raised $4,000 less than Forbes did.

Even if they were fair-minded, government and corporate debate managers are not clairvoyant. They cannot foretell who is going to win: the whole point of campaigns is to change public opinion. Third-party candidates *can* win, especially if given the chance to debate. Vermont gives us the refreshing examples of an independent House member, socialist Bernie Sanders, and an independent senator, Jim Jeffords, elected as a Republican but likely to change his party affiliation. Consider also the dramatic example of Minnesota Governor Jesse Ventura. A giant bald former all-pro wrestler derided as frivolous and unelectable, Ventura challenged the two-party system as the Reform candidate in 1998. On September 20, he was at 10 percent in the polls and thus would have been excluded from the debates had the CPD been running things. But he was invited to participate in every debate. On October 18, after the debates began, he was up to 21 percent in the polls, and by October 30 his numbers had risen to 27 percent (Appleseed Citizens Task Force 2000). On Election Day he won and has since emphasized he could not have won had he been excluded from the debates.

AETN's judgment that Forbes was not viable was pure guesswork, but the CPD relies on polling, which seems superficially scientific. Polls fluctuate madly: at best, they capture the present moment but tell us nothing reliable about the future. If AETN had sponsored a debate for candidates in the U.S. Senate Democratic primary in Wisconsin in 1992, it would have excluded the eventual winner of the election, Russ Feingold, because a major poll showed him at 10 percent of the vote compared to 42 percent for Congressman Jim Moody and 40 percent for businessman Joe Checota. Yet Feingold went on to overcome his rivals *less than three weeks after this poll was taken*, collecting 69 percent of the vote to 14 percent each for Moody and Checota. Feingold then went on to defeat incumbent Republican Senator Bob Kasten in the general election. No mainstream pollster ever predicted Governor Ventura's victory because polling vastly understates first-time and independent voters. In general, polling response rates have fallen dramatically, to 20 percent in some cases.

Besides, an election campaign is more than a mechanical contest over who will take office when the election is over. It is democracy's way of promoting robust political debate among citizens and allowing candidates and parties to inject new ideas and messages into popular discussion in order to influence the public agenda. Candidates often run to establish legitimacy for an alternative political position and to position themselves for a future race. Sometimes a defeat can propel a candidate's political career, such as was the case not only with Abraham Lincoln but with Bill Clinton, who actually lost his first race for the House in Arkansas's Third Congressional District in 1974, but then went on to be elected attorney general of Arkansas two years later. Many politicians have faced multiple losses before finding success with the voters. For example, Robert Casey "made a second career out of running for governor" in Pennsylvania, where over the course of twenty years from 1966 to 1986, he continuously ran and lost for the Democratic nomination before finally winning in 1986. He narrowly won in the general election, and was reelected to a second term in 1990 with 68 percent of the vote. Another Pennsylvania politician, Arlen Specter, waged an unsuccessful bid for mayor in 1967, lost his reelection campaign for district attorney of Philadelphia, and piled up back-to-back losses in the 1976 Senate primary and the 1978 gubernatorial primary before succeeding in his bid for Senate in 1980.

Given the declining party allegiance in modern American politics, and the increased interest in new parties and independent candidacies, third-party candidates today can affect electoral outcomes decisively, as shown by Ralph Nader's potent and extremely controversial impact on the 2000 presidential election. Debate exclusion is never a neutral journalistic act, as AETN would have it, or a neutral public policy judgment, as the CPD suggests, but an aggressive interference with the course and outcome of a political campaign.

THE CACOPHONY FALLACY

The only serious argument made for exclusionary debates is that if government debate sponsors are not allowed broad discretion to pick and choose participating candidates, they will be "faced with the prospect of cacophony," as Justice Kennedy put it, and "might choose not to air candidates' views at all. . . . In this circumstance, a [g]overnment-enforced right of access inescapably dampens the vigor and limits the variety of public debate" (*Forbes v. Arkansas* 1998). Justice Kennedy's conclusion incorporated AETN's argument before the Court that removing the viability filter will cause huge numbers of candidates to flood debates and "public broadcasters would abandon the effort" (*Forbes v. Arkansas* 1998).

There is not even the slightest empirical basis for saying that opening up debates to all balloted candidates will produce "cacophony." Over the past fifty years, in the last twenty-five general elections for the U.S. House of Representatives, there have been on average fewer than one independent or minor-party candidate running in each of America's 435 congressional districts. The idea that government debate sponsors could not handle nonmajor-party candidates is preposterous. The 1992 House races in Arkansas illustrate the national pattern. In the state's four congressional districts, Ralph Forbes was the *only* independent or minor-party candidate running.

Given that the incumbent reelection rate usually floats above 90 percent, it is difficult to get a *second* candidate to run in most districts. Witness, for instance, the weak major-party challengers in districts neighboring

Forbes's. With our excessively stringent ballot access laws, built-in incumbent advantages, and money-drenched elections, third-party and independent candidates are already discouraged to the point of despair. Can the wild suggestion that they will overwhelm government-run fora also be used to prevent them from debating with the other candidates?

The idea that multicandidate debates would dissolve into white noise contradicts our experience with nationally televised debates in Democratic and Republican presidential *primaries* that regularly feature many more than two candidates. For example, in the 1992 presidential primary season, there was a Democratic primary debate in St. Louis with Bob Kerrey, Jerry Brown, Bill Clinton, Tom Harkin, Paul Tsongas, and Douglas Wilder. In the 1988 season, six Republicans squared off in New Hampshire, including George Bush, Pete du Pont IV, Alexander Haig Jr., Bob Dole, Pat Robertson, and Jack Kemp. In recent years, we have been treated to large televised party primary debates that include long shots like Morry Taylor and Alan Keyes. No one was injured during any of these debates, no chairs were thrown. Far from creating a *cacophony*, they protected *democracy*.

Even if we accept the premise that government debate sponsors will be overrun, the whole concept that government can restrict the speech rights of citizens in order to prevent "cacophony" offends well-accepted First Amendment norms. In *Cohen v. California*, 403 U.S. 15, 24 (1971), the Supreme Court showed better perspective on the democratic necessity of multiple voices: "[The] constitutional right of free expression is powerful medicine in a society as diverse and populous as ours. It is designed and intended to remove governmental restraints from the arena of public discussion, putting the decision as to what views shall be voiced largely into the hands of each of us, in the hope that use of such freedom will ultimately produce a more capable citizenry and more perfect polity and in the belief that no other approach would comport with the premise of individual dignity and choice upon which our political system rests."

The unproven suggestion by AETN in *Forbes* that major-party candidates will pull out of debates if minor-party candidates are allowed to participate is pernicious. To exclude some candidates because their presence may cause others not to come is, in effect, to impose a prior restraint on their speech based on a heckler's veto. It is like saying public schools should not desegregate because white families may withdraw; that result would be unfortunate, but it would be *their* choice. It is wrong to deny people equal rights because it might cause others to decline to exercise theirs.

If cacophony were to become a real and compelling interest, there would obviously be an alternative much less restrictive than simply banishing all candidates but two. A debate sponsor should decide in advance how many candidates the voters can tolerate without losing focus: is it four? Five? Six? What is the evidence that this is the point at which the public loses attention? In any event, it must be a number the sponsor cannot alter for the purposes of major-party primary debates. If there are more candidates than places, the debate sponsor should add a second debate and divide the candidates up between the two. If time is so scarce that there is only time for a single debate and the judgment is made that only four candidates can participate, then names should be drawn out of a hat and each candidate given an equal chance to be included. This is surely the result suggested by the Supreme Court in *Rosenberger v. University of Virginia*, where it stated that "government cannot justify viewpoint discrimination among private speakers on the economic fact of scarcity" and declared it "incumbent on the State, of course, to ration or allocate the scarce resources on some acceptable neutral principle" (515 U.S. 819, 835 [1995]).

Of course, if the Democratic and Republican candidates in the Third District wanted to debate without Forbes being present, they had every First Amendment right to arrange a private meeting of their own. But, as a government actor, AETN had no right to set up and pay for a private debate between them and exclude Forbes, who met every requirement of candidate seriousness set by Arkansas and had a right to be treated as an equal in the government's forum. Similarly, in the case of presidential elections, the Democratic and Republican nominees have every right in the world to meet each other in a debate paid for jointly by their presidential campaigns and exclude all other candidates. But they cannot concoct an allegedly "nonpartisan" private corporation called the Commission on Presidential Debates to raise tens of millions of dollars from private corporations to send the message to the American people that these two are the official and legitimate candidates and all others frivolous and "unelectable."

2004 AND BEYOND: WHAT IS TO BE DONE?

We need America's much-praised but underutilized "civil society" to recapture presidential debates and others from the electoral-industrial complex. The League of Women Voters, the organization so humiliated by the CPD's 1988 takeover, should challenge the CPD's continued "hoodwinking" of the American people. It should be joined by uncorrupted parts of the nonprofit sector, universities, labor unions, and other popular associations. Currently, a Citizens' Debate Commission is being organized by www.ReclaimDemocracy.org, headquartered in Boulder, Colorado. Its efforts to wake up civil society should be endorsed—but need far broader and deeper support.

What form should fair debates take? In the spring of 2000, the Apple-seed Project on Electoral Reform convened a Citizens' Task Force on Fair Debate to study the problem of debate gerrymandering and develop plausible alternatives. The Task Force recommended that the CPD or a substitute organization extend an invitation to any presidential candidate who is constitutionally eligible and mathematically electable in the Electoral College and who registers at 5 percent in national public opinion polls or who registers a majority (50 percent or more) in polls asking eligible voters (not *likely* voters) which candidates they would like to see included in the debates. This now strikes me as a sensible standard for debates that take place after the very first one, but the first should include *all* presidential candidates on the ballot in enough states theoretically to win. In the last several elections this group would have included between four and six candidates.

The tricky question of who participates is the most prominent but certainly not the only one where we need a much broader analysis than the loyalists of the two-party system are willing to render. Who asks questions? Where should the debates be held? What format? What opportunities for public participation? The issue quickly becomes: Who decides all these things? Right now the CPD has ten commissioners selected for their loyalty to two parties. There are no independents, no Greens, no Libertarians. At least one-third of the public has no representation. A Citizens' Debate Commission could impanel from at large an old-fashioned American grand jury of twenty-three citizens chosen to deliberate these issues and invite presidential candidates to debate. They could also choose the moderators and questioners—who need not be journalists. Why not union leaders, university presidents, businesspeople, historians, artists? A truly popular and nonpartisan commission could choose the host cities and towns. Why should Anheuser-Busch have so much say about the site of our presidential debates?

If there is any hope of derailing another corporate takeover of the debates, the American people must demand a much more meaningful campaign. One of the wonderful things about the Lincoln–Douglas debates was the spirited interaction between the audience and the candidates. It remains a measure of our disempowerment today that the American people are passive spectators in our debates, consumers of a choreographed spectacle that wears "our expectations like an armored suit" in the words of REM. The Commission on Presidential Debates would gladly keep offering us a choice between "competitors" bankrolled by the same large corporations, the political equivalent of those two great Anheuser-Busch rivals, Budweiser and Bud Light.

13

The Electoral College: Constitutional Debate, Partisan Manipulation, and Reform Possibilities

JOEL LEFKOWITZ

The Executive Magistrate should be the guardian of the people . . . against the Great & the wealthy who in the course of things will necessarily compose the Legislative body. Wealth tends to corrupt the mind & to nourish its love of power, and to stimulate it to oppression. . . . The Executive therefore ought to be so constituted as to be the great protector of the Mass of the people. . . . If he is to be the Guardian of the people let him be appointed by the people.

—Gouverneur Morris at the Constitutional Convention (1787)

The Electoral College "accident waiting to happen" (Amar 1997) took place in slow motion. The difficulty in determining the vote in Florida distracted attention from the inconsistency between the popular vote and electoral vote, but the eventual result made clear that rules about how to count votes mattered more than the preferences of voters. As with impeachment, public attention returned to the intentions of the Framers of the Constitution. This chapter reviews the debate at the Constitutional Convention about how to choose a president and the partisan stacking of the Electoral College by the Republican Party in the 19th century without which George W. Bush would not have taken a majority of the electoral vote. A proposal at the convention to offer voters two choices for president sheds useful light on the controversy surrounding "over votes" and Nader votes in Florida. That proposal foreshadowed a reform now contemplated—an instant runoff election. Such an alternative would give voters the advantage that James Madison had foreseen at the Constitutional Convention: the chance to vote for the candidate they like best and to cast a second vote for a candidate more likely to win. While such a system could, with a constitutional amendment, eventually replace the entire Electoral College with a direct popular vote and instant runoff, it could also be adopted, without going through the difficult amendment process, as a method of allocating the electoral votes of some states.

THE CONSTITUTIONAL CONVENTION DEBATE

Often going around in circles, the Constitutional Convention spent months trying to decide how the United States would choose a president. The convention repeatedly approved election of the president by the Congress, but finally abandoned the idea, persuaded by James Madison, James Wilson, and Gouverneur Morris of the importance of separating the executive from the legislature. A decision by the judiciary, Madison "presumed . . . was out of the question" (July 25. All references to the Constitutional Convention debates are to Madison's notes for the dates of the cited passages, available at such sites on the World Wide Web as www.lcweb2.loc.gov/ammem/amlaw/lwfr.html). All three favored direct popular vote for the president instead. Madison asserted: "The people at large" was "the fittest in itself" to choose the president (July 19). Wilson's "opinion remained unshaken that we ought to resort to the people for the election" (July 24).

Popular vote, Morris argued, would protect the people "against the Great & the wealthy who in the course of things will necessarily compose the Legislative body. Wealth tends to corrupt the mind & to nourish its love of power, and to stimulate it to oppression. History proves this to be the spirit of the opulent. . . . The Executive therefore ought to be so constituted as to be the great protector of the Mass of the people. . . . If he is to be the Guardian of the people let him be appointed by the people" (July 19).

Elbridge Gerry, best known today through the term for partisan manipulation of electoral district maps that bears his name, replied, "The people are uninformed, and would be misled" (July 19). Gerry preferred "appointment of the Executive by Electors to be chosen by the State Executives" (July 19). In most states, Gerry's proposal would have meant that citizens would vote for state legislators, who would choose the governor, who in turn would choose electors, who then would choose the president. Gerry's fear of an "excess of democracy" (May 31) is presented as the wisdom of the Founders more often than Morris's warning against wealth as a source of corruption and oppression. However, in reviewing the objections to direct election, Madison "would only take notice of two difficulties which he admitted to have weight": disadvantage to the smaller states and to the slave states that might result from a popular vote.

"The principal objection [against] an election by the people," Hugh Williamson of North Carolina explained, was "the disadvantage under which it would place the smaller States" (July 25). The disadvantage, as Roger Sherman of Connecticut put it, was that people "will generally vote for some man in their own State, and the largest State will have the best chance for the appointment" (July 17). If people did vote for someone of their own state, then they would "never give a majority of votes to any one" (Sherman, July 17).

Williamson "suggested as a cure for this difficulty, that each man should vote for three candidates," two of whom would "probably " be from "other States" (July 25). Morris "liked the idea, suggesting as an amendment that each man should vote for two persons one of whom at least should not be of his own State" (July 25). Madison agreed. He thought voters would first choose someone from their own state, the candidate closest to them, and their second choice, necessarily from another state, would more likely be someone of national reputation, capable of winning the election. After speculating on the strategy voters might use with two votes, Madison concluded that "citizens" not being sure "of having their favorite elected" would "give their second vote with sincerity to the next object of their choice" (July 25).

Direct popular vote faced another obstacle according to Madison: "the disproportion of qualified voters in the [Northern and Southern] States, and the disadvantages which this mode would throw on the latter" (July 25). On July 25, 1787, then, the debate at the convention had arrived at a proposal for direct popular election of the president, with people casting two votes, first for the candidate closest to them and second for one with a greater chance of victory. At that point the convention defeated a motion to explore further "some such proposition as had been hinted by Mr. Williamson & others" by a vote of six states to five, with the smallest states, and most of the slave states, voting against further consideration of the proposal (July 25). Thus the convention approached but did not work out the mechanics of a plural popular election for president similar to a popular vote for president with an instant runoff.

The Connecticut Compromise gave the small states an advantage in the Senate by providing each state two senators, regardless of population. The Three-fifths Compromise gave slaveowners an advantage in the House of Representatives: the more people they held as slaves, the more representatives, they would get. Not convinced by Madison's arguments, the small states joined most of the slave states to defeat a popular vote for president. Professor Shlomo Slonim concisely describes "the Electoral College [as] an ingenious means of preserving the built-in advantages of those states while removing the choice from the legislature" (Slonim 1989, 54).

Williamson's proposal, amended by Morris, found its way into the Constitution in the provision that electors vote "for two persons, one of whom at least shall not be an inhabitant of the same state as themselves" (Article II Section 1). Electors did not indicate first and second choices. After the electoral vote tie in 1800, the Twelfth Amendment specified one vote for president and one for vice president, ending the idea of plural voting for president. The Twelfth Amendment received some attention in 2000 because it retained the idea of electors not casting both of their votes for residents of their own state, which led to Richard Cheney's formal reestablishment of a Wyoming residence in order to be eligible for the votes of Texas electors.

PARTISAN MANIPULATION

While at the Constitutional Convention large states made concessions to the interests of *existing* small states, in the second half of the 19th century the Republican Party set about *contriving new* and *smaller* states (in terms of population) in order to exploit the power of small states within the constitutional framework. In the late 18th century, Virginia, the most populous state, had about ten times as many people as the smallest existing state, Delaware. In the late 19th century, New York (then the most populous state) had about one hundred times as many people as the state of Wyoming, newly created by the Republican Party. From 1787 to 1858, a minimum population criterion "ensure[d] that any newly admitted state would be at least as large as the smallest state"; each of the new states admitted in that period met the criterion and most had a population sufficient to qualify for more than one representative (Stewart and Weingast 1992, 253–56). Political scientists Charles Stewart and Barry Weingast have carefully described the "Republican use of statehood politics to secure their hold on the presidency and the Senate" by "creating Republican 'rotten boroughs'" (places with very few voters but electoral power equal to more populous areas) in the second half of the 19th century (Stewart and Weingast 1992, 226, 228).

The admission of Nevada, Idaho, and Wyoming, all with far less than the standard population criterion, gained the Republicans additional Senate seats and electoral votes, as did a partisan plan to admit Dakota as two separate states. With about one-sixth of the population criterion, Nevada's admission in 1864 was "the most egregious effort in the nation's history to disregard population and economic criteria in order to admit a state for political reasons" (Stewart and Weingast 1992, 232). Republicans claimed during the debate on Nevada that the state would not only reach, but exceed, the population threshold within a year. In fact, it did not reach the population projected for 1864 until 1950, nor meet the minimum population criterion until 1970 (Stewart and Weingast 1992,

234 n31, 232). McCarty, Poole, and Rosenthal point out that "the Republicans' political ingenuity was quickly repaid in electoral votes" (1999, 36).

After the Dakota Territory had been reduced to the area of the current states of North and South Dakota, Republicans, led by Benjamin Harrison, "defeated a Democratic amendment to admit Dakota as a single state . . . on a strict party-line vote" (Stewart and Weingast 1992, 237–38). Instead they created two states, intending to gain two additional electoral votes and two additional Senate seats.

Harrison won the presidency while losing the popular vote in 1888, and the Republicans quickly moved to further strengthen their hold on the Electoral College by adding Wyoming and Idaho as new states although each had only about half the population criterion in 1890 (Stewart and Weingast 1992, 256). (Wyoming has never even met the population criterion.) Wyoming had been, after a number of territorial reorganizations, part of the Idaho Territory, before organization into separate territories and states. While Wyoming and Idaho could have been admitted as one state meeting the population criterion, Republicans once again created two states, seeking two extra Senate seats and two extra electoral votes. Republicans voted 138–1 for the admission of Wyoming while Democrats voted 0–126 against; Republicans voted 127–0 in favor of the admission of Idaho, while only one Democrat voted for it (McCarty, Poole, and Rosenthal 1999, table 7).

While generally such efforts yielded "only marginal help" in the Electoral College (McCarty, Poole, and Rosenthal 1999, 38), the impact of this partisan manipulation on the 2000 election is clear: without the additional electoral votes derived from the admission of underpopulated Republican states in the second half of the 19th century, George W. Bush would not have won the 2000 electoral vote. That is, if consistent with previous territorial organization, Nevada had been admitted as part of the Utah Territory, the Dakotas together, and Wyoming with Idaho, George W. Bush would have received six fewer electoral votes, losing both the Electoral College and the popular vote in 2000.

The most recent presidential election hinged, then, on the enduring success of the Republican packing of the Electoral College, which, along with the packing of the Senate, has received far less attention from political scientists and historians than Franklin D. Roosevelt's unsuccessful effort to pack the Supreme Court. Underlining the partisan nature of their statehood politics, Republicans did not uniformly support admitting new states, blocking the entry of states they thought would favor the Democrats (McCarty, Poole, and Rosenthal 1999, 46). Often "Democrats fail[ed] to emulate [the partisanship of] Republican strategies" in new state admissions (McCarty, Poole, and Rosenthal 1999, 39), frustrating Democratic partisans (see Stewart and Weingast 1992, 239).

While the Republicans manipulated the Electoral College, both parties engaged in systematic campaigns to reduce the popular vote. In 1876, for example, about three-fourths of eligible southerners voted, yet less than half that proportion voted a generation later. After the withdrawal of federal troops, terrorism, chicanery, and legislation reduced voter turnout sharply throughout the South, and voter participation declined in the North as well, with the institution of the requirement for personal voter registration (Piven and Cloward 2000).

One lesson of the efforts to reduce turnout, as well as of the 2000 election both in Florida and nationally, is that the decisions about the rules of electoral systems matter more than the decisions of individual voters. As E. E. Schattschneider put it, "politics deals largely with procedure rather than substance. . . . The grand strategy of politics has concerned itself first of all with the structure of institutions" (1960, 70).

REFORM POSSIBILITIES

By drawing attention to the way in which the rules may trump voter preferences, the election of 2000 provides an opportunity to consider alternative procedures and institutional structures. The central reason for deciding the presidency by popular vote is the principle of one person, one vote, cited by the Supreme Court (in a sharply limited context) in *Bush v. Gore*. The Court majority wrote that "the State may not, by later arbitrary and disparate treatment, value one person's vote over that of another." Dissenting, Justice Stevens observed that, even as they claimed to be providing equal protection, "the majority effectively orders the disenfranchisement of an unknown number of voters whose ballots reveal their intent—and are therefore legal votes under state law—but were for some reason rejected by ballot-counting machines." For the equal protection decision "to be completely consistent the Court would have had no choice but to invalidate the entire Florida election, since there is no question that votes lost in some counties because of the method of voting would have been recorded in others utilizing a different method" (Bugliosi 2001, 12). While Justice Souter asserted that "the Equal Protection Clause does not forbid the use of a variety of voting mechanisms within a jurisdiction, even though different mechanisms will have different levels of effectiveness in recording voters' intentions; local variety can be justified by concerns about cost, the potential value of innovation, and so on," it is hard to see how different levels of effectiveness in recording votes can be equal.

But the Court avoided dealing with arbitrary and disparate treatment in the actual balloting in the state of Florida as well as the disparities across states that the Constitution itself creates by weighing the votes of people in some states more than others in the Electoral College. Even more disproportionate than the Electoral College is the contingency procedure if no candidate receives a majority of the electoral vote: the House of Representatives chooses among the three leading electoral vote recipients, with each state having one vote.

Most people in the United States favor changing the Constitution to replace the Electoral College with direct popular vote for the president. In 1968, 81 percent of Gallup poll respondents favored replacing the Electoral College with a direct vote. In 1980, more than three-fifths of both Democrats and Republicans favored abolishing the Electoral College. However, in the wake of the 2000 elections, partisanship skewed attitudes about the Electoral College, Republicans support for abolition dropped sharply to 44 percent, while support among Democrats increased to 73 percent (Gallup News Service November 16, 2000). With such partisan polarization, the necessary two-thirds in the Congress for a constitutional amendment (in the usual manner) seems far beyond reach; in any case, the prospect of ratification of an amendment by three-fourths of the states, especially smaller, Republican states, is even less likely.

Increasing the number of states is one way to change the Electoral College without changing the Constitution, but it is unlikely to succeed. Solid Republican opposition and a divided Democratic Party defeated statehood for Washington, D.C., in 1993. Although that proposal would not affect the Electoral College (since Washington already has electoral votes), it makes clear how difficult it is to add new states. The Constitution requires approval by state legislatures and the Congress for any state to be created out of an existing one, as had occasionally been suggested with reference to dividing California into two states or making New York City a separate state. Another national-level change to the Electoral College would increase the size of the House of Representatives, which has been fixed at 435 for almost a century. The larger the House, the smaller the impact of the two additional votes each state receives regardless of population. Calculating the appropriate size of a legislature as the cube root of the population, Arend Lijphart (1998) suggests that the appropriate size of the House of Representatives would be 650 members, which would mean, if no new states were added, 753 electoral votes. While the less populous states would still be overrepresented in the Electoral College, the extent of that overrepresentation would decline somewhat. With a House of Representatives of 500 or 650, Al Gore would have won a three-vote majority in the Electoral College in 2000. Without any overrepresentation for small states in the Electoral College, assigning electoral votes only for the number of Representatives based on population, as James Wilson had once proposed (June 2), the popular vote winner in 2000 would have won a six-vote majority in the Electoral College.

Modifications within states are a little less unlikely than national changes. The Constitution allows state legislatures to determine how states choose electors, although not, as the Florida legislature believed, retroactively (Ackerman 2000, 33). A district plan in use in two states could create more problems, while an instant runoff election system might solve some.

The method used by Maine and Nebraska to allocate votes has received some attention since it allows for the possibility that the statewide winner would not receive all of the state's electoral votes. In those states electoral votes are assigned on the basis of the presidential vote in the congressional district, with one electoral vote going to the winner of the presidential vote in each congressional district, and the state's two additional electoral votes assigned to the statewide winner. Such a change is both unlikely and undesirable. Even if the gerrymandering of congressional districts did not increase with the stakes raised by relating the districts to the Electoral College, the plan would lessen the influence of those areas that strongly support one party—urban and minority residents concentrated in districts that overwhelmingly support the Democratic Party. States would be unlikely to adopt such a procedure because it could reduce their importance and the party in control of the decision might have to give up some electoral votes.

Both those obstacles could be avoided, and more active voter participation achieved, if states retain the winner-take-all system but allocate the electoral votes through an instant runoff vote. Just as James Madison at the Constitutional Convention favored allowing people to cast two votes for president, one for the candidate closest to a voter, and one for a candidate more likely to win, the instant runoff vote system would allow voters to select a first choice and other choices, with the other choices considered if the first candidate did not have sufficient votes to win (see the Robert Richie, Steven Hill, and Caleb Kleppner chapter in this volume).

While such a system could be used, with a constitutional amendment, in a national popular vote for president, it could also be used, without amending the Constitution, to determining a state's electoral vote. Although political scientists describe the vote as "a singularly blunt instrument for the communication of information" (Verba, Schlozman, and Brady 1995, 24), plural voting would allow voters to express a little more information about their preferences and, perhaps, gain more confidence in electoral institutions. But while people dissatisfied with the major parties may appreciate such a possibility even more after the election of 2000, the parties in control of the decision-making process may lack the will and the ability to reform the electoral system.

Part Five

Challenges and Prospects for Democratic Reform

14

What Makes Reform So Difficult: The Case of America's Cities and the Problems of Elites

LINCOLN MITCHELL

This book has proposed numerous democratic proposals that could expand political participation. In this chapter, I ask how the complicated role of political elites affects this process. I argue that while many elected officials claim to be friends of reform, and while some can even point to accomplishments in this area, these same people are part of a pervasive political culture that inhibits reform. My particular focus is on America's cities. This reflects not simply my professional background, but also the historical fact that progressive reform has always centered around urban areas (see the chapter by Mattson in this collection). With this said, I broaden my sites to understand the difficulties of reform outside of cities as well. Nonetheless, I believe the problems of cities often highlight the general difficulties of reform today.

The analysis and examples in this chapter clearly apply to national politics broadly. Disincentives for increasing voter participation apply just as much, if not more, in Republican-dominated suburban counties, where new voters might be immigrants and Democrats, as they do in big cities. It is not only big city legislators who behave contemptuously toward their constituents, although the urban examples often strike us as the most egregious. Politicians from all over the country use language suggesting a lack of a clear commitment to democracy. These phenomena are discussed in greater detail in a big city context throughout this chapter.

While I have worked in local politics in New York City, every now and then the deep contradictions running through the self-proclaimed reform, grassroots-oriented progressive Democratic Party leadership in urban America have become extremely stark. Urban politics today are filled by elected officials who will make speeches in support of the motor voter law, but resist doing voter registration in their own district and by legislators who will fight for political reform in the state capital and still seek

199

to knock an opponent off the primary ballot. None of these situations described above occur because politicians are hypocrites or phonies. In reality, these contradictions are quite complicated and reveal a great deal about the state of crisis in democracy in our cities today.

This crisis can be seen in a number of ways. First, in most American cities, voter turnout has declined consistently over the last decade. For example, in the 1989 Democratic mayoral primary in New York City over a million voters went to the polls, but this number had fallen to less than 500,000 in the 1997 mayoral primary. Second, the role of coalition politics has declined. Relationships between elites have supplanted genuine coalition making to the point where discussions of coalitions like those in Sonenshein (1993), DeLeon (1992), and numerous other works on urban elections seem almost quaint in 2001. To a great extent coalition building has been replaced by elite deal making. In today's political climate, leaders build relationships with other political leaders and base decisions on webs of favors, personal ties, and financial support of candidates. There is little incentive to bring people into the process and expand democracy. Instead, leaders know full well they need to work with a finite group of people and that politics is based largely on personal and financial relationships.

The skills that are needed to compete in the electoral arena have become increasingly complex and sophisticated in recent years. Correspondingly, these skills have become concentrated in a few hands. Those without the necessary skills are increasingly excluded from meaningful participation in the electoral arena. Complicated ballot access laws, expensive media campaigns, and sophisticated targeting mechanisms require professional skills that are not easy, or cheap, to acquire. The growing importance of these skills, even at the local level, represents a barrier to people seeking to become involved in politics.

The professionalization of politics is a national, and increasingly international, dynamic. It is not only urban areas where consultants with technical knowledge of targeting and political communication play a larger part in most elections than grassroots organizers and volunteers. The role of election lawyers is perhaps even more important than that of political consultants in cities like New York where ballot access is still very much a legal matter. (For discussion of the role of political professionals, particularly political consultants, see Johnson 2001; Salmore and Salmore 1989; Thurber and Nelson 2000; and Wade 1990.)

Because this crisis in urban democracy has become more intense over the last several years at a time when center and center-right mayors such as Richard Daley Jr., Rudolph Giuliani, Ed Rendell, and Richard Riordan have been mayors of our major cities, it is too easy to lay the blame at the feet of these Republicans and conservative Democrats. In fact, the responsibility is shared by many more people and institutions. Democratic organizations and leaders, including many who call themselves reformers, need to be called to task on their anti-reform behavior.

While some cities have elected Republican mayors, the crisis of democracy in America's cities has grown in a context where the overwhelming majority of city council members, mayors, and other local legislators remain Democratic; where Democrats still outnumber Republicans by margins between 3–1 and 6–1 in most big cities; and where cities still deliver solid majorities for Democrats for state and national office. Moreover, the Democratic-elected officials and party leaders in most of these cities look quite different from a generation ago. The number of African American, Asian American, and Latino legislators, and even mayors, has increased dramatically in recent decades. Cities as diverse as Atlanta, Chicago, Dallas, Los Angeles, New York, and San Francisco have elected African American mayors. Latinos and Asians have narrowly lost elections in Los Angeles.

Ironically, a substantial number of these elected leaders and political elites think of themselves as progressives. Many have the voting record or public profile to support that assertion. However, these are the same cities where voter turnout is down, where insurgent candidates still have trouble being taken seriously by the political community, where money heavily influences politics, and where the signs of democracy in trouble are present. The need for meaningful political reform in big cities should be apparent.

ELECTIONS AND PARTY POLITICS

Of course, politics is practiced differently in big cities than in the rest of the country. The unique structures of urban electoral politics have a tremendous effect on urban democracy. The density and population size of cities means that there are more elected officials. New York City, for example, has fifteen members of Congress, sixty state assembly members, fifty-one city council members, twenty state senators, and seven city or boroughwide elected officials. Chicago has nine members of Congress, fifty-seven state assembly members, fifty aldermen, twenty-eight state senators, and fourteen county commissioners. In comparison, in suburban or rural communities with light population density there may be only one state senator for a county.

Big cities create a stronger culture of political insiders who, in many cases, make their living from politics as consultants, lobbyists, or elected officials. This community of political elites has become an important institutional player in many cities. These political elites spend most of their time talking to each other, thus deemphasizing ideology and politics while underscoring the import of individuals and relationships in all aspects of politics. Those seeking office rely upon those insiders for information and advice (Richardson 1996).

In big cities, political insiders view grassroots political movements as rivals, vehicles for politicians to further their careers, or opportunities for consultants to make money. This is true even when the rest of the city does not interpret events this way. For example, the protests and arrests following the shooting of Amadou Diallo in 1999 in New York City was viewed by most of the city as an important political struggle, but to many political insiders it was deeply tied to the electoral ambitions of two of its leaders—Norman Siegel and Al Sharpton. Thus, for good reason, some were reluctant to lend their support because they did not want to strengthen these two people. It goes without saying that the loser in this situation is the movement that lies behind its leaders. A similar dynamic was evident in progressive Chicago politics after the death of Harold Washington. William Grimshaw describes how progressive politics in Chicago were "personalized not institutionalized" (Grimshaw 1992).

The most significant structural characteristic about urban politics is that most major cities have a de facto one-party system dominated by the Democratic Party. On the national and state level this means that cities like Chicago, New York, or Philadelphia can be relied upon to deliver substantial votes for Democratic candidates for president, Senate, and state constitutional offices such as governor or attorney general. This one-party system poses major problems for urban democracy. After all, political parties are the major way in which voters are offered meaningful electoral choice. In many respects democracies must have parties and party competition, otherwise they cannot be genuinely democratic. Parties help allow voters to see the difference between candidates and serve as an important cue to voters (Campbell 1960; Fiorina 1981; Popkin 1991). Exercising this right is very difficult in a primary, particularly when there is no incumbent because voters don't know which candidate to blame for the incumbent's failure.

For down ballot offices (i.e., state assembly and city council races), voters are often asked to choose between two candidates of whom they have never before heard without being able to rely on party distinctions. Virtually all down ballot races occur in low information contexts, but primaries generally have even less information. Voters often rely on endorsements, which may not always be the best solution. For the most part, even higher profile races like congressional or mayoral are decided in the primary in most cities. Although voters in these elections generally have more information than they do in elections for down ballot offices, the party is still useless as a tool for distinguishing between candidates.

The option of throwing out representatives who have not served well is much less clearly available to the voter in urban elections because of the one-party system. Equally importantly, categories such as liberal and conservative are not available to candidates in big city elections either. The breadth of opinions in the Democratic Party in cities like Philadelphia, Chicago, or New York is extreme. These parties include conservatives and liberals as well as individuals who represent the interests of a specific group.

In New York City, for example, Democrats from white ethnic areas of Staten Island or Queens are often social conservatives who oppose most forms of government spending, abortion rights, and other signature Democratic issues; some of these legislators even run with the joint support of the Democratic and Conservative Parties. However, Democrats in neighborhoods like Central Brooklyn and Chelsea are among the most liberal elected officials in the entire country. Similarly, liberal assembly members from South Central Los Angeles and council members from the San Fernando Valley in Los Angeles both identify themselves as Democrats. Essentially, the Democratic Party no longer has any clear political vision but rather factions united solely by political expediency.

Elected officials in urban one-party political systems have little incentive to expand democracy by increasing voter registration, mobilizing new voters, finding creative ways to involve new people into the political process, or incorporating new ethnic or political groups into the system. In a one-party system where elected officials must only win renomination in primaries rather than general elections, it is helpful for these elected officials to control the electorate, because bringing in new voters means introducing uncertainty into the election. For example, many African American legislators who have been reelected for decades represent districts that have become increasingly Caribbean, Latino, or African. However, native-born African Americans have higher rates of registration than these other groups. A voter registration drive bringing in 5,000 more Dominicans or Haitians could very well make the incumbent's seat substantially less safe in a primary. In Los Angeles, districts that are held by African Americans have become increasingly Mexican in recent years creating a strong disincentive for incumbents to register new voters.

Expanding democratic participation would force local elected officials to be more responsive and build relationships with new sectors of the electorate. This difficult and time-consuming work is avoided when the small electorate is maintained and elected officials must simply continue to work with the same small political elite year after year and election after election. Obviously, incumbents are not generally enthusiastic about voter registration drives because they know what a few thousand new voters can do to a Democratic primary electorate. Though most elected officials know better than to publicly oppose voter registration, as chapter 3 by Hayduk notes, their fear of an enlarged electorate generally keeps them from helping to fund registration and mobilization drives, particularly around primary time.

It is likely that few elected officials anywhere, even outside big cities, genuinely want to expand the electorate. However, many elected officials understand the need to enroll new members in their party, even if it may cause difficulties in the primary, because it brings more votes for their party in the general election. In one-party systems, this consideration is irrelevant.

The weakness of ideology in the one-party urban system makes it very difficult to build durable coalitions that might provide a viable substitute for political parties. Diverse groups within urban Democratic Parties are very rarely drawn together around a common set of interests, which is what would occur in a coalition. When this does occur, the coalition generally only lasts for a political moment and generally exists outside the formal, and informal, framework of the party. Wade (1990) goes so far as to describe the party apparatus as being an "embarrassment" to David Dinkins in 1989 when he brought a progressive coalition together to win the election for mayor of New York City.

Broad coalitions are a prerequisite for democratic governance. When they do not occur, groups are left out of the process and an important element of democracy is ignored. Without coalitions, governance and politics focus much more on elites. If a meaningful coalition cannot be built, elected officials must concentrate on deal making to ensure they have the support they need. This means that endorsements from elected officials and ethnic leaders become more important than working with and earning the support of actual citizens.

One example of this can be seen in the 2000 Democratic primary for president. This primary was unusual for several reasons, not least of which was the unprecedented relative ease with which Al Gore, a nonincumbent, won the nomination. One of the ways in which the Gore campaign precluded a strong primary challenge was to work very directly with African American and Latino leadership in big cities. However, this work was elite-focused and political, rather than broadly focused on policy. The best example of this was when Bronx leader Roberto Ramirez explained on local television that he was supporting Gore because the vice president's office always worked through the county organization when it was in the Bronx. Needless to say, this issue was probably not too important to most of New York's Latino or Bronx voters.

In this political system where coalitions, parties, and ideology are weak, politics becomes more personal. This weakness manifests itself in two ways. First, politicians must win election on the basis of their own personal appeal. They must deal in favors and keep key constituent groups happy. Accordingly, it is very difficult to beat incumbents because few challengers have strong enough name recognition or sufficiently powerful friends in a given community. Second, personal relations become the bedrock of virtually all aspects of political life. In addition to the role of individuals in local elections, personal relations dominate legislation, support in campaigns, and disbursement of public resources.

In short, the political community in most big cities is made up of elected and party leaders, political staff and operatives, consultants, and lobbyists who all know each other. In many cases these relationships go back for several decades, and in some cases several generations. Maintaining positive relationships and taking care of old friends generally outweigh policy considerations among those who must make their living in politics. It should also be understood that in many cases relationship is a euphemism for money. When people in politics speak about a relationship with somebody, in many cases they are referring to campaign contributions.

Perhaps the most devastating effect of the party system on democratic politics in big cities is that there are very few competitive elections in either primaries or general elections. For example, in the last round of city council elections in 1997 in New York City where all fifty-one seats were on the ballot, only nine out of forty-five Democratic council members had a Democratic primary that they won by less than 20 percentage points. Only six general elections for council were this close. Twenty-nine incumbent Democratic members of the city council had no primaries that year, while twenty-one incumbent Democrats had no Republican opponent in the November general election. Similarly, it is not uncommon to see mayors like Tom Bradley and Richard Riordan in Los Angeles face only token opposition in their reelection campaigns.

Politicians who remain in office for years without ever having to go before the voters often lose touch with the voters, and more importantly with the democratic nature of their position. This can be heard through the language politicians use. They begin to see the office that they hold as "their" office. This attitude is antithetical to true democracy where politicians are "public servants." Frequently legislators refer to the taxpayer dollars that they can spend with discretion through capital budgets as "their" money. It is not uncommon to hear a legislator claiming to have paid for some tax-funded project they authorized. The most outrageous and disturbing use of this sort of language reflecting the notion of elected office belonging to politicians not the people that I ever encountered occurred in a strategy meeting with top officials in the Gore campaign and several members of the New York city council early in 2000. Among the litany of complaints with which the council members were bombarding the Gore official was that one councilwoman who represented a heavily African American, low-income district was upset because people in her district knew things about the Gore campaign before she did. This statement speaks for itself, but the lack of regard for the intellect, interest, or involvement of her constituents should not be missed as most of the information to which she was referring had been seen in the newspapers or on television.

As fewer competitive elections occur, voters become less interested in the process and democracy is weakened. Local elections, in many cases, are not elections in the true sense of the word—providing choice. Rather they are affirmations, where voters can either vote for the incumbent or not at all. Thus an urban politics has evolved where competitive elections rarely occur and are rarely the route to office. In the next section, I describe how political elites work to keep this system in place and use it to their advantage.

POLITICAL ORGANIZATIONS:
MEET THE NEW BOSS, SAME AS THE OLD BOSS

To understand the weakening of urban democracy in the electoral arena, one must look closely at the Democratic Party. An examination of how political elites behave, not when talking to the press or voting on legislation, but when acting within the structure of the Democratic Party, demonstrates the ambiguous relationship these elites have with efforts to democratize our cities. While Democratic Party machines are nowhere near as strong as they were during the early and middle parts of the century, in many cities they still have substantial influence. Frequently, while they cannot determine who will be mayor or senator, they still dominate who will be elected to the state house, to the city council, or to the bench. These contests, not surprisingly, remain the most important to local party leadership. More importantly, the rules and structures of the Democratic Party can be used to exclude people and reduce the opportunity for genuine democratic reform.

In some respects, the remnants of urban political machines that exist in our cities at the beginning of the 21st century represent much of the bad and little of the good that existed in early and mid-20th-century political machines. Political party organizations can still frequently control ballot access, determine the future of an aspiring politician, and hurt somebody who crosses them, but they rarely can deliver needed services, influence legislation, or get any real attention at the federal level.

To a great extent, the Democratic Party is still strong enough in most cities to control access to elected office. In some cases, as seen frequently in New York City, this means using legal means to limit access to the ballot (typically by challenging individual signatures on nomination petitions, something that consumes a great deal of time). In other cases it means creating a network of relationships and politics through which any aspiring politician must pass before winning an elected position. For the most part this network consists of writing checks and supporting incumbent legislators until a seat opens up. Once that seat opens up, the legislators will support the candidate who has navigated the web of relationships and politics best.

This dynamic is worth examining more closely because it clearly demonstrates the need for political reform in urban America. The typical way this works is that a young attorney decides she wants a career in politics. She either joins a political club or meets with a few local officials. In either case she might be cautiously encouraged to become active in local politics. This means two things: (1) volunteering in support of and (2) contributing money to local officials. Contributing money is a way to get one's name listed on fund-raising invitations and raising name recognition among political elites. In addition to contributing money, the attorney will try to get appointed to local boards and organizations in order to strengthen her resume. After several years of doing this the attorney, who may no longer be so young, will have achieved a certain amount of name recognition among political leadership and will herself have become part of the political elite. With luck a seat in the state assembly, city council, or state senate might open up after only five to fifteen years of this. In some cities this pace is somewhat accelerated due to term limits.

When the seat opens up, all of the elected officials who have benefited from all the years of campaign contributions from the ambitious young attorney will return the favor by endorsing her for the open seat. The attorney will have an impressive list of endorsers. This is particularly important in low-turnout primaries and special elections. Importantly, the young attorney-turned-elected-official has played the game successfully, but has never really had to be involved with the community at the grassroots level, or taken leadership on an issue important to the community she now represents. Her target audience has been a relatively small one of political elites. The voters, in this case, have delegated their decision making to their elected leadership and have little voice in policy formulation.

The role money plays in this system is crucial. Our young attorney proved herself to the political leadership, not by taking leadership on a local issue or by toiling in the trenches for the party, although she probably did volunteer on election days, but by writing checks to the political leadership. Obviously, not everybody can write several campaign checks every year in hopes of winning the future support of elected officials.

The system, however, is not impermeable. It is important to note that the attorney in the above example was a woman. In many cities she also could have been Latino, African American, Jewish, or lesbian as well. To its credit, urban democracy and its elected leaders reflect the diversity of our cities. Entry to this leadership is rarely denied due to gender, race, or sexual orientation as long as the entrant "pays her dues" in the way described above. Furthermore, the leaders of many big city Democratic parties are people of color. For example for the last five to ten years, three of New York City's five county organizations have been led by people of color—Brooklyn and Queens by African Americans and the Bronx by a Latino.

What then is the problem with a system that makes it possible for people from diverse backgrounds to have access to a political system by paying dues over a period of several years to elected officials who, generally speaking, have progressive voting records in city, state, and national legislatures? There are several areas where a structure like this one fails to meet democratic challenges. In the broader context of urban politics today, the results are troubling.

1) It creates a tremendous incentive for aspiring politicians to support incumbents. The value of incumbent support in a low-turnout primary is so great that in many cases it is almost insurmountable.
2) It draws a closed circle. The first, and in many cases only, audience that an aspiring politician has to win is that of the existing elected officials.
3) It encourages a political system based upon relationships and personalities rather than issues and service to a community.
4) It discourages other approaches to winning electoral office. People who do not take the approach to winning elected office described above are generally seen as threats and rarely supported in their bids for office, regardless of their community activism or political vision.

One of the best-kept secrets about big city Democratic politicians is that they are all vulnerable in primaries. It takes a lot to beat them, but it does not take much to run strongly against them. For this reason, avoiding primaries is a major goal of most urban elected officials. This is particularly problematic because in most cases primaries are the only real election these candidates face. Many incumbents' political skills lie not in their ability to win elections, but to preclude them in the first place.

Nonetheless, occasional primary challenges to incumbents occur. These challenges reveal a great deal about how urban Democratic politics work. Generally speaking, these challenges fall into one of several different categories. First, there are challenges based on ethnic secession. These occur when a longtime incumbent, usually white, although increasingly African American, is challenged by a member of a different ethnic or racial group due to changing demographics of the district. Second, there are challenges based on personal animus. Third, there are generational challenges where a younger, more energetic candidate seeks to unseat an older incumbent who is invariably described as "old and out of touch." Fourth, and most infrequently, there are challenges based on legitimate ideological grievances between the challenger and the incumbent. A fifth category may be emerging that is based on challengers who are running for office because they are term limited out of the office they currently hold.

Incumbents and party organizations also use other less savory tactics to discourage candidates from challenging incumbents. This includes trying to force challengers off the ballot through challenging their petition signatures. This is a particularly effective and nasty tactic because even when the courts rule in favor of the challenger, the incumbent succeeds in wasting the challenger's precious time and money.

The reverse tactic is used as well. The generally much better funded incumbent does not hesitate to spend money on directly winning the support of community leaders and others. These expenditures include items like buying ads in journals for an organization's annual dinner, hosting block parties and picnics, and in some cases hiring people. It is surprising how little money an incumbent has to use to win the support of local group or organization. This behavior is not illegal, but it is not entirely ethical either.

Another tactic frequently used by incumbents is to restrict access to the professionals and professional services that are needed to run a strong campaign. Similarly, many political professionals are discouraged from working with challengers by elected officials and other political elites. Without access to political professionals, challengers make strategic mistakes, have trouble getting on the ballot, waste money, and produce shoddy campaign materials. The tactic of dissuading political professionals from working with challengers is made easier because incumbents generally have more money, which can be distributed to several consultants. In 1999, Willie Brown used this approach in San Francisco as most of the prominent local consultants signed on to do independent expenditure campaigns in support of Mayor Brown. This hurt the campaign of challenger Tom Ammiano who had some difficulty putting his campaign team together.

Local political organization and elected officials working together in the ways described above contribute to a system that does not facilitate increased democracy in the electoral arena. Through party machinations, political strategies, and politics as usual a political context has emerged where incumbents are almost always reelected, competitive races are rare, and potential challengers are discouraged. These are not the signs of a healthy democracy.

CONCLUSION

In too many cases the business of politics is focused on distributing political resources. Staff jobs and elected positions (or at least the option to run) are awarded to people who have paid their dues and "earned" their job or promotion. Aspiring politicians write their checks to powerful incumbents who in turn write checks to constituent groups in their district. Incumbents take credit for using "their money" to provide street improvements, park beautification, or otherwise deliver basic services to their district. Community activists and leaders who are not part of the political community are discouraged from getting involved or running for office. Political decisions are driven by personal relationships, not by any notion of broadening democracy or participation. Most devastatingly, a closed loop is created where broad participation is at a minimum and turnout for primaries, the only elections that matter in most of these communities, is very low.

Big city politicians generally function in a context that is entirely different from that in which other American politicians function. Many urban politicians represent poorer, more compact districts. They frequently work as part of a larger community of elected officials and political professionals than is found in suburban and rural communities. Party competition is not part of their electoral environment as most cities and urban legislative districts are overwhelmingly Democratic. These politicians rarely face competitive elections and when they do it is usually in a primary, thus their relationship to political parties is very different from other politicians. The paradox is that urban politicians are perceived, perhaps rightly, as the most progressive and most committed to the poor and minorities. I have tried to show that these values are not always consistent with a commitment to building and fighting for real democracy.

The challenges that our cities will face over the next decades as new immigrant groups continue to become politically active, as older African American communities struggle to become part of the new economy, and as schools and infrastructure continue to lack the infrastructure they need, are substantial. Urban America in the 21st century will continue to need accountable elected officials, politics that are open and built upon more than financial and personal relations, politicians who truly see themselves as servants of the people, and a vibrant democratic system where participation is high and people feel a sense of ownership.

Changing this system is the major political challenge urban America faces. The building blocks for this will be easier ballot access and voter registration laws, radical campaign finance reform, aggressive efforts to increase access to political expertise, sunshine laws to demystify the working of government and the power of elected officials—precisely those proposals laid out in this book. However, this type of legislative reform will not be enough to bring about the type of profound political reform needed.

The most important, and difficult, challenge will be to create and institutionalize a competitive party system in urban America. As long as the Democratic Party continues its hegemony in urban politics it will be very difficult for voters to see real choice and feel a real stake in who their leaders are. This has been true for decades and remains an extremely daunting task, but it is essential for truly democratizing urban government.

We can strengthen third parties like the Green Party or the Working Families Party in New York. We can also try to reattach some meaning to the party label Democrat. If the Democratic Party can be more clearly defined, and if party candidates can be held to a set of positions, it will be possible to build a multiparty urban politics.

New electoral systems may also help breathe life into urban democracy and facilitate the growth of second and third parties in our cities. Many cities have nonpartisan elections; some have experimented with at-large representation, rank order voting, proportional representations, and other alternatives. It would be fruitful to closely examine the impact these systems have had on the democratic health of the cities where they have been tried.

I have argued that the conditions outlined in this chapter are in some ways unique to urban America. Nonetheless, the applications of this analysis to the broader polity cannot be ignored. Many Americans live in communities dominated by one of the major parties and are thus denied meaningful electoral choice and, in many cases, less responsive political institutions. Personal relationships between elites have supplanted genuine coalition building at virtually all levels of politics. Money is the key to winning access to government at many levels. It is not just urban elected officials who employ language suggesting a lack of understanding of the democratic process. Political elites across the country face the challenge of reconciling their public rhetoric, and perhaps genuine ideals, with the reality of functioning in a system that does not encourage democratic participation.

15

Looking Backward
While Looking Forward to
Democracy's Moment

RONALD HAYDUK AND KEVIN MATTSON

Poll after poll finds that Americans think their political system is corrupt. Clearly, far too many Americans are more than merely apathetic about politics—they are downright cynical. Their lack of trust of politicians and government has been growing over the past several decades, and has reached new heights in the wake of the 2000 presidential election fiasco. Alienation and anger about our political system is evident among nearly all segments of the population but is especially palpable among African Americans and other minorities, poorer citizens, young people, and people with disabilities—precisely the most vulnerable and disenfranchised who comprise close to a numerical majority of the voting age population but who rarely vote. Who can blame them for not participating? Revelations in the media about political corruption—from Florida's flawed election process to campaign finance abuses—are steady drumbeats that erode the public's confidence. Even with an upsurge of progovernment sentiment surrounding the September 11 tragedy of terror, there are few signs of increased political participation, even in terms of voting in the 2001 elections.

The authors of these chapters have examined different ways to reform and invigorate our polity. We have done this in order to combat political apathy and ensure a more dynamic public life in America. The essays here have analyzed a wide range of reform efforts in three broad categories: to reduce barriers to participation (both to voters and to progressive candidates and third parties); to engage citizens and improve the level of political debate; and to make the political system more responsive and representative. Taken together, these reform measures strive to make politics more open, accessible, accountable, and thereby, less corrupt and more democratic. We now want to step back and ask what progressive reformers have achieved and what are possibilities for future gains to democratize America.

Since the end of the 19th century, the goals of progressive reformers have remained the same: to create a democratic system of governance the public can fully participate and believe in. Yet tactics and emphases have changed throughout the course of the 20th century. To a significant degree, the leadership of the civil rights movement has shaped the reform terrain over the past several decades. Powerful political actors and interests, who responded to these reform campaigns, have also affected political dynamics. The interplay between reformers and elites has led reformers to reassess their goals, strategies and tactics.

For example, democracy reformers during the 1960s and 1970s focused on voter registration and education campaigns. They launched Freedom Summer and other community-based campaigns to empower the previously disenfranchised. They heroically challenged onerous election laws. By the late 1980s, due in part to gains made, traditional voter registration and voter education work started to appear less pressing. Yet, as Ron Hayduk has argued here, the reasons for such initiatives had not really disappeared. Many reformers continued to persevere, breaking new ground with get-out-the-vote campaigns and educational programs, while others turned their attention to shifting the onus of getting registered from the individual and registration groups to the government, primarily through motor voter programs. These were won in several states and eventually at the national level with the passage of the National Voter Registration Act of 1993.

At the same time that motor voter became a national reality, the reform landscape changed significantly. The democracy reform movement had grown broader, and, in many respects, more sophisticated about factors that posed barriers and what worked to remove them. Greater reform efforts were being made to get money out of politics, widen ballot access, and provide alternative voting systems. Nor were reform leaders content with changing the rules of politics; rather, they wanted to nurture citizen engagement by opening up public service to young people or deliberative sessions and community organizing to adults. In the 1990s, democracy reform moved beyond simply assuring formal institutions of political participation toward ensuring what one political theorist called "strong democracy" (Barber 1984).

Along with this growth in the movement's goals and achievements, however, a new weakness emerged. While, broadly speaking, much of the reform work from the 1960s until the 1980s focused on minority enfranchisement, the work of the 1990s came to center on issues of majority alienation. Today, progressive reformers are pursuing a number of approaches. Variety is good, of course, and it signals the health of this vital movement. Nonetheless, variety often reflects a fragmentation of organizations and thinking about the issues. And here we come up against one of the major problems within the democracy renewal movement—a problem that we have only cursorily discussed but needs more attention in a conclusion intended to ask what should be done in the future.

As both editors have personally experienced, many reformers feel hamstrung by the funding mechanisms available to them. The civil society organizations that Jamin Raskin mentions in his chapter, the organizations that promote deliberation discussed in R. Claire Snyder's piece, nonprofit groups that work on registering voters—all of these rely upon private philanthropic support. Foundations who give money to reformers are often intent on funding the next "big thing" and ironically (and often unwittingly) pressure leaders from organizations to sell themselves as the be-all-and-end-all. All too often reformers argue that *their* particular reform—whether removing barriers to registration, getting money out of politics, or creating more informed and deliberative citizens—will ultimately solve all the problems of our democracy. Leaders position themselves as having the cure-all. They pump up their proposals with the very easy rhetoric of democracy and citizenship—who could be opposed to such things?—while the foundations tout those they have blessed with funds as the next big thing in the world of reform. Many reformers argue that only their initiative can really enhance progressive politics.

ONE FOR ALL, AND ALL FOR ALL

As should be evident from this book, we believe this logic is shortsighted. The real challenge for the contemporary democracy reform movement is to find a basis—both practical and intellectual—to *unite* diverse democracy reform groups and strategies. Only then can each reform initiative truly meet its particular goal and work in consort with other initiatives. Fortunately, the 2000 presidential election provided a shot in the arm to this movement. But even here there is a danger: Too quickly the debate surrounding Florida focused solely on fixing the technology of voting machines. Of course, as we have shown in this book, the problem is much larger and multifaceted. Only if a variety of reforms are implemented can we hope that democracy will be strengthened in the future. For this reason, this book draws together different reform options under one umbrella. We view all of them as critical pieces in the larger puzzle of democracy. Thus, we argue, the American political system can only be democratized if the various parts of the reform movement work in tandem.

For instance, the first step in democracy reform is to renew the original civil rights movement's strategy—to remove barriers to participation. This means reforming election laws but also getting money out of politics and more political parties and candidates on the ballots. Once barriers are removed, we believe that citizens must be availed of opportunities at political education—through educational programs in public schools, community organizing initiatives that might show them how politics affects their daily lives, and deliberative sessions with other citizens both online and offline. Only then will the removal of barriers allow educated citizens to enter a more healthy polity. While providing citizens with opportunities to learn more about politics, we then have to ensure that they can have their voices heard. That requires creating new ways for voting to reflect a plurality of choices, opening up political debates to a wider range of candidates and opinions, making certain that direct legislation really reflects citizens' wishes and not the whims of millionaires, and reforming the Electoral College so that votes actually matter in national elections. This is the way the bigger democratic picture presented here should look—all of these reforms operating together and enhancing one another. Removing barriers to voter participation is intimately tied to methods of producing engaged citizens who, in the context of a more limited role of money in campaigns, might turn out to provide the margin of victory for progressive third parties and independent candidates. In this way, the various reforms analyzed in this book, when taken as a whole, produce a broader vision of progressive reform.

BEING REALISTIC

The ideas of unity and working in tandem sound nice, but we face very real problems in initiating these reforms. Elites often stand in their way (as Lincoln Mitchell points out), and much of our current political system allies against the reforms called for here. Besides, even if we get beyond these problems, we also have to heed the teachings of reformers who came before us: As the philosophy of pragmatism teaches us, we need to test our reforms in the often messy world of politics, with its conflict and contestation. We are not arguing that all of these reforms will enhance democratic participation, for that is an empirical question that remains open. Nor can we be assured that reforms will operate the way we intend.

As history has shown, progress is a slippery idea; or to use academic parlance, progress is a "meta-narrative" now destined for the trash heap of history. In the case of democracy reform, this lesson is not at all academic. Winning particular reforms might provide gains that are not easy to hold on to. Progress by democracy reformers in one area might not amount to gains for groups in another area. And it is not merely conflicts among reformers that have contributed to limited achievements. We have witnessed how progress even in one area can sometimes be reversed or undermined by the very targets or opponents of reform efforts. For example, democracy reformers hoped to stem the tide of money in politics by passing the Federal Election Campaign Act of 1971. Yet, these reforms actually created new pathways for the wealthy and powerful—namely political action committees (PACs). Similarly, achieving important registration reform in the 1980s and 1990s, such as motor voter, did not enfranchise all groups equally. We have also seen how mechanisms to provide voters with direct policy-making capacity—that is, direct legislation intended to get around corrupt politicians—have ironically empowered wealthy citizens to enact legislation in their self-interest. And programs to provide forums for greater public education and deliberation have sometimes produced citizens with *higher* levels of alienation.

We must therefore be careful about implementing and evaluating reforms. We must not only see how different initiatives work best in tandem but also how reform can have unintended consequences in the real world of politics. We must take into account the pluralistic world that we live in. Different combinations and reform might be called for in different states and locales, let alone at the national level. The trick to revitalizing democracy, or more properly, to expanding and deepening democracy in America, may lie in building bridges across historical rifts and between divergent groups. None of this is easy work.

It is especially not easy work considering that some reformers are in conflict with one another. This goes beyond competing for foundation dollars. Different groups present different visions of democracy and propose different reforms. One of the most important results of Florida might be an opening for various reformers to grapple with each other on more equal footing, especially as they rapidly move to address an overarching and pressing question: How to move forward? Perhaps groups can now put aside their differences and work more effectively with each other to produce changes in the immediate context, while at the same time, forcing groups to grapple with sorting out past conflicts and set their priorities. Democracy reformers are committed to leveraging their capacities and the public's disaffection in order to keep the window of opportunity of reform open. This may also provide space for reformers to assess what short-, medium-, and long-range goals and various reforms organizations will pursue, who will fight on which fronts with whom, and which strategies might be employed to enact desired changes.

SEIZING DEMOCRACY'S MOMENT

With these tough lessons in mind, we believe the reform movements outlined in this book, taken as a whole and with an eye toward historical dynamics, could help make the American political system more democratic and progressive. Removing barriers—both to voters and to progressive candidates and third parties—would make the system more open, accessible, and inclusive. Furthering voter registration reform, changing the patronage-ridden election administrative system, and creating substantial ballot access and campaign finance reform are crucial steps toward this end as well. Rediscovering old and finding new spaces—town halls, schools, the Internet—in which an often demoralized public can deliberate and educate itself about political affairs must accompany reforms aimed at increasing political choice. These sorts of reforms would help make the political system more transparent and politicians more accountable. Instituting alternative methods for selecting representatives and allocating political power, and providing public platforms for all viable candidates and parties to convey their messages, would go a long way to make the system more responsive and representative.

In the wake of the Florida fiasco, the American public woke up—even if just for a brief moment—to the fact that our political system faces a gapping democratic deficit. It is a rare moment when problems bubbling below the surface come out into the open for all to see. But that is exactly what occurred in Florida. For this crisis to become *democracy's moment*, though, reformers must push hard to show the American public that something can be done to make the political system more transparent, deliberative and responsive. This book has tried to shed light on this possibility, arguing that reformers must move on several fronts simultaneously. We sincerely believe that democracy's moment is here. Now we must see if we can live up to it.

Appendix
National and Regional
Democracy Organizations

This appendix has been compiled by Dēmos: A National Network of Ideas and Actions, www.demos-vsa.org

NATIONAL ORGANIZATIONS

ACORN
The Association of Community Organizations for Reform Now (ACORN), a national organization with 500 neighborhood chapters, focuses primarily on issues of felony disenfranchisement, housing, predatory lending, living wage, and community development in low-income communities.

739 8th Street South East
Washington, DC 20003
Phone: (202) 547-2500
www.acorn.org

Action Agenda for Electoral Reform
The Action Agenda for Electoral Reform (AAER) is a Web site that serves as a clearinghouse of information on election reform and democracy reform organizations. It is affiliated with the Institute for Policy Studies.

www.ips-dc.org/electoral/index.htm

Advancement Project
The Advancement Project provides legal and policy resources for people working to solve public policy problems across lines of race, ethnicity, and culture in three major areas: education for students of color and poor children, law enforcement reform, and democracy.

1730 M Street NW, Suite 401
Washington, DC 20036
Phone: (202) 728-9557
www.advancementproject.org

Advocacy Institute

The Advocacy Institute strengthens the capacity of political, social, and economic justice advocates and works with other organizations to make democratic institutions accountable in the areas of public health, gender equity, peace, poverty, sustainable development, and the environment.

1629 K Street NW, Suite 200
Washington, DC 20006-1629
Phone: (202) 777-7575
www.advocacy.org

AFL-CIO

The AFL-CIO is a federation of labor unions that represents most of America's unionized workers and advances the interests of working people on the job, in government, in a changing global economy, and in their communities.

815 16th Street NW
Washington, DC 20006
Phone: (202) 637-5000
www.aflcio.org

Alliance for Better Campaigns

The Alliance for Better Campaigns (ABC) seeks to persuade or require television broadcasters to provide free airtime for candidates in an effort to promote election participation by an informed, unbiased American electorate.

1150 17th Street NW, Suite 600
Washington, DC 20036
Phone: (202) 659-1300
www.bettercampaigns.org

Alliance for Democracy

The Alliance for Democracy seeks campaign finance reform to halt corporate influence of our economy, our government, our culture, our media, and the environment.

681 Main Street
Waltham, MA 02451
Phone: (781) 894-1179
www.thealliancefordemocracy.org

American Association of People with Disabilities: Disabilities Vote Project

The American Association of People with Disabilities (AAPD) is a strong voice for the rights of disabled voters in the electoral process at the state and national levels.

1629 K Street NW, Suite 802
Washington, DC 20006
Phone: (202) 955-6114
www.aadp-dc.org

The American Bar Association

The American Bar Association (ABA) Commission on Public Financing of Judicial Campaigns urges public financing of judicial campaigns.

740 15th Street NW
Washington, DC 20005-1019
www.abanet.org/home.html

The American Civil Liberties Union

The American Civil Liberties Union (ACLU) advocates free speech, voting rights (including for ex-offenders), and other individual rights and liberties guaranteed by the Constitution and laws of the United States.

125 Broad Street, 17th Floor
New York, NY 10004
Phone: (212) 344-3005
www.aclu.org

American Council of the Blind

American Council of the Blind (ACB) works to improve the well-being of the blind and visually impaired, including working to ensure that the election process is accessible to people with impaired vision.

1155 15th Street NW, Suite 1004
Washington, DC 20005
Phone: (202) 467-5081
www.acb.org

America*Speaks*

America*Speaks* seeks to strengthen democratic institutions and processes and enhance citizen trust in democracy by engaging citizens in policy making, governance, and thoughtful dialogue.

1612 U Street, Suite 408
Washington, DC 20009
Phone: (202) 299-0126
www.americaspeaks.org

Asian American Legal Defense and Education Fund
Asian American Legal Defense and Education Fund (AALDEF) strives to build an informed and active Asian American community that is involved in the civic and political life of this country and to ensure maximum access to the electoral process.

99 Hudson Street, 12th Floor
New York, NY 10013
Phone: (212) 966-5932
www.aaldef.org/index.html

Asian Pacific American Legal Center of Southern California
Asian Pacific American Legal Center (APALC) works on voting rights, immigration and naturalization, workers' rights, family law and domestic violence, immigrant welfare, and antidiscrimination issues on behalf of Asian Pacific Islander Americans.

1145 Wilshire Boulevard, 2nd Floor
Los Angeles, CA 90017
Phone: (213) 977-7500
www.apalc.org

Ballot Initiatives Strategy Center
Ballot Initiatives Strategy Center (BISC) provides advice and assistance to organizations working on ballot initiatives and tracks donations to ballot measure campaigns.

33 Long Avenue
Allston, MA 02134
Phone: (617) 254-0207
www.ballotfunding.org

Black Youth Vote!
Black Youth Vote! educates black youth about the political process and encourages them to influence public policy decisions through participation in elections.

1629 K Street NW, Suite 801
Washington, DC 20006
Phone: (202) 659-4929
www.bigvote.org

The Brennan Center for Justice at NYU Law School
The Brennan Center combines scholarship, public education, and legal action to address problems in three areas: democracy, poverty, and criminal justice.

161 Avenue of the Americas, 12th Floor
New York, NY 10013

Phone: (212) 998-6730
www.brennancenter.org

The Campaign for America's Future/The Institute for America's Future
These related organizations are working to revitalize a progressive agenda emphasizing economic security and campaign finance and democracy reform.

1025 Connecticut Avenue NW, Suite 205
Washington, DC 20036
Phone: (202) 955-5665
www.ourfuture.org

Center for Constitutional Rights
CCR is dedicated to advancing and protecting the rights guaranteed by the U.S. Constitution and the U.N. Declaration of Human Rights.

666 Broadway, 7th Floor
New York, NY 10012
Phone: (212) 614-6464
www.ccr-ny.org

The Center for Democracy and Citizenship
Center for Democracy and Citizenship (CDC) aims to increase participation and stimulate discussion on the workings of democracy and government, promote youth involvement, and encourage attention by candidates to youth issues.

1301 K Street NW, Suite 450 West
Washington, DC 20005
Phone: (202) 728-0418
www.excelgov.org/demandcit/index.htm

Center for Policy Alternatives
Center for Policy Alternatives (CPA) is a resource center for legislators and advocates on state-level policy, leadership, and networking. CPA's Democracy Program monitors and advances state legislation on democracy issues.

1875 Connecticut Avenue NW, Suite 710
Washington, DC 20009
Phone: (202) 956-5120
www.stateaction.org

Center for Public Integrity
Center for Public Integrity (CPI) investigates and analyzes public service, government accountability, and ethics-related issues and disseminates their findings through books, reports, and newsletters.

910 17th Street NW, 7th Floor
Washington, DC 20006
Phone: (202) 466-1300
www.publicintegrity.org

Center for Responsive Politics
CRP is a research organization that tracks money in politics and its effect
on elections and public policy.

1101 14th Street NW, Suite 1030
Washington, DC 20005-5635
Phone: (202) 857-0044
www.opensecrets.org

Center for Third World Organizing
Center for Third World Organizing (CTWO) promotes civic engagement
in democratic processes through direct action organizing in communities
of color in the United States.

1218 East 21st Street
Oakland, CA 94606
Phone: (510) 533-7583
www.ctwo.org

Center for Voting and Democracy
Center for Voting and Democracy (CVD) studies how voting systems affect participation, representation, and governance, with a particular focus
on proportional representation and instant runoff voting.

6930 Carroll Avenue, Suite 901
Tacoma Park, MD 20912
Phone: (301) 270-4616
www.fairvote.org

The Century Foundation
The Century Foundation (formerly the 20th Century Fund) researches
and analyzes major economic, political, and social institutions and issues,
including democracy and election reform.

41 East 70th Street
New York, NY 10021
Phone: (212) 535-4441
www.tcf.org

Committee for Economic Development

Committee for Economic Development (CED) is a business-oriented reform group that conducts policy research on a wide range of economic and social issues, including globalization and trade, welfare reform, education and childcare, and campaign finance reform.

2000 L Street NW, Suite 700
Washington, DC 20036
Phone: (202) 296-5860
www.ced.org

Committee for the Study of the American Electorate

The Committee publishes reports on voter participation and registration laws, campaign advertising, campaign finance, the impact of media on politics, and citizen education.

601 Pennsylvania Avenue NW, Suite 900
Washington, DC 20004
Phone: (202) 546-3221
www.gspm.org/csae

Common Cause

Common Cause is a national membership organization with state affiliates that promotes open, honest, and accountable government; campaign finance reform; and increased election participation.

1250 Connecticut Avenue NW, Suite 600
Washington, DC 20036
Phone: (202) 833-1200
www.commoncause.org

Constitution Project's Election Reform Initiative

The Initiative undertakes studies and advances recommendations for long-term solutions to problems of election administration. One of their major reports made recommendations for federal election reform.

1717 Massachusetts Avenue NW, Suite 801
Washington, DC 20036
Phone: (202) 299-9540
www.constitutionproject.org/eri/index.htm

Council on Government Ethics and Election Laws

Council on Government Ethics and Election Laws (COGEL) serves as an information clearinghouse for its members, many of whom are election and ethics officials, on information in the areas of ethics, elections, campaign finance, lobbying and freedom of information.

P.O. Box 417
Locust Grove, VA 22508
Phone: (540) 972-3662
www.cogel.org

Democracy 21

Democracy 21 focuses on campaign finance reform, particularly on educating the public about policy, constitutional and legal issues related to "soft money."

1825 I Street NW
Washington, DC 20006
Phone: (202) 429-2008
www.democracy21.org

The Democracy Collaborative

The Democracy Collaborative engages public and private universities across the country in encouraging students toward civic engagement, building democratic communities, and fostering genuine democratic renewal.

University of Maryland
c/o Civil Society/Community Building Initiative
1241 Tawes Hall
College Park, MD 20742
Phone: (301) 405-9834

Democracy Compact

Democracy Compact encourages voter registration, democratic participation and voting through outreach, education, and volunteer efforts.

505 Park Avenue, 5th Floor
New York, NY 10022
Phone: (212) 763-4824
www.pledgetovote.com

Democracy Matters

Democracy Matters informs and engages college students and communities in efforts to strengthen our democracy, focusing particularly on the issue of money in politics and campaign finance reform.

2170 Bonney Road
Hamilton, NY 13346
Phone: (315) 824-8866
www.democracymatters.org

Dēmos: A Network of Ideas and Action

Dēmos is a new research, public policy, and advocacy organization that generates reports and ideas into the public debate on issues of democracy and economic security and is working to develop a diverse network of democracy reform organizations and advocates.

155 Avenue of the Americas, 4th Floor
New York, NY 10013
Phone: (212) 633-1405
www.demos-usa.org

Election Center

The Election Center, a service bureau and association for election officials, updates its members on recent legislation and court decisions that affect voting and registration. The Center works closely with election officials on issues of election administration and voter registration.

12543 Westella Street, Suite 100
Houston, TX 77077-3929
Phone: (281) 293-0101
www.electioncenter.org

Election Reform Information Project

Election Reform Information Project (ERIP) serves as a comprehensive clearinghouse for data, news, and analysis on election reform from many viewpoints.

1101 30th Street NW, Suite 210
Washington, DC 20007
Phone: (202) 338-9860
www.electionline.org

Fannie Lou Hamer Project

Fannie Lou Hamer Project (FLHP) serves as a vehicle for traditional civil rights organizations and communities of color to engage in campaign finance reform initiatives, helping to create a national grassroots movement to redefine campaign finance as a civil rights issue.

729 Academy Street
Kalamazoo, MI 49007
Phone: (616) 349-9760
www.flhp.org

Institute for Policy Studies

Institute for Policy Studies (IPS) is a multi-issue progressive think tank in Washington, D.C., that has undertaken significant democracy work that includes: producing a comprehensive website on electoral reform information with *The Nation* [www.ips-c.org/electoral/index.html]; developing a ten-point Voters' Bill of Rights; and organizing Democracy Summer, a program to train and place young activists with organizations working on democracy issues.

733 15th Street NW
Washington, DC 20005
Phone: (202) 234-9382
www.ips-dc.org

Jefferson Center
Jefferson Center seeks to strengthen the democratic process by generating thoughtful citizen input on important civic issues, determining the will of an informed public, and actively presenting those views to policy makers.

3100 West Lake Street, Suite 405
Minneapolis, MN 55416
Phone: (612) 926-3292
www.jefferson-center.org

Justice at Stake Campaign
JSC is a new national grassroots effort that supports the judicial independence movement, conducts public education campaigns, works in the states with local and national partners to keep courts impartial, accessible, and fair by reforming campaign financing for judicial elections.

1717 Massachusetts Avenue NW, Suite 801
Washington, DC 20036
Phone: (202) 588-9700
www.justiceatstake.org

Lawyers' Committee for Civil Rights Under Law
The Lawyers' Committee provides legal services to address racial discrimination. Its Voting Rights Project litigates voting rights cases and monitors U.S. Justice Department enforcement of federal voting rights statutes.

1401 New York Avenue NW, Suite 400
Washington, DC 20005
Phone: (202) 662-8600
www.lawyerscomm.org

Leadership Conference on Civil Rights
Leadership Conference on Civil Rights (LCCR), consisting of more than 185 national organizations, has coordinated the national legislative cam-

paign on behalf of every major civil rights law since 1957 and has extended its advocacy work to promote the national effort for election reform.

1629 K Street NW, Suite 1010
Washington, DC 20006
Phone: (202) 466-3311
www.civilrights.org

League of Women Voters

League of Women Voters (LWV), through its fifty state chapters and their local affiliates, supports election reform, campaign finance reform, civic education, and other parts of the democracy agenda through advocacy, education and outreach, and coalition-building efforts.

1730 M Street NW, Suite 1000
Washington, DC 20036
Phone: (202) 429-1965
www.lwv.org

Local Initiative Support Training and Education Network

Local Initiative Support Training and Education Network (LISTEN, Inc.) develops the leadership potential of urban youth for civic engagement and community problem solving and seeks to be a source of information on policy issues and trends affecting urban youth.

1436 U Street NW, Suite 201
Washington, DC 20009
Phone: (202) 483-4494
www.lisn.org

Mexican American Legal Defense and Educational Fund

Mexican American Legal Defense and Educational Fund (MALDEF) is a Latino litigation, advocacy, and educational outreach organization. Democracy efforts include voting rights litigation, legislative advocacy, and community mobilization for fair census enumeration and redistricting.

634 South Spring Street
Los Angeles, CA 90014
Phone: (213) 629-2512
www.maldef.org

Miller Center of Public Affairs, University of Virginia

Miller Center of Public Affairs (MCPA) is a nonpartisan research center that studies the national and international policies of the United States. It cosponsored the National Commission on Federal Election Reform.

2201 Old Ivy Road
P.O. Box 400406
Charlottesville, VA 22904-4406
Phone: (804) 924-7236
www.millercenter.virginia.edu

NAACP Legal Defense and Education Fund
The NAACP Legal Defense and Education Fund is serves as a legal resource for the nation's African American communities. Its pro-democracy
efforts include voting rights litigation, legislative advocacy, and community mobilization for fair census enumeration and redistricting.

99 Hudson Street, 16th Floor
New York, NY 10013
Phone: (212) 965-2200
www.naacp.org

NAACP Voter Empowerment Program
The Voter Empowerment Program of the NAACP advances the African
American community's inclusion in the American political system by promoting African American political awareness and participation and ad-
vocating for electoral reform.

4805 Mt. Hope Drive
Baltimore, MD 21215
Phone: (410) 580-5013
www.naacp.org

National Asian Pacific American Legal Consortium
National Asian Pacific American Legal Consortium (NAPALC) works to
advance the legal and civil rights of Asian Pacific Americans through litigation, public education, and public policy. Efforts include violence prevention and education, voting rights, immigration, naturalization, affirmative action, language rights, and the census.

1140 Connecticut Avenue NW, Suite 1200
Washington, DC 20036
Phone: (202) 296-2300
www.napalc.org

National Association of Counties
National Association of Counties (NACo) is the national representative of
county governments in the United States. Areas of focus include election
reform.

440 First Street NW, Suite 800
Washington, DC 20001
Phone: (202) 393-6226
www.naco.org

National Association of Latino Elected and Appointed Officials

National Association of Latino Elected and Appointed Officials (NALEO) is a nonprofit, nonpartisan membership organization of the nation's Latino elected and appointed officials and their supporters. Efforts include workshops on redistricting and voting rights and mobilization of young Latino Voters.

5800 S. Eastern Avenue, Suite 365
Los Angeles, CA 90040
Phone: (323) 720-1932
www.naleo.org

National Association of Secretaries of State

National Association of Secretaries of State (NASS), the nonpartisan professional organization of state secretaries of state, promotes exchange of information among the secretaries of state and fosters development of public policy at the national level. In the last year, NASS has been actively involved in pursuing election reform at the local, state and federal levels.

Hall of States
444 North Capitol Street NW, Suite 401
Washington, DC 20001
Phone: (202) 624-3525
www.nass.org

National Association of State Elections Directors

National Association of State Elections Directors (NASED) is a professional, nonpartisan organization of state election directors. It has been very involved in election reform work, testifying before Congress and working closely with NASS and the Election Center to develop new voting practices and standards.

444 North Capitol Street NW
Washington, DC 20001
Phone:(202) 624-5460
www.nased.org

National Association of State PIRGs

The National Association of State PIRGs works to coordinate all of the state member organizations, and with U.S. PIRG, to expand campaigns beyond the state level. Democracy issues on the PIRGs' agenda include campaign finance reform, instant runoff voting, and voting technology upgrades.

926 J Street, Suite 523
Sacramento, CA 95814
Phone: (916) 448-4516
www.pirg.org/democracy

National Black Caucus of State Legislators
National Black Caucus of State Legislators (NBCSL) has a primary mission to develop, conduct, and promote educational, research, and training programs that enhance the effectiveness of its members as they consider legislation and issues of public policy that impact the general welfare of African American constituents within their respective jurisdictions.

444 North Capitol Street NW, Suite 622
Washington, DC 20001
Phone: (202) 624-5457
www.nbcsl.com

National Civic League
National Civic League (NCL) is a research, network building, and advocacy center focused on strengthening citizen democracy by transforming democratic institutions. Its New Politics Program encourages campaign finance reform at the local level, codes of conduct for candidates, and instant runoff voting and other electoral reforms.

1445 Market Street, Suite 300
Denver, CO 80202
Phone: (303) 571-4343
www.ncl.org

National Congress of American Indians
National Congress of American Indians (NCAI), the oldest and largest tribal government organization in the U.S., informs the public and the federal government of tribal self-government, treaty rights, and a broad range of federal policy issues affecting tribal governments.

1301 Connecticut Avenue NW, Suite 200
Washington, DC 20036
Phone: (202) 466-7767
www.ncai.org

National Coalition on Black Civic Participation

National Coalition on Black Civic Participation (NCBCP) is a nonprofit, nonpartisan organization with eighty-six member affiliates that promotes democratic inclusion of African Americans in the political and voting process.

1629 K Street NW, Suite 801
Washington, DC 20006
Phone: (202) 659-4929
www.bigvote.org

National Commission on Federal Election Reform

National Commission on Federal Election Reform (NCFER) was organized by the Miller Center of Public Affairs of the University of Virginia and the Century Foundation after the 2000 presidential elections and held hearings on electoral reform and election administration. The Commission's Report was released on July 31, 2001.

The Federal Election Reform Network
c/o The Century Foundation
41 East 70th Street
New York, NY 10021
Phone: (212) 452-7750
www.reformelections.org

National Conference of State Legislatures

National Conference of State Legislatures (NCSL) is a bipartisan organization that works to improve state legislatures by increasing interstate communication and cooperation and by bringing the voices of state legislatures to the federal level. Following the 2000 election, NCSL developed an Election Reform Task Force that made recommendations for reform.

444 North Capitol Street NW, Suite 515
Washington, DC 20001
Phone: (202) 624-5400
www.ncsl.org

National Council of La Raza

National Council of La Raza (NCLR) is a national organization that supports community-based groups in the Latino community on issues of poverty and discrimination. NCLR works to expand participation and representation of the nation's growing Latino community.

1111 19th Street NW, Suite 1000
Washington, DC 20036
Phone: (202) 785-1670
www.nclr.org

National Immigration Forum
The Immigration Forum engages in advocacy, media work, targeted research, and public education in order to provide reliable immigration-related data to policy makers, the press, and the general public. It has published a report on immigrant voting.

220 I Street NE, Suite 220
Washington, DC 20002-4362
Phone: (202) 544-0004
www.immigrationforum.org

National Institute on Money in State Politics
The Institute is a nonpartisan organization dedicated to collecting information and research on the financing of state electoral campaigns and disseminating the information electronically and through reports.

648 North Jackson Street, Suite 1
Helena, MT 59601
Phone: (406) 449-2480
www.followthemoney.org

National Organization on Disabilities
National Organization on Disabilities (NOD) promotes the full and equal participation of persons with disabilities of all ages in all aspects of life. Its Political Participation Program works to increase the participation of people with disabilities in elections and the political process.

910 16th Street NW, Suite 600
Washington, DC 20006
Phone: (202) 293-5960
www.nod.org

National Urban League
The Urban League works to secure economic self-reliance, parity and power, full participation, and civil rights for African Americans.

120 Wall Street
New York, NY 10005
Phone: (212) 558-5300
www.nul.org

National Voting Rights Institute

National Voting Rights Institute (NVRI) is a legal advocacy center that focuses on campaign finance reform as a voting rights issue by working on primary systems; participation barriers; corporate funding of presidential debates; campaign spending limits; campaign finance reform and civil rights; campaign finance at the state and local level; and public awareness about voting rights.

One Bromfield Street, 3rd Floor
Boston, MA 02108
Phone: (617) 368-9100
www.nvri.org

People for the American Way

People for the American Way (PFAW) is a large, multi-issue progressive advocacy organization committed to justice, civil rights, democracy, and monitoring the right wing. They are strong supporters of election reform and are principal organizers of a collaborative project to monitor elections and insure full access for voters.

2000 M Street NW, Suite 400
Washington, DC 20036
Phone: (202) 467-4999
www.pfaw.org

Project Vote Smart

Project Vote Smart provides free information to citizens on the political system, issues, candidates, and elected officials through their Voter Research Hotline and comprehensive website.

One Common Ground
Philipsburg, MT 59858
Phone: (406) 859-8683; 1-888-VOTE-SMART
www.vote-smart.org

Public Agenda

Public Agenda is a nonpartisan, nonprofit public opinion research and citizen education organization whose publications and Web site help leaders better understand the public's point of view on major policy issues, and help citizens better understand critical policy issues so they can make their own more informed and thoughtful decisions.

6 East 39th Street
New York, NY 10016
Phone: (212) 686-6610
www.publicagenda.org

Public Campaign

Public Campaign serves as a national coordinating center for comprehensive campaign finance reform, defined mainly as winning voluntary public financing as an alternative to the current campaign finance system. Public Campaign's principal work has been at the state level, where several states have enacted public financing systems.

1320 19th Street NW, Suite M-1
Washington, DC 200036
Phone: (202) 293-0222
www.publicampaign.org

Public Citizen

Public Citizen fights for health, trade, environmental, and democracy issues. It produces research and publications on issues such as "soft money" and the Independent Counsel Act.

1600 20th Street NW
Washington, DC 20009
Phone: (202) 588-1000
www.citizen.org

Puerto Rican Legal Defense and Education Fund

Puerto Rican Legal Defense and Education Fund (PRLDEF) is a national civil rights organization established to protect the civil rights of Puerto Ricans and other Latinos through litigation, advocacy, and creative legal education programs. PRLDEF has been deeply involved in redistricting efforts and in building support for election reforms within the Puerto Rican and Latino communities.

99 Hudson Street, 14th Floor
New York, NY 10013-2815
Phone: (212) 219-3360
www.igc.org/IPR

Rainbow/PUSH Coalition

The Rainbow/PUSH Coalition was actively involved in pointing out the obstacles and barriers voters faced in the 2000 election. It promotes the economic, social, and political empowerment of the African American community and is involved in electoral reform activities through its Voter Registration and Education Project.

930 East 50th Street
Chicago, IL 60615-2702
Phone: (773) 373-3366
www.rainbowpush.org

The Reform Institute
The Reform Institute is a research and education organization for election administration debates and the issue of campaign finance. Senator John McCain founded and chairs its Advisory Committee, which hopes to attract moderate Republican support to the field of election reform.

211 North Union Street, Suite 250
Alexandria, VA 22314
Phone: (703) 535-6897
www.reforminstitute.org

Rock the Vote
Rock the Vote involves and empowers youth in the political process. It has conducted numerous voter registration and youth involvement activities.

10635 Santa Monica Boulevard, Box 22
Los Angeles, CA 90025
Phone: (310) 234-0665
www.rockthevote.org

The Sentencing Project
The Sentencing Project advocates alternative sentencing programs and criminal justice reform, including reenfranchisement of ex-offenders. It has released reports on the impact of the disenfranchisement of ex-offenders and continues to promote the restoration of voting rights.

514 10th Street NW, Suite 1000
Washington, DC 20004
Phone: (202) 628-0871
www.sentencingproject.org

**Southwest Voter Registration Education Project /
William C. Velasquez Institute**
SVREP is dedicated to involving more Latinos in our democracy through education about the importance of voter registration and voter participation and electoral reform. The affiliated WCVI conducts research and education on issues of concern in the Latino community.

403 E. Commerce, Suite 220
San Antonio, TX 78205
Phone: (210) 222-0224
www.svrep.org

Study Circles Resource Center
Study Circles Resource Center (SCRC) promotes and supports study circles, a method of deliberative dialogue, providing study guides and training

manuals for facilitators. Many study circles have been on race and community issues, but recently they have also been held on the issues of campaign finance and election reform.

P.O. Box 203
697 Pomfret Street
Pomfret, CT 06258
Phone: (860) 928-2616
www.studycircles.org

United States Commission on Civil Rights

The U.S. Commission on Civil Rights investigates any charges of civil rights violations, most recently studying voting rights violations in Florida during the 2000 elections. Their 2001 report sharply criticized the Florida elections process.

624 9th Street NW
Washington, DC 20425
Phone: (202) 376-8312
www.usccr.gov

United States Hispanic Leadership Institute

United States Hispanic Leadership Institute (USHLI) empowers Latinos and similarly disenfranchised groups by maximizing civic awareness and participation in the electoral process. It pays particular attention to developing leadership through a number of programs that target youths.

431 South Dearborn Street, Suite 1203
Chicago, IL 60605
Phone: (312) 427-8683
www.ushli.com

USAction

USAction is a national coalition of statewide citizen action organizations that come together on a series of national and multistate campaigns. Their efforts have included medical care and tax fairness, and they are involved in several state election reform campaigns.

1341 G Street NW, 10th Floor
Washington, DC 20005
Phone: (202) 661-0216
www.usaction.org

Voter Integrity Project
Voter Integrity Project (VIP) works on voter rights and election integrity issues with a particular focus on voting technology, poll watching, and youth outreach.

P.O. Box 6470
Arlington, VA 22206
Phone: 1-888-578-4343
www.voter-integrity.org

Youth Vote Coalition
Youth Vote Coalition (YVC) mobilizes young voters and conducts efforts aimed at improving youth participation in government.

1010 Vermont Avenue NW, Suite 715
Washington, DC 20005
Phone: (202) 783-4751
www.youthvote.org

REGIONAL ORGANIZATIONS

Democracy South
Democracy South is a regional network of state-based organizations in the Southeast dedicated to helping build, strengthen, and link progressive multiracial and multi-issue coalitions that address issues of social, environmental, and economic justice, as well as election reform.

105 West Main Street
Carrboro, NC 27510
Phone: (919) 967-9942
www.all4democracy.org/demsouth

Midwest States Center
Midwest States Center (MSC) helps develop state coalitions in several states and does public education campaigns on issues of agriculture and small farmers, affordable health care, encouragement of civic participation, and campaign finance reform.

P.O. Box 104
Prairie Farm, WI 54762
Phone: (715) 455-1758

Northeast Action
Northeast Action is a support center for progressive organizing efforts in New England and New York on a number of issues, including health care,

corporate accountability, tax reform, poverty and economic security issues, and campaign finance and electoral reform

30 Germania Street, Building L
Boston, MA 02130
Phone: (617) 541-0500
www.neaction.org

Southern Regional Council
SRC works to improve voting and democratic rights for African Americans and all citizens in the South. Their work has included redistricting efforts and the promotion of racial justice and tolerance.

133 Carnegie Way NW, Suite 900
Atlanta, GA 30303-1031
Phone (404) 522-8764
www.southerncouncil.org

Western States Center
Western States Center (WSC) works to build a progressive movement for social, economic, racial and environmental justice in the Western states through organizing, building coalitions, and encouraging a new generation of citizen leaders to run for public office. They support campaign finance and electoral reform efforts.

P.O. Box 40305
Portland, OR 97240
Phone: (503) 228-8866
www.westernstatescenter.org

Bibliography

Ackerman, Bruce. "As Florida Goes. . . . *New York Times,* December 12, 2000.

Advancement Project. "Claims of Fraud under 'Motor Voter' Are Meritless." Memo. Washington, D.C.: Advancement Project, August 2001a.

———. "America's Modern Poll Tax: How Structural Disenfranchisement Erodes Democracy." Washington, D.C.: Advancement Project, November 2001b. [www.advancement.org]

Addams, Jane. *Twenty Years at Hull House.* New York: Penguin, 1910 (1998).

———. *Twenty Years at Hull House.* New York: Signet, 1960 (originally 1910).

Adventure in American Education (Volume II). Exploring the Curriculum: The Work of the Thirty from the Viewpoint of Curriculum Consultants. New York: Harper & Brothers, 1943.

Alberty, H. *Reorganizing the High School Curriculum.* New York: Macmillan, 1953.

Alinsky, Saul. *Revile for Radicals.* New York: Vintage Books, 1969.

Allen, Howard W., and Kay Warren Allen. "Voter Fraud and Data Validity." In *Analyzing Electoral History,* edited by Jerome Clubb, William H. Flanigan, and Nancy Zingale, 153–93. Beverly Hills, Calif.: Sage Publications, 1981.

Amar, Akhil Reed. "Testimony of Professor Akhil Amar." House of Representatives Subcommittee on the Constitution Hearing on "Proposals for Electoral College Reform." September 4, 1997. [www.house.gov/judiciary/222315.htm]

Anderson, John B., and Rob Richie. "Let the Voters Decide Their Representation." *Legal Times,* February 23, 1998.

Anderson, David M., and Michael Cornfield, eds. *The Civic Web: Online Politics and Democratic Values.* Lanham, Md.: Rowman & Littlefield, 2002.

Appleseed Project on Electoral Reform. *A Blueprint for Fair and Open Presidential Debates in 2000.* Washington College of Law, American University, May 2000. [www.wcl.american.edu]

Argersinger, Peter H. "New Perspectives on Electoral Fraud in the Gilded Age." *Political Science Quarterly,* 100, 4 (Winter 1985–1986).

Avey, Michael J. *The Demobilization of American Voters: A Comprehensive Theory of Voter Turnout.* New York: Greenwood Press, 1989.

241

Ballot Initiative Strategy Center Foundation. Boston, Mass. [www.ballotfunding .org]

Barber, Benjamin. *Strong Democracy: Participatory Politics for a New Age.* Berkeley: University of California Press, 1984.

———. *The Conquest of Politics.* Princeton, N.J.: Princeton University Press, 1988.

———. *Jihad vs. McWorld: How Globalism and Tribalism Are Reshaping the World.* New York: Ballantine Books, [1995] 1996a.

———. "Foundationalism and Democracy." In *Democracy and Difference: Contesting the Boundaries of the Political,* edited by Seyla Benhabib, 348–60. Princeton, N.J.: Princeton University Press, 1996b.

Barber, Kathleen. *A Right to Representation: Proportional Election Systems for the Twenty-first Century.* Columbus: Ohio University Press, 2000.

Barbook, Richard. "The Hi-Tech Gift Economy." In *FirstMonday,* 1998. [www .firstmonday.org]

Barstow, David, and Don Van Natta Jr. "How Bush Took Florida: Mining the Overseas Absentee Vote." *New York Times,* July 15, 2001.

Beck, Paul Allen, and Marjorie Hershey. *Party Politics in America.* New York: Addison Wesley Longman, Inc., 2000.

Benhabib, Seyla. "Toward a Deliberative Model of Democratic Legitimacy." In *Democracy and Difference: Contesting the Boundaries of the Political,* edited by Seyla Benhabib, 67–94. Princeton, N.J.: Princeton University Press, 1996.

Benkler, Yochai. "From Consumers to Users: Shifting the Deeper Structures of Regulation Toward Sustainable Commons and User Access." *Federal Communications Law Journal,* 52 (2000): 561–79.

Bennett, James. *Oral History and Delinquency: The Rhetoric of Delinquency.* Chicago: University of Chicago Press, 1981.

Bennett, Stephen Earl, and Linda L. M. Bennett. "What Political Scientists Should Know about the Survey of First-Year Students in 2000." *PS: Political Science and Politics* 34 (2001): 295–99.

Berman, S. *Children's Social Consciousness and the Development of Social Responsibility.* New York: Teachers College Press, 1997.

Bimber, Bruce. "The Internet and Political Transformation: Populism, Community, and Accelerated Pluralism." *Polity,* 31, 1 (1998): 138.

Blake, Casey Nelson. *Beloved Community: The Cultural Criticism of Randolph Bourne, Van Wyck Brooks, Waldo Frank, and Lewis Mumford.* Chapel Hill: University of North Carolina Press, 1991.

Boggs, Carl. *The End of Politics: Corporate Power and the Decline of the Public Sphere.* New York: The Guilford Press, 2000.

Bode, Boyd. *Progressive Education at the Crossroads.* New York: Newson and Company, 1938.

Bohman, James. *Public Deliberation.* Cambridge: MIT Press, 1996.

Bollier, David. *Public Assets, Private Profits: Reclaiming the American Commons in an Age of Market Enclosure.* Washington, D.C.: New America Foundation, 2001.

Boyte, Harry, and Nancy Kari. *Building America: The Democratic Promise of Public Work.* Philadelphia: Temple University Press, 1996.

Brady, Henry E., Justin Buchler, Matt Jarvis, and John McNulty. *Counting All The Votes: The Performance of Voting Technology in the United States.* Berkeley, Calif.: Institute of Government Studies, September 2001.

Brinton, Henry. "What You Lose by Looking on Your Own." *Washington Post,* March 18, 2001, p. B2

Broder, David. *Democracy Derailed: Initiative Campaigns and the Power of Money.* New York: Harcourt, 2000.

Brody, Richard A. "The Puzzle of Political Participation in America." In *The New American Political System,* edited by Anthony King, 287–324. Washington, D.C.: American Enterprise Institute, 1978.

Bugliosi, Vincent. "None dare call it treason." *The Nation,* February 5, 2001.

Burnham, Walter Dean. "The Changing Shape of the American Political Universe." *American Political Science Review* 65, 1 (March 1965).

——. *Critical Elections and the Mainsprings of American Politics.* New York: W.W. Norton, 1970.

——. "Theory and Voting Research: Some Comments On Converse' 'Change in the American Electorate.'" *American Political Science Review* 68, 3 (September 1974a).

——. "Rejoinder to Comments by Philip Converse and Jerold Rusk." *American Political Science Review* 68, 3 (September 1974b).

Button, Mark, and Kevin Mattson. "Deliberative Democracy in Practice: Challenges and Prospects for Civic Deliberation." *Polity* 31, 4 (1999): 609–37.

CalTech/MIT, Voting Technology Project. "Voting: What Is, What Could Be." 2001. [www.vote.caltech.edu]

Campbell, Angus, Philip E. Converse, Warren Miller, and Donald Stokes. *The American Voter.* New York: John Wiley, 1960.

Castells, Manuel. *The Rise of the Network Society.* Oxford: Blackwell, 2000.

Cazenhave, Noel A. "Chicago Influences the War on Poverty." *Journal of Policy History,* 5, 1 (2000).

Center for Voting and Democracy. "Black Representation Under Cumulative Voting in IL," a report. May 2001. [www.fairvote.org/vra/ilcv.htm]

Center for Voting and Democracy, videotaped interviews, 1998.

Chambers, Simone. *Reasonable Democracy: Jurgen Habermas and the Politics of Discourse.* Ithaca, N.Y.: Cornell University Press, 1996.

Chester, Jeffrey. *The Center for Media Education and the Center for Digital Democracy: Response to the Public Telecommunications Service Proposal.* Chicago: University of Chicago Press, 2001.

Chivers, C. J. "After Arresting 31 Protesters, City Bulldozes Prized Garden." *New York Times,* February 16, 2000, p. A1.

Cohen, Julie E. "Information Rights and Intellectual Freedom." In *Ethics and the Internet,* edited by Anton Vedder. Oxford: Intersentia Publishing, 2001.

Converse, Philip E. "Change in the American Electorate." In *The Human Meaning of Social Change,* edited by Angus Campbell and Philip Converse, 263–338. New York: Russell Sage Foundation, 1972.

——. "Comment on Burnham's 'Theory and Voting Research.'" *American Political Science Review,* 68, 3 (September 1974).

Cooper, John Milton. *The Warrior and the Priest: Woodrow Wilson and Theodore Roosevelt.* Cambridge: Belknap Press, 1983.

Cotkin, George. *William James, Public Philosopher.* Baltimore: Johns Hopkins University Press, 1990.

Counts, G. "Dare Progressive Education be Progressive?" *Progressive Education,* 9 (1932): 257–63.

Cremin, Lawrence. *The Transformation of the School: Progressivism in American Education, 1876–1957.* New York: Vintage, 1961.

———. *American Education, the Metropolitan Experience, 1876–1980.* New York: Harper & Row, 1988.

Croly, Herbert. *Progressive Democracy.* New York: Macmillan, 1914.

Crotty, William J., ed. *Paths to Political Reform.* Lexington, Mass.: Lexington Books, 1980.

Crunden, Robert. *Ministers of Reform: The Progressives' Achievement in American Civilization.* Urbana: University of Illinois Press, 1984.

Cyler, Keith. "Creating a Caring Community from ACT UP to Housing Works." In *From ACT UP to the WTO: Urban Protest and Community Building in the Era of Globalization,* edited by Benjamin Shepard and Ronald Hayduk. New York: Verso, 2002.

DeLeon, Richard. *Left Coast City: Progressive Politics in San Francisco 1975–1991.* Lawrence: University Press of Kansas, 1992.

Delli Carpini, Michael X., and Scott Keeter. *What Americans Know About Politics and Why It Matters.* New Haven: Yale University Press, 1996.

Dewey, J. "The Way Out of Educational Confusion." In *John Dewey: The Later Works, 1925–53.* Vol. 6., edited by A. Boydston, 75–81. Carbondale: Southern Illinois University Press, 1931.

Dewey, John. "The School and Society." In *The Child and the Curriculum and the School and Society.* Chicago: University of Chicago Press, 1900 (1956).

———. *The Public and Its Problems.* New York: H. Holt and Company, 1927.

Dionne, E. J. *Why Americans Hate Politics.* New York: Simon & Schuster, 1991.

———. *They Only Look Dead: Why Progressives Will Dominate the Next Political Era.* New York: Simon and Schuster, 1996.

Downs, Anthony. *An Economic Theory of Democracy.* New York: Addison-Wesley, 1957.

Driver, R., H. Asoko, J. Leach, E. Mortimer, and P. Scott. "Constructing Scientific Knowledge in the Classroom." *Educational Researcher,* 23, 7 (1994): 5–12.

Duneier, Mitchell. *Slim's Table: Race, Respectability, Masculinity.* Chicago: University of Chicago Press, 1994.

Dynneson, T. L., and R. E. Gross, eds. *Social Science Perspectives on Citizenship Education.* New York: Teachers College Press, 1991.

Effrat, Marcia Pelly. *The Community Approaches and Applications.* New York: The Free Press, 1974.

Ehrenhalt, Alan. "Political Pawns." *Governing* (July 2000): 20.

Election Reform Information Project. October 2001.

Elshtain, Jean Bethke. "A Pilgrim's Progress: Jane Addams in America." A Lecture in the Inaugural Lecture Series, Swift Hall, Chicago Divinity School. November 7, 1995.

Everson, David. "The Effect of the 'Cutback' on the Representation of Women and Minorities in the Illinois General Assembly." In *United States Electoral Systems: Their Impact on Women and Minorities,* edited by Wilma Rule and Joseph Zimmerman, 111–19. New York: Praeger, 1992.

Fagan, Patrick. "Presidential Election 2000: Political Bibliography." [http:// workingpapers.org/bibliography/twothousbib.htm]

Fallows, James. "Internet Illusions." *New York Review of Books,* November 26, 2000.

Faunce, R.C., and N. L. Bossing, *Developing the Core Curriculum.* Englewood Cliffs, N.J.: Prentice Hall, 1951.

Fine, M. *Habits of Mind: Struggling over Values in America's Classrooms.* San Francisco: Jossey-Bass, 1995.

Fiorina, Morris. *Retrospective Voting in American National Elections.* New Haven: Yale University Press, 1981.

Fishkin, James. *Democracy and Deliberation.* New Haven: Yale University Press, 1991.

Fitch, Robert. *The Assassination of New York.* New York: Verso, 1993.

Follett, Mary Parker. *The New State,* with a historical introduction by Kevin Mattson. University Park: Penn State Press, 1998 (originally 1918).

Fose, Max. Testimony to the Democracy Online Project, April 17, 2000.

Franklin, Donna L. "Mary Richmond and Jane Addams: From Moral Certainty to Rational Inquiry in Social Work Practice." *Social Service Review* (December 1986).

Fuchs, Ester R. *Mayors and Money: Fiscal Policy in New York and Chicago.* Chicago: University of Chicago Press, 1992.

Gallup News Service. "Americans Have Long Questioned Electoral College." November 16, 2000. [www.gallup.com/poll/releases/pr010105]

General Accounting Office. *Elections: Perspectives on Activities and Challenges across the Nation.* Washington, D.C: U.S. General Accounting Office, GAO-02-3, October 2001.

Gerber, Elisabeth. *The Populist Paradox.* Princeton, N.J.: Princeton University Press, 1999.

Giles, H. H., S. P. McCutchen, and A. N. Zechiel. *Exploring the Curriculum: The Work of Thirty Schools from the Viewpoint of Curriculum Consultants.* New York: Harper, 1942.

Gosnell, Harold G. *Getting out the Vote.* Chicago: University of Chicago Press, 1927.

Gosnell, Harold G., with Richard Smolka. *American Parties and Elections.* Chicago: University of Chicago Press, 1976.

Graham, P. A. *Progressive Education, from Arcady to Academe: A History of the Progressive Education Association, 1919–1955.* New York: Columbia University, Teachers College, 1967.

Grimshaw, William J. *Bitter Fruit: Black Politics and the Chicago Machine 1931–1991.* Chicago: University of Chicago Press, 1992.

Groarke, Margaret, and Jordan Moss. "The Northwest Bronx Community and Clergy Coalition." In *From ACT UP to the WTO: Urban Protest and Community-Building in the Era of Globalization,* edited by Benjamin Shepard and Ronald Hayduk. New York: Verso, 2002.

Grob, Gerald, and George Billias. *Interpretations of American History.* New York: The Free Press, 1987.

Grossman, Lawrence K. *The Electronic Republic: Reshaping Democracy in the Information Age.* New York: Penguin, 1996.

Grossman, Lawrence, and Newton N. Minow. *The Digital Promise Report,* 2001. [www.digitalpromise.org]

Gutmann, Amy, and Dennis Thompson. *Democracy and Disagreement.* Cambridge: Belknap Press, 1996.

Habermas, Jurgen. *The Structural Transformation of the Public Sphere: An Inquiry into a Category of Bourgeois Society.* Trans. Thomas Burger with the assistance of Frederick Lawrence. Cambridge, Mass.: MIT Press, 1989.

———. *Moral Consciousness and Communicative Action*. Trans. Christian Lenhardt and Shierry Weber Nicholson. Cambridge, Mass.: MIT Press, 1990.

Hanna, P. R. "The Need for Teacher Training." *Progressive Education*, 9 (1932): 273–74.

Hardin, Garrett. "The Tragedy of the Commons." *Science*, 62 (1968): 1243–48.

Harris, Joseph P. *Registration of Voters in the United States*. Washington, D.C.: Brookings Institution, 1929.

———. *Election Administration in the United States*. Washington, D.C.: Brookings Institution, 1934.

———. "Election Reform: The Perspective of Forty Years." In *Issues of Electoral Reform*, edited by Richard J. Carlson, 101–16. New York: National Municipal League, 1974.

Harvard University Institute of Politics. *Campaign for President: The Managers Look at 96*. Cambridge, Mass.: Harvard University, 1997.

Harwood, Richard C. "The Nation's Looking Glass." *The Kettering Review* (Spring 2000).

Hayduk, Ronald. "Gatekeepers to the Franchise: Election Administration and Voter Participation in New York." Ph.D. diss., City University of New York Graduate Center, 1996.

Heilprin, John. "105.4 Million Voters Cast Ballots," Associated Press story, December 18, 2000.

Herbert, Bob. "Championing Cities." *New York Times*, April 26, 2001, p. A23.

Hill, Kim Quaile, and Jan E. Leighley. "The Policy Consequences of Class Bias in State Electorates." *American Journal of Political Science*, 36 (May 1992).

Hill, Steven, and Robert Richie. "Should the Democrats favor Majority–Minority Districts in the 2001 Redistricting?" *American Prospect Online*, March 20, 2001. [www.prospect.org/controversy/districts/hill-richie-1.html#round1]

Hoeffel, John. "Six incumbents are a week away from easy election." *Winston–Salem Journal*, January 27, 1998.

Hofstadter, Richard. *The Age of Reform*. New York: Knopf, 1955.

Holzer, Harold. *The Lincoln–Douglas Debates*. New York: HarperCollins, 1993.

House Committee on the Judiciary, Democratic Investigative Staff. "How to Make Over One Million Votes Disappear: Electoral Sleight of Hand in the 2000 Presidential Election." August 20, 2001. [www.house.gov/judiciary_democrats/electionreport.pdf]

Howe, Frederic. *Confessions of a Reformer*. New York: Quadrangle, 1967 (originally 1925).

Hunter, James Davison. *Culture Wars: The Struggle to Define America*. New York: Basic Books, 1991.

Initiative and Referendum Institute, Washington, D.C. [www.iandrinstitute.org]

Institute for Government and Public Affairs at the University of Illinois, "Illinois Assembly on Political Representation and Alternative Electoral Systems, Executive Summary," 2001. [www.fairvote.org/op_eds/illinoisreport.htm]

Internet Policy Institute. *Report of the National Workshop on Internet Voting*. Washington, D.C.: Internet Policy Institute, 2001.

Isaac, Jeffrey. "The Poverty of Progressivism." In *Democracy in Dark Times*, 139–49. Ithaca, N.Y.: Cornell University Press, 1998.

Issacharoff, Samuel, Pamela S. Karlan, and Richard H Pildes. *The Law of Democracy: Legal Structure of the Political Process*. Westbury, N.Y.: Foundation Press, 1998.

Jackman, Robert W. "Political Institutions and Voter Turnout in the Industrial Democracies." *American Political Science Review*, 81, 2 (1987): 405–23.

James, William. *Pragmatism and the Meaning of Truth*. Cambridge, Mass.: Harvard University Press, 1978.

Johnson, Dennis W. *No Place for Amateurs : How Political Consultants are Reshaping American Democracy.* New York: Routledge, 2001.

Kamarck, Elaine C., and Joseph S. Nye Jr. *Democracy.com? Governance in a Networked World*. Hollis, Md.: Hollis Publishing, 1999.

Kant, Immanuel. *Groundwork of the Metaphysic of Morals*. Trans. H. J. Paton. New York: Harper & Row Publishers, 1956.

Kelly, Stanley Jr., Richard Ayers, and William C. Bowen. "Registration and Voting: Putting First Things First." *American Political Science Review*, 61, 2 (June 1967).

Key, V. O. *Southern Politics in State and Nation*. New York: Knopf, 1949.

Keyssar, Alexander. *The Right To Vote: The Contested History of Democracy in the United States*. New York: Basic Books, 2000.

Kilpatrick, W. "The Project Method." *Teachers College Record*, 19, 4 (1918): 319–35.

Klein, Naomi. "The fate of the end of the end of history." *The Nation*, March 19, 2001.

Kleppner, Paul. *Who Voted? The Dynamics of Electoral Turnout*. New York: Praeger, 1982.

———. *Continuity and Change in Electoral Politics, 1893–1928*. New Haven, Conn.: Greenwood Press, 1987.

Kleppner, Paul, and Stephen C. Baker. "The Impact of Voter Registration Requirements on Electoral Turnout, 1900–1916." *Journal of Political and Military Sociology*, 8, 2 (Fall 1980).

Kliebard, H. *The Struggle for the American Curriculum: 1893–1958*. New York: Routledge, 1995.

Knack, Stephen. "Does 'Motor Voter' Work? Evidence from State-Level Data." *Journal of Politics*, 57, 3 (August 1995).

Kousser, J. Morgan. *The Shaping of Southern Politics: Suffrage Restrictions and the Establishment of the One-Party South*. New Haven, Conn.: Yale University Press, 1974.

Larry Sabato, and Glenn Simpson. *Dirty Little Secrets: The Persistence of Corruption in American Politics*. New York: Times Books, 1996.

League of Women Voters Education Fund. "Administrative Obstacles to Voting." Mimeo, 1972.

LeDuc, Lawrence, Richard Niemi, and Pippa Norris. *Comparing Democracies: Elections and Voting in Global Perspective*. Thousand Oaks, Calif.: Sage Publications, 1996.

Lessig, Lawrence. "Jail Time in the Digital Age." *New York Times*, July 30, 2001, p. A21.

Levine, Peter. *The New Progressive Era: Toward a Fair and Deliberative Democracy*. Lanham, Md.: Rowman & Littlefield, 2000.

———. Interview with Mitch Ogden, St. Paul, Minnesota, June 27, 2001a.

———. "The Legitimacy of Labor Unions." Forthcoming in the *Hofstra Labor and Employment Law Journal* 18 (2001b): 529–73.

———. "Campaign Web Pages and the Public Interest." Forthcoming in David M. Anderson and Michael Cornfield, *The Civic Web: Online Politics and Democratic Values*. Lanham, Md.: Rowman & Littlefield, 2002.

Lichtman, Allan J. "Report on the Racial Impact of the Rejection of Ballots Cast in the 2000 Presidential Election in the State of Florida." For the U.S. Commission on Civil Rights, 2001. [www.usccr.gov/vote2000/stdraft1.htm]

Lijphart, Arend. "Unequal Participation: Democracy's Unresolved Dilemma." *American Political Science Review,* 91, 1 (1997): 1–14.

———. "Reforming the House: Three Moderately Radical Proposals." *PS: Political Science and Politics* (March 1998): 10–13.

Lind, Michael. *The Next American Nation: The New Nationalism and the Fourth American Revolution.* New York: The Free Press, 1996.

Lippmann, Walter. *Drift and Mastery.* Madison: University of Wisconsin Press, 1985 [originally published in 1914].

Lobbia, J. A. "War of the Roses, Garden Vote Could Settle a Perennial Problem." *The Village Voice* (July 31, 2001): 28.

Lueck, Thomas J. "Democrats Fault Mayor over Garden." *New York Times,* February 19, 2000, p. B2.

Lustig, R. Jeffrey. *Corporate Liberalism: The Origins of American Political Theory.* Berkeley: University of California Press, 1982.

Lux, Mike. Unpublished analysis on file with the author, 2000.

Mansbridge, Jane. *Beyond Adversary Democracy.* Chicago: University of Chicago Press, 1983.

Manza, Jeff, Christopher Uggen, and Marcus Britton. "The Truly Disenfranchised: Felon Voting Rights and American Politics." The Institute for Policy Research, Electronic Policy Network, 2001. [www.epn.org.]

Mathews, David. *Politics for People,* 2nd ed. Chicago: University of Illinois Press, [1994] 1999.

Mattson, Kevin. *Creating a Democratic Public: The Struggle for Urban Participatory Democracy During the Progressive Era.* University Park: Penn State Press, 1998.

May, Henry. *The End of American Innocence: A Study of the First Years of Our Own Time.* Chicago: Quadrangle, 1964.

McCarty, Nolan M., Keith T. Poole, and Howard Rosenthal. "Congress and the Territorial Expansion of the United States." Paper prepared for the Stanford–UCSD Conference on the History of Congress, 1999.

McChesney, Robert W. *Rich Media, Poor Democracy: Communication Politics in Dubious Times.* Chicago: University of Illinois Press, 1999.

McCormick, Richard L. "The Discovery that Business Corrupts Politics: A Reappraisal of the Origins of Progressivism." *American Historical Review* 86 (1981a): 247–74.

———. *From Realignment to Reform: Political Change in New York State, 1893–1910.* Ithaca, N.Y.: Cornell University Press, 1981b.

McCormick, Richard P. *The History of Voting in New Jersey: A Study of the Development of Election Machinery, 1664–1911.* New Brunswick, N.J.: Rutgers University Press, 1953.

McCrary, George W. *A Treatise on the American Law of Elections,* 3d ed. Chicago: Callaghan & Co., 1887.

McGerr, Michael. *The Decline of Popular Politics: The American North, 1865–1928.* New York: Oxford, 1986.

McLaren, P., and M. Pruyn. "Indoctrination." In *Philosophy of Education: An Encyclopedia,* edited by J. J. Chambliss. New York: Garland, 1996.

McNight, John. "Regenerating Community." *Social Policy* (Winter 1987): 54–55.

Meier, Deborah. *The Power of Their Ideas.* Boston: Beacon Press, 1995.

Merriam, Charles E., and Harold Gosnell. *Non-Voting: Causes and Methods of Control.* Chicago: University of Chicago Press, 1924.

Michels, Robert. *Political Parties: A Sociological Study of the Oligarchical Tendencies of Modern Democracy.* Trans. Eden and Cedar Pail. New York: Hearst's International Library, 1915.

Milkis, Sidney, and Jerome Mileur, eds. *Progressivism and the New Democracy.* Amherst: University of Massachusetts Press, 1999.

Moglen, Eben. "Anarchism Triumphant: Free Software and the Death of Copyright." *FirstMonday,* 1999. [www.firstmonday.org]

Moos, E. "Steps Toward the American Dream." *Progressive Education,* 9 (1932): 264–65.

Morin, Richard. "Misperceptions Cloud Whites' View of Blacks." *The Washington Post,* July 11, 2001, p. A1.

National Commission on Federal Election Reform. *To Assure Pride and Confidence in the Electoral Process.* Charlottesville, Va.: Miller Center of Public Affairs, August 2001.

National Municipal League. Richard J. Carlson, ed. *Issues of Electoral Reform.* New York: National Municipal League and Ann Arbor: University Microfilms International, 1974.

National Voting Rights Institute, Boston, Mass. [www.nvri.org]

Nye, Joseph S., Jr. "Introduction: The Decline of Confidence in Government." In *Why People Don't Trust Government,* edited by Joseph S. Nye Jr., Philip D. Zelikow, and David C. King. Cambridge, Mass.: Harvard University Press, 1997.

Orren, Gary. "Fall from Grace: The Public's Loss of Faith in Government." In *Why People Don't Trust Government,* edited by Joseph S. Nye Jr., Philip D. Zelikow, and David C. King. Cambridge, Mass.: Harvard University Press, 1997.

Ostrom, Elinor. *Governing the Commons: The Evolution of Institutions for Collective Action.* Cambridge: Cambridge University Press, 1990.

Parsons, Christi. "New Legislature Reform Push." *Chicago Tribune,* July 8, 2001.

Pateman, Carole. *Participation and Democratic Theory.* Cambridge: Cambridge University Press, 1970.

Pew Research Center for the People of the Press. "Internet Gapping Broadcast News Audience." Washington, D.C.: Pew Research Center for the People of the Press, 2000.

Piven, Frances Fox, and Richard A. Cloward. *Why Americans Don't Vote.* New York: Pantheon, 1988.

———. *Why Americans Still Don't Vote: And Why Politicians Want It That Way.* Boston, Mass.: Beacon Press, 2000.

Plummer, Ken. *Telling Sexual Stories: Power, Change, and Social Worlds.* Routledge: London, 1995.

Popkin, Samuel L. *The Reasoning Voter: Communication and Persuasion in Presidential Campaigns.* Chicago: University of Chicago Press, 1991.

Poster, Mark. "CyberDemocracy: Internet and the Public Sphere," 1995. [www.hnet.uci.edu/mposter/writings/democ.html]

Powell, G. Bingham Jr. "American Voter Turnout in Comparative Perspective." *American Political Science Review,* 80, 1 (1986): 17–43.

Pressman, Jeffrey, and Aaron Wildavsky. *Implementation.* Berkeley: University of California Press, 1973.

Putnam, Robert D. *Bowling Alone: The Collapse and Revival of American Community.* New York: Simon & Schuster, 2000.

Raskin, Jamin. "The Debate Gerrymander" *Texas Law Review,* 77 (1999).

———. "Non-Citizen Voting." *Pennsylvania Law Review* (1993).

Reilly, Ben. "Preferential Voting and Political Engineering: A Comparative Study." *Journal of Commonwealth and Comparative Politics,* 35, 1 (March 1997): 1–19.

Richardson, James. *Willie Brown: A Biography.* Berkeley: University of California Press, 1996.

Richie, Robert, and Steven Hill. *Whose Vote Counts.* New York: Beacon Press, 2001.

Robbins, Tom, et al. "Garden Was Razed for a Rudy Contributor." *New York Daily News,* February 18, 2000, p. 45.

Robinson, James Harvey. *The New History.* New York: The Free Press, 1912.

Rosenstone, Steven, and John Mark Hansen. 1993. *Mobilization, Participation, and Democracy in America.* New York: Macmillan, 1993.

Roth, Susan King. "Disenfranchised by Design: Voting Systems and the Electoral Process." The American Political Science Association, March 2001. [www .apsanet.org/new/briefing.cfm]

Rugg, H. "Reconstructing the Curriculum: An Open Letter to Professor Henry Johnson Commenting on Committee Procedure As Illustrated by the Report of the Joint Committee on History and Education for Citizenship." In *Educating the Democratic Mind,* edited by W. Parker, 45–60. New York: State University of New York Press, 1996.

Rusk, Jerold G. "Effect of the Australian Ballot Reform on Split-Ticket Voting, 1896–1908." *American Political Science Review* 64, 4 (December 1970).

———. "Comment." *American Political Science Review* 68, 3 (September 1974).

Sabatier, Paul A., and Daniel A. Mazmanian. "Policy Implementation." In *Encyclopedia of Policy Studies,* edited by Stuart S. Nagel. New York: Marcel Dekker, 1983.

Sabato, Larry, and Glenn Simpson. *Dirty Little Secrets: The Persistence of Corruption in American Politics.* New York: Times Books, 1996.

Salmore, Barbara, and Stephen Salmore. *Candidates, Parties, and Campaigns: Electoral Politics in America.* Washington, D.C.: Congressional Quarterly Inc., 1989.

Sandel, Michael. *Democracy's Discontent: America in Search of a Public Philosophy.* Cambridge: Belknap Press, 1996.

Schattschneider, E. E. *The Semisovereign People.* New York: Holt, Rinehart & Winston, 1960.

Schlossman, Steven, Gail Zellman, Richard Schavelson with Michael Sedlack and Jane Cobb. *Delinquency Prevention in South Chicago: A Fifty-Year Assessment of the Chicago Area Project.* Report by the Rand Corp. prepared for National Institute of Education. Santa Monica, Calif.: Rand Corporation, 1984.

Shapiro, Andrew. *The Control Revolution.* New York: Century Foundation/Public Affairs, 1999.

Shaw, Clifford. *An Experimental Neighborhood Program for the Prevention and Treatment of Juvenile Delinquency and Crime.* A Chicago Area Project Report. March 1939. Mimeo.

Sheffner, Benjamin. "Will 'Unholy Alliance' Be Back in 2001? Redistricting Could Team Republicans, Blacks Again," *Roll Call,* January 13, 1997, p. 13.

Shefter, Martin. *Political Parties and the State: The American Historical Experience.* Princeton: Princeton University Press, 1994.

Shepard, Benjamin. "Culture Jamming a Sexpanic!" In *From ACT UP to the WTO: Urban Protest and Community Building in the Era of Globalization,* edited by Benjamin Shepard and Ronald Hayduk. Verso: New York, 2002.

Shepard, Benjamin, and Ronald Hayduk. "Introduction." In *From ACT UP to the WTO: Urban Protest and Community Building in the Era of Globalization,* edited by Shepard and Hayduk. Verso: New York, 2002.

Short, James F. "Introduction." In *Juvenile Delinquency in Urban Areas,* rev. ed., edited by Shaw and McKay, 1–18. Chicago: University of Chicago Press, 1972.

Shultz, Jim. *The Initiative Cookbook.* San Francisco: Democracy Center, 1996.

Sidel, Ruth. "Introduction." In *Twenty Years at House.* New York: Penguin, 1998.

Siegel, H. *Educating for Reason: Rationality, Critical Thinking, and Education.* New York: Routledge, 1988.

Simonds, R. "A Plea for the Children." *Educational Leadership,* 51, 4 (1994): 12–15.

Slonim, Shlomo. "Designing the Electoral College." In *Inventing the American Presidency,* edited by Thomas E. Cronin, 33–60. Lawrence: University Press of Kansas, 1989.

Smith, Daniel. "Campaign Financing of Ballot Initiatives in the American States." In *Dangerous Democracy? The Battle over Ballot Initiatives in America,* edited by Larry Sabato, Howard Ernst, and Bruce Larson. Lanham, Md.: Rowman & Littlefield, 2001.

Sonenshein, Raphael J. *Politics in Black and White: Race and Power in Los Angeles.* Princeton: Princeton University Press, 1993.

Squire, Pervill, David P. Glass, and Raymond Wolfinger. "Residential Mobility and Voter Turnout." *American Political Science Review,* 81, 1 (March 1987).

Startin, Nicholas. "Lessons from the Livingstone Campaign." *Representation: Journal of Representative Democracy,* 38, 1 (Spring 2001).

Stewart, Charles III, and Barry R. Weingast. "Stacking the Senate, Changing the Nation: Republican Rotten Boroughs, Statehood Politics, and American Political Development." *Studies in American Political Development* (Fall 1992): 223–71.

Sullivan, J. W. *Direct Legislation by the Citizenship Through the Initiative and Referendum.* New York: Twentieth Century Publishing Company, 1892.

Sunstein, Cass. *Republic.Com.* Princeton, N.J.: Princeton University Press, 2001.

Taylor, Michael. *The Possibility of Cooperation.* Cambridge: Cambridge University Press, 1987.

Teixeira, Ruy A. *Why Americans Don't Vote: Turnout Decline in the United States, 1960–1984.* Westport, Conn.: Greenwood Press, 1987.

———. *The Disappearing American Voter.* Washington, D.C.: Brookings Institution Press, 1992.

Throgmorton, James A. *Planning as Persuasive Storytelling: The Rhetorical Construction of Chicago's Electric Future.* Chicago: University of Chicago Press, 1996.

Thurber, James A., and Candice J. Nelson *Campaign Warriors: The Role of Political Consultants in Elections.* Washington, D.C.: Brookings Institution Press, 2000.

Tocqueville, Alexis de. *Democracy in America.* Trans. by Henry Reeve and others. New York: Vintage Books, 1954.

Tolchin, Susan. *The Angry American: How Voter Rage Is Changing the Nation,* 2nd ed. Boulder, Colo.: Westview Press, 1999.

Trattner, Walter. *From Poor Law to the Welfare State*, 5th ed. New York: The Free Press, 1994.

Traugott, Michael. "Why Electoral Reform Has Failed: If You Build It, Will They Come?" The American Political Science Association, March 2001. [www .apsanet.org/new/briefing.cfm]

U.S. Census. "Voting and Registration in the Election of November 1998." 2000a. Available at [www.census.gov/prod/2000pubs/p20-523.pdf].

U.S. Census Bureau. *Falling Through the Net, Toward Digital Inclusion*. For the National Telecommunications and Information Administration (NTIA). 2000b. Available at [www.ntia.doc.gov/ntiahome/digitaldivide/index.html].

U.S. Commission on Civil Rights. "The 2000 Presidential Election." [www.usccr.gov]

Van Alstyne, Marshall, and Erik Brynjolfsson. "Electronic Communities: Global Village or Cyberbalkans?" 1997. Available at [web.mit.edu/marshall/www/ papers/CyberBalkans.pdf].

Varelas, M. "Between Theory and Data in a 7th Grade Science Class." *Journal of Research in Science Teaching*, 33, 3 (1996): 229–63.

Verba, Sidney, and Norman H. Nie. *Participation in America: Political Democracy and Social Equality*. Chicago: University of Chicago Press, 1972.

Verba, Sidney, Kay Lehman Schlozman, and Henry E. Brady. *Voice and Equality: Civic Voluntarism in American Politics*. Cambridge, Mass.: Harvard University Press, 1995.

Wade, Richard. "The Withering Away of the Party System." In *Urban Politics New York Style*, edited by Jewel Bellush, and Dick Netzer, 271–96. Armonk, N.Y.: M.E. Sharpe Inc., 1990.

Ware, Alan. *The Breakdown of Democratic Party Organization, 1940–1980*. New York: Oxford University Press, 1985.

Warner, Michael, editor for the Social Text Collective. "Introduction." In *Fear of a Queer Planet: Queer Politics and Social Theory*, 1–7. Minnesota: University of Minnesota Press, 1994.

Wattenberg, Martin P. *The Decline of American Political Parties: 1952–1988*. Cambridge, Mass.: Harvard University Press, 1990.

Wayne, Leslie. "On the Web, Voters Reinvent Grassroots Activism." *New York Times*, May 21, 2000, p. A22.

Weisberg, Jacob. *In Defense of Government*. New York: Scribner, 1996.

Westbrook, Robert. *John Dewey and American Democracy*. Ithaca, N.Y.: Cornell University Press, 1991.

Westen, Tracy. "Can Technology Save Democracy?" *National Civic Review*, 87, 1 (1998).

Westheimer, J. *Among Schoolteachers: Community, Autonomy, and Ideology in Teachers' Work*. New York: Teachers College Press, 1998.

White, Morton. *Social Thought in America: The Revolt Against Formalism*. New York: Oxford, 1976.

Wiebe, Robert. *The Search for Order, 1877–1920*. Westport, Conn.: Greenwood, 1980.

Wigginton, E. *Sometimes a Shining Moment: The Foxfire Experience*. Garden City, N.Y.: Anchor Press/Doubleday Books, 1986.

Wilson, Peter Lamborn, and Bill Weinberg. *Avant Gardening: Ecological Struggles in the City & the World*. New York: Autonomedia, 1999.

Wilson, William Julius. *The Truly Disadvantaged*. Chicago: University of Chicago Press, 1987.

———. "When Work Disappears." *New York Times Magazine*, August 18, 1996, sec. 6, p. 26.

Wolfinger, Raymond, and Steven Rosenstone. *Who Votes?* New Haven, Conn.: Yale University Press, 1980.

Wood, G. *Schools that Work: America's Most Innovative Public Education Programs*. New York: Dutton, 1992.

Woods, David, and Peter Hancock. "Ballot Disaster Reveals Machines Do Not Accurately Recognize and Tabulate Our Votes." The American Political Science Association. March 2001. [www.apsanet.org/new/briefing.cfm]

Zeller, Belle, and Hugh A. Bone. "Repeal of Proportional Representation in New York City: Ten Years in Retrospect." *American Political Science Review*, 42 (December 1948).

Index

About the Contributors

Ronald Hayduk teaches political science at the Borough of Manhattan Community College of the City University of New York (CUNY). He was the director of the New York City Voter Assistance Commission from 1993 to 1996 and consults to research and policy organizations, including the Aspen Institute, Demos, and the Century Foundation. Hayduk has written about political participation, immigration, regionalism, and social movements in *From ACT UP to the WTO: Urban Activism and Community Building in the Era of Globalization* (which he also coedited; Verso, 2002); essays in *In Defense of the Alien*, edited by Lydio Tomasi (Center for Migration Studies, 2001), *Leftist Movements in the United States*, edited by John Berg (Rowman & Littlefield, forthcoming), and *Structural Racism and Community Building* (forthcoming); and in journals and public affairs magazines. Hayduk is currently finishing a book, *Gatekeepers to the Franchise: Election Administration and Voter Participation* (forthcoming). He continues to engage in democracy-building efforts in New York and at the national level.

Steven Hill is the western regional director of the Center for Voting and Democracy. He is the coauthor of *Whose Vote Counts?* (Beacon Press, 2001) and author of a book on politics to be published by Routledge Press in Spring 2002. He is a frequent contributor of political commentaries to the Knight-Ridder wire service, and his articles and commentaries have appeared in dozens of newspapers and magazines, including the *Washington Post, New York Times, Los Angeles Times, Wall Street Journal, New York Daily News, The Nation, Ms., Roll Call, Miami Herald, Baltimore Sun, Chicago Tribune, Houston Chronicle, San Antonio Express-News, Atlanta Journal-Constitution, Providence Journal, Hartford Courant, Salon.com, Mother Jones Wire, TomPaine.com, Asian Week, Christian Science Monitor, San Francisco Chroni-

cle, Seattle Times, Arizona Republic, Boston Review, Social Policy, In These Times, and many others. His work has also been published in the academic press, including *Representation: Journal of Representative Democracy* (Winter 1998), *Inroads, a Journal of Opinion* (Issue 7, 1998), and the anthologies *Making Every Vote Count* (Broadview Press, 1999) and *Civil Rights Since 1787* (New York University Press, 2000). He coauthored a paper presented at the Western Political Science Association convention in 1997. He is a frequent guest on radio and TV shows and has given presentations, testimony, and workshops to numerous conferences, charter commissions, legislative committees, and organizations. He is a researcher of European politics and political institutions, having conducted recent research trips to Brussels, Paris, Rome, Amsterdam, and Bonn.

Joseph Kahne is an associate professor of educational policy at Mills College where he directs the doctoral program in educational leadership and the Institute for Civic Leadership. His work focuses on the academic, social, and civic development of youth in school and community settings. Kahne's book, *Reframing Educational Policy: Democracy, Community, and the Individual,* was published by Teachers College Press in 1996. He has worked as a high school teacher in the New York City Public Schools.

Caleb Kleppner directs the Majority Rule Project of the Center for Voting and Democracy, which aims to implement cost-efficient voting systems that ensure majority rule with wide participation. He has drafted legislation to implement or allow instant run-off voting at local, state, and federal levels and worked with election officials to address all aspects of voting equipment and election administration. His articles and commentaries have appeared in newspapers and magazines across the country, and he regularly comments on radio and television. He has made presentations on electoral reform to numerous audiences, including students, local Leagues of Women Voters, Chambers of Commerce, Sierra Club, political groups, and other civic organizations. Prior to joining the Center, he was the executive director of a small nonprofit organization that educates the public about the systemic causes of environmental degradation. He works in San Francisco.

Joel Lefkowitz teaches classes on American political thought, campaigns and elections, and other political science topics at the State University of New York at New Paltz. He is the author of "Student Power and the Movement Against Sweatshops," published in *From ACT UP to the WTO: Urban Protest and Community-Building in the Era of Globalization,* edited by Benjamin Shepard and Ronald Hayduk (New York: Verso, 2002) and, with Christine Kelly, "Radical and Pragmatic: United

Students against Sweatshops," published in *Leftist Movements in the United States*, edited by John Berg (Rowman & Littlefield, forthcoming, 2002).

Peter Levine has published four books including *The New Progressive Era* (Rowman & Littlefield, 2000). He graduated from Yale in 1989 with a B.A. in philosophy. He studied at Oxford as a Rhodes Scholar, receiving his doctorate in 1992. For the next two years, Levine was a research associate at Common Cause helping the organization to lobby for campaign finance reform and government ethics. In 1993, he became a research scholar at the Institute for Philosophy and Public Policy at the University of Maryland. Since 1987, Levine has worked part-time for the Charles Kettering Foundation, of which he is now an associate. He is also deputy director of CIRCLE, the Center for Information and Research on Civic Learning and Engagement.

Kevin Mattson is associate professor of American history at Ohio University (Athens). Before entering academia, he was a political activist in Washington, D.C., where he organized youth groups working on issues of peace and social justice during the 1980s (one group was recently featured in *The Nation*). After acquiring a Ph.D., Mattson came to the Walt Whitman Center for the Culture and Politics of Democracy at Rutgers University in 1995 where he served as associate director. There he oversaw numerous projects combining academic research with community-based practice, all aimed at enhancing democratic participation. As a historian, he has published *Creating a Democratic Public: The Struggle for Urban Participatory Democracy During the Progressive Era* (Penn State Press, 1998); an introduction to the reissue of Mary Parker Follett's 1918 work in democratic political theory, *The New State* (Penn State Press, 1998); and *Intellectuals in Action: The Origins of the New Left and Radical Liberalism, 1945–1970* (Penn State, forthcoming). He has written essays, editorials, and reviews for magazines and journals including *The Nation, In These Times, Commonweal, The Baffler, Dissent,* and *Social Policy* on numerous subjects such as public education reform, youth culture, generational politics, the academic labor movement, community service, the revival of progressive politics, and issues of democracy and citizenship in 20th-century America. In addition, he has researched and written reports on youth political participation for the Carnegie Corporation of New York and the Century Foundation.

Lincoln Mitchell is a political scientist and consultant based in New York City. He has an extensive background in local and state politics in New York City and elsewhere, including serving as the manager of C. Virginia

Fields's successful race for Manhattan Borough president, general consultant for Kathryn Freed for Public Advocate, and numerous other positions. Mitchell has also worked on campaigns for Representative Charles Rangel, Speaker Peter Vallone, and former Mayor David Dinkins. He has been a course facilitator in the Democratic National Committee's national campaign training program in Washington, D.C., and has trained party activists and political candidates in Bosnia-Herzegovina and Bulgaria. Mitchell has a Ph.D. in political science from Columbia University and has taught courses on the media, campaigns and elections, and urban politics at Columbia, as well as at Brown University and at Hunter College. He has also worked as a consultant for the Rockefeller Foundation's building democracy program and the New York City Community Leadership Institute. His political observations have been heard on New York One, WNYC, MSNBC, Fox News, Bronxtalk, and in the *Village Voice, Jewish Week, El Diario,* and the other New York City daily newspapers.

Galen Nelson is executive director and founder of the Ballot Initiative Strategy Center (BISC). BISC was founded in 1996 to help defeat right-wing ballot initiatives and to catalyze the development of a proactive, national initiative strategy for progressives. Nelson also directs the Ballot Initiative Strategy Center Foundation's Money in Ballot Measures project. Nelson served as assistant field director and a field organizer at People For the American Way (PFAW) from 1992 to 1998 where he led organizing and lobbying efforts around state legislation, conducted trainings, and spearheaded national organizing efforts around federal cabinet nominees and legislation related to gay civil rights, religious freedom, reproductive choice, and public education. Nelson also worked on several ballot measure campaigns and managed a PFAW-sponsored presidential primary campaign in New Hampshire. Prior to that, Nelson worked for two national arts advocacy organizations. Nelson serves on the steering committee of Massachusetts Voters for Clean Elections, the state's campaign finance reform advocacy group.

Jamin Raskin is the codirector of the Washington College of Law (WCL) Program on Law and Government and a professor at American University. He has edited books on democratic issues and written dozens of articles for the *Harvard Law Review, Columbia Law Review, University of Pennsylvania Law Review, American University Journal of Gender and the Law, Yale Law and Policy Review, Hastings Law Journal, Howard Law Journal,* and *Catholic University Law Review.* Additionally, Raskin has written popular essays on law and politics for the *Washington Post, Los Angeles Times, Philadelphia Inquirer, Minneapolis Star Tribune, Z Magazine, Nation, California Lawyer,* and *In These Times.* He recently published a crucial article on opening up political debates: "The Debate Gerrymander," 77 *Texas Law Review* 1943 (1999). Raskin has been an expert witness and delivered testimony before the U.S. House of Representatives, U.S. Senate, U.S. Commission on Civil Rights, the Maryland General Assembly, and Council of the District of Columbia. Raskin was a member of the Clinton–Gore Justice Department Transition Team, 1992; the assistant attorney general, Commonwealth of Massachusetts, 1987–1989; and the general counsel, National Rainbow Coalition, 1989–1990.

Robert Richie is the executive director of the Center for Voting and Democracy, a nonprofit organization that researches and advocates election reforms that promote voter turnout, accountable governance, and fair representation. Richie is an expert on both international and domestic electoral systems and has directed the Center, whose president chair is former member of Congress John Anderson, since its founding in 1992. His writings appeared in four books in 1999, including the feature essay on proportional representation in *Whose Votes Count?* (Beacon, 2001). Richie has published commentary in the *New York Times, Washington Post, Wall Street Journal, Roll Call, Nation, National Civic Review, Social Policy, Boston Review, Christian Science Monitor,* and *Legal Times.* Among his other activities, Richie has worked with the staff of Congresswoman Cynthia McKinney in developing the Voters' Choice Act, as introduced in each year since 1995 (to allow states to use PR systems) and the staff of Congressman Melvin Watt in developing the similar States' Choice of Voting Systems Act in 1999. He has testified in special sessions before charter commissions in numerous jurisdictions. Richie edits the Center's newsletter and other publications like its Voting and Democracy reports and its biannual analyses of congressional elections that have received prominent news coverage around the nation. He is a frequent source for print, radio, and television journalists. Richie has been a guest on many radio and television programs, including C-SPAN, NPR, MSNBC, FOX, CNN, and NBC.

Mark Schmitt was a senior adviser to Bill Bradley's campaign for president. He was involved in issues development, communications, and debate preparation. He is presently director for governance and public policy at the Open Society Institute (OSI), a New York–based grant-making and operating foundation established by George Soros. At OSI, he developed the foundation's Initiative on Campaign Finance Reform and Democratic Participation, as well as a program that strengthened the capacity of state and local nonprofits to respond to the devolution of government services from the federal level to the states. Before joining OSI, Mark Schmitt was policy director to Senator Bradley for seven years.

In that capacity, Schmitt helped develop major legislation on student loans, an Urban Community-Building Initiative, the child support enforcement system, and a distinctive campaign finance reform proposal. His writings on U.S. politics have appeared in *Foreign Policy, The New Republic, Foreign Affairs, The National Civic Review,* and *The Los Angeles Times.*

Benjamin Shepard is a social worker moonlighting as a social historian. By day he combines his work as a program director of an AIDS housing program with his doctoral studies in social welfare at Hunter College, CUNY; by night he is involved in campaigns to save New York's public spaces. Shepard is coeditor of *From ACT UP to the WTO: Urban Protest and Community Building in the Era of Globalization* (Verso, 2002), and author of *White Nights and Ascending Shadows: An Oral History of the San Francisco AIDS Epidemic* (Cassell, 1997). His work has appeared in *Monthly Review, WorkingUSA: A Journal of Labor, Minnesota Review, Antioch Review,* and two other book collections: John Berg's *Leftist Movements in the United States* (Rowman & Littlefield, forthcoming) and David Colbert's *Eyewitness to the American West: 500 Years of Firsthand History* (Penguin, 1999).

R. Claire Snyder is assistant professor of government and politics in the Department of Public and International Affairs at George Mason University where she teaches political theory. Her publications include *Citizen-Soldiers and Manly Warriors: Military Service and Gender in the Civic Republican Tradition* (Rowman & Littlefield, 1999) and "Social Capital: The Politics of Race and Gender," published in *Robert Putnam and Social Capital: Critical Perspectives on American Democracy and Social Engagement* (New York University Press, forthcoming), as well as a number of articles on higher education and public life. Snyder currently serves as executive director of the Virginia Citizenship Institute (VCI), which runs a state-focused civic leadership training program for young Virginians. In addition, she is a longtime associate of the Kettering Foundation and the former director of their projects on the History of Higher Education and the Evolution of Public Life. Snyder holds a Ph.D. from Rutgers University and a B.A. cum laude from Smith College.

Joel Westheimer is an associate professor of education at the University of Ottawa and fellow of the Center for the Study of American Culture and Education at New York University. A former New York City public schools teacher and musician, he currently writes about democracy and community in education, service learning, and civic and social goals of schooling. Westheimer's 1998 book *Among Schoolteachers: Community, Autonomy, and Ideology in Teacher's Work* was published by Teachers College Press.

Richard Winger is a leading expert on ballot access. He is presently editor of *Ballot Access News*, a nonpartisan newsletter. His writings on these matters have appeared in *Multiparty Politics in America*, edited by Paul Herrnson and John C. Green (Rowman & Littlefield, 1997); *The Encyclopedia of Third Parties in America*, edited by Immanuel Ness and James Ciment (M.E. Sharpe, 2000); and *The New Populist Reader*, edited by Karl Trautman (Praeger, 1997). Winger's writing has also appeared in the *Wall Street Journal*, *American Review of Politics*, and *California Journal*. In addition, he has appeared as a commentator on ballot access on NBC, ABC, CNN, and NPR.

My home, my life

Practical ideas for people with dementia and carers

Colm Cunningham and Natalie Duggan
with Agnes Houston

Published by HammondCare 2018

Sydney, Australia, Edinburgh, Scotland.
hammondcaremedia@hammond.com.au
hammondcare.com.au
dementiacentre.com.au

ISBN 978-0-9945461-9-7

Design: Melissa Summers of SD Creative

 A catalogue record for this
book is available from the
National Library of Australia

Important: Dementia care knowledge and research is continually changing and as new
understanding develops, so to does the support provided for people with dementia. All care
has been taken by the authors and publishers, as far as possible at time of publication, to
ensure information is accurate and up-to-date. You can contribute to future editions of this
book by going to myhomemylifebook.com

The information in this book is not intended to be used to diagnose, treat, cure or prevent any
disease, nor should it be used for therapeutic purposes or as a substitute for your own health
professional's advice. The authors do not accept liability for any injury, loss or damage incurred
by use of or reliance on the information contained in this book.

Thank you: The Dementia Centre and HammondCare Media are committed to providing
excellence in dementia care. Older and younger people living with dementia deserve services
that are designed and delivered based on evidence and practice knowledge of what works.
This is achieved through providing research, training and education, publications and
information, consultancy and conferences. Thank you to everyone who supported the
publication of *My home, my life: Practical ideas for people with dementia and carers.*

Contents

'No one is pretending there are not challenges for people with dementia living at home. But neither should we lose sight of the fact that the person with dementia can be an active and engaged citizen with quality of life, full of rich experiences, tears and laughter and, of course, love and respect.'

~Agnes Houston

Foreword

Supporting the person living with dementia involves a partnership—a bringing together of the voices of people with dementia and carers, together with the best learning from research and practice experience.

That is what I believe is helpful in *My home, my life: Practical ideas for people with dementia and carers.* It presents many insightful tips and strategies that support the person who has dementia and their carer to live more independently at home and away from home—active in their community.

As well, better understanding the impacts of dementia may help both the person with dementia and the people supporting them. Learning how to communicate with more than words will be useful for the carer. And it will also help to understand that what appears to be a behaviour of the person with dementia is most often a form of communication—to be understood and interpreted, not dismissed or worse still, treated incorrectly with drugs or disdain.

Thinking about design features at home may offer enhancements that further enable the independence of the person with dementia, without losing familiarity which is so important.

Considering how best to approach a range of common activities outside the home promotes the value of people with dementia continuing to engage with the people and interests that are important to them.

No one is pretending there are not challenges for people with dementia living at home. But neither should we lose sight of the fact that the person with dementia can be an active and engaged citizen with quality of life–full of rich experiences, tears and laughter and, of course, love and respect.

We hope you enjoy the book and look forward to reading your tips, suggestions and stories too through myhomemylifebook.com on the Dementia Centre website.

~ Agnes and Donna Houston

Introduction

Respecting and better understanding the experience of a person living with dementia is essential to providing enabling environments and supporting the person to live at home.

This is why we are seeing the latest technologies employed to achieve this. One example is the Virtual Reality Empathy Platform[1]. It assists architects, designers and project managers to better understand the impact of good dementia design in the context of the impairments often experienced by people with dementia.

It's great that technology can provide these insights. And it highlights the value, for those who support people living with dementia, of understanding what the person's daily experience may be like, and how this may change over time.

People with dementia[2] have led the way in making it better known that the symptoms of dementia are more than memory loss, that they also include many sensory changes and challenges.

We hope to build on that awareness through this book by providing the person with dementia, carers and other supporters with practical information to create enabling and dignified living environments at home (in the community and also in residential care), as well as the means to move beyond home to have an active life in the world outside.

Maximising independence

One important discovery from our research and by listening to and supporting people with dementia is that environment can either help maximise independence (and enhance a sense of dignity) or it can highlight disabilities, creating feelings of dependence on others. No matter how advanced dementia is, there is opportunity to see the person's capacity and make room for it to be expressed.

That's the purpose of *My home, my life*. It is designed to enable living at home for as long as possible—supporting both the person with dementia and carer. It includes enough theoretical information to answer the many 'why' questions, and backs this up with lots of practical details to provide the 'how to'.

How *My home, my life* works

My home, my life has three sections:

- Me, dementia and growing older

- Enjoying life at home

- Being active beyond the home

Chapters are easy to read and include the aim (what will be learned), real-life stories and summary points at the end of each chapter. Then right at the end of the book there are some additional resources, tips and information.

Some people living with dementia may like to read all or part of the book alone or with a carer. In other cases, the carer may read it with or on behalf of the person with dementia, depending on the person's capacity and choice. You can start at the beginning and go through to the end (it's not too long) or dive in to whatever part is most relevant.

Because we recognise readers will approach the book in different ways, and from a variety of starting points, we have allowed some repetition of ideas so that they are not missed.

Everything included is backed up by research but we've kept referencing to a minimum to avoid making the book seem too daunting and complicated. Instead, look for our further reading lists at the end of many chapters.

> *Caring tip:* Those parts of the book that describe the symptoms and progress of dementia may in some cases be distressing to both the person with dementia and carers, so take it at your own pace and remember you are not alone, there are a range of supports listed towards the end of the book in the 'Useful organisations' section.

To change or not to change

Many suggestions in this book involve changes to design and approach that could be helpful to implement at home. Some are minor (many do-it-yourself) and inexpensive, others are larger and could incur substantial cost.

Whatever the case, any changes should be paced and balanced with the benefits of familiarity. A person with dementia may initially welcome the extra light in the room because you've changed the window coverings, only to feel confused later by the unfamiliar changes. This is why the personal dynamic of support and knowing the person is as important as any design insights presented.

Of course, if there are plans to move home (such as to live with a relative or move into a retirement village), or changes are needed for other reasons (carpets worn out, necessary refurbishments) then this might present the opportunity to implement some of the ideas presented here.

Everyone is different

It's important to emphasise that each person with dementia is unique (as is their carer and the other people supporting them) even though there are some common experiences of dementia. So the starting point is always recognising:

- the person as an individual
- there are personal preferences for care and support
- different things that bring pleasure or are triggers for frustration or confusion.

Our recommendations are purely that—recommendations. Support and care needs to be individualised.

Some earlier books have provided good information on how to make the most of the home environment. But we hear from people with dementia that this is not the end of the story. For example, people with dementia recently contributed to dementia-inclusive guidelines[3] for internal and external public spaces. Having an enabling environment at home includes being able to go out as well! So you will find plenty of practical information for getting the most out of your time away from home.

How you can contribute

As a companion to this book, a section on the Dementia Centre website will become a hub for sharing your tips, ideas and experiences. Please use www.myhomemylifebook.com in your internet browser to discover more—we'd love to hear from you!

Part 1
Me, dementia and growing older

01 Dementia and its symptoms

What we will learn

- What dementia is
- Symptoms and tips for managing
- Stages of dementia
- The impacts of ageing
- When behaviour changes

Dementia is a term used to describe a range of progressive disorders that affect the brain. There are younger people living with dementia, but it is more commonly a condition of older age, accompanied by age-related issues which we address in Chapter 2.

Our brain controls everything we do, with messages travelling to and from the body so if the brain is being affected by dementia, our daily lives will be affected too.

Different parts of the brain are responsible for different functions e.g. frontal lobe—planning and behaviour; temporal lobe—memory; limbic system—sleep, hunger.[4] The varying forms of dementia impact the brain differently which means the experience of dementia is highly individual but with some similar themes.

Forms of dementia

The most common form of dementia is Alzheimer's disease and it is usually characterised by a gradual but persistent decline in cognitive functioning. Vascular dementia is the next most common and usually involves a stepped cognitive decline due to a series of vascular events that affect blood circulation to the brain.

Lewy body disease is another form of dementia caused by the death of nerve cells in the brain. Symptoms can be characterised by fluctuations in mental state such as periods of extreme confusion and hallucinations. Falls are also common. Frontotemporal dementia (formerly known as Pick's disease), Huntington's disease, alcohol-related brain damage, HIV and AIDs-related dementia are some of the other forms of the condition. There are many other diseases that can cause dementia.

While the experience of dementia is different for everyone, and the different forms of dementia also vary in impact, it is almost always a progressive condition, with increased symptoms over time.

The human impact of dementia

When we consider the range of symptoms that people living with dementia may experience, it is clear why a dementia-inclusive approach to design and lifestyle can help support improved quality of life at home and in the community.

Below we provide some additional detail about the more common impacts of dementia along with one or two simple tips for the person with dementia and carer. These are addressed in more detail later in the book when we look at 'Enjoying life at home' (Part 2) and 'Being active beyond the home' (Part 3).

Problems with memory

Impaired memory is very common and can impact many aspects of life from remembering a name, knowing where you are or what season of life you are in. People with dementia are more likely to retain and rely on their long-term memory, while losing their short-term memory more quickly. For example, a carer may find the person with dementia believes their dead husband is still alive (or has only just died), that there son is their husband, or that they generally approach life as if they are living 30 or 40 years in the past.

Depending on the stage of dementia, memory changes might also mean the person with dementia doesn't remember he or she needs to wear glasses, or might not recognise family or friends. The person might not identify familiar places or usual routes they would have taken and may not remember what they've done today.

John misses his wife

John's wife, Helen died two years ago after a short illness. At the time, it was important to John to be part of planning her funeral and to speak at the service about their many years of marriage. John used to remember that Helen had died, but as his dementia progressed he no longer recalled this fact. Now, when John asks for Helen, his grief is as real as the first day he received this sad news. John's daughter realises the importance of her father being able to talk about Helen and remember their life together, but that it is no longer helpful to focus on the fact of her death. His daughter put together a photo album so that now when John talks about Helen, instead of reminding him of the sad news, she starts by mentioning a part of Helen's life and opening the album at this part. She has also written about some of their life together, so that visiting care staff can also be supportive of John.

Caring tip: When faced with memory symptoms, we recommend to not constantly correct the person with dementia. Due to cognitive impairment, a person with dementia may often be 'incorrect' about the accuracy or timeline of information, but to them it seems 'right', so correction is of little value. Another approach is 'validation' where we identify aspects of what is being understood, said or remembered that are valid and purposeful. And don't set up the person for failure by asking questions like 'what did you do today?' or 'where did you put your brush?' as the answer might be a brusque 'I'd tell you if I could remember!'

Sensory changes and challenges

Most people who receive a diagnosis of dementia are aware they may experience (or already have) memory problems. But they are often surprised when they begin to encounter 'unexplained' sensory changes such as reduced or confused vision and hypersensitivity to noise.[5] We'll look at these changes more closely in Chapter 4, along with of strategies to support people with dementia experiencing sensory challenges. But the starting point is to be aware they occur and encouraging the person with dementia to describe what they are experiencing.

> 'I did not think that getting a diagnosis affecting cognition would affect senses so when I started to have sensory challenges I did not think it had anything to do with dementia...'[6]

Difficulty with planning, organising and problem solving

These symptoms are particularly relevant to our book because life at home, as well as the activity of going out, both involve aspects of planning, organising and problem solving. There may be challenges in getting organised to prepare a meal, make a cup of tea, get ready for the day or to go out to a meeting. Simple problems may become insurmountable such as getting the TV remote to work, hanging the washing on the line or working out what train or bus to catch to arrive for an appointment on time. This is because damage to the brain and impaired memory make it hard to make the dozens of little connections that allow these things to occur.

'Most people who receive a diagnosis of dementia are aware they may experience memory problems. But they are often surprised when they begin to encounter 'unexplained' sensory changes...'

Keeping essential items in plain view and reducing clutter can make life easier. Good contrast in the kitchen also helps, as does keeping things familiar.

Caring tip: One (obvious) tip is 'making it easier' for the person with dementia. Being able to continue to live at home is a good start as the familiarity of home is a strong enabling factor. This can be further enhanced by placing in plain view things that will be needed or wanted in the day such as tea and coffee, while putting out of sight less essential items and clutter. An easy to read clock (analogue tends to work best) with day and date accompanied by a list of meaningful tasks or activities for the day may make it easier for the person with dementia to exercise greater independence. But remember if the list is not updated (another task for a busy carer) it may cause further confusion. Finally, for now, (more in Part 2), design enhancements might include labels, (with pictures, not just words) such as on drawers or useful items so the person can undertake tasks with more independence.

While every person with dementia is different, it is common for more complex activities—such as family finances—to become difficult in the earlier stages of dementia, while more basic activities such as bathing and dressing are challenging in the moderate and later stages of dementia. In the next chapter, we'll take a closer look at the stages of dementia and impacts of the ageing process, remembering that most people with dementia are older.

Key points

- Dementia is a term describing a range of progressive conditions that affect the brain.
- Younger people are diagnosed with dementia but it is more commonly a condition of older age.
- Memory problems, sensory changes and difficulties with problem solving and planning are some of the common impacts of dementia.
- Correcting a person with dementia is of less value than validating their feelings and experience.

02 Stages of dementia and the impact of ageing

What we will learn

- Impacts of dementia at different stages
- Developing support strategies
- Ageing and dementia

The onset and development of the symptoms of dementia are gradual and so when being described, are often grouped into three stages—early, middle and late.[7]

It's important not to think of these stages as 'boxes' that define people. Rather, it's helpful is to be aware that dementia is a progressive condition that impacts people in different ways at different times. And this doesn't mean there is nothing we can do when receiving a diagnosis of dementia. Just as treatment or rehabilitation is available for other serious illnesses, we are learning more about ways to manage the impacts of dementia, particularly in the early stages.[8] Things such as healthy lifestyle and diet, exercise and keeping active and creative, may assist. But there is no cure (yet!) and so being aware of how symptoms might progress is important.

Early stage dementia

In mild or early stage dementia, many people might not actually be aware that they have the condition. The person can live independently—and strongly desire this—but may need some assistance. This might include strategies to overcome memory problems or support with some aspects of personal care.

The following symptoms may be experienced[9]:

- memory loss, particularly of recent events
- disorientation, particularly towards time

- problem solving difficulties
- less interest in usual hobbies or tasks
- difficulties with activities of personal care.

Middle stage dementia

In moderate or middle stage dementia, symptoms may sometimes be more obvious and can include:

- more significant memory loss
- needing more help at home and getting out in the community
- disorientation towards time as well as place
- difficulty finding appropriate words
- lack of judgement and problem-solving.

Some assistance can help maintain favourite pastimes and connections.

When Amy was first diagnosed with dementia some of her family were surprised as they had barely noticed any changes. She did sometimes reply to emails multiple times but she was using her computer mostly without assistance, cooking meals and generally managing the household. But when her husband became very unwell, it was apparent that he had been quietly providing a lot of support such as sorting out computer issues, helping to plan and cook meals and regularly taking time with Amy to consult their diaries and record or read about what was coming up. In time, Amy was unable to use the computer at all and could not reply to emails. However it was still important to her to keep in touch with 'online' friends, so family enjoyed turning on her computer and helping her to read about her friendship group on social media, sometimes assisting her to post her usual cheeky comments. Eventually the day came when Amy's computer was packed away as she had lost interest and the focus was now on enjoying other activities and life in the moment.

In mild or middle stage dementia, and depending on the person, they will be aware (perhaps painfully so) of the challenges they are experiencing. This may present the opportunity for the person to talk with others about what they are experiencing which will help better support them and may also help other people who are experiencing similar challenges.

Advanced dementia

Caring tip: If you live with dementia, or have recently begun caring for someone with dementia, you may still be learning what to expect. The following description is of more advanced dementia and it may be confronting or distressing. Perhaps consider reading this with a supportive person present or skip to the next section. Remember everyone is different, and so the details below are general descriptions and don't apply to everyone.

In the later stages of dementia, the person usually requires more extensive assistance to function.

Symptoms and care needs when dementia is advanced may include:

- severe memory loss
- limited or no language or verbalisation
- very little problem-solving ability
- difficulties remembering even familiar people
- incontinence
- extensive assistance with personal care such as showering
- difficulty recognising day and night
- loss of interest in food and mealtimes.

Alongside the symptoms above, people with dementia can also experience:

- hallucinations
- delirium as a result of infections, dehydration, medications
- other illnesses
- stress related to the challenges being experienced
- side effects of medications.

Finally, people with more advanced dementia are also more likely to experience changes in their behaviour and psychological symptoms which can include 'anxiety, sadness, despair, or anger.'[10]

Caring tip: Some strategies for supporting a person with dementia with personal care or daily routines may be very successful at some point and less so in other stages of dementia. The success of strategies is also impacted (as for any of us) by mood, emotions, tiredness, illness and even the weather. As the carer you may need to be ready to set aside a previously effective strategy and try new ideas. At other times you might find yourself returning to earlier strategies.

Effects of ageing

Dementia is not a natural part of ageing—it is an illness or disorder. But there are many natural effects of ageing that may occur alongside or even compound the impact of dementia. These include:

- impaired or reduced eyesight
- loss of hearing
- reduced muscle strength and motility (ability to mobilise independently)
- increased prevalence of other chronic conditions.

When we consider the natural trajectory and associated changes that come with ageing, coupled with the symptoms of dementia, it is not surprising that the person with dementia may feel vulnerable and need reassurance and support while also trying to retain their independence.

Dementia can also contribute to people feeling frustrated by their interactions with people around them and the environment.[11]

Bringing all of this together—we can see the importance of considering design in the home or public environment to minimise disability, increase independence and reduce feelings of frustration and vulnerability.

Key points

- Dementia progresses and so different people experience a range of symptoms at different times.
- Support strategies that are helpful at some point may be less so at a later time, so being flexible and adaptable as a carer is important.
- Ageing may contribute other effects such as impaired eyesight, loss of hearing and reduced mobility.

03 Understanding changed behaviour

What we will learn

- What is meant by 'behaviours'?
- Why behaviours might change
- How to support distressed behaviour
- Good communication

As we have seen, dementia describes a range of conditions that affect the brain and this can result in direct or indirect changes to personality, memory, social interactions, sensory perception, language and behaviour. In this chapter we focus on what, clinically, has often been described as behavioural and psychological symptoms of dementia (BPSD). We prefer to simply say changed or distressed behaviour.

Some behaviours associated with dementia may never occur for you or the person you care for, or may only be for a limited time.

What is changed behaviour?

Behaviour is a complex phenomenon that exists in every human being. Everyone has behaviour that is an expression of who they are and generally fits within broad social norms (but not always!). Behaviour can be influenced by internal factors such as joy, anxiety, past habits and experiences and external factors as diverse as overcrowding and loud noises through to beautiful scenery and pleasant music. Cognitive impairment can also influence behaviour.

In the context of dementia, reoccurring behaviour may be linked to dementia itself, or wrongly attributed to being 'just the dementia' when in fact there is another cause such as an unmet need.

These behaviours come to notice when they:

- seem different to what we know of the person
- demonstrate a person with dementia's distress
- are distressing for the people providing care.

They can be active behaviours such as aggression, repeated calling out and wanting to leave, or passive behaviours such as apathy or withdrawal.

We all communicate through our behaviours—people with dementia are no different. What may be different is how dementia is the main factor, but that it interacts with a need that should be addressed but can't be expressed.

> '…research shows that much of this behaviour is a reaction to the physical environment or to things happening around the resident, and is also a form of communication.'[12]

Why do changed behaviours occur?

A common emotional experience for the person with dementia is distress—this can emerge (for example) from frustration with being unable to communicate, confusion as to what is going on around them or feelings of being dependent on other people. This distress may lead to changed behaviours which are indicative of the underlying issue.

In Australia, the national Dementia Support Australia service estimates[13] up to 70 per cent of people referred to them for distressed behaviours are experiencing unrecognised and/or under treated pain. Other common triggers are issues with the environment such as restricted access to outdoors or intrusive noise.

Caring tip: It's important not to see the person as one and the same as the behaviour. Instead, when there is changed behaviour, try to discover:

- the underlying cause
- what the person may be communicating
- how they want us to respond, or how we should respond
- what support they need.

Knowing the person

Many carers know the person with dementia very well, and this is the starting point for responding to changed or distressed behaviour. If the person can't verbally express what is causing their distress, you may be able work it out through your personal knowledge of their likes and dislikes, fears and anxieties, routines and rituals. Consider the person as they were before being diagnosed with the dementia.

Here are some further carer ideas for supporting a person with distressed behaviour, particularly aggression or agitation:

Listening to personalised music may reduce feelings of distress.

- **Leaving the room** gives the person and yourself some safe space. Allowing the person time to calm may be very helpful. This is especially true when you are unsure of the cause of agitation or distress.

- **Pain** is a common cause of distress, as mentioned. Ask about pain where possible and look for non-verbal signs of discomfort from pain. Discuss with your GP or dementia consultant.

- **Using touch** to show appropriate levels of affection may help the person with dementia feel calm or connected to you. Be careful and sensitive to avoid further irritation or confusion and avoid touch if it is unwelcome.

- **Staying calm** and using calm words can be difficult when faced with anger or agitation, but this is not the time to insist on being right or to argue. Apologise if it helps and move the focus if possible.

- **Regular exercise** such as going for a walk, swimming or gardening is extremely beneficial in reducing feelings of distress and burning up energy. The positive effects of exercise and being outdoors are numerous.[14]

- **Music engagement** using personalised music (iPod, singing or listening together) is shown to reduce feelings of distress, increase connection, provide calm and prompt reminiscence and conversation.[15]

- **Life story activities** are a great tool for people with dementia and their carers, supporting connection and familiarity. It can be a box or book or anything that contains a collection of familiar, interesting and important items (photos, letters, music, written-down memories) to the person with dementia.

- **Keep a journal** to help identify triggers, describing things that cause the person with dementia to feel distressed or frustrated. If possible, have conversations to identify the various things that trigger anxiety. In the same way, identify what is calming.

- **Massages or aromatherapy** (such as a hand massage or bath with lavender oil) may help some people. Try a few options and if they work, keep doing them as needed.

- **Pets** and animals can support relaxation and be pleasurable for people who are familiar with them and programs such as Dogs4Dementia have shown a range of benefits[16].

It's important to re-emphasise that care and support for people with dementia benefits from an individual approach. Each person with dementia is different and has different tendencies, idiosyncrasies, triggers and habits. Knowing these things will enrich their care and also help you connect with the person.

A word about 'wandering'

Not everyone is happy with the term 'wandering' but it's widely used and is a common behaviour that may occur with dementia. What it really describes is when a person with dementia wants to leave home or another location at a time or in a way that may not be safe or appropriate.

It can be very concerning for the carer. It can also be distressing for the person with dementia if they realise they are lost, aren't dressed for the outdoors or there is traffic or other hazards.

It's a behaviour that may have a range of underlying causes such as:

- pain which cannot be communicated

- needing to go to the bathroom but being confused about what to do or where to find it

- feeling trapped, stressed and anxious and looking for a way out

- being confused about important tasks from the past, like going to work or collecting the children

- feeling lost and wanting to go 'home'

- being bored and frustrated

- the environment being too noisy

- any combination of the above.

Identifying the main causes will help, as may any of the tips from the previous section, particularly having regular exercise such as walks planned around times the person becomes anxious. Easy access to a safe outdoor space is also key.

Communicating with the person with dementia

Another way to avoid distressed behaviour is seeking to communicate as effectively as possible. It's important to compensate for the communication challenges experienced by the person with dementia. This means adjusting your communication both verbally and non-verbally while still ensuring the person with dementia feels dignified and respected.

In the context of distressed behaviour, it is vital to consider the feelings behind what might be being said or done and, as a carer, to be mindful of your gestures and body language—what impression might they be giving?

For more tips and advice on communication, see Chapter 7.

Keeping a journal can help track distressing triggers and activities that promote calm.

Key points

- There are almost always underlying reasons for changed behaviour.
- Use your knowledge of the person with dementia to identify possible sources of changed behaviours, perhaps through a process of elimination.
- Remembering the person before dementia—what their personality was like and what caused frustration—can help in understanding current behaviours
- Don't underestimate the person's ability to pick up on your non-verbal cues.

Further reading

The room outside: Designing outdoor living for older people and people with dementia, A Pollock & C Cunningham, HammondCare Media, Sydney (2018).

Music remembers me: Connection and wellbeing in dementia, K Beilharz, HammondCare Media, Sydney (2017).

Better for everyone: Tools for managers, staff and families, M Gresham & R Forbes, HammondCare Media, Sydney (2017). A free download is available from dementiacentre.com

The 36 hour day (6th ed), N Mace & P Rabins, John Hopkins Press, Baltimore (2017).

04 More than memory: sensory challenges

Most people will initially associate dementia with memory loss. This can be frustrating for the person with dementia who is also trying to understand a range of other challenges and changes in their life. As we have explored, there are many changes happening in the body as a result of dementia, as well as ageing. The brain controls not only our memory, but also our executive functioning, our senses and even our personality. As a person's dementia progresses, it gradually impacts more of these different aspects of brain activity.

One of the main challenges for people with dementia is the impact on the senses: sight, smell, touch, taste, and hearing. All of these changes affect the person with dementia's ability to interpret the environment around them and make decisions about what is happening and how to respond.

These sensory changes obviously need to be considered when thinking about living at home and when going out into public spaces.

Also, we cannot over-emphasise the importance in personalising care and the environment of the person being cared for—each person experiences these symptoms differently and for different lengths of time.

What's on the path?

Margaret was going for a walk with her grandson on a sunny day when they came to a recently laid section of concrete footpath that was much whiter than previous sections. Margaret paused and looked intently at the white concrete, keeping her feet away from the edge. After a few moments her grandson, sensing her uncertainty gave her a gentle hug and spoke some reassuring words about continuing. Margaret tentatively crossed the white concrete, which may have appeared to her at first as water glistening in the sun, before looking up and enjoying her walk once more.

Sensory changes

The following information comes from *Dementia and Sensory Challenges* edited by author Agnes Houston with contributions from many other people living with dementia. Agnes writes:

> We are ordinary people living ordinary lives, who happen to have a long-term condition called dementia. Please help us continue to live in our homes and our communities, which is something we can do very well if society understood how to support us with our sensory challenges.[17]

The table[18] on the next page is an adaptation of material from the booklet showing sensory challenges and tips for those providing care and support.

An example from residential care (HammondCare Wahroonga) of good lighting, plain colours with contrast, not to mention well designed seating!

Sensory challenge	Tips and ideas
Seeing: Visuo-perceptual and perception challenges	• Provide more time to process information before acting on it. • Check glasses prescription and ensure they are clean. • Ensure bright, even lighting. • Contrast colours (e.g. contrast colour of the plate of food with the colour of the tablecloth or the table). • Have plain backgrounds, especially carpets. • Use talking books. • Prisms (ask your ophthalmologist —a medical specialist who is expert in the diagnosis and management of disorders of the eye and visual system) • Coloured overlays for reading. • Folding white stick to help with vision and perception and as a way of warning others there might be a visual problem. • See an optician if experiencing double vision.

Sensory challenge	Tips and ideas
Hearing: hypersensitivity to noise or specific tones; sensitivity to noisy environments	• Give the person with dementia enough time to hear what is being said. • Ask one question at a time. • Make sure you can be heard in the first place. • Allow the brain enough time to process information. • Repeat what the person with dementia has said back to them. • If it has been a busy or loud morning, give the person with dementia some time to rest and recover. • Try and avoid unexpected noises. • Avoid sensory overload. • Pick a quiet time when going out for a meal. • Use earplugs to reduce noise. • Sit at the end of the table (which may avoid loud noise). • If a space or setting is very loud, leave for a short time to take a break.

Sensory challenge	Tips and ideas
Touch taste and smell: Unable to differentiate between hot and cold; taste changing, affecting appetite and eating habits. Smells that are intense or overpowering; sense of smell has decreased.	• Fit special taps to ensure temperature regulation. Make sure they are also taps familiar to people with dementia (distinct hot and cold taps instead of a lever) • Explore various solutions to loss of appetite
Hallucinations: Sights and sounds that are not real. Intense life-like dreams.	• Check for signs of infection and delirium and/or side effects of medication

Access to daylight, good lighting and contrasting colours all make life easier in this bedroom.

Key points

- Visuo-perceptual and sensory challenges may require design modifications in your home to cater for changes in the person such as increased sensitivity to noise, perceptual changes and vision difficulties.
- Changes to senses can result in the person being overwhelmed, but remember our senses are also important for engaging with a person who is no longer able to communicate verbally.
- Be aware of the impacts of ageing on the older person with dementia. Make sure they have the correct glasses and hearing aids. Check the glasses are clean and that you also know how to work the hearing aids.

Further reading

Dementia & Sensory Challenges, Agnes Houston ed. Life changes trust (UK), Dementia Centre (Australia), 2016. Also available as a free download: www.dementiacentre.com/resources/37-dementia-and-sensory-challenges

Part 2
Enjoying life
at home

05 Living at home with dementia

What we will learn

- How to make the most of home
- Some of the main challenges and what to do
- Ideas for being calm and relaxed

The vast majority of people with dementia say they prefer to live at home. In Australia up to 70 per cent[19] of people with dementia live in their own homes while in the United Kingdom the figure is about 61 per cent[20].

That's why it's vital to consider how to make living at home as successful as possible for people with dementia and their carers.

Familiar is good, some change can help

Familiarity is enabling for the person living with dementia whereas an unfamiliar environment may cause increased stress and confusion. Living at home usually means being surrounded by familiar rooms, furniture, belongings, gardens, neighbourhood, people and accompanying sights and sounds. This stabilising familiarity makes functioning easier for the person with dementia than would be the case where everything is new—and at a time when learning new things is very difficult.

'I don't have to worry about being frightened'

Evelyn lives with mild dementia in her Cronulla home in the south-east of Sydney (Australia). Throughout the house are memories of her life. A beautiful photo collage that Evelyn made herself takes pride of place near the front door. Seeing all this history on display, it comes as no surprise that Evelyn wants to stay at home as long as she can. 'I'm by myself now but I'm quite comfortable. I don't have to worry about being frightened or anything like that,' Evelyn says. 'There's something about a place like this. I feel very safe here.'

While familiarity is key, most people's homes weren't designed with dementia or ageing in mind. So while retaining familiarity wherever possible, there are a range of positive changes that can be made to enhance the home environment for a person with dementia. Some changes may help support the person physically while others may be aimed at assisting the person to understand their environment and overcome specific challenges. We'll address many of the design-related changes at home that can benefit a person with dementia in Chapters 8, 9 and 10.

Challenges of daily activities

In the meantime, some of the rhythms, routines and occurrences that are part of living at home can also be challenging over time. For the carer, it may take some adjustment to realise that daily activities that they previously took for granted are now sometimes frustratingly difficult for the person for whom they care.

Some of these challenges may be:

- getting up and going in the morning
- night-time and sleeping well
- receiving visitors
- leaving the home for planned outings
- mealtimes and eating
- making sense of home with memory and sensory changes.

The good news is that there are approaches and strategies that can be used to address these challenges, remembering as previously mentioned, that these strategies may need to change over time.

Serving a familiar and favourite breakfast can help with morning routines. But keep in mind good tonal contrast with plates where possible.

Relying on routines morning and night

Routines can often help difficult times of the day such as morning and night. These can be particularly challenging times as the person with dementia may have:

- slept poorly
- a disturbed circadian rhythm (body clock)
- been distressed before sleeping
- uncertainty about if or why it is night-time
- impaired interpretation of regular day and night cues[21].

For morning, routines may include opening the window coverings and turning on the lights, putting out daytime clothes, serving a favourite breakfast, turning on a breakfast radio program or the news—anything that has a familiar morning feel.

During the day, get outside as much as possible as this will further maintain a person's body clock while exercise will tire the body and make sleep easier.

For night-time and going to bed, routines may include playing calming music before and while getting ready for bed, having a bath with some calming oils, a warm milk drink or nightcap, turning off or down radio or television, turning off main lights and turning on night lights. Again, whatever is familiar.

See the next chapter for a more extensive discussion of ways to support night-time and a good night's sleep.

Planning for visitors

In general, social interactions are positive for the person with dementia. If approached in a dementia-inclusive and sensitive way, having visitors can help with increasing socialisation and improving mood.

Having visitors over, however, can also be an overwhelming experience, particularly if the person with dementia is at a stage where they may not recognise familiar faces. This may cause some anxiety, thinking there is a stranger in their home. They may also be worried about having to entertain these guests. Keep in mind the following strategies that can ensure a positive experience.

Talk about the visit

Talk with the person with dementia about who will be coming to visit that day, reminding them who they are and how they know them. You can write this down for them, or provide a photo of the person.

Try and be present

Try to be present when the visit begins, and monitor how it goes, staying or leaving as is appropriate. Depending on the person, you may prefer to limit the number of visitors so that it doesn't overwhelm the senses. A person with dementia may withdraw within themselves in a crowded room, finding it difficult to follow conversation, which would lessen the value of the visit. And remember hypersensitivity to noise may be an issue.

Discuss with the visitor

Discuss the visit with the person who is visiting. You can give the person some strategies on communication, for example, telling them to avoid asking too many questions, or questions that may rely on memory. The visitor should introduce themselves upon arrival, reminding the person who they are (in a relaxed, non-patronising way) and how they might know them. The visitor should also expect that there may be times when the person is feeling tired, or not talkative, and perhaps even feeling distressed. At these points, the visitor can try using gentle touch to help comfort the person, or enjoy sitting in silence. If struggling to find something to do, you can advise the visitor to do something together e.g. get out the photo scrapbook or listen to individualised music together.

Other visitor tips

Other tips for visitors include establishing a visitor routine—having specific visitors at regular and consistent times and even provide the person with a dementia-inclusive daily or weekly schedule if that is manageable.

And to maximise independence, for example, leave out a teapot ready to go with a plate of biscuits so that practising hospitality is obvious and easy.

For unplanned visitors, employ as many of these strategies as possible and learn from what occurs. If it seems too hard, invite them to come at another time.

Adjusting routines when visiting Aunty Mary

During recent visits to Aunty Mary we thought her dementia may be advancing. We found several bags of food in the kitchen, some of which had gone rotten. Then we worked out a connection. Mary was a great host and liked to bake in advance of our visits. In the time soon after her diagnosis of dementia, our routine was to phone a week before visits and then again a few days before. We realised this could now be the problem! Aunty Mary's desire to host was triggered by our advanced calls and so she would head out to the shops a week before to get fresh cream and ingredients to bake scones. She then did this again when we called a few days in advance. It's true Mary was struggling more with dates and times, but an adjustment to our routine was the solution. We now phone Aunty Mary the evening before, just enough time for her to pop out to the shops, and feel settled that she is ready for the next day. We learned the value of adapting our routine to support the person with dementia in their routines and what matters to them.

Leaving the house

As much as we may enjoy the comfort and familiarity of home, and welcoming people's visits, it is also a normal part of life to go out to work, run errands, visit friends and families, to enjoy the outdoors, take part in entertainment activities or events and many more reasons.

For most of our lives we 'go out' without thinking much about it. So it is understandable that if going out has become a stressful challenge—for both the person with dementia and carer—this can be frustrating and produce feelings of loss, anger, disappointment and fear.

This is such an important issue that we have devoted more space to it in Part 3.

Mealtimes and eating

Eating may seem the most natural thing in the world, with shared mealtimes being a highlight of the day. But this can change if you are:

- finding tastes and appetite have changed
- struggling to use or recognise cutlery
- not really remembering the right order of eating

- having trouble swallowing
- finding food doesn't appear or smell as it used to.

In this case, meals may actually become quite unpleasant. These are all things that may occur for a person with dementia due to impairment to the brain and sensory changes.[22]

If the person is older, there are also the physical impacts of ageing such as slower stomach emptying, lower appetite, reduced ability to taste salt and reduced smell. [23]

These challenges may mean eating takes longer, that both carer and the person with dementia are discouraged and food and drink may need to change in texture and presentation. As eating, nutrition and mealtimes are a big part of anyone's life at home helping to support this area is vital.

Keep on cooking

In this context, it is vital to support the person with dementia to keep cooking as long as possible. This is the most powerful cue to eating and maintains enjoyment, independence and engagement. Cooking together can help prolong independent eating as well as being a great opportunity for social interaction. Studies have shown that involving the person with dementia in meaningful activities has positive effects on quality of life and wellbeing.[24]

This can be extended to shopping together—lists are very helpful to support the involvement of the person with dementia.

Caring tip: If meals have become challenging or weight loss is a concern some helpful 'foodie' strategies (more in Chapter 10 and the Appendix section) may include:

- using your knowledge of the person's food likes and dislikes, memories (good and bad), preferred times to eat, mealtime routines, favourite dining locations (breakfast in bed, barbecue outside)

- not being offended if a favourite meal is turned away because tastes change and many older people will leave a large meal untouched rather than 'waste food'

- having smaller meals more regularly across the day that are packed with protein, energy and flavour

- serving finger foods if cutlery is an issue, particularly foods that are traditionally eaten by hand so it won't be seen as rude or childish.[25]

Calm, relaxed and easy to understand

Living with dementia, as with any serious illness, can be very stressful both for the person and those caring for and supporting them. On the other hand, any of the challenges experienced will be solved more easily in a calm setting that is easy to understand and doesn't over-stimulate. But how do we stay calm when there are stressful things occurring and many things to worry about?

Making the home environment as calm, relaxed and easy to understand as possible is a good start. Some simple steps that may help include:

Reducing clutter and keeping important things visible like keys, tea and coffee, kettle and teapot, can all help make life easier at home.

- reducing clutter by clearing benches and work spaces of occasionally used items and leaving out those things that are needed every day such as tea and coffee making items

- thinking about what signs and cues would reduce confusion or uncertainty such as in the kitchen (words and pictures work well)

- adjusting light levels, remembering that people with dementia and older people generally benefit from more light (more details in Chapter 8)

- reducing distracting noises such as both a radio and television going nearby or operating loud equipment during meals, instead having more calming sounds such as personalised music

- creating a special, calming space for the person with dementia where they have favourite and familiar items and to which they can retreat if feeling tired or overwhelmed

- removing trip hazards, avoiding glare and reflections (some people with dementia can be startled by mirrors) and getting outside for some exercise

- not sitting the person with dementia at the dinner table where they will have a lot of noise and activity happening behind or near them as this can be stressful, e.g. next to the kitchen door where people come and go serving food and drink and clearing the table.

Caring tip: Stress is infectious and a person with dementia will be aware if their carer or support person is feeling stressed, even if it's through body language. So, carers, looking after yourself is also good for the person you care for. If organising a massage, have one yourself! If making a cup of tea, stop and have one too. Listen to music you both enjoy and make use of support services that give you time out and other assistance.

- The majority of people with dementia live at home and that's where they want to be.
- The familiarity of home is enabling for the person with dementia and the carer, but there are still discreet changes you can make to further create a calm, relaxed and understandable environment.
- Some parts of home life may be more difficult but there are ways to minimise distress.
- When carers look after themselves, it also benefits the person being supported. Make use of available resources —you are not alone.

Further reading:

Enlighten: Lighting design for older people and people with dementia, D McNair, R Pollock & C Cunningham, HammondCare Media, Sydney (2017).

Don't give me eggs that bounce: 118 cracking recipes for people with Alzheimer's, P Morgan-Jones, D McIntosh, E Colombage, P Ellis, HammondCare Media, Sydney (2018).

It's all about the food not the fork! 101 easy to eat meals in a mouthful, P Morgan-Jones, L Greedy, P Ellis, D McIntosh. HammondCare Media, Sydney (2016).

06 A good night's sleep

What we will learn

- Why sleep can be difficult
- Encouraging good sleep
- What 'sundowning' really is

A good night's sleep is a key part of having a healthy body, mind and emotions and yet many people with dementia will become light sleepers and find a good night's sleep harder to achieve. Add to this, common age-related struggles with sleeping through the night[26], and night-time and sleeplessness can be taxing issues for the person with dementia and those supporting them.

Why sleeplessness?

People with dementia may struggle to respond to night-time cues such as darkness, quietness or wearing pyjamas. Circadian rhythms (body clock) might also be disturbed by the cognitive impairment caused by dementia[27] and it is not uncommon for a person with dementia to switch day and night. The person may wake up in the middle of the night hungry and ready for some activity, which can be very challenging for an exhausted carer.

Often medications will be suggested for sleep disturbances and while they have their place, a better understanding of what may cause sleeplessness and learning some non-drug interventions should be considered first.[28]

Some age and dementia-related factors causing sleep disturbance include:

- pain—both acute (temporary) or chronic (long term)— with acute causes including toothache, earache, or pulled muscles; and chronic pain including conditions such as arthritis
- reflux and other digestive issues

- depression and anxiety
- needing to go to the toilet
- side effects of medication—e.g. sedatives can cause sleepiness during the day but make it harder to sleep at night, while some medications that need to be taken at night act as stimulants
- sleep apnoea
- not enough exposure to sun and light to synchronise the body's circadian rhythm
- lack of exercise (i.e. missing out on natural body tiredness)[29]
- daytime sleepiness
- restless legs syndrome—the sensation of something crawling on or tingling in your legs. The disorder causes the person to feel constant urges to move their legs.[30]

Getting ready for bed

George uses lighting and music to help Joan get ready for sleep. He closes up the house and pulls the curtains in the early evening, and then dims all the lights. George and Joan listen to soft, soothing music and look at photographs or magazines. Within an hour or two, Joan is yawning and ready to go to bed and sleep.

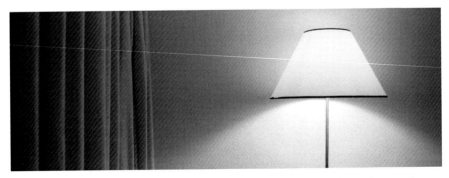

Closing the curtains and reducing lighting are good cues for going to sleep. Light coloured curtains are less stark, and be careful that reduced lighting doesn't create confusion.

Here are some tips to encourage a good night's sleep for the person with dementia:

- Make the room as dark as possible at night. If the person you are caring for does not like being in total darkness, then consider a night-light.

- Introduce more light in the morning to activate the 'awake' hormones.[31]

- Put on pyjamas (carer too) as the time for sleep approaches. Some aged care homes have night-time staff wearing dressing gowns—another cue to show the person it is time for sleep.

- Try and exercise or have activities planned during the day so by the time evening comes, everyone's tired and ready for bed.

- Have night-time routines as mentioned above.

- Where necessary, provide pain medication before sleeping.

- Have some night-time snacks and drinks on standby if the person with dementia is waking up hungry and thirsty. This will minimise getting up and walking around which makes it harder to continue sleeping.

- Enlist the help of your GP in addressing any medical issues listed above, such as sleep apnoea and pain.

You will find some helpful bed and bedroom design tips to support good sleeping in Chapter 8.

Caring tip: To nap or not to nap? With all these possible challenges to getting a good night sleep, it's not surprising that people with dementia (and carers!) might be quite keen on a daytime nap. Avoiding a daytime nap is the advice often given as a way of increasing the person's ability to sleep through the night. However, if the person is tired, don't stop them from napping (and have one yourself when you can). We all deserve the right to nap!

The truth about sundowning

'Sundowning' is a largely unhelpful term that has been widely used to describe changed behaviours (such as agitation, pacing) for a person with dementia that often occur late in the afternoon or early evening. The idea that these behaviours are inevitable and might be associated with the sun going down means it may be overlooked that these behaviours express needs or distress.

As this period of time leads in closely to bedtime routines it is important to understand that causes may include:

- exhaustion
- a lapse in the body's circadian rhythm
- responding to the non-verbal cues of caregivers who may themselves be tired, frustrated or preparing for some end of the day errands
- anxiety or confusion caused by lengthening shadows and diminishing light
- feelings emerging from long term memories that there are tasks that need to be done such as picking the children up from school or cooking dinner.

It's time to pick up Brian!

Rose was often angry at 4pm. She would shout and threaten her carer from the care agency for trying to stop her leaving home at that time. When Bridget, her carer, started to pay attention to what Rose was saying, she noticed Rose kept talking about Brian. Soon after, a friend was visiting and Bridget told her what was happening. The friend explained that Brian is Rose's adult son and, when he was younger, Rose would often dash from work so she could get to school in time to pick up Brian and her other children. Bridget realised that she herself often talked to Rose about the need to dash off and pick up her own daughter. People with dementia cannot always filter out information around them that is not about them. Three pieces of information were staying in Rose's mind: my children (as they were always on her mind); I cannot be late;

and pick the children up from school! So of course when Bridget came to offer support in the afternoon (the time Rose used to pick up her children), Rose was distressed and determined. Sometimes the solution can be simple and in this case it was not to talk about certain things that were about Bridget's life because they triggered important emotions in Rose that she could not process easily and in the context of today.

Caring tips: Familiar afternoon routines, a pre-dinner drink or walk outside, playing with pets, listening to personally-tailored music or involvement in cooking the evening meal may all help everyone through the late afternoon. Avoid creating barriers to a person who wants to walk (see outdoor access in Chapter 11) but do discuss with your doctor if concerns persist. Be alert to information that might trigger anxiety in a person with dementia either from your conversations or other sources like the TV. Consider talking later or in another room about things that relate to what you might need to do. In a care home context, agree as a team that these conversations are best to happen in the staff room.

Playing with pets may help everyone feel more relaxed in the late afternoon.

Needing to go to the toilet

A common reason for night-time sleep disturbance and perhaps night walking is the need to find and go to the toilet. The obvious answer is to make sure going to the toilet is easy to do—even at night.

One option is a commode—a portable toilet—placed near the bed so it is immediately visible when the call of nature occurs! However they can be quite unfamiliar to many people and simply bypassed by the person as they head for the toilet.

Ensuites are probably the best option for people with dementia. Positioning the bed so that the toilet in the ensuite can be seen is ideal. Assistive technology can also help such as an infrared sensor that monitors movement and turns on a light to help wayfinding. A night-light might be a less intrusive option. If the toilet is out in the hall, watch out not to leave the outside porch light on as the person may be drawn to this and end up locked out and lost.

Supporting successful night-time access to the toilet promotes continued confidence and independence and hopefully won't interrupt sleep too much. Solutions such as adult continence pads or night-time pads may become necessary in advanced dementia.

There are many styles of motion sensors that will turn on a light if someone gets up to go to the toilet at night. [Creative Commons photo licence: Versatile Techno.]

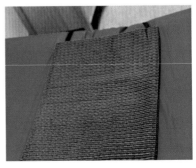

Bed sensors can quietly let a carer know if someone has got up in night, and this may help prevent falls or leaving the house in an unsafe way.

Midnight munchies

A person with dementia may wake up in the middle of the night feeling hungry or thirsty. It's a good idea to leave out some finger foods and a drink (avoiding caffeine), particularly if these are familiar night-time snacks which may trigger a sleep-time routine. Having them available may mean a quick bite to eat and drink and then back to sleep without disturbing the home too much.

Wanting to be active

Some people are more 'night owls' than others and may need to keep busy for a while at night as part of being ready for a good night sleep. While people with dementia may find it hard to instigate activities, this does not mean they don't want to do them. Some suggestions include:

- Life story collections (described in Chapter 4) are a good activity to have ready for both day and night. Leaving them out to be engaged with if waking at night may promote positive reminiscence and reduce feelings of agitation and distress. The carer and the person with dementia might work together building these collections in the evening before bed as well, to bring on tiredness and calm feelings.

- A relaxing bath or massage may be a sleep-promoting activity and there is some evidence that aromatherapy can help. This is the use of fragrant essential oils, such as lavender, to reduce feelings of agitation.[32]

- Any other bedtime or night-time activities that the person with dementia is familiar with.

Going outside at night

Sometimes people with dementia may wake up and being confused about the time of day or what they are doing, decide to leave the house. This is understandably distressing for a carer and worrying about this can significantly interfere with good sleep.

Apart from the activities on the previous page to promote less sleep disturbance, assistive technology can be very useful. There are a range of sensors that quietly let the carer know (e.g. a vibration under their pillow) that the person with dementia has left their bed.

> *Carer tip:* Sleep is important for the person with dementia. Sleep is also incredibly important for you. From time to time, try and get family or other support to come for a 'sleep over', so you can get a good night sleep.

Key points

- There are many non-drug interventions that can help with sleeplessness before considering medications.
- Aged and dementia-related factors along with common issues such as pain, needing the toilet, getting hungry and preferring to stay up, can all contribute to sleep disturbance.
- Assistive technology can make a difference at night, such as sensors that turn on the bathroom light or alert the carer when a person with dementia hops out of bed.

Further reading:

Providing good care at night for older people and people with dementia, D Kerr & H Wilkinson, Jessica Kingsley Publishers, London (2011).

Night-time care: A practice guide, D Kerr & C Cunningham, HammondCare Media, Sydney (2016).

07 Maintaining good communication

What we will learn

- Communication is vital

- Dementia affects communication

- Simple steps to help

Before we look more closely at specific design improvements for the home, we want to take a moment to consider an issue that is central to quality of life—communication.

Communication is a two-way activity involving verbal and non-verbal expression and reception of feelings, ideas, opinions and information. It involves words, gestures, body language, listening, affirmation and relationship.

Good communication is just as important for people with dementia and those that support them as for anyone, perhaps even more so. And obviously it's important at home and beyond the home.

When am I going home?

Lisa had come to believe that she was visiting, rather than living with her daughter and that her husband would be arriving soon to take her home to a small town where they lived many years before. Her daughter Joy understood good communication involved validating the feelings and memories of her mum, rather than arguing over the facts. Joy would agree that it was wonderful that Lisa was visiting, that she had plenty of time to stay longer and then ask what were some of her favourite things about living in that town? This respected the feelings Lisa was expressing, even though her facts were confused, and she was soon happily recalling some fond memories of this former home.

Dementia and communication

Dementia impacts communication in a number of ways and this will depend on the parts of the brain affected. Trouble remembering, reduced concentration, hypersensitivity to noise, feeling overwhelmed, depression and anxiety may all affect responses from the person with dementia. This is in turn can make carers feel they have failed or been ignored. Neither is true.

Cognitive impairment can also cause a range of conditions affecting communication such as aphasia and dysphasia which is:

> …a break down in the understanding and/or use of language, losing the ability to comprehend language or even gestures/signing, to read or write and/or to speak. It can range in severity from very mild to very severe. If a person is unable to communicate at all or to comprehend, this is known as global aphasia.[33]

It would be easy to understand if both the person with dementia and carer became discouraged and frustrated because of these communication challenges, but don't give up. Here are five 'S' steps that may help:

Slow—speak more slowly and clearly and be patient if responses take some time. And don't be anxious when there is silence (have a breather too).

Simple—use sentences that contain just one idea that is relevant to the activity at hand rather than a list or sequence of events. 'Let's go to the supermarket' or 'Time to get dressed'.

Specific—describe things in terms of place, time and who is involved. 'Your niece, Judy, is visiting us here at home, today, Thursday.'

Show—use familiar gestures or hold up items being discussed, but don't go overboard.

Smile—whenever it is appropriate, and communicate at eye-level. Relaxing your body to smile is reassuring for the person with dementia and calming for you.[34]

As mentioned in the previous chapter, third-party conversations (including phone calls or those on TV or radio) may intrude on good communication because people with dementia may not be able to separate what they overhear from their own reality. The conversations of others may trigger concerns, confusion or memories and hamper good communication.

Communicate at eye level when possible, use familiar gestures and don't forget to smile

Finally, here are some helpful communication tips based on research, care practice and the advice of people with dementia and carers:

- Give reassurance of who you are and what you are doing.
- Be aware of your facial expression, posture, gesture and tone and pitch of our voice.
- Give the person time to say what they are thinking.
- Keep sentences short and simple, asking one question at a time. As well, it's important not to use a childish tone.
- Show the person what you want them to do. Pointing towards the item you are referring to can be helpful.
- Make sure you have the person's attention. You can gently touch their arm or hand and say their name.
- Make eye contact and sit where the person can see you.
- Be prepared to wait for an answer.
- Avoid asking questions that test memory.
- Observe the feelings behind the words being said.
- Think carefully about your gestures—what impression will they give the person with dementia?
- Try providing visual clues for the person about what is going on.
- You can make conversations enjoyable by focusing on longer-term memories that enable the person with dementia to be included.
- Avoid arguing with the person as that can cause distress to both parties.
- Focus on the person's remaining abilities and use this as a starting point for your communication. For example, if they enjoy looking at images and respond more to visual information, use photos to remind them of people or memories.

- Help connection by asking open-ended questions that don't rely on memory.

- Be prepared to communicate about the reality being experienced by the person with dementia. The person may be switching between the past and the present to make sense of conflicts, reliving past experiences.

- Avoid correcting facts, but observe the context of the information.

> *Caring tip:* Before beginning a conversation with someone with dementia try to make sure they are aware of you and give them a moment to concentrate on the conversation. Say their name, face them directly and where appropriate or comforting, use touch to help them focus on you (pat their arm, hold their hand). If you start the conversation with the most important point, they may miss it, if you take too long, the person may lose concentration!

Key points

- Good communication is important for everyone but perhaps especially for a person with dementia and those who support them.
- Dementia may impact communication in a variety of ways depending on areas of the brain affected.
- Try not to give up on communication, despite frustrations that may occur, as there are steps that can help.
- A person with dementia may find it hard to filter out conversations they overhear, leading them to reinterpret information as something needing to be done, causing confusion and concern.

08 Supportive design ideas

What we will learn
- Dementia-inclusive design principles
- Getting light and noise right
- Colour contrast and signage that enables
- Good ideas for floors and furnishings

To make the most of living at home for the person with dementia, it is helpful sometimes to consider a range of design changes and adjustments, which will increase enablement while retaining familiarity.

This is true whether the person is living at home by themselves, with a full-time family carer or friend, or receiving in-home help from professional services and carers.

Changes made to the domestic environment may involve lighting, noise, textures, tonal contrasts, wayfinding and hazards. Changes can be minute or major, and will similarly vary from inexpensive, do-it-yourself options to more expensive changes.

Changes also require a delicate balance—try not to lose the familiarity of the home environment and be aware of changes that cause confusion or frustration.

An example of a change that might be well intended but could cause confusion, relates to plumbing fixtures. The more traditional style of cross-head taps will be better understood and they usually clearly display hot and cold. Mixer taps on the other hand, while sleek and modern, are less intuitive and may prove confusing for a person with dementia or any older person.

As you make changes at home, continue to assess the person and how they are responding, abandoning changes that are too distressing.

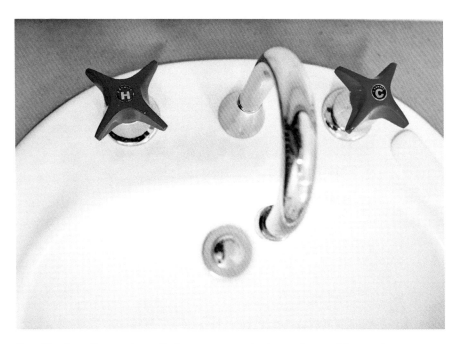

Familiar handles and tap fittings support independence. These also clearly identify hot and cold.

Supporting dad's bathroom independence

Julie noticed her dad, Joseph, had been having some toileting difficulties recently and often seemed quite distressed afterwards. Julie thought Joseph may have been unwell, but then noticed when assisting him to the newly renovated, all white-bathroom, that he was unsure about locating the toilet. Later, he fumbled with the new modern tap fitting at the basin, and left without washing his hands—unusual for Joseph as he was fastidious about hygiene. When discussing this with a support person, she learned that greater contrast benefits older eyes and people with dementia, and that the shiny mixer tap would be unfamiliar to her dad. A new black toilet seat and easy to understand tap seem to have addressed most of Joseph's difficulties and distress.

Dementia-inclusive design

A dementia-inclusive environment includes being:

- small in size
- familiar, domestic and homely in style
- suitable for ordinary, passive and active activities
- safe and free of fall or dangerous hazards
- inclusive of assistive technology.

Ideally your home or other living environment will have:

- various rooms for specific uses
- furniture and fittings appropriate for age and culture
- an outdoor space which is safe and easy to access and navigate
- good signage and multiple cues where possible
- objects for orientation rather than colour contrasts
- the person's sensory needs in mind—not too noisy, too colourful or having patterns on walls or carpets that can be interpreted as 3D objects.

Caring tip: An important understanding is that sometimes in our desire to make a person with dementia 'safe' we may unduly limit their independence. Good design and care can achieve both because we know that 'dependency may negatively impact on… well-being'.[35] Good design can help someone with dementia make safe and non-confused decisions without compromising feelings of dignity and independence.

Five areas of design that relate to most areas of the home (and also out in the community) are lighting, acoustics (sound), colour contrasts, choice of furnishings/flooring and signage.

Light that's right

When creating an enabling environment for a person with dementia who is most likely older, not only do we need to account for the ageing eye, but also sensory and memory challenges that can be symptoms of dementia. Lighting can help in many ways—increasing visual acuity, helping with perception, synchronising the body.

Lights inside this wardrobe are an example of good 'task' lighting for older eyes.

Ageing eyes need double the lighting of younger eyes[36]. To brighten up your home:

- adjust light bulbs to ensure brightness (many power-saver bulbs are not as bright)

- ensure your windows allow in as much natural light as possible—perhaps they need a good clean or to have nearby foliage and branches trimmed

- consider the use of curtains and blinds over doors and windows. If they reduce glare, it's important to retain them but if blocking natural daylight, ensure they are drawn back for some time in the day.

We often take lighting for granted, but the right level of lighting can avoid frustration for the person who can't remember where they put something and is searching for it, or in poor light sees a shape or shadow and thinks it's a stranger or is confused by a dimly lit pattern on the wall.

Wider benefits of light

Apart from using brighter light to see and make paths and rooms clear, sunlight also contributes to increased muscle strength through healthier levels of vitamin D and nitric oxide, which in turn may reduce falls. Up to 10 minutes of sunlight exposure on the hands and forearms can help with this, but don't forget to follow guidelines on exposure to sun in the country you live in.[37] Light is also known to help improve mood and perhaps most importantly—stabilise or synchronise the body clock.[38]

Being exposed to light in the morning and in the same way making sure it's dark when it is time for sleep, is a good method of synchronising the body with day and night. When a room doesn't let in proper levels of light in the morning, or the lighting levels are too dim for an older person, their body might not be aware it's time to be awake. This can lead to all day snoozing or sleepiness, which in turn leads to lack of sleeping through the night. Rooms at night should be dark so light doesn't disturb sleep. If the person is more comfortable with a night-light, then be sure to leave one in the room.

Caring tip: Leaving the bathroom light on might seem the simplest way to help the person with dementia, but not always. Many older people are budget conscious and so may get up in the night and turn it off, being worried about wasting electricity. A more subtle night-light or a sensor light would work better in this case.

Light for getting around

Light also helps with finding your way around. Some examples include brighter lighting in places where tasks might be performed, even lighting (avoid spotlights) along halls and paths to avoid dark or shadowed areas, or having sensor lights come on when the person is walking so they can see where they are going.

Good lighting is particularly important for staircases. It can prevent the person with dementia from perceiving stairs as shapes or holes they have to avoid stepping on. This can be a major risk for falls.

The stairs are not only poorly lit, the shadows across them are confusing and the steps themselves are low contrast.

These stairs are well lit and there is good contrast; but make sure the steps aren't slippery or shiny if possible.

Sound that supports

As mentioned in Chapter 4, a common sensory challenge experienced by the person with dementia is hypersensitivity to noise. This can be a major issue in residential care because of the larger number of people and additional equipment, not to mention buzzers and alerts. This should be easier to control at home—e.g. be aware of appliances that beep loudly (perhaps turn this function off if possible), or of having televisions on when a person is trying to concentrate on eating or talking. Often people with dementia find it hard to discern the direction from which sound is coming, which is why someone talking on radio or television in the background may be very confusing.

Alarm causing alarm!

When Bruce was diagnosed with dementia he received support so that he and his wife Marie could live well at home. A year later, Bruce's daughter asked for help from Dementia Support Australia (DSA).[39] She explained to the DSA consultant that her dad had started being 'aggressive' toward Marie and that this had never happened before. In talking with the consultant, important information came to light. Bruce had been in the army and served in many dangerous situations. Also, the 'aggressive behaviour' was described as Bruce pushing Marie on occasion. The consultant asked had anything changed in their routine before this behaviour began and one thing noted was the installation of a pendant alarm system. The system was tested regularly and this involved it making a loud beep. A helpful person from the alarm call centre would then speak through the system to say all was in working order. For Bruce, the noise and the voice coming from the alarm was just like a 'walkie talkie' in the army that warned when there might be danger. What do you do when there is danger? 'Get down'! Bruce was attempting to protect Marie by pushing her to the floor, away from danger such as flying bullets. To check if this was the trigger, the testing for the pendant system was done in a different way and suddenly, the so-called aggressive behaviour went away. Importantly this critical piece of background in Bruce's life was recorded, so that if he ever needed residential care it should be in a home that understood that alarms and audio announcements don't help the people who actually live there, especially those with dementia!

Reducing unwanted background noise

Design features that may help further reduce disturbing noises include:

- soft furnishings such as curtains and cushions to absorb noise
- carpet tiles and floor coverings (cleaned and kept odour free) reduce the noise of moving furniture and clattering feet
- doors and windows that can be closed to keep out unwanted noise (and opened to let in fresh air and pleasant sounds such as birds singing or children playing)
- turning off audio alerts and beeping noises on machines (and shading flashing lights)

Remember, personalised music provides many benefits and in this context, may screen unwanted and disturbing noises.

Monitor hearing ability and hearing aids

Because of the natural process of ageing, an older person with dementia may have trouble hearing. This can often be the cause of further confusion and more difficult communication. Check for any build-up of earwax, arrange regular hearing checks and check that properly prescribed hearing aids are on and working properly. A carer may need to help with working the hearing aid and adjusting the controls, as they can be small and fiddly to adjust.

If the person does have a hearing aid, reduction in noise is especially important because meaningless squeaks are magnified just as fiercely as helpful and encouraging words.

This all white bedroom might be fashionable but a person with dementia may have trouble even locating the bed, not to mention being concerned by reflections in the giant mirror! Avoid this at home or in a motel on holidays.

Contrasting colours

For the ageing eye and for people with dementia sensory changes, colour contrast is very important. The simple step of introducing, in some situations, contrasting colours, helps people understand the room and find their way. At other times, keeping colour uniform avoids drawing attention to things that are confusing or to be avoided. Some basic colour and decorating tips include:

- resisting pastel or white on white colours that blend into each other on things you want people to see

- caution about patterns in wallpaper as this may be mistaken for real objects on the wall

- using a plain, matte, consistent surface and colouring for floor covering, ideally with contrast between the floor and the wall

- having contrasting bed linen so the bed is more obvious and consider a different colour top and bottom sheet to make getting into bed easier

- stairs that contrast in colour with the staircase frame and walls

- painting traditional skirting boards (or an approximation) around any room in a colour that contrasts with walls to make it clear where the floor ends and the wall begins

- a toilet seat that contrasts with the toilet bowl, so it can be seen clearly as a toilet rather than a very white cupboard. Even better, try to have contrast between the toilet and the wall colour behind it.[40] In one case, a person with dementia was found to be using the mop bucket for a toilet because it was clearly visible in the bathroom while the toilet had very poor contrast. We want to be able to see where to sit or aim!

Signs at home won't suit everyone but if you have them (e.g. for the toilet), a sign with words and pictures is ideal, placed not too high. Many public toilets have unfamiliar fittings and so a good sign (as above) could help. Clocks are often better analogue with good contrast.

Furnishings and flooring

If you are in a position to choose flooring, pick a smooth, matte surface and ensure the same flooring is across as many rooms as possible. These surfaces are safer and easier for people with dementia. In kitchens and other wet areas, opt for a surface that is not shiny and reflective as this may look like water on the floor and a person with dementia may wisely refuse to enter!

Between rooms, make the carpet bar or strip the same colour as the flooring. This can also reduce the risk of falls and prevent perceptual confusion—the person may perceive the change in colour or texture as an object in their path to be stepped over, likewise with patterns and shapes. Here are some other tips:

- Assess and remove trip hazards from floors.

- Make sure ramp finishes are slip-resistant and have a kerb on exposed edges or a brightly visible toe-guard (an occupational therapist can advise on ramp design).

- Don't visually deceive without good cause (i.e. painting fire places or landscape views) as often people with dementia are working hard enough to understand their surroundings. If wanting to 'de-emphasise' a door to utilities or another area it can be 'hidden' by painting it the same colour as the surrounding wall, with a 'skirting board' painted along the bottom to trick the eye into not seeing it. (These are known colloquially around HammondCare as 'Harry Potter doors'.)

- Have light-coloured curtains, which are not only good for reflecting light during the day, but will be less stark at night when they are closed.

- Be aware that mirrors or reflections (such as in a framed picture with reflective glass) may startle a person with dementia who may believe they are being watched by a stranger. If the person with dementia reports that there is someone in their room, try covering their mirror with a blind so it can be used at other times.

Sensible signs

People with dementia often describe making signs for themselves as a practical aid to finding their way and locating useful items. While it may seem institutional for us to introduce signs into a home, appropriate signage may have a significant enabling effect. Even more so if it's possible to work alongside the person with dementia to develop the signage.

Signs that are accompanied by images (e.g. a sign with an image of a garden and the description 'garden') can help a person who has lost the ability to read, but can still recognise visually.

Signs on doors should be at the right height for the person. We recommend that the base of the sign is no higher than 4 ft/122 cm from the floor.

Having looked at design principles that affect the whole house and also can be applied to other spaces, let's focus in the next chapter on some of the most important rooms in the house.

Key points

- Older people need twice as much light as younger people.
- Light can help reduce confusion and with finding the way, as well as providing many physical and emotional benefits.
- Colour contrast can be used to make rooms and hallways more understandable and finding the way clearer.
- Avoid patterned wallpapers and carpets and reflective flooring which may be confused for objects or water.
- Appropriate signage can help with recognition of items, spaces and finding the way.
- Assess the success of your changes by continually checking the person's verbal and non-verbal behaviour for signs of distress.

Further reading:

DesignSmart: The rating tool for environments that work for people with dementia, C Cunningham and D McIntosh with S Thorne and M Gresham, HammondCare Media, Sydney (2015).

09 Better bathrooms and bedrooms

What we will learn

- How to enhance independence in personal care
- Care and design that supports
- Filling in the gaps of processes

Bathrooms and dignity in personal care

There are certain moments in the day when the bathroom is the most important room in the house! Going to the bathroom and attending to personal care can become difficult depending on the progression of dementia. So it is important to consider bathroom design to promote dignity and independence.[41]

As a general principle it is good to support independent showering, dressing and going to the toilet for as long as possible. This will be easier with safe bathrooms that are easy to find and designed to reduce the risk of falls.

Of course we all would prefer bathing and showering to be a relaxing—and not stressful—experience and this is more likely if the person feels that their privacy and dignity is protected and they are safe.

Some common bathroom and personal care challenges are:

- finding the toilet (in time)
- recognising the toilet or seeing it clearly
- reluctance to undress and wash
- knowing if the water is too hot or too cold
- mobility issues such as getting on and off the toilet or in and out of the bath or shower
- loss of awareness (in more advanced dementia) of the need to go to the bathroom, or what to do if the need becomes apparent.

An easily visible toilet with contrasting seat, rail and wall colour.

Design that enhances

A range of design changes and adjustments may help provide support for these challenges and they include:

- signs, light and cues for navigating to the bathroom

- removing items such as waste bins which could be mistaken as a toilet seat

- anti-slip finish for flooring and robust rails (in contrasting colours) to support use of the toilet and bath/shower

- appropriate bath and toilet aids or frames providing they don't increase confusion or distress

- contrasting colour for the toilet seat (avoid white on white) and easy to see and reach toilet paper and holder

- traditional cross-head tap fittings preferably colour coded for hot and cold, with water temperature adjusted so as not to scald

- avoiding any inconsistencies (loose or cracked tiles) in the floor to help prevent falls.

Care that complements design

These design features are complemented by a variety of dementia care approaches which can be tailored to suit care needs:

- If the person with dementia is finding dressing difficult, make it easier by providing pants with an elastic or Velcro waist.

- Use anti-slip mats in low contrast colour around the bath or the shower. A person might not step in to the bath if there is a mat in front of it that looks like a hole.

- Ensure bathroom products that may present a risk are put away including razors, medicines, shampoo and conditioners.

- If the person has difficulty with the lock from inside the bathroom door, consider changing to an easier, safer lock.

- No one enjoys being cold when undressing so provide an appropriate heater in the bathroom (heating lamps in a light fitting are safest).

- Try playing relaxing personally-tailored music before and during shower time (or sing together). This can promote calmness at a time when a person with dementia might otherwise feel anxiety.

- If the person finds that certain smells also help relax them, try using this in the shower or bath—e.g. coconut shampoo and conditioner or lavender soap—depending on what the person likes.

- Exhaust fans help reduce steam which otherwise may add to feelings of confusion or anxiety.

- Try putting a commode chair near the bed if the person struggles to get up at night to find the bathroom. This can be more dignifying then putting on a night-time pad.

Sometimes dementia may affect the person's ability to start or continue a process or activity and so rather than taking over, a carer can support by filling in the gaps. Providing assistance for going to the toilet may be as simple as a carer saying, 'I am going to the toilet before we head out,' which triggers that thought for the person with dementia.

At other times, it might be that the person needs help with another part of the process which is easy for others to take for granted such as standing up and getting moving, or locating the toilet. Either way, remember that filling in the gaps might be the care needed to support independence.

It's timely to mention that appropriate seating can make a difference—make sure it enables the person to stand up and get going.[42]

Caring tip: Contrasting colours for toilet seats, bath edges and also for taps will make it easier for people who are experiencing sensory challenges or weakening eyesight. Another colour tip may be to paint all the bathroom doors in the home the same colour so they are more easily recognised. Of course not every person with dementia needs any or all of the supports listed— look for what helps in your home.

A word on ensuites

Ensuites warrant some additional advice as they can play a big role in promoting independence. Some incontinence can be a result of a person with dementia not being able to find or get to the toilet in time, or simply forgetting that it might be time to do so. As ensuites are positioned adjacent to bedrooms, they can be an important cue that reduces incontinence.

Many homes have ensuites nowadays, others may have bedrooms adjacent to bathrooms which could be turned into an ensuite. But where it is not possible or too expensive, having clear visual cues (signs, lighting) to the nearest toilet or bathroom.

Where you have an ensuite, it can further assist to position the bed in the adjacent room so the toilet can be seen from the head of the bed.

Being able to see the toilet from bed can aid getting there in time!

Help with incontinence

Where incontinence is a serious and repetitive issue, regardless of the measures above, some common supports include:

- using waterproof mattress (and chair) protectors
- continence pads
- a linen service to clean sheets—this will reduce workload considerably
- contacting continence support organisations such as the Continence Foundation of Australia, Continence NZ, UK Continence Society or National Association for Continence in the US.

Bedrooms are one of our most private places where we sleep, dress and undress, and share intimacy. It's important these familiar associations are maintained while also considering design enhancements that support both the person with dementia and carers.

Start with a comfortable bed that caters for any particular health conditions and personal preference and make it more obvious as a destination with brightly coloured covers. As mentioned, ensuring the ensuite toilet is visible when in bed can help with going to the toilet, especially at night.

To promote better sleep (covered in more detail in Chapter 6) a warm, cosy bed in a cooler, darkened room will make it the place to be!

Having just a few choices of coordinated outfits can maximise independence.

What to do with wardrobes

Sometimes wardrobes full of clothes, shoes and other items can be overwhelming. We all have days where we stand in front trying to decide what to wear (or just find what we're looking for). The additional memory, planning and sensory challenges of dementia can make this a demoralising and frustrating task.

To make it easier to independently choose an outfit, try hanging the components together (e.g. shirt, trousers, jacket), laying them out the night before and/or having minimal clothing in the wardrobe.

To help with remembering where clothes are, one solid door could be replaced with a glazed one (but be careful with reflection) so clothes are visible. Then hang the clothes for the day (or evening) behind the glazed door, so it becomes even easier to get dressed.

As mentioned throughout this book, signs with pictures and text are often most effective, so consider labelling drawers, cupboards and wardrobe doors to reduce confusion or frustration.

Assistive technology

Depending on the sleeping arrangements in the home, one of the varieties of bed-related sensors may give carers some reassurance if they are concerned about the person with dementia falling or walking around at night in an unsafe way.

Key points:

- Bathrooms are best warm, non-slip, with robust contrasting rails and good colour contrast for the toilet seat—and paper easily reached!
- Make finding the toilet easier with good signs and lighting—an ensuite can help!
- Preserve the privacy and intimacy of the bedroom while introducing subtle design ideas to support independence.
- Wardrobes and choosing clothing can be overwhelming so reduce options and use a glazed door to make clothes obvious.
- Be aware that mirrors and other reflective surfaces can alarm some people with dementia so consider ways to cover.
- Sometimes filling in the gaps in a process can help the person with dementia complete tasks independently.

10 Inclusive kitchens and dining

What we will learn

- Creating an enabling kitchen
- Cooking together
- Dining by design

Kitchens are often the heart of the home where not only the household's meals are prepared, but there is an overflow of conversation, shared activity and eating and drinking. For people with dementia who have enjoyed cooking or been responsible for providing meals for others and themselves, there may be a strong desire to remain active in the kitchen.

At the same time, kitchens do present risks and can cause anxiety for both the person with dementia and the carer. People with dementia have reported risks such as pouring scalding water over their hands and not realising, or not being able to tell if food has gone off, because of sensory changes.[43] Carers may be concerned about food left to burn while cooking on a hot plate or cleaning products inadvertently being consumed, among a range of other risks.

Rather than total risk avoidance, there are a number of design improvements (balanced with keeping things familiar) that can minimise many of these risks and support independence in the kitchen and an improved quality of life.

Shane helps Shirley follow recipes by splitting the recipe into the hard parts, and the easy parts. Shane has simplified and rewritten the easy steps of the recipe in large writing for Shirley to follow, and while Shirley follows these steps, Shane manages the harder parts of the recipe. They work together to complete the food preparation, and both enjoy the sense of accomplishment and the tasty end result!

Putting more dangerous items in one locked draw makes the rest of the kitchen more safely accessible.

Creating an enabling kitchen

Finding or understanding things in the kitchen may be frustrating due to memory loss and other changes. Consider:

- replacing some solid cupboard doors with clear safety glass or removing cupboard doors where commonly-used items are stored

- using open shelving or including signs with words and images on closed drawers

- signs for any other appliances that may not be obvious such as custom-fitted dishwashers

- decluttering the kitchen so that often-used appliances, utensils and food are plainly visible on the bench

- using traditional cross-head taps which are easier to use and understand rather than a mixer.

To minimise kitchen risks, a few helpful hints include:

- placing dangerous items in cupboards with standard doors, perhaps high up or low down so they are less obvious—or have one locked cupboard

- installing scald control devices on hot water taps or even turning the temperature down at the hot water heater ('DIY' or a plumber could help)

- avoiding floods with overflow drains or plugs which empty the sink when it is full

- having an isolation switch for the cooktop and oven and make sure your smoke alarm is working correctly.[44]

Encouraging eating and drinking

As mentioned previously (Chapter 5), people with dementia may develop problems with eating and drinking related to memory loss, sensory challenges, swallowing difficulties or age-related issues such as appetite loss, sore teeth and arthritis in fingers (using cutlery).

So when a person with dementia gravitates to the kitchen—as we all tend to do, looking for something to eat—having favourite (and nutritious where possible) snacks and drinks plainly in view can encourage eating and drinking e.g. a fruit bowl, mid meal finger foods, tea and coffee or biscuits (cookies).

When you see it, you can do it!

Betty loved her many daily cups of tea, but recently had stopped being able to make these. It was assumed this was due to Bettys' dementia progressing. In fact, it was caused, unintentionally, by her loving son paying for new kitchen cabinets. Previously when Betty went to make tea, she could see the kettle, cups and teabags on the shelf—everything needed to make her cuppa, including the fridge to get the milk. With her new kitchen, everything looked beautiful, but was hidden. For example, the fridge was fitted with a cover door that matched the new kitchen cupboards and was no longer familiar to. Because Betty could no longer see her teapot, the first cue or trigger to thinking about making a pot of tea was hidden. Thankfully, Betty's visiting care worker had learned about design that supports eating and drinking[45] and explained to the family what needed to change. The cupboard with the teapot and the other with the fridge had the doors removed. Betty could again see the tea-making items and could plan her pots of tea.

Healthy snacks in plain view can encourage good nutrition.

Dining by design

Design of dining rooms or eating areas is also important for supporting independence and good nutrition and should take into account the familiar routines and preferences of the person with dementia.

If eating in a designated dining room or area is the best option for the person with dementia and carer, there are many design tips[46] that can help. Let's start with the general dining environment:

- Provide sufficient light so dining tasks are easier and, most importantly, there's no confusion about what's being served.

- Minimise noisy distractions and movement which might draw a person with dementia away from their meal (put away the mobile phone).

- There's evidence that personalised background music can support better dining experiences.[47]

- As much as possible, have everyone in the home eating together which may mean giving thought to where the person with dementia is seated (for hearing and support) and reminding everyone to take their time!

- Remember that we often eat in other locations (in front of the television, outside near the barbecue, breakfast in bed) and some variety is good for everyone!

Tables, table settings and seating are central to a good dining experience. Here are some key recommendations:

- Use a sturdy table to cater for people with mobility issues who may lean on them for support.

- Look for clear legroom and rounded edges and corners where possible—corner protectors can also be an option.

- Provide a comfortable, supportive chair with arms (for aiding mobility) which is the right height for the table and allows the person to have their feet on the floor.

- Use plates that contrast with the tablecloth and also the food—mashed potato on a white plate on a white tablecloth will be harder to see.

- Set only the necessary cutlery for each stage of the meal and keep the table setting generally simple and uncluttered (including a plain contrasting table cloth)

- Place meals directly in front of the person with dementia with the carer sitting opposite, modelling eating and use of cutlery.

- If the person with dementia is no longer comfortable with cutlery, there are dozens of nutritious finger food recipes which can serve as meals and which everyone at the table will enjoy.

- Avoid sitting the person with their back to the dining room door, where coming and going and conversation could provoke anxiety.

- Browse our two cookbooks[48] for people with dementia to discover more practical mealtime information and hundreds of appropriate recipes including for people on texture-modified diets.

Smaller meals served on an uncluttered table with good contrast will all support positive mealtimes.

Caring tip: For some people with dementia, eating and mealtimes will be happy and comfortable experiences. But for others, they could become very difficult. If you are used to cooking for your loved one this change can be discouraging. Be assured it's no one's fault. Be flexible and try new things and remember, there are services and businesses that help with meal preparation and delivery so don't feel as if you always need to be cooking! As well, going out for dinner is a relaxing option— we'll look at this in Part 3.

- Use clever design ideas to enable use of the kitchen while keeping safe.
- Encourage the person with dementia to stay involved with cooking for as long as possible.
- Make regularly used kitchen items as visible as possible and hide away dangerous items.
- The dining environment should have plenty of light and be free of distracting noise and movement.
- A robust table and a supportive chair with plenty of legroom is the starting point for good dining.
- Contrasting colours for plates, food and tablecloths will help, as will a simple but familiar table setting with only necessary cutlery.

Further reading

Don't give me eggs that bounce, 118 cracking recipes for people with Alzheimer's, 2014, HammondCare Media, Sydney.

It's all about the food not the fork! 107 easy to eat meals in a mouthful, 2016, HammondCare Media, Sydney.

Music remembers me: Connection and wellbeing in dementia, 2017, HammondCare Media, Sydney.

A variety of articles giving background to assistive technology for the home are available from the Independent Living Centre: ilcaustralia.org.au/Using_Assistive_Technology/in_the_home

Further advice and access to technology is available from Assistive Technology Australia: at-aust.org/

'Considering how best to approach a range of common activities outside the home promotes the value of people with dementia continuing to engage with the people and interests that are important to them.'

Part 3
Being active beyond the home

11 The great outdoors

What we will learn

- Tips for well-designed outdoor spaces
- Barriers and solutions to going outside

It's time to turn our attention to life beyond the house. People with dementia want to remain active citizens in their communities and we know this is important to their wellbeing. This is reflected in developments such as the recent guidelines for dementia-inclusive indoor and outdoor public spaces, written with input and assessment from people living with dementia.[49]

First, let's take a closer look at life beyond the home that may often begin right outside the front or back door—outdoor spaces.

The room outside

Being outside is a vital part of life for a person with dementia, as it is for carers and any human being. The outdoors offers fresh air, sunshine, a place to clear the head and the emotions, to exercise, have peaceful reflection and to enjoy a range of pastimes and meaningful activities.

Key guidelines for dementia-enabling outdoor spaces around your home, such as your garden or yard, include:

- views to the outdoor space from inside
- easy (unlocked and visible) access to a secure outdoor space or garden
- flat, plain paths that are wide enough for wheelchairs, walkers or for two people and, preferably,
- contrasting edges on paths to help with finding the way
- familiar plants that are not sharp, prickly or poisonous
- ideally some plants that involve the senses such as herbs or flowers with pleasant perfume
- clear sight lines (remove low hanging branches, busy hedges and shrubs) so people can see clearly across the garden
- destinations along the path such as a seat for resting, or gazebo or pergola, so going for a walk doesn't seem too daunting.

These are just a few key points and there are many more in *The room outside*—details in 'Further reading' at the end of the chapter.

Meaningful engagement with familiar tasks in a safe outdoor space is ideal.

Barriers and solutions

It's important to consider the various barriers preventing people with dementia from going outside. Here we've listed various barriers and possible solutions.

Barrier	Solution
Not feeling confident to re-enter the house after going outdoors	Appropriate signage, using both words and images, to show the way to the outdoors; keeping access doors unlocked.
Fear of needing to go the bathroom	Appropriate signage, again using both words and images, to show the way back inside; an outside toilet where possible.
Feeling too cold or too hot to go outdoors	Store coats (on a coat rack), umbrellas, hats, boots (and maybe sunglasses!) near the door to outside.
Not having someone to help them get outdoors	A well-designed space may be safe for the person on their own. If that's not appropriate, try and schedule a time each day to take the person with dementia outside. If this is not possible, try and get a family member or friend to help.
Not having a comfortable space to sit and enjoy the outdoors	Robust, smooth wooden seating with back and arms, preferably visible from the doorway. If using cushions, consider colour contrast and stability.
No reason to go outdoors	If the person associates positive feelings with outdoors, they will feel more inclined to spend more time there. Activities such as morning tea, barbecues, gardening, playing with the grandkids may all help.

| Nothing to do outside | Passive options include watching and listening to a water feature, bird feeder or bird bath or listening to music outside. Active options include playing with pets, feeding birds, gardening, picking fruit, vegetables or flowers or even raking the leaves! |

Outdoor spaces beyond the home

Some homes may not have a yard or garden but even when they do, a visit to a park or gardens can be a time of reminiscence or an enjoyable change from home.

When planning to visit parks, it can help to check if it is dementia-inclusive. This might include accessible toilets, places to sit, level pathways that are in good condition, parking nearby (if driving) and cover in case of bad weather.

Key points

- Being active outside the home begins with the outdoor spaces of your own home.
- Simple design ideas such as trimming low branches in the garden to improve sight lines can help make gardens dementia-inclusive.
- When planning a park visit, check first for features such as level paths, accessible toilets and ease of parking.

Further reading

The room outside: Designing outdoor living for older people and people with dementia, Annie Pollock, Colm Cunningham. HammondCare Media, Sydney (2018).

Designing outdoor spaces for people with dementia, eds Annie Pollock, Mary Marshall, HammondCare Media/ Stirling University (2015).

12 Leaving the house

What we will learn

- Checklist for a positive shopping trip
- Preparing for events
- Enjoying a restaurant meal

Going shopping

Heading to the shops is a very familiar activity for most people and if it remains enjoyable, it should be continued as long as possible for the person with dementia. For some people it will be possible to do this alone, particularly if close to a local shopping centre where they are well known and feel comfortable and safe. For other people, it will be an outing with a carer or support person.

Some things that will support shopping outings for the person with dementia include:

- having a clear shopping and task list—if going to a local grocer, they may be happy to keep a copy as well
- assistive technology sometimes known as safer walking technology which locates or tracks a person with dementia if shopping on their own and there is a risk of getting lost
- a specially-adapted mobile phone which allows the person with dementia to call the carer by simply pushing a button with their photo on it
- doing the shopping together and making it a social outing by stopping for lunch or cup of tea or coffee.

While often a positive experience, the hustle and bustle of shopping can also become tiring for the carer and confusing or stressful for the person with dementia. This might be time to see the shopping outing as an opportunity for some 'me time'—for both the person with dementia and carer. The Dogs4Dementia program has some useful learning around this, including that if you have a dog, they may be able to sit in a café with the person who has dementia, offering reassurance for them as they enjoy a coffee or cup of tea, allowing time for the carer to shop on their own.[50]

Dogs4Dementia has shown how an assistance dog can help anchor a person comfortably and independently in a cafe while a carer is involved in other tasks.

Of course there may be a time when the thought of anyone going shopping for the household seems too hard—most major supermarkets and shops offer internet shopping and home delivery with accounts keeping track of regularly ordered items.

Attending events

Events can be exciting and anticipated items on the calendar and include birthdays, dinner parties, community activities, festivals, religious services, concerts and conferences. Events at private homes may be familiar and it is easy to ask family or friends to be dementia-inclusive. Events in public spaces may require a little more research.

Recent guidelines on dementia-inclusive public spaces with input from people with dementia say the following features are ideal:

- an easy to access, well signed and welcoming entrance with parking nearby, obvious disability access and easy to locate reception
- internal areas that are easy to navigate with good signage that has words and pictures
- a toilet that can be readily accessed with clear signage and, once inside, traditional or easy to use taps, fittings, and buttons with good colour contrast
- floors that are not slippery, rough, shiny (looks like water) or too steep, with plain rather than patterned colouring, and preferably no black mats (look like holes)
- minimal clutter and distractions and preferably minimal mirrors
- not too much noise from overly loud music or machines and preferably a choice to attend in quieter times or sit in quieter locations.

Letting staff at the venue know that you have dementia, or that the person you are caring for has dementia, and how they can support this, may encourage them to follow these guidelines and/or take the time to personally assist.

Another helpful way to prepare for attending events is to have reminders on calendars or on phones prompting discussion about the event and what the person with dementia can expect.

Dining out at restaurants

Going out for dinner is for most people an enjoyable way to spend an evening and this is usually the case for people with dementia as well. A favourite restaurant, café or eatery may continue to be especially enjoyed and provide a positive social experience.

All of the guidelines mentioned above will assist when attending a restaurant as well as:

- avoiding restaurants that are very full, noisy or that play loud music (or ask when there are quieter times)

- allowing the person with dementia to sit with their back to other people in the restaurant so they are not overwhelmed by the variety of faces, conversation, noises and movement

- sitting opposite the person to model use of cutlery and correct steps for eating various dishes to minimise confusion

- if possible, minimising items on the table to just the essentials

- going to places the person is familiar with so they feel more secure and the staff understand their needs. You can search 'review' platforms such as TripAdvisor to check for comments about the restaurant's approach to people with dementia.

See food to help order!

Don helps Brian order what he likes at the coffee shop by spending time with him looking at the food in the counter windows before they sit down. Brian is able to look at what is available, and points out to Don what he would like to eat, often choosing the chocolate croissant! When they go to a restaurant for lunch, Don chooses restaurants that have pictures of the food on their menus so that Brian can easily identify what he would like to order.

For all of these occasions when leaving the house, monitor the person's wellbeing and if something particularly distresses them or they become tired, withdrawn or otherwise overwhelmed, it may be time to head home. This experience will be good learning to inform subsequent outings.

Caring tip: Carers may worry about unknown risks when the person with dementia is away from home, especially on their own. Not only may this anxiety be 'picked up' by the person with dementia, it may be that carers choose to put aside the idea of outings in favour of being entirely safe. But avoiding risk in this way may open up another risk—of the person with dementia feeling agitated, miserable, despondent or bored. A better option is to find ways to manage risk so that at least some outings are possible, with the related benefits. Assistive technology can provide some reassurance. And using your knowledge of the person and thinking through their needs, will usually lead to solutions that do not compromise safety, but enable the person for whom you are caring to exercise freedom and independence.

- Manage the risks of leaving home to enjoy outings such as shopping, events and dining out at restaurants.
- Avoid overwhelming the senses, particularly hearing, and assess if venues are dementia-inclusive.
- Continually assess the person's response to check for distress.

Further reading

Supportive telephones and mobiles:
www.unforgettable.org/telephones-and-mobiles

Trackers and object locators:
www.unforgettable.org/trackers-and-object-locators

13 Appointments, advice and emergencies

What we will learn
- How to reduce the pressure of appointments
- The role of GPs and health professionals
- What to do in emergencies

Going to appointments

People with dementia may have many external appointments relating to their health or personal affairs. They may be working hard every day to overcome the challenges of dementia and so it will be helpful to reduce the pressure that can come with important appointments.

Alongside all of the practical solutions for living at home with dementia throughout this book, there are a few specific tips to help make going out a positive and enabling experience.

When an appointment is approaching, try leaving a sign or note on the door, coffee table, fridge or kitchen bench—you'll both know the best place—that tells the person what and when the appointment is. Always use the same place for these notes, to build familiarity.

Often there are important things to communicate at a long-awaited appointment and it can be difficult for the person with dementia and the carer to have all of these points in mind. Consider writing some notes together beforehand to build confidence and create a list of things you need to say or ask—ticking them off when done. Maybe even taking some notes during the meeting to aid remembrance afterward.

Caring tip: Helping a person with dementia to be a partner in appointments concerning their wellbeing or personal affairs is vital, for as long as this is appropriate. As a carer, try to communicate with the person with dementia to see what concerns they have and where ever possible enable them to raise these at the appointment. Most health professionals should understand the need to take time, to not have distracting noise (alarms, alerts, beeping computers) and to be still and focused in the appointment. A friendly reminder is always an option.

Let's look at some of the most common appointments that may occur:

Family doctor or GP

The local or family doctor, known as a General Practitioner (GP), is often the first place to go for:

- general advice on health and diagnosis
- health check ups such as weight, blood pressure, cholesterol
- medication prescriptions
- understanding the side effects of medication
- assessing the progress of dementia
- referrals to other medical specialists
- advice and referrals for allied health support.

Most people are aware of the benefits of visiting the same GP or clinic so they can build personal knowledge of your health needs, keep track of your progress and have all health records at hand. This may be particularly important for people with dementia—if they have attended the same medical practice for a long time it may remain familiar and this will support trust and confidence.

Learning to talk to doctors

Jodie had noticed that when she took her mum, Anne, to the doctor, she would invariably tell the doctor there was nothing wrong with her, even when she had been unwell. Jodie realised that in addition to memory difficulties, her mum was quite enjoying the outing and social interaction and had always been a positive person who tended not to dwell on her own problems. Jodie learned that rather than contradict her, it was more supportive to affirm how Anne was feeling at that moment but also have with her a list of specific concerns or symptoms Anne had expressed previously. She would explain what the list was and often in reading it out, her mum would confirm these concerns. The GP learned to phrase her questions differently as well.

Dietitian

Dietitians and nutritionists will assist with understanding general and specific dietary needs such as for older people and people with dementia. They will assess your particular needs and help create strategies for:

- good nutrition

- maintaining healthy weight

- addressing changing tastes

- presenting meals (smaller, more regular) to stimulate appetite

- identifying diet or nutrition related disease or conditions.[51]

Speech pathologist

For people with dementia, a speech pathologist may assist with understanding and supporting speech-related changes of dementia. But they are more likely to assist with diet, as swallowing difficulties are quite common as dementia progresses. If texture-modified food and drink is recommended, the speech pathologist will help with understanding the different kinds of texture-modified diets and foods and how to prepare them.

Occupational therapist

This group of health professionals provide support for any daily 'occupation' of life such as eating, showering, sleeping or getting around your home. The OT can provide strategies and help functioning through the processes of 'compensation or adaptation'[52] which may occur with conditions such as dementia. Some OTs may have a particular expertise with dementia (you'll find them through the Dementia Centre and similar services) and they'll help evaluate strengths and impairments and areas needing specific support.

Physiotherapist

Physiotherapists will encourage independence by supporting mobility and strength, as well as providing strategies to prevent falls. Another important role of the physiotherapist is to identify sources of pain and to recommend exercises and other treatments to manage pain. Physiotherapists will also provide detailed assessments of the 'impairments, activity restrictions and participatory limitations' faced by people with dementia so positive strategies can be developed.[53]

Physiotherapists may assist the person with dementia with mobility, strength and falls prevention.

Preparing for emergencies

In emergency situations there is often uncertainty, requiring us to use our judgment and weigh the options based on the information we have available. This means that in a disaster there are additional risks that must be assessed for people with dementia.

Expect the unexpected

Regardless of the setting, much will depend on the stage of the person's illness and on the level of need they have for support or assistance. Emergency situations are difficult for everyone and there are additional challenges for the person with dementia. It is important to keep in mind that reactions may be hard to anticipate.

Changes in surroundings and routines can be unsettling, as can the heightened activity and excitement in the environment overall, as reflected in television and radio coverage of the events. People with dementia may also have trouble distinguishing reality from what is occurring on TV.

Whether people with dementia are still living on their own or with family members, maintaining daily routines as much as possible is extremely helpful. Dementia may affect people's ability to think abstractly, make sound judgments, and to plan and carry out complex tasks. So if there is a need to make a change in plans, it may prove overwhelming for people with dementia, even if they have been doing fine on their own until that point. Someone else may need to take responsibility for making a new plan.

Caring tip: Any changes in the normal routine can be extremely upsetting and sometimes results in an exaggerated response from the person with dementia: yelling, making what may appear to be unreasonable demands or accusations, or experiencing extreme emotions or agitation. While this may happen on other occasions as well, the added stress in an emergency can further limit the person's ability to handle frustration. Being hungry, thirsty, in pain, fearful, or unable to express oneself can exacerbate this, so to the extent possible try to anticipate and respond to these needs. Even when they may not be able to understand exactly what is happening, people with dementia will pick up on emotional cues. Remain as calm as possible and speak slowly using short, simple sentences. Provide continued reassurance. Try to move the person to a quieter environment. Attempt to redirect attention and, if possible, get the person involved in doing something enjoyable or meaningful.

It is always good to have on hand an emergency bag (which can also be helpful in the event of an unexpected trip to hospital), which could include a list of medications and dosages, some clothing, water, favourite foods or snacks, and small items that are comforting to the person with dementia. It is a bit like thinking about the bag that someone would have on hand when preparing to have a baby. Because the timing of the baby's arrival is usually not known, a bag is packed and ready. It can be like this if the person with dementia is prone to physical health issues, that may require a hospital trip. It is also a good idea to be aware of evacuation routes, emergency telephone numbers and local websites that contain emergency information.

Once the emergency has passed
No matter where the person resides, there may be lingering effects from the emergency. The event itself could also trigger reactions from past traumatic experiences. It will be most helpful if those around people with dementia keep orienting to the present, providing reassurance of safety, and engaging in distracting and relaxing activities. And while it may be difficult, try establishing a consistent schedule as soon as possible, because knowing what to expect helps people with dementia feel safe. While carers may understandably feel relief that the disaster has passed, the person with dementia may experience difficulty readjusting even to what was previously normal.

Key points

- Living with dementia will often involve appointments with a range of health professionals as part of a multidisciplinary approach to care and support.
- Appointments are important and promote independence but can add pressure and stress to daily challenges.
- Prepare for appointments beforehand with reminders, take a list of points and questions and make notes while there.
- Emergencies introduce sometimes overwhelming change for the person with dementia and responses may be unexpected.
- Once the emergency has passed, try and point people to the present and engage in relaxing, distracting activities.
- Try to have a grab and go bag in the cupboard if the person with dementia needs to go somewhere like hospital at short notice.

Further reading

Preparing for a natural disaster: Carer ready guide. Free download from dementiakt.com.au/resource/carer-ready-guide/ viewe3d April 23, 2018.

Dementia Support Australia offers a range of free resources for people living at home and health care professionals: www.dementia.com.au/resources/library

14 Going on holiday or staying with friends

What we will learn

- How to plan for a holiday
- Considering different kinds of holidays
- Preparing and packing

Planning for your holiday

Going on holiday can be relaxing and enjoyable for people with dementia and their carer as it can offer new experiences and a break from routine.

It is important to plan carefully in order to avoid potential problems. People with dementia might find a new environment confusing or may have difficulties readjusting once they return home. Meanwhile, a travel companion might be so concerned about giving the person with dementia a good holiday that they themselves forget to relax. For these reasons, it is important to make plans for the most suitable holiday for everyone involved.

When organising a holiday, try to be open with others (for example, hotel staff) about the person with dementia's needs. Trying to hide challenges can make life more stressful for everyone.

Types of holidays

People enjoy various types of breaks, depending on their interests, personal preferences, availability and finances. The extent to which the person's dementia affects their daily life will also determine the type of holiday that is most suitable.

Visiting family or friends may be a familiar and supportive way to enjoy a holiday.

- **Staying with friends and relatives**—If you are considering visiting friends or relatives, or if a number of you are going away together, discuss a plan and suggest how each person might be able to help. For example, some members of the group might spend regular time with the person with dementia during the mornings or afternoons. This can give the person and their usual carer a break from each other. Alternatively, they might provide extra help with particular tasks, such as preparing dinner. People are usually more willing to offer support or share responsibilities once they are clear about how they can contribute.

- **Independent travel**—This option offers the greatest choice and flexibility. It may be suitable for some people with dementia, but you will be responsible for arranging your own travel and accommodation. Speak to the hotel before you book to check that it is the right place for you. Look for places that offer a friendly, welcoming atmosphere and where staff will be understanding if any difficulties occur. A smaller hotel without too many corridors may be less confusing. It may be a good idea to book out of peak season, when staff are less busy and can give you more time and attention. Asking for a room in a quiet area of the hotel and on the ground floor can also help.

- **Packaged holiday**—You may want to go on a holiday where everything is arranged on your behalf. If you choose this option, talk to the travel agency before you book. Make sure they are aware of your needs and can advise how they will be met. There are travel agents who are willing to offer more support.

- **Specialist provision**—A range of holiday and travel services are available for people needing special support. A person with dementia may be accompanied by a friend, relative or carer, or may use respite services. As mentioned previously, reviewing platforms such as TripAdvisor may provide insight into how accommodation and other services approach people with dementia.

Whatever type of holiday you choose, try to find out as much as you can beforehand about the place you intend to visit. Are there interesting places to see, activities you can enjoy and pleasant places to relax? If anyone travelling has a physical disability, will it be easy for you to get around? Local tourist offices and websites can provide useful information.

Be aware that someone with dementia who is independent in familiar surroundings may need extra support when coping with a new environment or changes to their routine.

Preparing and packing

The earlier you start preparing for your holiday, the less stressful it will be. Allow plenty of time to organise passports, insurance and other administration. It can be helpful to write a list of all the belongings that you are taking with you. This list should state what is in each piece of luggage and how many pieces of luggage there are. Each person travelling should carry one copy of the list with them, and another copy can also be left with someone at home.

Packing tip: Make a list of what is in each suitcase and bag and have a copy for each person on the trip.

There are aids available that might help if a person with dementia becomes disorientated in an unfamiliar environment. An occupational therapist can advise you. Make sure all luggage is clearly labelled with your name and address. Also, put a sheet of paper with your name and address inside each separate bag or suitcase, in case luggage labels are removed or lost.

A medical alert bracelet or similar identification may be useful for a person with dementia in case they become separated from the person they are travelling with, become confused or experience communication problems.

Medicines

If you are likely to be separated from your luggage during your journey, keep medication in a carry-on bag, together with a list of the medicines and dosage routines. Medication must be kept with you at all times. If any medication needs to be kept refrigerated, tell the airline in advance and make sure you will have access to a fridge where you are staying.

Travel insurance

Ensure that you are protected in case of eventualities such as sickness or lost items. You will need a travel insurance policy that covers all passengers for any relevant medical conditions. Some policies do not cover claims arising from a 'pre-existing medical condition or defect', which could mean that any illness or accident linked to dementia may not be covered. Policies that do not have this clause sometimes have higher premiums, so it might be necessary to shop around. There are specialist insurers that cater for people with special needs. You might also consider making sure you are covered for travel delay.

The journey

Airports, railway stations, bus stations, ships, trains and even large airplanes are usually busy and confusing places and it can be very easy to get lost or to lose touch with someone. If you are travelling with someone with dementia, always make a mental note of what they are wearing and consider carrying a recent photograph of them. If you need help, look for people who are wearing official uniforms (for example, security staff, airline counter staff or train conductors).

Consider travelling at quieter times if possible, avoiding weekends and public holidays.

Travelling by car

If you are planning a long car journey, try not to travel for more than two hours before having a break. Consider using a taxi service or asking a relative or friend to drive. Try to ensure that everyone is comfortable and that seatbelts are properly fitted. If you are planning to stop at service areas along the way, be aware that these can be large complexes and it is easy to get lost or disorientated, or separated from travelling companions. It might help for people with memory problems to keep on them a record of the model, colour and registration number of the car (a clear photograph would be ideal).

Plan your journey carefully, factoring in regular breaks from driving, and listen to traffic updates before you set off.

Arrival

A person with dementia may feel tired or unsettled on arrival. It may help to have a cup of tea, relax and leave the unpacking until later.

Key points

- Holidays are a normal part of life that can be relaxing and enjoyable and break from the normal routine.
- As holidays may involve new and unfamiliar places and people, think ahead and plan well to minimise confusion or anxiety.
- Involving friends and family in accompanying the person with dementia during the visit will provide a welcome change.
- Having medicines available at all times and special considerations with travel insurance are important issues for planning.

15 Life at home and beyond: final thoughts

Living with dementia presents many challenges and changes that progress over time, making the ordinary activities of life harder to achieve. It's easy to be overwhelmed by limitations or problems and respond by withdrawing from life, family and community.

While not minimising or hiding from these difficulties—this is not a helpful approach either—there are many practical tips, solutions and advice (such as those in this book) that can help to enable the person with dementia and carer to enjoy life at home and beyond.

Understanding dementia, its symptoms and progression, including sensory changes, is important when considering what kind of support may be needed to maximise capacity and independence.

Learning more about dementia-inclusive support and discovering dementia-enabling design ideas, that are often relatively easy to introduce, will also support the person with dementia living at home.

Of course one of the privileges of living at home is choosing to go out! People with dementia are increasingly highlighting the importance of being actively engaged in life at home and beyond.

Once again, *My home, my life* offers a range of practical solutions, design principles and planning ideas that support people with dementia as they engage with the world around them.

We hope that all of this encourages people with dementia, their carers and support network to meet challenges with courage, creativity, honesty and let's not forget, a sense of humour!

Your feedback needed

We understand that for some readers, there will be many relevant points in this book that can be implemented, while for others, there may be very little. Which is why we want to hear from you!

As mentioned in the 'Introduction', the story is not complete without your contribution of ideas, tips and experiences that can enhance our understanding and support many others facing similar challenges. Visit myhomemylifebook.com to learn more, we look forward to hearing from you!

Appendix: A collection of tips, strategies and resources

Tips to aid memory[54]

Memory loss is a progressive symptom of dementia than can be stressful and frustrating. But as with many of the challenges presented by dementia, there are practical solutions that may maximise capacity.

These are recommendations of which some may work for you, and you may have your own ideas that work well. It's also very important to consider that while remembering is important, there are many other valuable parts of who we are and beautiful ways in which we relate to others.

1. **Routines:** Patterns of behaviour act as an aid to memory. Routines can include preparing for bed by having a cup of tea or warm milk, having a glass of wine, dressing in pyjamas, turning off the TV.

2. **Keeping a diary or a notebook:** You can use this to write about everyday tasks, things to remember, appointments. It might be a good idea to have a day per page diary so as to avoid confusion about what day of the week it is and what is planned for that day.

3. **Noticeboards:** This can be a place where you consistently put up information, ideas or reminders.

4. **Labels:** Labels or signs (words and pictures) may help remind you of what's in drawers and cupboards.

5. **Sticky notes or instructions:** Leave out simple operating instructions near the kettle and next to the stove, and sticky notes at the front door, reminding you to close it or to take certain items with you.

6. **Address book and phone numbers:** Have these ready by the phone. Keep those most important and needed on

Support memory by keeping a journal, making notes, using photos, compiling lists and instructions.

speed dial. If you start to forget people's names, but can remember their faces, put a picture of the face next to the person you are calling. Some mobile phones have this option.

7. **Electronic prompt services:** Alarms or reminders on smartphones or other devices can be used to prompt you to take medication or do other tasks. If the alarm causes anxiety and you can't remember why the phone or device is beeping, then it's best to avoid this.

8. **Place for keys:** Get into the habit of putting keys, phone, money, glasses all in the same, obvious place.

9. **Clocks with dates display:** Sometimes analogue clocks are easier to use. Ensure the clock is big enough to use and see easily.

10. **Newspaper:** Some people are very interested in current events and reading newspapers can be a great aid to your memory about what day it is and what is happening in the world around you.

11. **Photographs:** take photos of the service providers you use—the carers that might clean your house, or the people that drop off your meals. Write a description (or have them do it) under each of the photos so you know who they are and what they do. Take photos of family and friends and write their names underneath.

12. **Relax:** Don't rush or stress as this will make it harder to remember things.

It's not surprising that a popular book for people caring for someone with dementia is called the *36 Hour Day*. Such is your commitment to support your family member or friend amidst the many changes and challenges they are experiencing that there never seems to be enough hours in the day. Here are some practical ideas for helping you do what you do:[55]

1. **Avoid isolation:** Make sure you talk to people about your challenges and feelings and try to be in contact with other carers.

2. **Understand dementia:** Developing your understanding of the medical side of dementia will give you better insight into what is occurring for the person you care for and also help you understand the terminology of doctors and other health professionals.

3. **Plan for the future:** Plan for emergencies such as hospitalisation or death, or if something happens to you and you are unable to care for the person anymore. Think about driving, financial aspects, wills and legal.

4. **Taking over:** You may need to sensitively take over some roles the person with dementia used to do. Where possible continue doing tasks together (finances, cooking) for as long as is appropriate.

5. **Engaging activities:** Meaningful activity is an important component of care at home but remember to concentrate more on the process than the outcomes. Provide instructions, work alongside, fill in gaps and ask for feedback as to what is enjoyed or disliked.

6. **Care for yourself:** Acknowledge that while you may get exhausted, you are a caring person doing a great job. Care for yourself by meeting friends, going for a walk, playing with pets, doing some gardening, going to a movie, buying some flowers, joining in family celebrations.

People living with dementia can find eating and drinking challenging. This may be the result of short attention spans and an appetite that changes day to day. Additionally, age related changes such as decline of taste, smell, chewing and swallowing can impact the ability to initiate or finish a meal.

Weight loss and malnutrition affects between 10 and 30 per cent of older people in the community and is a common struggle for those living with dementia. Malnutrition is where the body does not receive enough vitamins, minerals, energy (calories) and protein to maintain a healthy body. The result is a loss of muscle mass, strength and capacity to do everyday tasks such as getting out of bed, walking and getting dressed. Some food and nutrition tips include:

1. **Good meal planning:** Thinking through plans and strategies for food is vital for maintaining good nutrition for people living with dementia.

2. **More meals:** Providing six to eight smaller meals a day (instead of the usual three larger meals) can be helpful for the person with a small appetite or reduced concentration.

3. **Mid meals:** In keeping with the previous tip, providing mid meals (morning tea, afternoon tea and supper) as part of the day can help fill nutritional gaps. Offering food regularly also allows more opportunities to eat and absorb vital nutrients.

4. **Finger foods:** Providing finger food allows a person to pick up suitable foods with their hands to eat. This strategy can support independence and dignity around mealtime, which is often lost with inability to use cutlery and recognise food. As well, providing each portion 'one at a time' can reduce the feeling of being overwhelmed and the person is more likely to finish the meal provided.

5. **Finger food ideas:** Some nourishing but easy to prepare finger foods include:

- sliced boiled eggs
- savoury dips with crackers
- soft finger sandwiches
- raisin toast
- pieces of fruit
- sliced meat
- pieces of steamed vegetables
- omelette squares or mini quiches
- antipasto platter
- fruit cake or nut meal cake
- modified foods such as moulded fruit or moulded yoghurt can be useful for those with swallowing difficulties.

6. **Nourishing drink:** This is another strategy that can support good nutrition for a person losing weight or unable to finish a meal. This is because a drink can be easier to manage than a meal, particularly for those easily fatigued. Providing a nourishing drink as part of a mid meal can increase the nutritional intake. Milk or dairy based drinks are generally a better nutritional choice compared to water, juice or tea as they contain more energy (calories), protein and vitamins. Commercial based supplement drinks can provide additional calories but should be considered with the guidance of a dietitian.

What's important when planning meals and going to the shops?

When planning a meal, a careful balance of protein, energy and nutrients will help ensure it is as nourishing as possible. When we are unwell and as we age, our dietary requirements change, so it is important seek medical advice before making any significant changes.

For a person with a small appetite or losing weight, including foods which are naturally rich in protein and energy can make the most of every mouthful that they eat.

As people with dementia are at risk of losing weight rapidly, avoid choosing low calorie or diet foods and choose full fat products. High calorie products such as butter or oil can be used to enrich cakes and biscuits. Foods containing protein can be incorporated with each meal or snack to give a good amount of protein to maintain muscles. Keep in mind that red meat, chicken and nuts can be difficult for some to chew, so these foods should be prepared so they are easy to eat.

Your tips and strategies

As mentioned earlier, please share the tips, strategies and resources that are helpful for you and may be helpful for others by visiting myhomemylifebook.com or the dementiacentre.com. We'd love you to join the conversation and your ideas may be incorporated into future editions of My home, my life: Practical ideas for people with dementia and carers.

Helpful organisations

Australia

Dementia Centre: dementiacentre.com or +61 (0) 2 8437 7355

Dementia Support Australia: www.dementia.com.au or
AU 1800 699 799

Dementia Australia: dementia.org.au or AU 1800 100 500

Carer Gateway: carergateway.gov.au or AU 1800 422 737

Independent Living Centres: ilcaustralia.org.au or
AU 1300 885 886

United Kingdom

Dementia Centre: dementiacentre.com or +44 (0) 7787 168168

Alzheimer's Society: alzheimers.org.uk or +44 (0) 300 222 1122

Dementia UK (Admiral Nurses): dementiauk.org or
0800 888 6678

Carers UK: www.carersuk.org or +44 (0) 20 7378 4999

United States

Alzheimer's Association: www.alz.org or US 1800 272 3900

Dementia Society of America: dementiasociety.org or
US 1800 336 3684

Dementia Care Central: dementiacarecentral.com

International

Dementia Alliance International:
dementiaallianceinternational.org

Alzheimer's Diseases International: alz.co.uk or info@alz.co.uk

World Health Organisation:
who.int/mental_health/neurology/dementia

Agnes Houston MBE is a dementia activist who has always put others first. She was diagnosed with younger onset Alzheimer's disease in 2006 at the age of 57. She has campaigned for best practice and improving the lives of people with dementia (especially those experiencing sensory issues) in Scotland and received a lifetime achievement award from Alzheimer Scotland in 2013. Agnes is former Chair of the Scottish Dementia Working Group and currently Vice Chair of the European Dementia Working Group and a board member of Dementia Alliance International. In 2015 Agnes was awarded an MBE and in 2016 was awarded a Churchill Fellow. In 2016 she was the editor of *Dementia and sensory challenges: Dementia can be more than memory.*

Colm Cunningham is the Director of HammondCare's Dementia Centre and leads an Australian and international team of more than 200 staff involved in research, education and consultancy as well as the translation of this knowledge into accessible publications and tools to improve practice. The centre's priorities are building design, life engagement, models of care, understanding behaviour and end of life care. Colm has more than 30 years' experience in older age care. Colm leads national dementia behaviour response services, Dementia Support Australia (see 'Helpful organisations'), with the aim of reconsidering the understanding of what is happening when people with dementia are perceived to have 'behaviours' related to dementia. A nurse and social worker by background, he has written extensively and undertaken research on a wide range of issues about dementia including design, pain care, hospital care, night-time care and intellectual disability. Colm is a Conjoint Associate Professor at the University of New South Wales School of Public Health and Community Medicine and a Visiting Fellow in Dementia Design and Practice at the University of Edinburgh School of Health in Social Science. Colm is also a member of the Wicking Strategic Review Panel.

Natalie Duggan is an aged care specialist with 25 years experience in senior leadership and education, including roles as Head of the Dementia Centre and Head of Hammond College. Natalie's academic journey includes a Master of International Dementia Studies and authorship of numerous aged care and dementia training programs. Natalie has been a Visiting Fellow at the University of Edinburgh, regularly presents at conferences and collaborates with leading experts in dementia care around the world. Natalie is passionate about people with dementia leading the life they choose and her current role in community services has made her a passionate advocate and proponent of innovations in models of community support.

Thank you

The authors and publishers would like to thank the many people living with dementia, carers, family members, care workers, nurses, service managers and consultants who have contributed to *My home, my life*. A special thanks to all those people whose stories are told in these pages—your experiences will encourage, inform and support our readers!

References

Introduction

[1] vr-ep.com viewed April 20, 2018

[2] Agnes Houston ed. *Dementia and Sensory Challenges,* 2016

[3] dementiacentre.com/resources/64-is-this-outside-public-space-dementia-inclusive viewed April 20, 2018

01 Dementia and its symptoms

[4] M Gresham, R Forbes, Going to Stay at Home facilitator's guide, HammondCare/Dementia Centre/DCRC, 2015

[5] A Houston ed. Dementia and Sensory Challenges, 2016

[6] ibid – quote from contributor Peter McLauchlan

02 Stages of dementia and the impact of ageing

[7] www.who.int/mediacentre/factsheets/fs362/en/ viewed April 20, 2018

[8] http://sydney.edu.au/medicine/cdpc/news-events-participation/hammondcare-reable-wshop.php viewed April 20, 2018. Also M Marshall ed. *Perspectives on rehabilitation and dementia,* Jessica Kingsley Publishers (2005)

[9] *Dementia in Australia,* Australian Institute of Health and Welfare 2012. p. 3

[10] E Lykkesle, et al, 'Sensory stimulation—A way of creating mutual relations in dementia care', *International Journal of Qualitative studies on Health and Well-being,* 2014, p. 1.

[11] Ibid., p. 1

03 Understanding changed behaviour

[12] M Gresham, R Forbes, *Better for everyone,* HammondCare Media 2017, p. 5

[13] S Macfarlane, C Cunningham, 'The need for holistic management of behavioural disturbances in dementia', *International Psychogeriatrics,* vol. 29, no. 7, 2017, pp. 1055-1058

[14] A Pollock & C Cunningham, *The room outside: Designing outdoor living for older people and people with dementia,* HammondCare Media, 2018.

[15] K Beilharz, *Music remembers me: Connection and wellbeing in dementia,* HammondCare Media, 2017

[16] www.hammond.com.au/news/significant-benefits-from-dogs4dementia-program-interim-report viewed April 20, 2018

04 More than memory: sensory challenges

[17] A Houston, ed. *Dementia and Sensory Challenges*, 2016.

[18] ibid – adapted to table format

05 Living at home with dementia

[19] www.nsw.fightdementia.org.au/files/20131011-NSW-PUB-LivingAlone_ServiceGuide.pdf viewed April 20., 2018

[20] www.dementiastatistics.org/statistics/care-services viewed April 20, 2018

[21] D McNair et al, *Enlighten: Lighting design for older people and people with dementia,* HammondCare Media, Sydney, 2017, pp. 8-9

[22] P Morgan-Jones et al, *Don't give me eggs that bounce,* p.19, HammondCare Media, Sydney, 2014

[23] P Morgan-Jones et al, *It's all about the food not the fork!,* HammondCare Media, Sydney, 2016

[24] Dieneke Smit et al, 'Activity involvement and quality of life of people at different stages of dementia in long term care facilities', *Aging & Mental Health,* vol. 20, no. 1, pp. 100-109.

[25] P Morgan-Jones et al, *It's all about the food not the fork!,* HammondCare Media, Sydney, 2016.

06 A good night's sleep

[26] D Kerr & H Wilkinson, *Providing Good Care at Night for Older People, Practical Approaches for Use in Nursing and Care Homes,* 2011, Jessica Kingsley Publishers, London.

[27] Alzheimer's Association, *Treatments for Sleep Changes,* www.alz.org/ alzheimers_disease_10429.asp viewed April 20, 2018

[28] Seek the help of a medical professional if it gets to this point.

29 *Providing Good Care at Night.* pp. 60-61

30 *Treatments for Sleep Changes*

31 For more information on circadian rhythms see *Enlighten: Lighting design older people and people with dementia* pp. 25-30

32 Ballard CG, O'Brien JT, Reichelt K, Perry EK, 'Aromatherapy as a safe and effective treatment for the management of agitation in sever dementia: the results of a double-blind placebo-controlled trial with Melissa. *Journal of Clinical Psychiatry,* 2002, vol. 63, no. 7, pp. 5533 – 558.

07 Maintaining good communication

33 M Gresham, R Forbes, Going to Stay at Home facilitator's guide

34 M Gresham & R Forbes, *Going to Stay at Home facilitator's guide*

08 Supportive design ideas

35 CM Giebel et al, 'Activities of daily living and quality of life across different stages of dementia: a UK study', in Ageing & Mental Health, 2015, vol. 19, no. 1, 63-71.

36 McNair D et al, *Enlighten: Lighting design for older people and people with dementia,* HammondCare Media, 2017

37 ibid

38 ibid

39 Dementia Support Australia – dementia.com.au

40 M Marshall, *Toilet talk: Accessible design for people with dementia,* HammondCare Media, Sydney (2018)

09 Better bathrooms and bedrooms

41 *At home with dementia*

10 Inclusive kitchens and dining

42 *10 tips about seating and postural care for older people.* Free download from www.dementiacentre.com/resources/14-10-tips-about-seating-and-postural-care-for-older-people

10 Inclusive kitchens and dining

43 A Houston ed. *Dementia and Sensory Challenges,* 2016

44 P Morgan-Jones et al, *Don't give me eggs that bounce*

45 P Morgan-Jones et al, *Don't give me eggs that bounce*

46 C Cunningham, D McIntosh et al, *DesignSmart. The rating tool for environments that work for people with dementia,* HammondCare Media, Sydney (2015)

47 K Beilharz, *Music remembers me,* HammondCare Media, Sydney, 2017

48 *Don't give me eggs that bounce (2104) and It's all bout the food not the fork!* (2016)

11 The great outdoors

49 Free download from https://www.dementiacentre.com/resources/64-is-this-outside-public-space-dementia-inclusive viewed April 23, 2018

12 Leaving the house

50 www.dogs4dementia.com.au

13 Appointments, advice and emergencies

51 https://www.bda.uk.com/improvinghealth/healthprofessionals/keyfacts/dementia_kf_sheet

52 www.aota.org/About-Occupational-Therapy/Professionals/MH/Dementia.aspx viewed April 23, 2018

53 www.csp.org.uk/professional-union/practice/evidence-base/physiotherapy-works/dementia-care viewed April 23, 2018

Appendix

54 Adapted from *Going to stay at home facilitator's guide,* p. 88

55 Going to Stay at Home